W9-AUL-778

SECOND EDITION

Python for Data Analysis
Data Wrangling with Pandas, NumPy, and IPython

Wes McKinney

Beijing · Boston · Farnham · Sebastopol · Tokyo

Python for Data Analysis

by Wes McKinney

Copyright © 2018 William McKinney. All rights reserved.

Published by O'Reilly Media, Inc., 1005 Gravenstein Highway North, Sebastopol, CA 95472.

O'Reilly books may be purchased for educational, business, or sales promotional use. Online editions are also available for most titles (*http://oreilly.com/safari*). For more information, contact our corporate/institutional sales department: 800-998-9938 or *corporate@oreilly.com*.

Editor: Marie Beaugureau	**Indexer:** Lucie Haskins
Production Editor: Kristen Brown	**Interior Designer:** David Futato
Copyeditor: Jasmine Kwityn	**Cover Designer:** Karen Montgomery
Proofreader: Rachel Monaghan	**Illustrator:** Rebecca Demarest

October 2012:	First Edition
October 2017:	Second Edition

Revision History for the Second Edition

2017-09-25:	First Release
2017-10-20:	Second Release
2017-11-03:	Third Release
2018-09-21:	Fourth Release

See *http://oreilly.com/catalog/errata.csp?isbn=9781491957660* for release details.

The O'Reilly logo is a registered trademark of O'Reilly Media, Inc. *Python for Data Analysis*, the cover image, and related trade dress are trademarks of O'Reilly Media, Inc.

While the publisher and the author have used good faith efforts to ensure that the information and instructions contained in this work are accurate, the publisher and the author disclaim all responsibility for errors or omissions, including without limitation responsibility for damages resulting from the use of or reliance on this work. Use of the information and instructions contained in this work is at your own risk. If any code samples or other technology this work contains or describes is subject to open source licenses or the intellectual property rights of others, it is your responsibility to ensure that your use thereof complies with such licenses and/or rights.

978-1-491-95766-0

[LSI]

Table of Contents

Preface

New for the Second Edition

The first edition of this book was published in 2012, during a time when open source data analysis libraries for Python (such as pandas) were very new and developing rapidly. In this updated and expanded second edition, I have overhauled the chapters to account both for incompatible changes and deprecations as well as new features that have occurred in the last five years. I've also added fresh content to introduce tools that either did not exist in 2012 or had not matured enough to make the first cut. Finally, I have tried to avoid writing about new or cutting-edge open source projects that may not have had a chance to mature. I would like readers of this edition to find that the content is still almost as relevant in 2020 or 2021 as it is in 2017.

The major updates in this second edition include:

- All code, including the Python tutorial, updated for Python 3.6 (the first edition used Python 2.7)
- Updated Python installation instructions for the Anaconda Python Distribution and other needed Python packages
- Updates for the latest versions of the pandas library in 2017
- A new chapter on some more advanced pandas tools, and some other usage tips
- A brief introduction to using statsmodels and scikit-learn

I also reorganized a significant portion of the content from the first edition to make the book more accessible to newcomers.

Conventions Used in This Book

The following typographical conventions are used in this book:

Italic
> Indicates new terms, URLs, email addresses, filenames, and file extensions.

`Constant width`
> Used for program listings, as well as within paragraphs to refer to program elements such as variable or function names, databases, data types, environment variables, statements, and keywords.

`Constant width bold`
> Shows commands or other text that should be typed literally by the user.

`Constant width italic`
> Shows text that should be replaced with user-supplied values or by values determined by context.

This element signifies a tip or suggestion.

This element signifies a general note.

This element indicates a warning or caution.

Using Code Examples

You can find data files and related material for each chapter is available in this book's GitHub repository at *http://github.com/wesm/pydata-book*.

This book is here to help you get your job done. In general, if example code is offered with this book, you may use it in your programs and documentation. You do not need to contact us for permission unless you're reproducing a significant portion of the code. For example, writing a program that uses several chunks of code from this book does not require permission. Selling or distributing a CD-ROM of examples from O'Reilly books does require permission. Answering a question by citing this book and quoting example code does not require permission. Incorporating a significant amount of example code from this book into your product's documentation does require permission.

We appreciate, but do not require, attribution. An attribution usually includes the title, author, publisher, and ISBN. For example: *"Python for Data Analysis* by Wes McKinney (O'Reilly). Copyright 2017 Wes McKinney, 978-1-491-95766-0."

If you feel your use of code examples falls outside fair use or the permission given above, feel free to contact us at *permissions@oreilly.com*.

O'Reilly Safari

 Safari (formerly Safari Books Online) is a membership-based training and reference platform for enterprise, government, educators, and individuals.

Members have access to thousands of books, training videos, Learning Paths, interactive tutorials, and curated playlists from over 250 publishers, including O'Reilly Media, Harvard Business Review, Prentice Hall Professional, Addison-Wesley Professional, Microsoft Press, Sams, Que, Peachpit Press, Adobe, Focal Press, Cisco Press, John Wiley & Sons, Syngress, Morgan Kaufmann, IBM Redbooks, Packt, Adobe Press, FT Press, Apress, Manning, New Riders, McGraw-Hill, Jones & Bartlett, and Course Technology, among others.

For more information, please visit *http://oreilly.com/safari*.

How to Contact Us

Please address comments and questions concerning this book to the publisher:

O'Reilly Media, Inc.
1005 Gravenstein Highway North
Sebastopol, CA 95472
800-998-9938 (in the United States or Canada)
707-829-0515 (international or local)
707-829-0104 (fax)

We have a web page for this book, where we list errata, examples, and any additional information. You can access this page at *http://bit.ly/python_data_analysis_2e*.

To comment or ask technical questions about this book, send email to *bookquestions@oreilly.com*.

For more information about our books, courses, conferences, and news, see our website at *http://www.oreilly.com*.

Find us on Facebook: *http://facebook.com/oreilly*

Follow us on Twitter: *http://twitter.com/oreillymedia*

Watch us on YouTube: *http://www.youtube.com/oreillymedia*

Acknowledgments

This work is the product of many years of fruitful discussions, collaborations, and assistance with and from many people around the world. I'd like to thank a few of them.

In Memoriam: John D. Hunter (1968–2012)

Our dear friend and colleague John D. Hunter passed away after a battle with colon cancer on August 28, 2012. This was only a short time after I'd completed the final manuscript for this book's first edition.

John's impact and legacy in the Python scientific and data communities would be hard to overstate. In addition to developing matplotlib in the early 2000s (a time when Python was not nearly so popular), he helped shape the culture of a critical generation of open source developers who've become pillars of the Python ecosystem that we now often take for granted.

I was lucky enough to connect with John early in my open source career in January 2010, just after releasing pandas 0.1. His inspiration and mentorship helped me push forward, even in the darkest of times, with my vision for pandas and Python as a first-class data analysis language.

John was very close with Fernando Pérez and Brian Granger, pioneers of IPython, Jupyter, and many other initiatives in the Python community. We had hoped to work on a book together, the four of us, but I ended up being the one with the most free time. I am sure he would be proud of what we've accomplished, as individuals and as a community, over the last five years.

Acknowledgments for the Second Edition (2017)

It has been five years almost to the day since I completed the manuscript for this book's first edition in July 2012. A lot has changed. The Python community has grown immensely, and the ecosystem of open source software around it has flourished.

This new edition of the book would not exist if not for the tireless efforts of the pandas core developers, who have grown the project and its user community into one of the cornerstones of the Python data science ecosystem. These include, but are not limited to, Tom Augspurger, Joris van den Bossche, Chris Bartak, Phillip Cloud, gfyoung, Andy Hayden, Masaaki Horikoshi, Stephan Hoyer, Adam Klein, Wouter Overmeire, Jeff Reback, Chang She, Skipper Seabold, Jeff Tratner, and y-p.

On the actual writing of this second edition, I would like to thank the O'Reilly staff who helped me patiently with the writing process. This includes Marie Beaugureau, Ben Lorica, and Colleen Toporek. I again had outstanding technical reviewers with Tom Augpurger, Paul Barry, Hugh Brown, Jonathan Coe, and Andreas Müller contributing. Thank you.

This book's first edition has been translated into many foreign languages, including Chinese, French, German, Japanese, Korean, and Russian. Translating all this content and making it available to a broader audience is a huge and often thankless effort. Thank you for helping more people in the world learn how to program and use data analysis tools.

I am also lucky to have had support for my continued open source development efforts from Cloudera and Two Sigma Investments over the last few years. With open source software projects more thinly resourced than ever relative to the size of user bases, it is becoming increasingly important for businesses to provide support for development of key open source projects. It's the right thing to do.

Acknowledgments for the First Edition (2012)

It would have been difficult for me to write this book without the support of a large number of people.

On the O'Reilly staff, I'm very grateful for my editors, Meghan Blanchette and Julie Steele, who guided me through the process. Mike Loukides also worked with me in the proposal stages and helped make the book a reality.

I received a wealth of technical review from a large cast of characters. In particular, Martin Blais and Hugh Brown were incredibly helpful in improving the book's examples, clarity, and organization from cover to cover. James Long, Drew Conway, Fernando Pérez, Brian Granger, Thomas Kluyver, Adam Klein, Josh Klein, Chang She, and Stéfan van der Walt each reviewed one or more chapters, providing pointed feedback from many different perspectives.

I got many great ideas for examples and datasets from friends and colleagues in the data community, among them: Mike Dewar, Jeff Hammerbacher, James Johndrow, Kristian Lum, Adam Klein, Hilary Mason, Chang She, and Ashley Williams.

I am of course indebted to the many leaders in the open source scientific Python community who've built the foundation for my development work and gave encouragement while I was writing this book: the IPython core team (Fernando Pérez, Brian Granger, Min Ragan-Kelly, Thomas Kluyver, and others), John Hunter, Skipper Seabold, Travis Oliphant, Peter Wang, Eric Jones, Robert Kern, Josef Perktold, Francesc Alted, Chris Fonnesbeck, and too many others to mention. Several other people provided a great deal of support, ideas, and encouragement along the way: Drew Conway, Sean Taylor, Giuseppe Paleologo, Jared Lander, David Epstein, John Krowas, Joshua Bloom, Den Pilsworth, John Myles-White, and many others I've forgotten.

I'd also like to thank a number of people from my formative years. First, my former AQR colleagues who've cheered me on in my pandas work over the years: Alex Reyfman, Michael Wong, Tim Sargen, Oktay Kurbanov, Matthew Tschantz, Roni Israelov, Michael Katz, Chris Uga, Prasad Ramanan, Ted Square, and Hoon Kim. Lastly, my academic advisors Haynes Miller (MIT) and Mike West (Duke).

I received significant help from Phillip Cloud and Joris Van den Bossche in 2014 to update the book's code examples and fix some other inaccuracies due to changes in pandas.

On the personal side, Casey provided invaluable day-to-day support during the writing process, tolerating my highs and lows as I hacked together the final draft on top of an already overcommitted schedule. Lastly, my parents, Bill and Kim, taught me to always follow my dreams and to never settle for less.

## CHAPTER 1

Preliminaries

1.1 What Is This Book About?

This book is concerned with the nuts and bolts of manipulating, processing, cleaning, and crunching data in Python. My goal is to offer a guide to the parts of the Python programming language and its data-oriented library ecosystem and tools that will equip you to become an effective data analyst. While "data analysis" is in the title of the book, the focus is specifically on Python programming, libraries, and tools as opposed to data analysis methodology. This is the Python programming you need *for* data analysis.

What Kinds of Data?

When I say "data," what am I referring to exactly? The primary focus is on *structured data*, a deliberately vague term that encompasses many different common forms of data, such as:

- Tabular or spreadsheet-like data in which each column may be a different type (string, numeric, date, or otherwise). This includes most kinds of data commonly stored in relational databases or tab- or comma-delimited text files.

- Multidimensional arrays (matrices).

- Multiple tables of data interrelated by key columns (what would be primary or foreign keys for a SQL user).

- Evenly or unevenly spaced time series.

This is by no means a complete list. Even though it may not always be obvious, a large percentage of datasets can be transformed into a structured form that is more suitable for analysis and modeling. If not, it may be possible to extract features from a dataset into a structured form. As an example, a collection of news articles could be processed into a word frequency table, which could then be used to perform sentiment analysis.

Most users of spreadsheet programs like Microsoft Excel, perhaps the most widely used data analysis tool in the world, will not be strangers to these kinds of data.

1.2 Why Python for Data Analysis?

For many people, the Python programming language has strong appeal. Since its first appearance in 1991, Python has become one of the most popular interpreted programming languages, along with Perl, Ruby, and others. Python and Ruby have become especially popular since 2005 or so for building websites using their numerous web frameworks, like Rails (Ruby) and Django (Python). Such languages are often called *scripting* languages, as they can be used to quickly write small programs, or *scripts* to automate other tasks. I don't like the term "scripting language," as it carries a connotation that they cannot be used for building serious software. Among interpreted languages, for various historical and cultural reasons, Python has developed a large and active scientific computing and data analysis community. In the last 10 years, Python has gone from a bleeding-edge or "at your own risk" scientific computing language to one of the most important languages for data science, machine learning, and general software development in academia and industry.

For data analysis and interactive computing and data visualization, Python will inevitably draw comparisons with other open source and commercial programming languages and tools in wide use, such as R, MATLAB, SAS, Stata, and others. In recent years, Python's improved support for libraries (such as pandas and scikit-learn) has made it a popular choice for data analysis tasks. Combined with Python's overall strength for general-purpose software engineering, it is an excellent option as a primary language for building data applications.

Python as Glue

Part of Python's success in scientific computing is the ease of integrating C, C++, and FORTRAN code. Most modern computing environments share a similar set of legacy FORTRAN and C libraries for doing linear algebra, optimization, integration, fast Fourier transforms, and other such algorithms. The same story has held true for many companies and national labs that have used Python to glue together decades' worth of legacy software.

Many programs consist of small portions of code where most of the time is spent, with large amounts of "glue code" that doesn't run often. In many cases, the execution time of the glue code is insignificant; effort is most fruitfully invested in optimizing the computational bottlenecks, sometimes by moving the code to a lower-level language like C.

Solving the "Two-Language" Problem

In many organizations, it is common to research, prototype, and test new ideas using a more specialized computing language like SAS or R and then later port those ideas to be part of a larger production system written in, say, Java, C#, or C++. What people are increasingly finding is that Python is a suitable language not only for doing research and prototyping but also for building the production systems. Why maintain two development environments when one will suffice? I believe that more and more companies will go down this path, as there are often significant organizational benefits to having both researchers and software engineers using the same set of programming tools.

Why Not Python?

While Python is an excellent environment for building many kinds of analytical applications and general-purpose systems, there are a number of uses for which Python may be less suitable.

As Python is an interpreted programming language, in general most Python code will run substantially slower than code written in a compiled language like Java or C++. As *programmer time* is often more valuable than *CPU time*, many are happy to make this trade-off. However, in an application with very low latency or demanding resource utilization requirements (e.g., a high-frequency trading system), the time spent programming in a lower-level (but also lower-productivity) language like C++ to achieve the maximum possible performance might be time well spent.

Python can be a challenging language for building highly concurrent, multithreaded applications, particularly applications with many CPU-bound threads. The reason for this is that it has what is known as the *global interpreter lock* (GIL), a mechanism that prevents the interpreter from executing more than one Python instruction at a time. The technical reasons for why the GIL exists are beyond the scope of this book. While it is true that in many big data processing applications, a cluster of computers may be required to process a dataset in a reasonable amount of time, there are still situations where a single-process, multithreaded system is desirable.

This is not to say that Python cannot execute truly multithreaded, parallel code. Python C extensions that use native multithreading (in C or C++) can run code in parallel without being impacted by the GIL, so long as they do not need to regularly interact with Python objects.

1.3 Essential Python Libraries

For those who are less familiar with the Python data ecosystem and the libraries used throughout the book, I will give a brief overview of some of them.

NumPy

NumPy (*http://numpy.org*), short for Numerical Python, has long been a cornerstone of numerical computing in Python. It provides the data structures, algorithms, and library glue needed for most scientific applications involving numerical data in Python. NumPy contains, among other things:

- A fast and efficient multidimensional array object *ndarray*
- Functions for performing element-wise computations with arrays or mathematical operations between arrays
- Tools for reading and writing array-based datasets to disk
- Linear algebra operations, Fourier transform, and random number generation
- A mature C API to enable Python extensions and native C or C++ code to access NumPy's data structures and computational facilities

Beyond the fast array-processing capabilities that NumPy adds to Python, one of its primary uses in data analysis is as a container for data to be passed between algorithms and libraries. For numerical data, NumPy arrays are more efficient for storing and manipulating data than the other built-in Python data structures. Also, libraries written in a lower-level language, such as C or Fortran, can operate on the data stored in a NumPy array without copying data into some other memory representation. Thus, many numerical computing tools for Python either assume NumPy arrays as a primary data structure or else target seamless interoperability with NumPy.

pandas

pandas (*http://pandas.pydata.org*) provides high-level data structures and functions designed to make working with structured or tabular data fast, easy, and expressive. Since its emergence in 2010, it has helped enable Python to be a powerful and productive data analysis environment. The primary objects in pandas that will be used in this book are the `DataFrame`, a tabular, column-oriented data structure with both row and column labels, and the `Series`, a one-dimensional labeled array object.

pandas blends the high-performance, array-computing ideas of NumPy with the flexible data manipulation capabilities of spreadsheets and relational databases (such as SQL). It provides sophisticated indexing functionality to make it easy to reshape, slice and dice, perform aggregations, and select subsets of data. Since data manipulation, preparation, and cleaning is such an important skill in data analysis, pandas is one of the primary focuses of this book.

As a bit of background, I started building pandas in early 2008 during my tenure at AQR Capital Management, a quantitative investment management firm. At the time, I had a distinct set of requirements that were not well addressed by any single tool at my disposal:

- Data structures with labeled axes supporting automatic or explicit data alignment —this prevents common errors resulting from misaligned data and working with differently indexed data coming from different sources
- Integrated time series functionality
- The same data structures handle both time series data and non–time series data
- Arithmetic operations and reductions that preserve metadata
- Flexible handling of missing data
- Merge and other relational operations found in popular databases (SQL-based, for example)

I wanted to be able to do all of these things in one place, preferably in a language well suited to general-purpose software development. Python was a good candidate language for this, but at that time there was not an integrated set of data structures and tools providing this functionality. As a result of having been built initially to solve finance and business analytics problems, pandas features especially deep time series functionality and tools well suited for working with time-indexed data generated by business processes.

For users of the R language for statistical computing, the DataFrame name will be familiar, as the object was named after the similar R `data.frame` object. Unlike Python, data frames are built into the R programming language and its standard library. As a result, many features found in pandas are typically either part of the R core implementation or provided by add-on packages.

The pandas name itself is derived from *panel data*, an econometrics term for multidimensional structured datasets, and a play on the phrase *Python data analysis* itself.

matplotlib

matplotlib (*http://matplotlib.org*) is the most popular Python library for producing plots and other two-dimensional data visualizations. It was originally created by John D. Hunter and is now maintained by a large team of developers. It is designed for creating plots suitable for publication. While there are other visualization libraries available to Python programmers, matplotlib is the most widely used and as such has generally good integration with the rest of the ecosystem. I think it is a safe choice as a default visualization tool.

IPython and Jupyter

The IPython project (*http://ipython.org*) began in 2001 as Fernando Pérez's side project to make a better interactive Python interpreter. In the subsequent 16 years it has become one of the most important tools in the modern Python data stack. While it does not provide any computational or data analytical tools by itself, IPython is designed from the ground up to maximize your productivity in both interactive computing and software development. It encourages an *execute-explore* workflow instead of the typical *edit-compile-run* workflow of many other programming languages. It also provides easy access to your operating system's shell and filesystem. Since much of data analysis coding involves exploration, trial and error, and iteration, IPython can help you get the job done faster.

In 2014, Fernando and the IPython team announced the Jupyter project (*http://jupyter.org*), a broader initiative to design language-agnostic interactive computing tools. The IPython web notebook became the Jupyter notebook, with support now for over 40 programming languages. The IPython system can now be used as a *kernel* (a programming language mode) for using Python with Jupyter.

IPython itself has become a component of the much broader Jupyter open source project, which provides a productive environment for interactive and exploratory computing. Its oldest and simplest "mode" is as an enhanced Python shell designed to accelerate the writing, testing, and debugging of Python code. You can also use the IPython system through the Jupyter Notebook, an interactive web-based code "notebook" offering support for dozens of programming languages. The IPython shell and Jupyter notebooks are especially useful for data exploration and visualization.

The Jupyter notebook system also allows you to author content in Markdown and HTML, providing you a means to create rich documents with code and text. Other programming languages have also implemented kernels for Jupyter to enable you to use languages other than Python in Jupyter.

For me personally, IPython is usually involved with the majority of my Python work, including running, debugging, and testing code.

In the accompanying book materials (*http://github.com/wesm/pydata-book*), you will find Jupyter notebooks containing all the code examples from each chapter.

SciPy

SciPy (*http://scipy.org*) is a collection of packages addressing a number of different standard problem domains in scientific computing. Here is a sampling of the packages included:

`scipy.integrate`
   Numerical integration routines and differential equation solvers

`scipy.linalg`
   Linear algebra routines and matrix decompositions extending beyond those provided in `numpy.linalg`

`scipy.optimize`
   Function optimizers (minimizers) and root finding algorithms

`scipy.signal`
   Signal processing tools

`scipy.sparse`
   Sparse matrices and sparse linear system solvers

`scipy.special`
   Wrapper around SPECFUN, a Fortran library implementing many common mathematical functions, such as the `gamma` function

`scipy.stats`
   Standard continuous and discrete probability distributions (density functions, samplers, continuous distribution functions), various statistical tests, and more descriptive statistics

Together NumPy and SciPy form a reasonably complete and mature computational foundation for many traditional scientific computing applications.

scikit-learn

Since the project's inception in 2010, scikit-learn (*http://scikit-learn.org*) has become the premier general-purpose machine learning toolkit for Python programmers. In just seven years, it has had over 1,500 contributors from around the world. It includes submodules for such models as:

- Classification: SVM, nearest neighbors, random forest, logistic regression, etc.
- Regression: Lasso, ridge regression, etc.
- Clustering: *k*-means, spectral clustering, etc.
- Dimensionality reduction: PCA, feature selection, matrix factorization, etc.
- Model selection: Grid search, cross-validation, metrics
- Preprocessing: Feature extraction, normalization

Along with pandas, statsmodels, and IPython, scikit-learn has been critical for enabling Python to be a productive data science programming language. While I won't be able to include a comprehensive guide to scikit-learn in this book, I will give a brief introduction to some of its models and how to use them with the other tools presented in the book.

statsmodels

statsmodels (*http://statsmodels.org*) is a statistical analysis package that was seeded by work from Stanford University statistics professor Jonathan Taylor, who implemented a number of regression analysis models popular in the R programming language. Skipper Seabold and Josef Perktold formally created the new statsmodels project in 2010 and since then have grown the project to a critical mass of engaged users and contributors. Nathaniel Smith developed the Patsy project, which provides a formula or model specification framework for statsmodels inspired by R's formula system.

Compared with scikit-learn, statsmodels contains algorithms for classical (primarily frequentist) statistics and econometrics. This includes such submodules as:

- Regression models: Linear regression, generalized linear models, robust linear models, linear mixed effects models, etc.
- Analysis of variance (ANOVA)
- Time series analysis: AR, ARMA, ARIMA, VAR, and other models
- Nonparametric methods: Kernel density estimation, kernel regression
- Visualization of statistical model results

statsmodels is more focused on statistical inference, providing uncertainty estimates and p-values for parameters. scikit-learn, by contrast, is more prediction-focused.

As with scikit-learn, I will give a brief introduction to statsmodels and how to use it with NumPy and pandas.

1.4 Installation and Setup

Since everyone uses Python for different applications, there is no single solution for setting up Python and required add-on packages. Many readers will not have a complete Python development environment suitable for following along with this book, so here I will give detailed instructions to get set up on each operating system. I recommend using the free Anaconda distribution. At the time of this writing, Anaconda is offered in both Python 2.7 and 3.6 forms, though this might change at some point in the future. This book uses Python 3.6, and I encourage you to use Python 3.6 or higher.

Windows

To get started on Windows, download the Anaconda installer (*http://anaconda.com/downloads*). I recommend following the installation instructions for Windows available on the Anaconda download page, which may have changed between the time this book was published and when you are reading this.

Now, let's verify that things are configured correctly. To open the Command Prompt application (also known as *cmd.exe*), right-click the Start menu and select Command Prompt. Try starting the Python interpreter by typing **python**. You should see a message that matches the version of Anaconda you installed:

```
C:\Users\wesm>python
Python 3.5.2 |Anaconda 4.1.1 (64-bit)| (default, Jul  5 2016, 11:41:13)
[MSC v.1900 64 bit (AMD64)] on win32
>>>
```

To exit the shell, press Ctrl-D (on Linux or macOS), Ctrl-Z (on Windows), or type the command **exit()** and press Enter.

Apple (OS X, macOS)

Download the OS X Anaconda installer, which should be named something like *Anaconda3-4.1.0-MacOSX-x86_64.pkg*. Double-click the *.pkg* file to run the installer. When the installer runs, it automatically appends the Anaconda executable path to your *.bash_profile* file. This is located at */Users/$USER/.bash_profile*.

To verify everything is working, try launching IPython in the system shell (open the Terminal application to get a command prompt):

```
$ ipython
```

To exit the shell, press Ctrl-D or type **exit()** and press Enter.

GNU/Linux

Linux details will vary a bit depending on your Linux flavor, but here I give details for such distributions as Debian, Ubuntu, CentOS, and Fedora. Setup is similar to OS X with the exception of how Anaconda is installed. The installer is a shell script that must be executed in the terminal. Depending on whether you have a 32-bit or 64-bit system, you will either need to install the x86 (32-bit) or x86_64 (64-bit) installer. You will then have a file named something similar to *Anaconda3-4.1.0-Linux-x86_64.sh*. To install it, execute this script with bash:

```
$ bash Anaconda3-4.1.0-Linux-x86_64.sh
```

Some Linux distributions have versions of all the required Python packages in their package managers and can be installed using a tool like apt. The setup described here uses Anaconda, as it's both easily reproducible across distributions and simpler to upgrade packages to their latest versions.

After accepting the license, you will be presented with a choice of where to put the Anaconda files. I recommend installing the files in the default location in your home directory—for example, */home/$USER/anaconda* (with your username, naturally).

The Anaconda installer may ask if you wish to prepend its *bin/* directory to your $PATH variable. If you have any problems after installation, you can do this yourself by modifying your *.bashrc* (or *.zshrc*, if you are using the zsh shell) with something akin to:

```
export PATH=/home/$USER/anaconda/bin:$PATH
```

After doing this you can either start a new terminal process or execute your *.bashrc* again with `source ~/.bashrc`.

Installing or Updating Python Packages

At some point while reading, you may wish to install additional Python packages that are not included in the Anaconda distribution. In general, these can be installed with the following command:

```
conda install package_name
```

If this does not work, you may also be able to install the package using the pip package management tool:

```
pip install package_name
```

You can update packages by using the `conda update` command:

```
conda update package_name
```

pip also supports upgrades using the `--upgrade` flag:

```
pip install --upgrade package_name
```

You will have several opportunities to try out these commands throughout the book.

While you can use both conda and pip to install packages, you should not attempt to update conda packages with pip, as doing so can lead to environment problems. When using Anaconda or Miniconda, it's best to first try updating with conda.

Python 2 and Python 3

The first version of the Python 3.x line of interpreters was released at the end of 2008. It included a number of changes that made some previously written Python 2.x code incompatible. Because 17 years had passed since the very first release of Python in 1991, creating a "breaking" release of Python 3 was viewed to be for the greater good given the lessons learned during that time.

In 2012, much of the scientific and data analysis community was still using Python 2.x because many packages had not been made fully Python 3 compatible. Thus, the first edition of this book used Python 2.7. Now, users are free to choose between Python 2.x and 3.x and in general have full library support with either flavor.

However, Python 2.x will reach its development end of life in 2020 (including critical security patches), and so it is no longer a good idea to start new projects in Python 2.7. Therefore, this book uses Python 3.6, a widely deployed, well-supported stable release. We have begun to call Python 2.x "Legacy Python" and Python 3.x simply "Python." I encourage you to do the same.

This book uses Python 3.6 as its basis. Your version of Python may be newer than 3.6, but the code examples should be forward compatible. Some code examples may work differently or not at all in Python 2.7.

Integrated Development Environments (IDEs) and Text Editors

When asked about my standard development environment, I almost always say "IPython plus a text editor." I typically write a program and iteratively test and debug each piece of it in IPython or Jupyter notebooks. It is also useful to be able to play around with data interactively and visually verify that a particular set of data manipulations is doing the right thing. Libraries like pandas and NumPy are designed to be easy to use in the shell.

When building software, however, some users may prefer to use a more richly featured IDE rather than a comparatively primitive text editor like Emacs or Vim. Here are some that you can explore:

- PyDev (free), an IDE built on the Eclipse platform
- PyCharm from JetBrains (subscription-based for commercial users, free for open source developers)
- Python Tools for Visual Studio (for Windows users)
- Spyder (free), an IDE currently shipped with Anaconda
- Komodo IDE (commercial)

Due to the popularity of Python, most text editors, like Atom and Sublime Text 2, have excellent Python support.

1.5 Community and Conferences

Outside of an internet search, the various scientific and data-related Python mailing lists are generally helpful and responsive to questions. Some to take a look at include:

- pydata: A Google Group list for questions related to Python for data analysis and pandas
- pystatsmodels: For statsmodels or pandas-related questions
- Mailing list for scikit-learn (*scikit-learn@python.org*) and machine learning in Python, generally
- numpy-discussion: For NumPy-related questions
- scipy-user: For general SciPy or scientific Python questions

I deliberately did not post URLs for these in case they change. They can be easily located via an internet search.

Each year many conferences are held all over the world for Python programmers. If you would like to connect with other Python programmers who share your interests, I encourage you to explore attending one, if possible. Many conferences have financial support available for those who cannot afford admission or travel to the conference. Here are some to consider:

- PyCon and EuroPython: The two main general Python conferences in North America and Europe, respectively
- SciPy and EuroSciPy: Scientific-computing-oriented conferences in North America and Europe, respectively
- PyData: A worldwide series of regional conferences targeted at data science and data analysis use cases
- International and regional PyCon conferences (see *http://pycon.org* for a complete listing)

1.6 Navigating This Book

If you have never programmed in Python before, you will want to spend some time in Chapters 2 and 3, where I have placed a condensed tutorial on Python language features and the IPython shell and Jupyter notebooks. These things are prerequisite knowledge for the remainder of the book. If you have Python experience already, you may instead choose to skim or skip these chapters.

Next, I give a short introduction to the key features of NumPy, leaving more advanced NumPy use for Appendix A. Then, I introduce pandas and devote the rest of the book to data analysis topics applying pandas, NumPy, and matplotlib (for visualization). I have structured the material in the most incremental way possible, though there is occasionally some minor cross-over between chapters, with a few isolated cases where concepts are used that haven't necessarily been introduced yet.

While readers may have many different end goals for their work, the tasks required generally fall into a number of different broad groups:

Interacting with the outside world
Reading and writing with a variety of file formats and data stores

Preparation
Cleaning, munging, combining, normalizing, reshaping, slicing and dicing, and transforming data for analysis

Transformation
Applying mathematical and statistical operations to groups of datasets to derive new datasets (e.g., aggregating a large table by group variables)

Modeling and computation
Connecting your data to statistical models, machine learning algorithms, or other computational tools

Presentation
Creating interactive or static graphical visualizations or textual summaries

Code Examples

Most of the code examples in the book are shown with input and output as it would appear executed in the IPython shell or in Jupyter notebooks:

```
In [5]: CODE EXAMPLE
Out[5]: OUTPUT
```

When you see a code example like this, the intent is for you to type in the example code in the In block in your coding environment and execute it by pressing the Enter key (or Shift-Enter in Jupyter). You should see output similar to what is shown in the Out block.

Data for Examples

Datasets for the examples in each chapter are hosted in a GitHub repository (*http://github.com/wesm/pydata-book*). You can download this data either by using the Git version control system on the command line or by downloading a zip file of the repository from the website. If you run into problems, navigate to my website (*http:// wesmckinney.com*) for up-to-date instructions about obtaining the book materials.

I have made every effort to ensure that it contains everything necessary to reproduce the examples, but I may have made some mistakes or omissions. If so, please send me an email: *book@wesmckinney.com*. The best way to report errors in the book is on the errata page on the O'Reilly website (*http://bit.ly/pyDataAnalysis_errata*).

Import Conventions

The Python community has adopted a number of naming conventions for commonly used modules:

```
import numpy as np
import matplotlib.pyplot as plt
import pandas as pd
import seaborn as sns
import statsmodels as sm
```

This means that when you see `np.arange`, this is a reference to the `arange` function in NumPy. This is done because it's considered bad practice in Python software development to import everything (`from numpy import *`) from a large package like NumPy.

Jargon

I'll use some terms common both to programming and data science that you may not be familiar with. Thus, here are some brief definitions:

Munge/munging/wrangling
Describes the overall process of manipulating unstructured and/or messy data into a structured or clean form. The word has snuck its way into the jargon of many modern-day data hackers. "Munge" rhymes with "grunge."

Pseudocode
A description of an algorithm or process that takes a code-like form while likely not being actual valid source code.

Syntactic sugar
Programming syntax that does not add new features, but makes something more convenient or easier to type.

## CHAPTER 2

Python Language Basics, IPython, and Jupyter Notebooks

When I wrote the first edition of this book in 2011 and 2012, there were fewer resources available for learning about doing data analysis in Python. This was partially a chicken-and-egg problem; many libraries that we now take for granted, like pandas, scikit-learn, and statsmodels, were comparatively immature back then. In 2017, there is now a growing literature on data science, data analysis, and machine learning, supplementing the prior works on general-purpose scientific computing geared toward computational scientists, physicists, and professionals in other research fields. There are also excellent books about learning the Python programming language itself and becoming an effective software engineer.

As this book is intended as an introductory text in working with data in Python, I feel it is valuable to have a self-contained overview of some of the most important features of Python's built-in data structures and libraries from the perspective of data manipulation. So, I will only present roughly enough information in this chapter and Chapter 3 to enable you to follow along with the rest of the book.

In my opinion, it is *not* necessary to become proficient at building good software in Python to be able to productively do data analysis. I encourage you to use the IPython shell and Jupyter notebooks to experiment with the code examples and to explore the documentation for the various types, functions, and methods. While I've made best efforts to present the book material in an incremental form, you may occasionally encounter things that have not yet been fully introduced.

Much of this book focuses on table-based analytics and data preparation tools for working with large datasets. In order to use those tools you must often first do some munging to corral messy data into a more nicely tabular (or *structured*) form. Fortunately, Python is an ideal language for rapidly whipping your data into shape. The greater your facility with Python the language, the easier it will be for you to prepare new datasets for analysis.

Some of the tools in this book are best explored from a live IPython or Jupyter session. Once you learn how to start up IPython and Jupyter, I recommend that you follow along with the examples so you can experiment and try different things. As with any keyboard-driven console-like environment, developing muscle-memory for the common commands is also part of the learning curve.

 There are introductory Python concepts that this chapter does not cover, like classes and object-oriented programming, which you may find useful in your foray into data analysis in Python.

To deepen your Python language knowledge, I recommend that you supplement this chapter with the official Python tutorial (*http://docs.python.org*) and potentially one of the many excellent books on general-purpose Python programming. Some recommendations to get you started include:

- *Python Cookbook*, Third Edition, by David Beazley and Brian K. Jones (O'Reilly)
- *Fluent Python* by Luciano Ramalho (O'Reilly)
- *Effective Python* by Brett Slatkin (Pearson)

2.1 The Python Interpreter

Python is an *interpreted* language. The Python interpreter runs a program by executing one statement at a time. The standard interactive Python interpreter can be invoked on the command line with the python command:

```
$ python
Python 3.6.0 | packaged by conda-forge | (default, Jan 13 2017, 23:17:12)
[GCC 4.8.2 20140120 (Red Hat 4.8.2-15)] on linux
Type "help", "copyright", "credits" or "license" for more information.
>>> a = 5
>>> print(a)
5
```

The >>> you see is the *prompt* where you'll type code expressions. To exit the Python interpreter and return to the command prompt, you can either type **exit()** or press Ctrl-D.

Running Python programs is as simple as calling python with a *.py* file as its first argument. Suppose we had created *hello_world.py* with these contents:

```
print('Hello world')
```

You can run it by executing the following command (the *hello_world.py* file must be in your current working terminal directory):

```
$ python hello_world.py
Hello world
```

While some Python programmers execute all of their Python code in this way, those doing data analysis or scientific computing make use of IPython, an enhanced Python interpreter, or Jupyter notebooks, web-based code notebooks originally created within the IPython project. I give an introduction to using IPython and Jupyter in this chapter and have included a deeper look at IPython functionality in Appendix A. When you use the %run command, IPython executes the code in the specified file in the same process, enabling you to explore the results interactively when it's done:

```
$ ipython
Python 3.6.0 | packaged by conda-forge | (default, Jan 13 2017, 23:17:12)
Type "copyright", "credits" or "license" for more information.

IPython 5.1.0 -- An enhanced Interactive Python.
?         -> Introduction and overview of IPython's features.
%quickref -> Quick reference.
help      -> Python's own help system.
object?   -> Details about 'object', use 'object??' for extra details.

In [1]: %run hello_world.py
Hello world

In [2]:
```

The default IPython prompt adopts the numbered In [2]: style compared with the standard >>> prompt.

2.2 IPython Basics

In this section, we'll get you up and running with the IPython shell and Jupyter notebook, and introduce you to some of the essential concepts.

Running the IPython Shell

You can launch the IPython shell on the command line just like launching the regular Python interpreter except with the ipython command:

```
$ ipython
Python 3.6.0 | packaged by conda-forge | (default, Jan 13 2017, 23:17:12)
Type "copyright", "credits" or "license" for more information.

IPython 5.1.0 -- An enhanced Interactive Python.
?         -> Introduction and overview of IPython's features.
%quickref -> Quick reference.
help      -> Python's own help system.
```

```
object?    -> Details about 'object', use 'object??' for extra details.

In [1]: a = 5

In [2]: a
Out[2]: 5
```

You can execute arbitrary Python statements by typing them in and pressing Return (or Enter). When you type just a variable into IPython, it renders a string representation of the object:

```
In [5]: import numpy as np

In [6]: data = {i : np.random.randn() for i in range(7)}

In [7]: data
Out[7]:
{0: -0.20470765948471295,
 1: 0.47894333805754824,
 2: -0.5194387150567381,
 3: -0.55573030434749,
 4: 1.9657805725027142,
 5: 1.3934058329729904,
 6: 0.09290787674371767}
```

The first two lines are Python code statements; the second statement creates a variable named data that refers to a newly created Python dictionary. The last line prints the value of data in the console.

Many kinds of Python objects are formatted to be more readable, or *pretty-printed*, which is distinct from normal printing with print. If you printed the above data variable in the standard Python interpreter, it would be much less readable:

```
>>> from numpy.random import randn
>>> data = {i : randn() for i in range(7)}
>>> print(data)
{0: -1.5948255432744511, 1: 0.10569006472787983, 2: 1.972367135977295,
3: 0.15455217573074576, 4: -0.24058577449429575, 5: -1.2904897053651216,
6: 0.3308507317325902}
```

IPython also provides facilities to execute arbitrary blocks of code (via a somewhat glorified copy-and-paste approach) and whole Python scripts. You can also use the Jupyter notebook to work with larger blocks of code, as we'll soon see.

Running the Jupyter Notebook

One of the major components of the Jupyter project is the *notebook*, a type of interactive document for code, text (with or without markup), data visualizations, and other output. The Jupyter notebook interacts with *kernels*, which are implementations of

---

the Jupyter interactive computing protocol in any number of programming languages. Python's Jupyter kernel uses the IPython system for its underlying behavior.

To start up Jupyter, run the command `jupyter notebook` in a terminal:

```
$ jupyter notebook
[I 15:20:52.739 NotebookApp] Serving notebooks from local directory:
/home/wesm/code/pydata-book
[I 15:20:52.739 NotebookApp] 0 active kernels
[I 15:20:52.739 NotebookApp] The Jupyter Notebook is running at:
http://localhost:8888/
[I 15:20:52.740 NotebookApp] Use Control-C to stop this server and shut down
all kernels (twice to skip confirmation).
Created new window in existing browser session.
```

On many platforms, Jupyter will automatically open up in your default web browser (unless you start it with `--no-browser`). Otherwise, you can navigate to the HTTP address printed when you started the notebook, here `http://localhost:8888/`. See Figure 2-1 for what this looks like in Google Chrome.

Many people use Jupyter as a local computing environment, but it can also be deployed on servers and accessed remotely. I won't cover those details here, but encourage you to explore this topic on the internet if it's relevant to your needs.

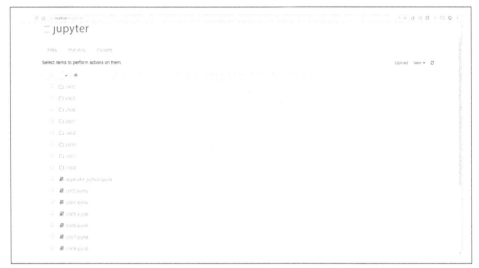

Figure 2-1. Jupyter notebook landing page

To create a new notebook, click the New button and select the "Python 3" or "conda [default]" option. You should see something like Figure 2-2. If this is your first time, try clicking on the empty code "cell" and entering a line of Python code. Then press Shift-Enter to execute it.

Figure 2-2. Jupyter new notebook view

When you save the notebook (see "Save and Checkpoint" under the notebook File menu), it creates a file with the extension *.ipynb*. This is a self-contained file format that contains all of the content (including any evaluated code output) currently in the notebook. These can be loaded and edited by other Jupyter users. To load an existing notebook, put the file in the same directory where you started the notebook process (or in a subfolder within it), then double-click the name from the landing page. You can try it out with the notebooks from my *wesm/pydata-book* repository on GitHub. See Figure 2-3.

While the Jupyter notebook can feel like a distinct experience from the IPython shell, nearly all of the commands and tools in this chapter can be used in either environment.

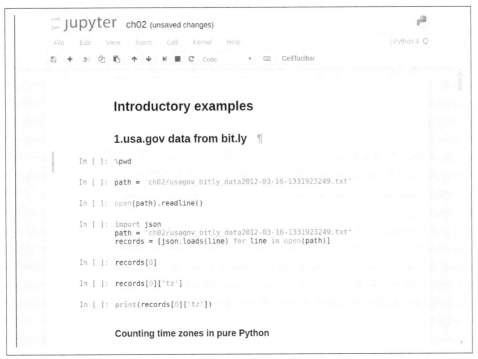

Figure 2-3. Jupyter example view for an existing notebook

Tab Completion

On the surface, the IPython shell looks like a cosmetically different version of the standard terminal Python interpreter (invoked with `python`). One of the major improvements over the standard Python shell is *tab completion*, found in many IDEs or other interactive computing analysis environments. While entering expressions in the shell, pressing the Tab key will search the namespace for any variables (objects, functions, etc.) matching the characters you have typed so far:

```
In [1]: an_apple = 27

In [2]: an_example = 42

In [3]: an<Tab>
an_apple    and        an_example  any
```

In this example, note that IPython displayed both the two variables I defined as well as the Python keyword and and built-in function any. Naturally, you can also complete methods and attributes on any object after typing a period:

```
In [3]: b = [1, 2, 3]

In [4]: b.<Tab>
b.append   b.count    b.insert   b.reverse
b.clear    b.extend   b.pop      b.sort
b.copy     b.index    b.remove
```

The same goes for modules:

```
In [1]: import datetime

In [2]: datetime.<Tab>
datetime.date            datetime.MAXYEAR      datetime.timedelta
datetime.datetime        datetime.MINYEAR      datetime.timezone
datetime.datetime_CAPI datetime.time          datetime.tzinfo
```

In the Jupyter notebook and newer versions of IPython (5.0 and higher), the auto-completions show up in a drop-down box rather than as text output.

 Note that IPython by default hides methods and attributes starting with underscores, such as magic methods and internal "private" methods and attributes, in order to avoid cluttering the display (and confusing novice users!). These, too, can be tab-completed, but you must first type an underscore to see them. If you prefer to always see such methods in tab completion, you can change this setting in the IPython configuration. See the IPython documentation to find out how to do this.

Tab completion works in many contexts outside of searching the interactive name-space and completing object or module attributes. When typing anything that looks like a file path (even in a Python string), pressing the Tab key will complete anything on your computer's filesystem matching what you've typed:

```
In [7]: datasets/movielens/<Tab>
datasets/movielens/movies.dat     datasets/movielens/README
datasets/movielens/ratings.dat    datasets/movielens/users.dat

In [7]: path = 'datasets/movielens/<Tab>
datasets/movielens/movies.dat     datasets/movielens/README
datasets/movielens/ratings.dat    datasets/movielens/users.dat
```

Combined with the %run command (see "The %run Command" on page 25), this functionality can save you many keystrokes.

Another area where tab completion saves time is in the completion of function key-word arguments (and including the = sign!). See Figure 2-4.

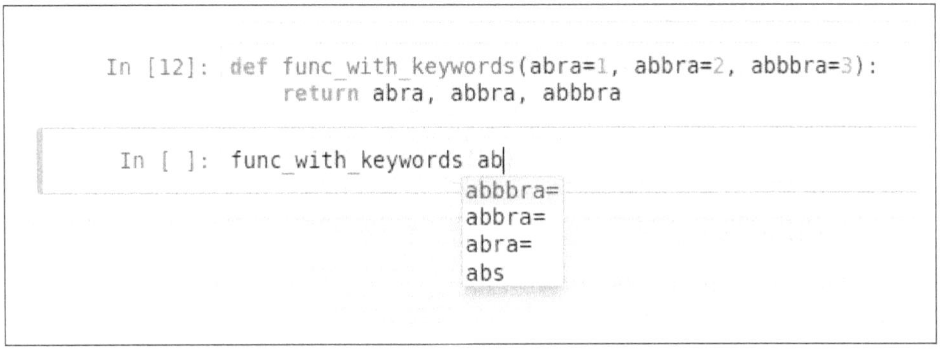

```
In [12]: def func_with_keywords(abra=1, abbra=2, abbbra=3):
             return abra, abbra, abbbra

   In [ ]: func_with_keywords ab|
                               abbbra=
                               abbra=
                               abra=
                               abs
```

Figure 2-4. Autocomplete function keywords in Jupyter notebook

We'll have a closer look at functions in a little bit.

Introspection

Using a question mark (?) before or after a variable will display some general information about the object:

```
In [8]: b = [1, 2, 3]

In [9]: b?
Type:        list
String Form:[1, 2, 3]
Length:      3
Docstring:
list() -> new empty list
list(iterable) -> new list initialized from iterable's items

In [10]: print?
Docstring:
print(value, ..., sep=' ', end='\n', file=sys.stdout, flush=False)

Prints the values to a stream, or to sys.stdout by default.
Optional keyword arguments:
file:  a file-like object (stream); defaults to the current sys.stdout.
sep:   string inserted between values, default a space.
end:   string appended after the last value, default a newline.
flush: whether to forcibly flush the stream.
Type:        builtin_function_or_method
```

This is referred to as *object introspection*. If the object is a function or instance method, the docstring, if defined, will also be shown. Suppose we'd written the following function (which you can reproduce in IPython or Jupyter):

```
def add_numbers(a, b):
    """
    Add two numbers together

    Returns
    -------
    the_sum : type of arguments
    """
    return a + b
```

Then using ? shows us the docstring:

```
In [11]: add_numbers?
Signature: add_numbers(a, b)
Docstring:
Add two numbers together

Returns
-------
the_sum : type of arguments
File:       <ipython-input-9-6a548a216e27>
Type:       function
```

Using ?? will also show the function's source code if possible:

```
In [12]: add_numbers??
Signature: add_numbers(a, b)
Source:
def add_numbers(a, b):
    """
    Add two numbers together

    Returns
    -------
    the_sum : type of arguments
    """
    return a + b
File:       <ipython-input-9-6a548a216e27>
Type:       function
```

? has a final usage, which is for searching the IPython namespace in a manner similar to the standard Unix or Windows command line. A number of characters combined with the wildcard (*) will show all names matching the wildcard expression. For example, we could get a list of all functions in the top-level NumPy namespace containing load:

```
In [13]: np.*load*?
np.__loader__
np.load
np.loads
np.loadtxt
np.pkgload
```

The %run Command

You can run any file as a Python program inside the environment of your IPython session using the %run command. Suppose you had the following simple script stored in *ipython_script_test.py*:

```
def f(x, y, z):
    return (x + y) / z

a = 5
b = 6
c = 7.5

result = f(a, b, c)
```

You can execute this by passing the filename to %run:

```
In [14]: %run ipython_script_test.py
```

The script is run in an *empty namespace* (with no imports or other variables defined) so that the behavior should be identical to running the program on the command line using `python script.py`. All of the variables (imports, functions, and globals) defined in the file (up until an exception, if any, is raised) will then be accessible in the IPython shell:

```
In [15]: c
Out [15]: 7.5

In [16]: result
Out[16]: 1.4666666666666666
```

If a Python script expects command-line arguments (to be found in `sys.argv`), these can be passed after the file path as though run on the command line.

 Should you wish to give a script access to variables already defined in the interactive IPython namespace, use `%run -i` instead of plain `%run`.

In the Jupyter notebook, you may also use the related %load magic function, which imports a script into a code cell:

```
>>> %load ipython_script_test.py

    def f(x, y, z):
        return (x + y) / z

    a = 5
    b = 6
    c = 7.5
```

```
result = f(a, b, c)
```

Interrupting running code

Pressing Ctrl-C while any code is running, whether a script through %run or a long-running command, will cause a KeyboardInterrupt to be raised. This will cause nearly all Python programs to stop immediately except in certain unusual cases.

 When a piece of Python code has called into some compiled extension modules, pressing Ctrl-C will not always cause the program execution to stop immediately. In such cases, you will have to either wait until control is returned to the Python interpreter, or in more dire circumstances, forcibly terminate the Python process.

Executing Code from the Clipboard

If you are using the Jupyter notebook, you can copy and paste code into any code cell and execute it. It is also possible to run code from the clipboard in the IPython shell. Suppose you had the following code in some other application:

```
x = 5
y = 7
if x > 5:
    x += 1

    y = 8
```

The most foolproof methods are the %paste and %cpaste magic functions. %paste takes whatever text is in the clipboard and executes it as a single block in the shell:

```
In [17]: %paste
x = 5
y = 7
if x > 5:
    x += 1

    y = 8
## -- End pasted text --
```

%cpaste is similar, except that it gives you a special prompt for pasting code into:

```
In [18]: %cpaste
Pasting code; enter '--' alone on the line to stop or use Ctrl-D.
:x = 5
:y = 7
:if x > 5:
:    x += 1
:
```

```
:    y = 8
:--
```

With the `%cpaste` block, you have the freedom to paste as much code as you like before executing it. You might decide to use `%cpaste` in order to look at the pasted code before executing it. If you accidentally paste the wrong code, you can break out of the `%cpaste` prompt by pressing Ctrl-C.

Terminal Keyboard Shortcuts

IPython has many keyboard shortcuts for navigating the prompt (which will be familiar to users of the Emacs text editor or the Unix bash shell) and interacting with the shell's command history. Table 2-1 summarizes some of the most commonly used shortcuts. See Figure 2-5 for an illustration of a few of these, such as cursor movement.

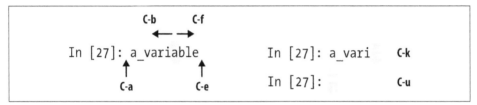

Figure 2-5. Illustration of some keyboard shortcuts in the IPython shell

Table 2-1. Standard IPython keyboard shortcuts

Keyboard shortcut	Description
Ctrl-P or up-arrow	Search backward in command history for commands starting with currently entered text
Ctrl-N or down-arrow	Search forward in command history for commands starting with currently entered text
Ctrl-R	Readline-style reverse history search (partial matching)
Ctrl-Shift-V	Paste text from clipboard
Ctrl-C	Interrupt currently executing code
Ctrl-A	Move cursor to beginning of line
Ctrl-E	Move cursor to end of line
Ctrl-K	Delete text from cursor until end of line
Ctrl-U	Discard all text on current line
Ctrl-F	Move cursor forward one character
Ctrl-B	Move cursor back one character
Ctrl-L	Clear screen

Note that Jupyter notebooks have a largely separate set of keyboard shortcuts for navigation and editing. Since these shortcuts have evolved more rapidly than IPython's, I encourage you to explore the integrated help system in the Jupyter notebook's menus.

About Magic Commands

IPython's special commands (which are not built into Python itself) are known as "magic" commands. These are designed to facilitate common tasks and enable you to easily control the behavior of the IPython system. A magic command is any command prefixed by the percent symbol %. For example, you can check the execution time of any Python statement, such as a matrix multiplication, using the %timeit magic function (which will be discussed in more detail later):

```
In [20]: a = np.random.randn(100, 100)

In [20]: %timeit np.dot(a, a)
10000 loops, best of 3: 20.9 µs per loop
```

Magic commands can be viewed as command-line programs to be run within the IPython system. Many of them have additional "command-line" options, which can all be viewed (as you might expect) using ?:

```
In [21]: %debug?
Docstring:
::

  %debug [--breakpoint FILE:LINE] [statement [statement ...]]

Activate the interactive debugger.

This magic command support two ways of activating debugger.
One is to activate debugger before executing code.  This way, you
can set a break point, to step through the code from the point.
You can use this mode by giving statements to execute and optionally
a breakpoint.

The other one is to activate debugger in post-mortem mode.  You can
activate this mode simply running %debug without any argument.
If an exception has just occurred, this lets you inspect its stack
frames interactively.  Note that this will always work only on the last
traceback that occurred, so you must call this quickly after an
exception that you wish to inspect has fired, because if another one
occurs, it clobbers the previous one.

If you want IPython to automatically do this on every exception, see
the %pdb magic for more details.

positional arguments:
  statement                 Code to run in debugger. You can omit this in cell
                            magic mode.

optional arguments:
  --breakpoint <FILE:LINE>, -b <FILE:LINE>
                            Set break point at LINE in FILE.
```

Magic functions can be used by default without the percent sign, as long as no variable is defined with the same name as the magic function in question. This feature is called *automagic* and can be enabled or disabled with %automagic.

Some magic functions behave like Python functions and their output can be assigned to a variable:

```
In [22]: %pwd
Out[22]: '/home/wesm/code/pydata-book'

In [23]: foo = %pwd

In [24]: foo
Out[24]: '/home/wesm/code/pydata-book'
```

Since IPython's documentation is accessible from within the system, I encourage you to explore all of the special commands available by typing %quickref or %magic. Table 2-2 highlights some of the most critical ones for being productive in interactive computing and Python development in IPython.

Table 2-2. Some frequently used IPython magic commands

Command	Description
%quickref	Display the IPython Quick Reference Card
%magic	Display detailed documentation for all of the available magic commands
%debug	Enter the interactive debugger at the bottom of the last exception traceback
%hist	Print command input (and optionally output) history
%pdb	Automatically enter debugger after any exception
%paste	Execute preformatted Python code from clipboard
%cpaste	Open a special prompt for manually pasting Python code to be executed
%reset	Delete all variables/names defined in interactive namespace
%page *OBJECT*	Pretty-print the object and display it through a pager
%run *script.py*	Run a Python script inside IPython
%prun *statement*	Execute *statement* with cProfile and report the profiler output
%time *statement*	Report the execution time of a single statement
%timeit *statement*	Run a statement multiple times to compute an ensemble average execution time; useful for timing code with very short execution time
%who, %who_ls, %whos	Display variables defined in interactive namespace, with varying levels of information/ verbosity
%xdel *variable*	Delete a variable and attempt to clear any references to the object in the IPython internals

Matplotlib Integration

One reason for IPython's popularity in analytical computing is that it integrates well with data visualization and other user interface libraries like matplotlib. Don't worry if you have never used matplotlib before; it will be discussed in more detail later in this book. The `%matplotlib` magic function configures its integration with the IPython shell or Jupyter notebook. This is important, as otherwise plots you create will either not appear (notebook) or take control of the session until closed (shell).

In the IPython shell, running `%matplotlib` sets up the integration so you can create multiple plot windows without interfering with the console session:

```
In [26]: %matplotlib
Using matplotlib backend: Qt4Agg
```

In Jupyter, the command is a little different (Figure 2-6):

```
In [26]: %matplotlib inline
```

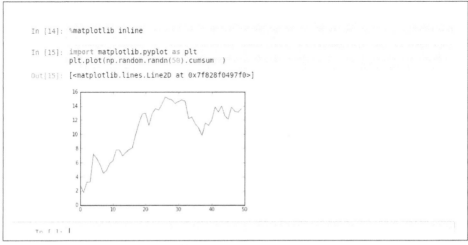

Figure 2-6. Jupyter inline matplotlib plotting

2.3 Python Language Basics

In this section, I will give you an overview of essential Python programming concepts and language mechanics. In the next chapter, I will go into more detail about Python's data structures, functions, and other built-in tools.

Language Semantics

The Python language design is distinguished by its emphasis on readability, simplicity, and explicitness. Some people go so far as to liken it to "executable pseudocode."

Indentation, not braces

Python uses whitespace (tabs or spaces) to structure code instead of using braces as in many other languages like R, C++, Java, and Perl. Consider a `for` loop from a sorting algorithm:

```
for x in array:
    if x < pivot:
        less.append(x)
    else:
        greater.append(x)
```

A colon denotes the start of an indented code block after which all of the code must be indented by the same amount until the end of the block.

Love it or hate it, significant whitespace is a fact of life for Python programmers, and in my experience it can make Python code more readable than other languages I've used. While it may seem foreign at first, you will hopefully grow accustomed in time.

 I strongly recommend using *four spaces* as your default indentation and replacing tabs with four spaces. Many text editors have a setting that will replace tab stops with spaces automatically (do this!). Some people use tabs or a different number of spaces, with two spaces not being terribly uncommon. By and large, four spaces is the standard adopted by the vast majority of Python programmers, so I recommend doing that in the absence of a compelling reason otherwise.

As you can see by now, Python statements also do not need to be terminated by semicolons. Semicolons can be used, however, to separate multiple statements on a single line:

```
a = 5; b = 6; c = 7
```

Putting multiple statements on one line is generally discouraged in Python as it often makes code less readable.

Everything is an object

An important characteristic of the Python language is the consistency of its *object model*. Every number, string, data structure, function, class, module, and so on exists in the Python interpreter in its own "box," which is referred to as a *Python object*. Each object has an associated *type* (e.g., *string* or *function*) and internal data. In practice this makes the language very flexible, as even functions can be treated like any other object.

Comments

Any text preceded by the hash mark (pound sign) # is ignored by the Python interpreter. This is often used to add comments to code. At times you may also want to exclude certain blocks of code without deleting them. An easy solution is to *comment out* the code:

```
results = []
for line in file_handle:
    # keep the empty lines for now
    # if len(line) == 0:
    #   continue
    results.append(line.replace('foo', 'bar'))
```

Comments can also occur after a line of executed code. While some programmers prefer comments to be placed in the line preceding a particular line of code, this can be useful at times:

```
print("Reached this line")  # Simple status report
```

Function and object method calls

You call functions using parentheses and passing zero or more arguments, optionally assigning the returned value to a variable:

```
result = f(x, y, z)
g()
```

Almost every object in Python has attached functions, known as *methods*, that have access to the object's internal contents. You can call them using the following syntax:

```
obj.some_method(x, y, z)
```

Functions can take both *positional* and *keyword* arguments:

```
result = f(a, b, c, d=5, e='foo')
```

More on this later.

Variables and argument passing

When assigning a variable (or *name*) in Python, you are creating a *reference* to the object on the righthand side of the equals sign. In practical terms, consider a list of integers:

```
In [8]: a = [1, 2, 3]
```

Suppose we assign a to a new variable b:

```
In [9]: b = a
```

In some languages, this assignment would cause the data [1, 2, 3] to be copied. In Python, a and b actually now refer to the same object, the original list [1, 2, 3] (see Figure 2-7 for a mockup). You can prove this to yourself by appending an element to a and then examining b:

```
In [10]: a.append(4)

In [11]: b
Out[11]: [1, 2, 3, 4]
```

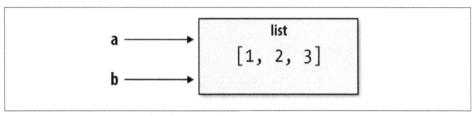

Figure 2-7. Two references for the same object

Understanding the semantics of references in Python and when, how, and why data is copied is especially critical when you are working with larger datasets in Python.

> Assignment is also referred to as *binding*, as we are binding a name to an object. Variable names that have been assigned may occasionally be referred to as bound variables.

When you pass objects as arguments to a function, new local variables are created referencing the original objects without any copying. If you bind a new object to a variable inside a function, that change will not be reflected in the parent scope. It is therefore possible to alter the internals of a mutable argument. Suppose we had the following function:

```
def append_element(some_list, element):
    some_list.append(element)
```

Then we have:

```
In [27]: data = [1, 2, 3]

In [28]: append_element(data, 4)

In [29]: data
Out[29]: [1, 2, 3, 4]
```

Dynamic references, strong types

In contrast with many compiled languages, such as Java and C++, object *references* in Python have no type associated with them. There is no problem with the following:

```
In [12]: a = 5

In [13]: type(a)
Out[13]: int

In [14]: a = 'foo'
```

```
In [15]: type(a)
Out[15]: str
```

Variables are names for objects within a particular namespace; the type information is stored in the object itself. Some observers might hastily conclude that Python is not a "typed language." This is not true; consider this example:

```
In [16]: '5' + 5
---------------------------------------------------------------
TypeError                             Traceback (most recent call last)
<ipython-input-16-f9dbf5f0b234> in <module>()
----> 1 '5' + 5
TypeError: must be str, not int
```

In some languages, such as Visual Basic, the string `'5'` might get implicitly converted (or *casted*) to an integer, thus yielding 10. Yet in other languages, such as JavaScript, the integer 5 might be casted to a string, yielding the concatenated string `'55'`. In this regard Python is considered a *strongly typed* language, which means that every object has a specific type (or *class*), and implicit conversions will occur only in certain obvious circumstances, such as the following:

```
In [17]: a = 4.5

In [18]: b = 2

# String formatting, to be visited later
In [19]: print('a is {0}, b is {1}'.format(type(a), type(b)))
a is <class 'float'>, b is <class 'int'>

In [20]: a / b
Out[20]: 2.25
```

Knowing the type of an object is important, and it's useful to be able to write functions that can handle many different kinds of input. You can check that an object is an instance of a particular type using the isinstance function:

```
In [21]: a = 5

In [22]: isinstance(a, int)
Out[22]: True
```

isinstance can accept a tuple of types if you want to check that an object's type is among those present in the tuple:

```
In [23]: a = 5; b = 4.5

In [24]: isinstance(a, (int, float))
Out[24]: True

In [25]: isinstance(b, (int, float))
Out[25]: True
```

Attributes and methods

Objects in Python typically have both attributes (other Python objects stored "inside" the object) and methods (functions associated with an object that can have access to the object's internal data). Both of them are accessed via the syntax *obj.attribute_name*:

```
In [1]: a = 'foo'
```

```
In [2]: a.<Press Tab>
a.capitalize  a.format     a.isupper    a.rindex      a.strip
a.center      a.index      a.join       a.rjust       a.swapcase
a.count       a.isalnum    a.ljust      a.rpartition  a.title
a.decode      a.isalpha    a.lower      a.rsplit      a.translate
a.encode      a.isdigit    a.lstrip     a.rstrip      a.upper
a.endswith    a.islower    a.partition  a.split       a.zfill
a.expandtabs  a.isspace    a.replace    a.splitlines
a.find        a.istitle    a.rfind      a.startswith
```

Attributes and methods can also be accessed by name via the getattr function:

```
In [27]: getattr(a, 'split')
Out[27]: <function str.split>
```

In other languages, accessing objects by name is often referred to as "reflection." While we will not extensively use the functions getattr and related functions hasattr and setattr in this book, they can be used very effectively to write generic, reusable code.

Duck typing

Often you may not care about the type of an object but rather only whether it has certain methods or behavior. This is sometimes called "duck typing," after the saying "If it walks like a duck and quacks like a duck, then it's a duck." For example, you can verify that an object is iterable if it implemented the *iterator protocol*. For many objects, this means it has a __iter__ "magic method", though an alternative and better way to check is to try using the iter function:

```
def isiterable(obj):
    try:
        iter(obj)
        return True
    except TypeError: # not iterable
        return False
```

This function would return True for strings as well as most Python collection types:

```
In [29]: isiterable('a string')
Out[29]: True
```

```
In [30]: isiterable([1, 2, 3])
```

```
Out[30]: True

In [31]: isiterable(5)
Out[31]: False
```

A place where I use this functionality all the time is to write functions that can accept multiple kinds of input. A common case is writing a function that can accept any kind of sequence (list, tuple, ndarray) or even an iterator. You can first check if the object is a list (or a NumPy array) and, if it is not, convert it to be one:

```
if not isinstance(x, list) and isiterable(x):
    x = list(x)
```

Imports

In Python a *module* is simply a file with the *.py* extension containing Python code. Suppose that we had the following module:

```
# some_module.py
PI = 3.14159

def f(x):
    return x + 2

def g(a, b):
    return a + b
```

If we wanted to access the variables and functions defined in *some_module.py*, from another file in the same directory we could do:

```
import some_module
result = some_module.f(5)
pi = some_module.PI
```

Or equivalently:

```
from some_module import f, g, PI
result = g(5, PI)
```

By using the as keyword you can give imports different variable names:

```
import some_module as sm
from some_module import PI as pi, g as gf

r1 = sm.f(pi)
r2 = gf(6, pi)
```

Binary operators and comparisons

Most of the binary math operations and comparisons are as you might expect:

```
In [32]: 5 - 7
Out[32]: -2
```

```
In [33]: 12 + 21.5
Out[33]: 33.5

In [34]: 5 <= 2
Out[34]: False
```

See Table 2-3 for all of the available binary operators.

To check if two references refer to the same object, use the is keyword. is not is also perfectly valid if you want to check that two objects are not the same:

```
In [35]: a = [1, 2, 3]

In [36]: b = a

In [37]: c = list(a)

In [38]: a is b
Out[38]: True

In [39]: a is not c
Out[39]: True
```

Since list always creates a new Python list (i.e., a copy), we can be sure that c is distinct from a. Comparing with is is not the same as the == operator, because in this case we have:

```
In [40]: a == c
Out[40]: True
```

A very common use of is and is not is to check if a variable is None, since there is only one instance of None:

```
In [41]: a = None

In [42]: a is None
Out[42]: True
```

Table 2-3. Binary operators

Operation	Description
a + b	Add a and b
a - b	Subtract b from a
a * b	Multiply a by b
a / b	Divide a by b
a // b	Floor-divide a by b, dropping any fractional remainder
a ** b	Raise a to the b power
a & b	True if both a and b are True; for integers, take the bitwise AND
a | b	True if either a or b is True; for integers, take the bitwise OR
a ^ b	For booleans, True if a or b is True, but not both; for integers, take the bitwise EXCLUSIVE-OR

Operation	Description
a == b	True if a equals b
a != b	True if a is not equal to b
a <= b, a < b	True if a is less than (less than or equal) to b
a > b, a >= b	True if a is greater than (greater than or equal) to b
a is b	True if a and b reference the same Python object
a is not b	True if a and b reference different Python objects

Mutable and immutable objects

Most objects in Python, such as lists, dicts, NumPy arrays, and most user-defined types (classes), are mutable. This means that the object or values that they contain can be modified:

```
In [43]: a_list = ['foo', 2, [4, 5]]

In [44]: a_list[2] = (3, 4)

In [45]: a_list
Out[45]: ['foo', 2, (3, 4)]
```

Others, like strings and tuples, are immutable:

```
In [46]: a_tuple = (3, 5, (4, 5))

In [47]: a_tuple[1] = 'four'
---------------------------------------------------------------------------
TypeError                                 Traceback (most recent call last)
<ipython-input-47-b7966a9ae0f1> in <module>()
----> 1 a_tuple[1] = 'four'
TypeError: 'tuple' object does not support item assignment
```

Remember that just because you *can* mutate an object does not mean that you always *should*. Such actions are known as *side effects*. For example, when writing a function, any side effects should be explicitly communicated to the user in the function's documentation or comments. If possible, I recommend trying to avoid side effects and *favor immutability*, even though there may be mutable objects involved.

Scalar Types

Python along with its standard library has a small set of built-in types for handling numerical data, strings, boolean (True or False) values, and dates and time. These "single value" types are sometimes called *scalar types* and we refer to them in this book as scalars. See Table 2-4 for a list of the main scalar types. Date and time handling will be discussed separately, as these are provided by the datetime module in the standard library.

Table 2-4. Standard Python scalar types

Type	Description
None	The Python "null" value (only one instance of the None object exists)
str	String type; holds Unicode (UTF-8 encoded) strings
bytes	Raw ASCII bytes (or Unicode encoded as bytes)
float	Double-precision (64-bit) floating-point number (note there is no separate double type)
bool	A True or False value
int	Arbitrary precision signed integer

Numeric types

The primary Python types for numbers are int and float. An int can store arbitrarily large numbers:

```
In [48]: ival = 17239871

In [49]: ival ** 6
Out[49]: 26254519291092456596965462913230729701102721
```

Floating-point numbers are represented with the Python float type. Under the hood each one is a double-precision (64-bit) value. They can also be expressed with scientific notation:

```
In [50]: fval = 7.243

In [51]: fval2 = 6.78e-5
```

Integer division not resulting in a whole number will always yield a floating-point number:

```
In [52]: 3 / 2
Out[52]: 1.5
```

To get C-style integer division (which drops the fractional part if the result is not a whole number), use the floor division operator //:

```
In [53]: 3 // 2
Out[53]: 1
```

Strings

Many people use Python for its powerful and flexible built-in string processing capabilities. You can write *string literals* using either single quotes ' or double quotes ":

```
a = 'one way of writing a string'
b = "another way"
```

For multiline strings with line breaks, you can use triple quotes, either ''' or """:

```
c = """
This is a longer string that
spans multiple lines
"""
```

It may surprise you that this string c actually contains four lines of text; the line breaks after """ and after lines are included in the string. We can count the new line characters with the count method on c:

```
In [55]: c.count('\n')
Out[55]: 3
```

Python strings are immutable; you cannot modify a string:

```
In [56]: a = 'this is a string'

In [57]: a[10] = 'f'
---------------------------------------------------------------------------
TypeError                                 Traceback (most recent call last)
<ipython-input-57-5ca625d1e504> in <module>()
----> 1 a[10] = 'f'
TypeError: 'str' object does not support item assignment

In [58]: b = a.replace('string', 'longer string')

In [59]: b
Out[59]: 'this is a longer string'
```

Afer this operation, the variable a is unmodified:

```
In [60]: a
Out[60]: 'this is a string'
```

Many Python objects can be converted to a string using the str function:

```
In [61]: a = 5.6

In [62]: s = str(a)

In [63]: print(s)
5.6
```

Strings are a sequence of Unicode characters and therefore can be treated like other sequences, such as lists and tuples (which we will explore in more detail in the next chapter):

```
In [64]: s = 'python'

In [65]: list(s)
Out[65]: ['p', 'y', 't', 'h', 'o', 'n']

In [66]: s[:3]
Out[66]: 'pyt'
```

The syntax s[:3] is called *slicing* and is implemented for many kinds of Python sequences. This will be explained in more detail later on, as it is used extensively in this book.

The backslash character \ is an *escape character*, meaning that it is used to specify special characters like newline \n or Unicode characters. To write a string literal with backslashes, you need to escape them:

```
In [67]: s = '12\\34'

In [68]: print(s)
12\34
```

If you have a string with a lot of backslashes and no special characters, you might find this a bit annoying. Fortunately you can preface the leading quote of the string with r, which means that the characters should be interpreted as is:

```
In [69]: s = r'this\has\no\special\characters'

In [70]: s
Out[70]: 'this\\has\\no\\special\\characters'
```

The r stands for *raw*.

Adding two strings together concatenates them and produces a new string:

```
In [71]: a = 'this is the first half '

In [72]: b = 'and this is the second half'

In [73]: a + b
Out[73]: 'this is the first half and this is the second half'
```

String templating or formatting is another important topic. The number of ways to do so has expanded with the advent of Python 3, and here I will briefly describe the mechanics of one of the main interfaces. String objects have a format method that can be used to substitute formatted arguments into the string, producing a new string:

```
In [74]: template = '{0:.2f} {1:s} are worth US${2:d}'
```

In this string,

- {0:.2f} means to format the first argument as a floating-point number with two decimal places.
- {1:s} means to format the second argument as a string.
- {2:d} means to format the third argument as an exact integer.

To substitute arguments for these format parameters, we pass a sequence of arguments to the format method:

```
In [75]: template.format(4.5560, 'Argentine Pesos', 1)
Out[75]: '4.56 Argentine Pesos are worth US$1'
```

String formatting is a deep topic; there are multiple methods and numerous options and tweaks available to control how values are formatted in the resulting string. To learn more, I recommend consulting the official Python documentation (*https://docs.python.org/3.6/library/string.html*).

I discuss general string processing as it relates to data analysis in more detail in Chapter 8.

Bytes and Unicode

In modern Python (i.e., Python 3.0 and up), Unicode has become the first-class string type to enable more consistent handling of ASCII and non-ASCII text. In older versions of Python, strings were all bytes without any explicit Unicode encoding. You could convert to Unicode assuming you knew the character encoding. Let's look at an example:

```
In [76]: val = "español"

In [77]: val
Out[77]: 'español'
```

We can convert this Unicode string to its UTF-8 bytes representation using the encode method:

```
In [78]: val_utf8 = val.encode('utf-8')

In [79]: val_utf8
Out[79]: b'espa\xc3\xb1ol'

In [80]: type(val_utf8)
Out[80]: bytes
```

Assuming you know the Unicode encoding of a bytes object, you can go back using the decode method:

```
In [81]: val_utf8.decode('utf-8')
Out[81]: 'español'
```

While it's become preferred to use UTF-8 for any encoding, for historical reasons you may encounter data in any number of different encodings:

```
In [82]: val.encode('latin1')
Out[82]: b'espa\xf1ol'

In [83]: val.encode('utf-16')
Out[83]: b'\xff\xfee\x00s\x00p\x00a\x00\xf1\x00o\x00l\x00'

In [84]: val.encode('utf-16le')
Out[84]: b'e\x00s\x00p\x00a\x00\xf1\x00o\x00l\x00'
```

It is most common to encounter `bytes` objects in the context of working with files, where implicitly decoding all data to Unicode strings may not be desired.

Though you may seldom need to do so, you can define your own byte literals by prefixing a string with b:

```
In [85]: bytes_val = b'this is bytes'

In [86]: bytes_val
Out[86]: b'this is bytes'

In [87]: decoded = bytes_val.decode('utf8')

In [88]: decoded  # this is str (Unicode) now
Out[88]: 'this is bytes'
```

Booleans

The two boolean values in Python are written as `True` and `False`. Comparisons and other conditional expressions evaluate to either `True` or `False`. Boolean values are combined with the and and or keywords:

```
In [89]: True and True
Out[89]: True

In [90]: False or True
Out[90]: True
```

Type casting

The `str`, `bool`, `int`, and `float` types are also functions that can be used to cast values to those types:

```
In [91]: s = '3.14159'

In [92]: fval = float(s)

In [93]: type(fval)
Out[93]: float

In [94]: int(fval)
Out[94]: 3

In [95]: bool(fval)
Out[95]: True

In [96]: bool(0)
Out[96]: False
```

None

None is the Python null value type. If a function does not explicitly return a value, it implicitly returns None:

```
In [97]: a = None

In [98]: a is None
Out[98]: True

In [99]: b = 5

In [100]: b is not None
Out[100]: True
```

None is also a common default value for function arguments:

```
def add_and_maybe_multiply(a, b, c=None):
    result = a + b

    if c is not None:
        result = result * c

    return result
```

While a technical point, it's worth bearing in mind that None is not only a reserved keyword but also a unique instance of NoneType:

```
In [101]: type(None)
Out[101]: NoneType
```

Dates and times

The built-in Python datetime module provides datetime, date, and time types. The datetime type, as you may imagine, combines the information stored in date and time and is the most commonly used:

```
In [102]: from datetime import datetime, date, time

In [103]: dt = datetime(2011, 10, 29, 20, 30, 21)

In [104]: dt.day
Out[104]: 29

In [105]: dt.minute
Out[105]: 30
```

Given a datetime instance, you can extract the equivalent date and time objects by calling methods on the datetime of the same name:

```
In [106]: dt.date()
Out[106]: datetime.date(2011, 10, 29)
```

```
In [107]: dt.time()
Out[107]: datetime.time(20, 30, 21)
```

The `strftime` method formats a `datetime` as a string:

```
In [108]: dt.strftime('%m/%d/%Y %H:%M')
Out[108]: '10/29/2011 20:30'
```

Strings can be converted (parsed) into `datetime` objects with the `strptime` function:

```
In [109]: datetime.strptime('20091031', '%Y%m%d')
Out[109]: datetime.datetime(2009, 10, 31, 0, 0)
```

See Table 2-5 for a full list of format specifications.

When you are aggregating or otherwise grouping time series data, it will occasionally be useful to replace time fields of a series of `datetimes`—for example, replacing the minute and second fields with zero:

```
In [110]: dt.replace(minute=0, second=0)
Out[110]: datetime.datetime(2011, 10, 29, 20, 0)
```

Since `datetime.datetime` is an immutable type, methods like these always produce new objects.

The difference of two `datetime` objects produces a `datetime.timedelta` type:

```
In [111]: dt2 = datetime(2011, 11, 15, 22, 30)

In [112]: delta = dt2 - dt

In [113]: delta
Out[113]: datetime.timedelta(17, 7179)

In [114]: type(delta)
Out[114]: datetime.timedelta
```

The output `timedelta(17, 7179)` indicates that the timedelta encodes an offset of 17 days and 7,179 seconds.

Adding a `timedelta` to a `datetime` produces a new shifted `datetime`:

```
In [115]: dt
Out[115]: datetime.datetime(2011, 10, 29, 20, 30, 21)

In [116]: dt + delta
Out[116]: datetime.datetime(2011, 11, 15, 22, 30)
```

Table 2-5. Datetime format specification (ISO C89 compatible)

Type	Description
%Y	Four-digit year
%y	Two-digit year

Type	Description
%m	Two-digit month [01, 12]
%d	Two-digit day [01, 31]
%H	Hour (24-hour clock) [00, 23]
%I	Hour (12-hour clock) [01, 12]
%M	Two-digit minute [00, 59]
%S	Second [00, 61] (seconds 60, 61 account for leap seconds)
%w	Weekday as integer [0 (Sunday), 6]
%U	Week number of the year [00, 53]; Sunday is considered the first day of the week, and days before the first Sunday of the year are "week 0"
%W	Week number of the year [00, 53]; Monday is considered the first day of the week, and days before the first Monday of the year are "week 0"
%z	UTC time zone offset as +HHMM or -HHMM; empty if time zone naive
%F	Shortcut for %Y-%m-%d (e.g., 2012-4-18)
%D	Shortcut for %m/%d/%y (e.g., 04/18/12)

Control Flow

Python has several built-in keywords for conditional logic, loops, and other standard *control flow* concepts found in other programming languages.

if, elif, and else

The `if` statement is one of the most well-known control flow statement types. It checks a condition that, if `True`, evaluates the code in the block that follows:

```python
if x < 0:
    print("It's negative")
```

An `if` statement can be optionally followed by one or more `elif` blocks and a catch-all `else` block if all of the conditions are `False`:

```python
if x < 0:
    print("It's negative")
elif x == 0:
    print("Equal to zero")
elif 0 < x < 5:
    print("Positive but smaller than 5")
else:
    print("Positive and larger than or equal to 5")
```

If any of the conditions is `True`, no further `elif` or `else` blocks will be reached. With a compound condition using `and` or `or`, conditions are evaluated left to right and will short-circuit:

```python
In [117]: a = 5; b = 7

In [118]: c = 8; d = 4
```

```
In [119]: if a < b or c > d:
   .....:     print('Made it')
Made it
```

In this example, the comparison c > d never gets evaluated because the first comparison was True.

It is also possible to chain comparisons:

```
In [120]: 4 > 3 > 2 > 1
Out[120]: True
```

for loops

for loops are for iterating over a collection (like a list or tuple) or an iterater. The standard syntax for a for loop is:

```
for value in collection:
    # do something with value
```

You can advance a for loop to the next iteration, skipping the remainder of the block, using the continue keyword. Consider this code, which sums up integers in a list and skips None values:

```
sequence = [1, 2, None, 4, None, 5]
total = 0
for value in sequence:
    if value is None:
        continue
    total += value
```

A for loop can be exited altogether with the break keyword. This code sums elements of the list until a 5 is reached:

```
sequence = [1, 2, 0, 4, 6, 5, 2, 1]
total_until_5 = 0
for value in sequence:
    if value == 5:
        break
    total_until_5 += value
```

The break keyword only terminates the innermost for loop; any outer for loops will continue to run:

```
In [121]: for i in range(4):
   .....:     for j in range(4):
   .....:         if j > i:
   .....:             break
   .....:         print((i, j))
   .....:
(0, 0)
(1, 0)
```

```
(1, 1)
(2, 0)
(2, 1)
(2, 2)
(3, 0)
(3, 1)
(3, 2)
(3, 3)
```

As we will see in more detail, if the elements in the collection or iterator are sequences (tuples or lists, say), they can be conveniently *unpacked* into variables in the for loop statement:

```
for a, b, c in iterator:
    # do something
```

while loops

A while loop specifies a condition and a block of code that is to be executed until the condition evaluates to False or the loop is explicitly ended with break:

```
x = 256
total = 0
while x > 0:
    if total > 500:
        break
    total += x
    x = x // 2
```

pass

pass is the "no-op" statement in Python. It can be used in blocks where no action is to be taken (or as a placeholder for code not yet implemented); it is only required because Python uses whitespace to delimit blocks:

```
if x < 0:
    print('negative!')
elif x == 0:
    # TODO: put something smart here
    pass
else:
    print('positive!')
```

range

The range function returns an iterator that yields a sequence of evenly spaced integers:

```
In [122]: range(10)
Out[122]: range(0, 10)
```

```
In [123]: list(range(10))
Out[123]: [0, 1, 2, 3, 4, 5, 6, 7, 8, 9]
```

Both a start, end, and step (which may be negative) can be given:

```
In [124]: list(range(0, 20, 2))
Out[124]: [0, 2, 4, 6, 8, 10, 12, 14, 16, 18]

In [125]: list(range(5, 0, -1))
Out[125]: [5, 4, 3, 2, 1]
```

As you can see, range produces integers up to but not including the endpoint. A common use of range is for iterating through sequences by index:

```
seq = [1, 2, 3, 4]
for i in range(len(seq)):
    val = seq[i]
```

While you can use functions like list to store all the integers generated by range in some other data structure, often the default iterator form will be what you want. This snippet sums all numbers from 0 to 99,999 that are multiples of 3 or 5:

```
sum = 0
for i in range(100000):
    # % is the modulo operator
    if i % 3 == 0 or i % 5 == 0:
        sum += i
```

While the range generated can be arbitrarily large, the memory use at any given time may be very small.

Ternary expressions

A *ternary expression* in Python allows you to combine an if-else block that produces a value into a single line or expression. The syntax for this in Python is:

```
value = true-expr if condition else false-expr
```

Here, *true-expr* and *false-expr* can be any Python expressions. It has the identical effect as the more verbose:

```
if condition:
    value = true-expr
else:
    value = false-expr
```

This is a more concrete example:

```
In [126]: x = 5

In [127]: 'Non-negative' if x >= 0 else 'Negative'
Out[127]: 'Non-negative'
```

As with if-else blocks, only one of the expressions will be executed. Thus, the "if" and "else" sides of the ternary expression could contain costly computations, but only the true branch is ever evaluated.

While it may be tempting to always use ternary expressions to condense your code, realize that you may sacrifice readability if the condition as well as the true and false expressions are very complex.

## CHAPTER 3

Built-in Data Structures, Functions, and Files

This chapter discusses capabilities built into the Python language that will be used ubiquitously throughout the book. While add-on libraries like pandas and NumPy add advanced computational functionality for larger datasets, they are designed to be used together with Python's built-in data manipulation tools.

We'll start with Python's workhorse data structures: tuples, lists, dicts, and sets. Then, we'll discuss creating your own reusable Python functions. Finally, we'll look at the mechanics of Python file objects and interacting with your local hard drive.

3.1 Data Structures and Sequences

Python's data structures are simple but powerful. Mastering their use is a critical part of becoming a proficient Python programmer.

Tuple

A tuple is a fixed-length, immutable sequence of Python objects. The easiest way to create one is with a comma-separated sequence of values:

```
In [2]: tup = 4, 5, 6

In [3]: tup
Out[3]: (4, 5, 6)
```

When you're defining tuples in more complicated expressions, it's often necessary to enclose the values in parentheses, as in this example of creating a tuple of tuples:

```
In [4]: nested_tup = (4, 5, 6), (7, 8)

In [5]: nested_tup
Out[5]: ((4, 5, 6), (7, 8))
```

You can convert any sequence or iterator to a tuple by invoking `tuple`:

```
In [6]: tuple([4, 0, 2])
Out[6]: (4, 0, 2)

In [7]: tup = tuple('string')

In [8]: tup
Out[8]: ('s', 't', 'r', 'i', 'n', 'g')
```

Elements can be accessed with square brackets [ ] as with most other sequence types. As in C, C++, Java, and many other languages, sequences are 0-indexed in Python:

```
In [9]: tup[0]
Out[9]: 's'
```

While the objects stored in a tuple may be mutable themselves, once the tuple is created it's not possible to modify which object is stored in each slot:

```
In [10]: tup = tuple(['foo', [1, 2], True])

In [11]: tup[2] = False
---------------------------------------------------------------------------
TypeError                                 Traceback (most recent call last)
<ipython-input-11-c7308343b841> in <module>()
----> 1 tup[2] = False
TypeError: 'tuple' object does not support item assignment
```

If an object inside a tuple is mutable, such as a list, you can modify it in-place:

```
In [12]: tup[1].append(3)

In [13]: tup
Out[13]: ('foo', [1, 2, 3], True)
```

You can concatenate tuples using the + operator to produce longer tuples:

```
In [14]: (4, None, 'foo') + (6, 0) + ('bar',)
Out[14]: (4, None, 'foo', 6, 0, 'bar')
```

Multiplying a tuple by an integer, as with lists, has the effect of concatenating together that many copies of the tuple:

```
In [15]: ('foo', 'bar') * 4
Out[15]: ('foo', 'bar', 'foo', 'bar', 'foo', 'bar', 'foo', 'bar')
```

Note that the objects themselves are not copied, only the references to them.

Unpacking tuples

If you try to *assign* to a tuple-like expression of variables, Python will attempt to *unpack* the value on the righthand side of the equals sign:

```
In [16]: tup = (4, 5, 6)

In [17]: a, b, c = tup

In [18]: b
Out[18]: 5
```

Even sequences with nested tuples can be unpacked:

```
In [19]: tup = 4, 5, (6, 7)

In [20]: a, b, (c, d) = tup

In [21]: d
Out[21]: 7
```

Using this functionality you can easily swap variable names, a task which in many languages might look like:

```
tmp = a
a = b
b = tmp
```

But, in Python, the swap can be done like this:

```
In [22]: a, b = 1, 2

In [23]: a
Out[23]: 1

In [24]: b
Out[24]: 2

In [25]: b, a = a, b

In [26]: a
Out[26]: 2

In [27]: b
Out[27]: 1
```

A common use of variable unpacking is iterating over sequences of tuples or lists:

```
In [28]: seq = [(1, 2, 3), (4, 5, 6), (7, 8, 9)]

In [29]: for a, b, c in seq:
   ....:     print('a={0}, b={1}, c={2}'.format(a, b, c))
a=1, b=2, c=3
a=4, b=5, c=6
a=7, b=8, c=9
```

Another common use is returning multiple values from a function. I'll cover this in more detail later.

The Python language recently acquired some more advanced tuple unpacking to help with situations where you may want to "pluck" a few elements from the beginning of a tuple. This uses the special syntax *rest, which is also used in function signatures to capture an arbitrarily long list of positional arguments:

```
In [30]: values = 1, 2, 3, 4, 5

In [31]: a, b, *rest = values

In [32]: a, b
Out[32]: (1, 2)

In [33]: rest
Out[33]: [3, 4, 5]
```

This rest bit is sometimes something you want to discard; there is nothing special about the rest name. As a matter of convention, many Python programmers will use the underscore (_) for unwanted variables:

```
In [34]: a, b, *_ = values
```

Tuple methods

Since the size and contents of a tuple cannot be modified, it is very light on instance methods. A particularly useful one (also available on lists) is count, which counts the number of occurrences of a value:

```
In [35]: a = (1, 2, 2, 2, 3, 4, 2)

In [36]: a.count(2)
Out[36]: 4
```

List

In contrast with tuples, lists are variable-length and their contents can be modified in-place. You can define them using square brackets [] or using the list type function:

```
In [37]: a_list = [2, 3, 7, None]

In [38]: tup = ('foo', 'bar', 'baz')

In [39]: b_list = list(tup)

In [40]: b_list
Out[40]: ['foo', 'bar', 'baz']

In [41]: b_list[1] = 'peekaboo'
```

```
In [42]: b_list
Out[42]: ['foo', 'peekaboo', 'baz']
```

Lists and tuples are semantically similar (though tuples cannot be modified) and can be used interchangeably in many functions.

The `list` function is frequently used in data processing as a way to materialize an iterator or generator expression:

```
In [43]: gen = range(10)

In [44]: gen
Out[44]: range(0, 10)

In [45]: list(gen)
Out[45]: [0, 1, 2, 3, 4, 5, 6, 7, 8, 9]
```

Adding and removing elements

Elements can be appended to the end of the list with the `append` method:

```
In [46]: b_list.append('dwarf')

In [47]: b_list
Out[47]: ['foo', 'peekaboo', 'baz', 'dwarf']
```

Using `insert` you can insert an element at a specific location in the list:

```
In [48]: b_list.insert(1, 'red')

In [49]: b_list
Out[49]: ['foo', 'red', 'peekaboo', 'baz', 'dwarf']
```

The insertion index must be between 0 and the length of the list, inclusive.

 insert is computationally expensive compared with append, because references to subsequent elements have to be shifted internally to make room for the new element. If you need to insert elements at both the beginning and end of a sequence, you may wish to explore `collections.deque`, a double-ended queue, for this purpose.

The inverse operation to `insert` is `pop`, which removes and returns an element at a particular index:

```
In [50]: b_list.pop(2)
Out[50]: 'peekaboo'

In [51]: b_list
Out[51]: ['foo', 'red', 'baz', 'dwarf']
```

Elements can be removed by value with `remove`, which locates the first such value and removes it from the list:

```
In [52]: b_list.append('foo')

In [53]: b_list
Out[53]: ['foo', 'red', 'baz', 'dwarf', 'foo']

In [54]: b_list.remove('foo')

In [55]: b_list
Out[55]: ['red', 'baz', 'dwarf', 'foo']
```

If performance is not a concern, by using `append` and `remove`, you can use a Python list as a perfectly suitable "multiset" data structure.

Check if a list contains a value using the `in` keyword:

```
In [56]: 'dwarf' in b_list
Out[56]: True
```

The keyword `not` can be used to negate `in`:

```
In [57]: 'dwarf' not in b_list
Out[57]: False
```

Checking whether a list contains a value is a lot slower than doing so with dicts and sets (to be introduced shortly), as Python makes a linear scan across the values of the list, whereas it can check the others (based on hash tables) in constant time.

Concatenating and combining lists

Similar to tuples, adding two lists together with + concatenates them:

```
In [58]: [4, None, 'foo'] + [7, 8, (2, 3)]
Out[58]: [4, None, 'foo', 7, 8, (2, 3)]
```

If you have a list already defined, you can append multiple elements to it using the extend method:

```
In [59]: x = [4, None, 'foo']

In [60]: x.extend([7, 8, (2, 3)])

In [61]: x
Out[61]: [4, None, 'foo', 7, 8, (2, 3)]
```

Note that list concatenation by addition is a comparatively expensive operation since a new list must be created and the objects copied over. Using `extend` to append elements to an existing list, especially if you are building up a large list, is usually preferable. Thus,

```
everything = []
for chunk in list_of_lists:
    everything.extend(chunk)
```

is faster than the concatenative alternative:

```
everything = []
for chunk in list_of_lists:
    everything = everything + chunk
```

Sorting

You can sort a list in-place (without creating a new object) by calling its `sort` function:

```
In [62]: a = [7, 2, 5, 1, 3]

In [63]: a.sort()

In [64]: a
Out[64]: [1, 2, 3, 5, 7]
```

`sort` has a few options that will occasionally come in handy. One is the ability to pass a secondary *sort key*—that is, a function that produces a value to use to sort the objects. For example, we could sort a collection of strings by their lengths:

```
In [65]: b = ['saw', 'small', 'He', 'foxes', 'six']

In [66]: b.sort(key=len)

In [67]: b
Out[67]: ['He', 'saw', 'six', 'small', 'foxes']
```

Soon, we'll look at the `sorted` function, which can produce a sorted copy of a general sequence.

Binary search and maintaining a sorted list

The built-in `bisect` module implements binary search and insertion into a sorted list. `bisect.bisect` finds the location where an element should be inserted to keep it sorted, while `bisect.insort` actually inserts the element into that location:

```
In [68]: import bisect

In [69]: c = [1, 2, 2, 2, 3, 4, 7]

In [70]: bisect.bisect(c, 2)
Out[70]: 4

In [71]: bisect.bisect(c, 5)
Out[71]: 6
```

```
In [72]: bisect.insort(c, 6)

In [73]: c
Out[73]: [1, 2, 2, 2, 3, 4, 6, 7]
```

 The bisect module functions do not check whether the list is sorted, as doing so would be computationally expensive. Thus, using them with an unsorted list will succeed without error but may lead to incorrect results.

Slicing

You can select sections of most sequence types by using slice notation, which in its basic form consists of start:stop passed to the indexing operator [ ]:

```
In [74]: seq = [7, 2, 3, 7, 5, 6, 0, 1]

In [75]: seq[1:5]
Out[75]: [2, 3, 7, 5]
```

Slices can also be assigned to with a sequence:

```
In [76]: seq[3:4] = [6, 3]

In [77]: seq
Out[77]: [7, 2, 3, 6, 3, 5, 6, 0, 1]
```

While the element at the start index is included, the stop index is *not included*, so that the number of elements in the result is stop - start.

Either the start or stop can be omitted, in which case they default to the start of the sequence and the end of the sequence, respectively:

```
In [78]: seq[:5]
Out[78]: [7, 2, 3, 6, 3]

In [79]: seq[3:]
Out[79]: [6, 3, 5, 6, 0, 1]
```

Negative indices slice the sequence relative to the end:

```
In [80]: seq[-4:]
Out[80]: [5, 6, 0, 1]

In [81]: seq[-6:-2]
Out[81]: [6, 3, 5, 6]
```

Slicing semantics takes a bit of getting used to, especially if you're coming from R or MATLAB. See Figure 3-1 for a helpful illustration of slicing with positive and negative integers. In the figure, the indices are shown at the "bin edges" to help show where the slice selections start and stop using positive or negative indices.

A `step` can also be used after a second colon to, say, take every other element:

```
In [82]: seq[::2]
Out[82]: [7, 3, 3, 6, 1]
```

A clever use of this is to pass -1, which has the useful effect of reversing a list or tuple:

```
In [83]: seq[::-1]
Out[83]: [1, 0, 6, 5, 3, 6, 3, 2, 7]
```

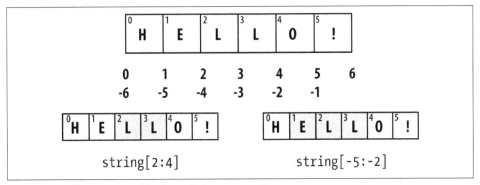

Figure 3-1. Illustration of Python slicing conventions

Built-in Sequence Functions

Python has a handful of useful sequence functions that you should familiarize your-self with and use at any opportunity.

enumerate

It's common when iterating over a sequence to want to keep track of the index of the current item. A do-it-yourself approach would look like:

```
i = 0
for value in collection:
    # do something with value
    i += 1
```

Since this is so common, Python has a built-in function, `enumerate`, which returns a sequence of `(i, value)` tuples:

```
for i, value in enumerate(collection):
    # do something with value
```

When you are indexing data, a helpful pattern that uses `enumerate` is computing a `dict` mapping the values of a sequence (which are assumed to be unique) to their locations in the sequence:

```
In [84]: some_list = ['foo', 'bar', 'baz']

In [85]: mapping = {}
```

```
In [86]: for i, v in enumerate(some_list):
   ....:     mapping[v] = i

In [87]: mapping
Out[87]: {'bar': 1, 'baz': 2, 'foo': 0}
```

sorted

The sorted function returns a new sorted list from the elements of any sequence:

```
In [88]: sorted([7, 1, 2, 6, 0, 3, 2])
Out[88]: [0, 1, 2, 2, 3, 6, 7]

In [89]: sorted('horse race')
Out[89]: [' ', 'a', 'c', 'e', 'e', 'h', 'o', 'r', 'r', 's']
```

The sorted function accepts the same arguments as the sort method on lists.

zip

zip "pairs" up the elements of a number of lists, tuples, or other sequences to create a list of tuples:

```
In [90]: seq1 = ['foo', 'bar', 'baz']

In [91]: seq2 = ['one', 'two', 'three']

In [92]: zipped = zip(seq1, seq2)

In [93]: list(zipped)
Out[93]: [('foo', 'one'), ('bar', 'two'), ('baz', 'three')]
```

zip can take an arbitrary number of sequences, and the number of elements it produces is determined by the *shortest* sequence:

```
In [94]: seq3 = [False, True]

In [95]: list(zip(seq1, seq2, seq3))
Out[95]: [('foo', 'one', False), ('bar', 'two', True)]
```

A very common use of zip is simultaneously iterating over multiple sequences, possibly also combined with enumerate:

```
In [96]: for i, (a, b) in enumerate(zip(seq1, seq2)):
   ....:     print('{0}: {1}, {2}'.format(i, a, b))
   ....:
0: foo, one
1: bar, two
2: baz, three
```

Given a "zipped" sequence, `zip` can be applied in a clever way to "unzip" the sequence. Another way to think about this is converting a list of *rows* into a list of *columns*. The syntax, which looks a bit magical, is:

```
In [97]: pitchers = [('Nolan', 'Ryan'), ('Roger', 'Clemens'),
   ....:            ('Curt', 'Schilling')]

In [98]: first_names, last_names = zip(*pitchers)

In [99]: first_names
Out[99]: ('Nolan', 'Roger', 'Curt')

In [100]: last_names
Out[100]: ('Ryan', 'Clemens', 'Schilling')
```

reversed

`reversed` iterates over the elements of a sequence in reverse order:

```
In [101]: list(reversed(range(10)))
Out[101]: [9, 8, 7, 6, 5, 4, 3, 2, 1, 0]
```

Keep in mind that `reversed` is a generator (to be discussed in some more detail later), so it does not create the reversed sequence until materialized (e.g., with `list` or a `for` loop).

dict

`dict` is likely the most important built-in Python data structure. A more common name for it is *hash map* or *associative array*. It is a flexibly sized collection of *key-value* pairs, where *key* and *value* are Python objects. One approach for creating one is to use curly braces {} and colons to separate keys and values:

```
In [102]: empty_dict = {}

In [103]: d1 = {'a' : 'some value', 'b' : [1, 2, 3, 4]}

In [104]: d1
Out[104]: {'a': 'some value', 'b': [1, 2, 3, 4]}
```

You can access, insert, or set elements using the same syntax as for accessing elements of a list or tuple:

```
In [105]: d1[7] = 'an integer'

In [106]: d1
Out[106]: {'a': 'some value', 'b': [1, 2, 3, 4], 7: 'an integer'}

In [107]: d1['b']
Out[107]: [1, 2, 3, 4]
```

You can check if a dict contains a key using the same syntax used for checking whether a list or tuple contains a value:

```
In [108]: 'b' in d1
Out[108]: True
```

You can delete values either using the del keyword or the pop method (which simultaneously returns the value and deletes the key):

```
In [109]: d1[5] = 'some value'

In [110]: d1
Out[110]:
{'a': 'some value',
 'b': [1, 2, 3, 4],
 7: 'an integer',
 5: 'some value'}

In [111]: d1['dummy'] = 'another value'

In [112]: d1
Out[112]:
{'a': 'some value',
 'b': [1, 2, 3, 4],
 7: 'an integer',
 5: 'some value',
 'dummy': 'another value'}

In [113]: del d1[5]

In [114]: d1
Out[114]:
{'a': 'some value',
 'b': [1, 2, 3, 4],
 7: 'an integer',
 'dummy': 'another value'}

In [115]: ret = d1.pop('dummy')

In [116]: ret
Out[116]: 'another value'

In [117]: d1
Out[117]: {'a': 'some value', 'b': [1, 2, 3, 4], 7: 'an integer'}
```

The keys and values method give you iterators of the dict's keys and values, respectively. While the key-value pairs are not in any particular order, these functions output the keys and values in the same order:

```
In [118]: list(d1.keys())
Out[118]: ['a', 'b', 7]
```

```
In [119]: list(d1.values())
Out[119]: ['some value', [1, 2, 3, 4], 'an integer']
```

You can merge one dict into another using the update method:

```
In [120]: d1.update({'b' : 'foo', 'c' : 12})

In [121]: d1
Out[121]: {'a': 'some value', 'b': 'foo', 7: 'an integer', 'c': 12}
```

The update method changes dicts in-place, so any existing keys in the data passed to update will have their old values discarded.

Creating dicts from sequences

It's common to occasionally end up with two sequences that you want to pair up element-wise in a dict. As a first cut, you might write code like this:

```
mapping = {}
for key, value in zip(key_list, value_list):
    mapping[key] = value
```

Since a dict is essentially a collection of 2-tuples, the dict function accepts a list of 2-tuples:

```
In [122]: mapping = dict(zip(range(5), reversed(range(5))))

In [123]: mapping
Out[123]: {0: 4, 1: 3, 2: 2, 3: 1, 4: 0}
```

Later we'll talk about *dict comprehensions*, another elegant way to construct dicts.

Default values

It's very common to have logic like:

```
if key in some_dict:
    value = some_dict[key]
else:
    value = default_value
```

Thus, the dict methods get and pop can take a default value to be returned, so that the above if-else block can be written simply as:

```
value = some_dict.get(key, default_value)
```

get by default will return None if the key is not present, while pop will raise an exception. With *setting* values, a common case is for the values in a dict to be other collections, like lists. For example, you could imagine categorizing a list of words by their first letters as a dict of lists:

```
In [124]: words = ['apple', 'bat', 'bar', 'atom', 'book']

In [125]: by_letter = {}
```

```
In [126]: for word in words:
     ....:     letter = word[0]
     ....:     if letter not in by_letter:
     ....:         by_letter[letter] = [word]
     ....:     else:
     ....:         by_letter[letter].append(word)
     ....:

In [127]: by_letter
Out[127]: {'a': ['apple', 'atom'], 'b': ['bat', 'bar', 'book']}
```

The `setdefault` dict method is for precisely this purpose. The preceding `for` loop can be rewritten as:

```
for word in words:
    letter = word[0]
    by_letter.setdefault(letter, []).append(word)
```

The built-in `collections` module has a useful class, `defaultdict`, which makes this even easier. To create one, you pass a type or function for generating the default value for each slot in the dict:

```
from collections import defaultdict
by_letter = defaultdict(list)
for word in words:
    by_letter[word[0]].append(word)
```

Valid dict key types

While the values of a dict can be any Python object, the keys generally have to be immutable objects like scalar types (int, float, string) or tuples (all the objects in the tuple need to be immutable, too). The technical term here is *hashability*. You can check whether an object is hashable (can be used as a key in a dict) with the `hash` function:

```
In [128]: hash('string')
Out[128]: 5330554102147468818

In [129]: hash((1, 2, (2, 3)))
Out[129]: 1097636502276347782

In [130]: hash((1, 2, [2, 3])) # fails because lists are mutable
---------------------------------------------------------------------------
TypeError                                 Traceback (most recent call last)
<ipython-input-130-800cd14ba8be> in <module>()
----> 1 hash((1, 2, [2, 3])) # fails because lists are mutable
TypeError: unhashable type: 'list'
```

To use a list as a key, one option is to convert it to a tuple, which can be hashed as long as its elements also can:

```
In [131]: d = {}

In [132]: d[tuple([1, 2, 3])] = 5

In [133]: d
Out[133]: {(1, 2, 3): 5}
```

set

A set is an unordered collection of unique elements. You can think of them like dicts, but keys only, no values. A set can be created in two ways: via the set function or via a *set literal* with curly braces:

```
In [134]: set([2, 2, 2, 1, 3, 3])
Out[134]: {1, 2, 3}

In [135]: {2, 2, 2, 1, 3, 3}
Out[135]: {1, 2, 3}
```

Sets support mathematical *set operations* like union, intersection, difference, and symmetric difference. Consider these two example sets:

```
In [136]: a = {1, 2, 3, 4, 5}

In [137]: b = {3, 4, 5, 6, 7, 8}
```

The union of these two sets is the set of distinct elements occurring in either set. This can be computed with either the union method or the | binary operator:

```
In [138]: a.union(b)
Out[138]: {1, 2, 3, 4, 5, 6, 7, 8}

In [139]: a | b
Out[139]: {1, 2, 3, 4, 5, 6, 7, 8}
```

The intersection contains the elements occurring in both sets. The & operator or the intersection method can be used:

```
In [140]: a.intersection(b)
Out[140]: {3, 4, 5}

In [141]: a & b
Out[141]: {3, 4, 5}
```

See Table 3-1 for a list of commonly used set methods.

Table 3-1. Python set operations

Function	Alternative syntax	Description
`a.add(x)`	N/A	Add element x to the set a
`a.clear()`	N/A	Reset the set a to an empty state, discarding all of its elements
`a.remove(x)`	N/A	Remove element x from the set a
`a.pop()`	N/A	Remove an arbitrary element from the set a, raising KeyError if the set is empty
`a.union(b)`	`a	b`	All of the unique elements in a and b
`a.update(b)`	`a |= b`	Set the contents of a to be the union of the elements in a and b
`a.intersection(b)`	`a & b`	All of the elements in *both* a and b
`a.intersection_update(b)`	`a &= b`	Set the contents of a to be the intersection of the elements in a and b
`a.difference(b)`	`a - b`	The elements in a that are not in b
`a.difference_update(b)`	`a -= b`	Set a to the elements in a that are not in b
`a.symmetric_difference(b)`	`a ^ b`	All of the elements in either a or b but *not both*
`a.symmetric_difference_update(b)`	`a ^= b`	Set a to contain the elements in either a or b but *not both*
`a.issubset(b)`	`<=`	True if the elements of a are all contained in b
`a.issuperset(b)`	`>=`	True if the elements of b are all contained in a
`a.isdisjoint(b)`	N/A	True if a and b have no elements in common

All of the logical set operations have in-place counterparts, which enable you to replace the contents of the set on the left side of the operation with the result. For very large sets, this may be more efficient:

```
In [142]: c = a.copy()

In [143]: c |= b

In [144]: c
Out[144]: {1, 2, 3, 4, 5, 6, 7, 8}

In [145]: d = a.copy()

In [146]: d &= b

In [147]: d
Out[147]: {3, 4, 5}
```

Like dicts, set elements generally must be immutable. To have list-like elements, you must convert it to a tuple:

```
In [148]: my_data = [1, 2, 3, 4]

In [149]: my_set = {tuple(my_data)}

In [150]: my_set
Out[150]: {(1, 2, 3, 4)}
```

You can also check if a set is a subset of (is contained in) or a superset of (contains all elements of) another set:

```
In [151]: a_set = {1, 2, 3, 4, 5}

In [152]: {1, 2, 3}.issubset(a_set)
Out[152]: True

In [153]: a_set.issuperset({1, 2, 3})
Out[153]: True
```

Sets are equal if and only if their contents are equal:

```
In [154]: {1, 2, 3} == {3, 2, 1}
Out[154]: True
```

List, Set, and Dict Comprehensions

List comprehensions are one of the most-loved Python language features. They allow you to concisely form a new list by filtering the elements of a collection, transforming the elements passing the filter in one concise expression. They take the basic form:

```
[expr for val in collection if condition]
```

This is equivalent to the following for loop:

```
result = []
for val in collection:
    if condition:
        result.append(expr)
```

The filter condition can be omitted, leaving only the expression. For example, given a list of strings, we could filter out strings with length 2 or less and also convert them to uppercase like this:

```
In [155]: strings = ['a', 'as', 'bat', 'car', 'dove', 'python']

In [156]: [x.upper() for x in strings if len(x) > 2]
Out[156]: ['BAT', 'CAR', 'DOVE', 'PYTHON']
```

Set and dict comprehensions are a natural extension, producing sets and dicts in an idiomatically similar way instead of lists. A dict comprehension looks like this:

```
dict_comp = {key-expr : value-expr for value in collection
             if condition}
```

A set comprehension looks like the equivalent list comprehension except with curly braces instead of square brackets:

```
set_comp = {expr for value in collection if condition}
```

Like list comprehensions, set and dict comprehensions are mostly conveniences, but they similarly can make code both easier to write and read. Consider the list of strings from before. Suppose we wanted a set containing just the lengths of the strings contained in the collection; we could easily compute this using a set comprehension:

```
In [157]: unique_lengths = {len(x) for x in strings}

In [158]: unique_lengths
Out[158]: {1, 2, 3, 4, 6}
```

We could also express this more functionally using the map function, introduced shortly:

```
In [159]: set(map(len, strings))
Out[159]: {1, 2, 3, 4, 6}
```

As a simple dict comprehension example, we could create a lookup map of these strings to their locations in the list:

```
In [160]: loc_mapping = {val : index for index, val in enumerate(strings)}

In [161]: loc_mapping
Out[161]: {'a': 0, 'as': 1, 'bat': 2, 'car': 3, 'dove': 4, 'python': 5}
```

Nested list comprehensions

Suppose we have a list of lists containing some English and Spanish names:

```
In [162]: all_data = [['John', 'Emily', 'Michael', 'Mary', 'Steven'],
   .....:             ['Maria', 'Juan', 'Javier', 'Natalia', 'Pilar']]
```

You might have gotten these names from a couple of files and decided to organize them by language. Now, suppose we wanted to get a single list containing all names with two or more e's in them. We could certainly do this with a simple for loop:

```
names_of_interest = []
for names in all_data:
    enough_es = [name for name in names if name.count('e') >= 2]
    names_of_interest.extend(enough_es)
```

You can actually wrap this whole operation up in a single *nested list comprehension*, which will look like:

```
In [163]: result = [name for names in all_data for name in names
   .....:           if name.count('e') >= 2]

In [164]: result
Out[164]: ['Steven']
```

At first, nested list comprehensions are a bit hard to wrap your head around. The for parts of the list comprehension are arranged according to the order of nesting, and any filter condition is put at the end as before. Here is another example where we "flatten" a list of tuples of integers into a simple list of integers:

```
In [165]: some_tuples = [(1, 2, 3), (4, 5, 6), (7, 8, 9)]

In [166]: flattened = [x for tup in some_tuples for x in tup]

In [167]: flattened
Out[167]: [1, 2, 3, 4, 5, 6, 7, 8, 9]
```

Keep in mind that the order of the for expressions would be the same if you wrote a nested for loop instead of a list comprehension:

```
flattened = []

for tup in some_tuples:
    for x in tup:
        flattened.append(x)
```

You can have arbitrarily many levels of nesting, though if you have more than two or three levels of nesting you should probably start to question whether this makes sense from a code readability standpoint. It's important to distinguish the syntax just shown from a list comprehension inside a list comprehension, which is also perfectly valid:

```
In [168]: [[x for x in tup] for tup in some_tuples]
Out[168]: [[1, 2, 3], [4, 5, 6], [7, 8, 9]]
```

This produces a list of lists, rather than a flattened list of all of the inner elements.

3.2 Functions

Functions are the primary and most important method of code organization and reuse in Python. As a rule of thumb, if you anticipate needing to repeat the same or very similar code more than once, it may be worth writing a reusable function. Functions can also help make your code more readable by giving a name to a group of Python statements.

Functions are declared with the def keyword and returned from with the return keyword:

```
def my_function(x, y, z=1.5):
    if z > 1:
        return z * (x + y)
    else:
        return z / (x + y)
```

There is no issue with having multiple `return` statements. If Python reaches the end of a function without encountering a `return` statement, `None` is returned automatically.

Each function can have *positional* arguments and *keyword* arguments. Keyword arguments are most commonly used to specify default values or optional arguments. In the preceding function, x and y are positional arguments while z is a keyword argument. This means that the function can be called in any of these ways:

```
my_function(5, 6, z=0.7)
my_function(3.14, 7, 3.5)
my_function(10, 20)
```

The main restriction on function arguments is that the keyword arguments *must* follow the positional arguments (if any). You can specify keyword arguments in any order; this frees you from having to remember which order the function arguments were specified in and only what their names are.

 It is possible to use keywords for passing positional arguments as well. In the preceding example, we could also have written:

```
my_function(x=5, y=6, z=7)
my_function(y=6, x=5, z=7)
```

In some cases this can help with readability.

Namespaces, Scope, and Local Functions

Functions can access variables in two different scopes: *global* and *local*. An alternative and more descriptive name describing a variable scope in Python is a *namespace*. Any variables that are assigned within a function by default are assigned to the local namespace. The local namespace is created when the function is called and immediately populated by the function's arguments. After the function is finished, the local namespace is destroyed (with some exceptions that are outside the purview of this chapter). Consider the following function:

```
def func():
    a = []
    for i in range(5):
        a.append(i)
```

When `func()` is called, the empty list a is created, five elements are appended, and then a is destroyed when the function exits. Suppose instead we had declared a as follows:

```
a = []
def func():
    for i in range(5):
        a.append(i)
```

Each call to func will modify the list a:

```
In [170]: func()

In [171]: a
Out[171]: [0, 1, 2, 3, 4]

In [172]: func()

In [173]: a
Out[173]: [0, 1, 2, 3, 4, 0, 1, 2, 3, 4]
```

Assigning variables outside of the function's scope is possible, but those variables must be declared as global via the global keyword:

```
In [174]: a = None

In [175]: def bind_a_variable():
     .....:     global a
     .....:     a = []
     .....: bind_a_variable()
     .....:

In [176]: print(a)
[]
```

 I generally discourage use of the global keyword. Typically global variables are used to store some kind of state in a system. If you find yourself using a lot of them, it may indicate a need for object-oriented programming (using classes).

Returning Multiple Values

When I first programmed in Python after having programmed in Java and C++, one of my favorite features was the ability to return multiple values from a function with simple syntax. Here's an example:

```
def f():
    a = 5
    b = 6
    c = 7
    return a, b, c

a, b, c = f()
```

In data analysis and other scientific applications, you may find yourself doing this often. What's happening here is that the function is actually just returning *one* object, namely a tuple, which is then being unpacked into the result variables. In the preceding example, we could have done this instead:

```
return_value = f()
```

In this case, `return_value` would be a 3-tuple with the three returned variables. A potentially attractive alternative to returning multiple values like before might be to return a dict instead:

```python
def f():
    a = 5
    b = 6
    c = 7
    return {'a' : a, 'b' : b, 'c' : c}
```

This alternative technique can be useful depending on what you are trying to do.

Functions Are Objects

Since Python functions are objects, many constructs can be easily expressed that are difficult to do in other languages. Suppose we were doing some data cleaning and needed to apply a bunch of transformations to the following list of strings:

```python
In [177]: states = ['   Alabama ', 'Georgia!', 'Georgia', 'georgia', 'FlOrIda',
   .....:           'south   carolina##', 'West virginia?']
```

Anyone who has ever worked with user-submitted survey data has seen messy results like these. Lots of things need to happen to make this list of strings uniform and ready for analysis: stripping whitespace, removing punctuation symbols, and standardizing on proper capitalization. One way to do this is to use built-in string methods along with the `re` standard library module for regular expressions:

```python
import re

def clean_strings(strings):
    result = []
    for value in strings:
        value = value.strip()
        value = re.sub('[!#?]', '', value)
        value = value.title()
        result.append(value)
    return result
```

The result looks like this:

```python
In [179]: clean_strings(states)
Out[179]:
['Alabama',
 'Georgia',
 'Georgia',
 'Georgia',
 'Florida',
 'South   Carolina',
 'West Virginia']
```

An alternative approach that you may find useful is to make a list of the operations you want to apply to a particular set of strings:

```python
def remove_punctuation(value):
    return re.sub('[!#?]', '', value)

clean_ops = [str.strip, remove_punctuation, str.title]

def clean_strings(strings, ops):
    result = []
    for value in strings:
        for function in ops:
            value = function(value)
        result.append(value)
    return result
```

Then we have the following:

```python
In [181]: clean_strings(states, clean_ops)
Out[181]:
['Alabama',
 'Georgia',
 'Georgia',
 'Georgia',
 'Florida',
 'South   Carolina',
 'West Virginia']
```

A more *functional* pattern like this enables you to easily modify how the strings are transformed at a very high level. The `clean_strings` function is also now more reusable and generic.

You can use functions as arguments to other functions like the built-in `map` function, which applies a function to a sequence of some kind:

```python
In [182]: for x in map(remove_punctuation, states):
   .....:     print(x)
Alabama
Georgia
Georgia
georgia
FlOrIda
south   carolina
West virginia
```

Anonymous (Lambda) Functions

Python has support for so-called *anonymous* or *lambda* functions, which are a way of writing functions consisting of a single statement, the result of which is the return value. They are defined with the `lambda` keyword, which has no meaning other than "we are declaring an anonymous function":

```
def short_function(x):
    return x * 2

equiv_anon = lambda x: x * 2
```

I usually refer to these as lambda functions in the rest of the book. They are especially convenient in data analysis because, as you'll see, there are many cases where data transformation functions will take functions as arguments. It's often less typing (and clearer) to pass a lambda function as opposed to writing a full-out function declaration or even assigning the lambda function to a local variable. For example, consider this silly example:

```
def apply_to_list(some_list, f):
    return [f(x) for x in some_list]

ints = [4, 0, 1, 5, 6]
apply_to_list(ints, lambda x: x * 2)
```

You could also have written `[x * 2 for x in ints]`, but here we were able to succinctly pass a custom operator to the `apply_to_list` function.

As another example, suppose you wanted to sort a collection of strings by the number of distinct letters in each string:

```
In [183]: strings = ['foo', 'card', 'bar', 'aaaa', 'abab']
```

Here we could pass a lambda function to the list's `sort` method:

```
In [184]: strings.sort(key=lambda x: len(set(list(x))))

In [185]: strings
Out[185]: ['aaaa', 'foo', 'abab', 'bar', 'card']
```

 One reason lambda functions are called anonymous functions is that , unlike functions declared with the `def` keyword, the function object itself is never given an explicit `__name__` attribute.

Currying: Partial Argument Application

Currying is computer science jargon (named after the mathematician Haskell Curry) that means deriving new functions from existing ones by *partial argument application*. For example, suppose we had a trivial function that adds two numbers together:

```
def add_numbers(x, y):
    return x + y
```

Using this function, we could derive a new function of one variable, `add_five`, that adds 5 to its argument:

```
add_five = lambda y: add_numbers(5, y)
```

The second argument to `add_numbers` is said to be *curried*. There's nothing very fancy here, as all we've really done is define a new function that calls an existing function. The built-in `functools` module can simplify this process using the `partial` function:

```
from functools import partial
add_five = partial(add_numbers, 5)
```

Generators

Having a consistent way to iterate over sequences, like objects in a list or lines in a file, is an important Python feature. This is accomplished by means of the *iterator protocol*, a generic way to make objects iterable. For example, iterating over a dict yields the dict keys:

```
In [186]: some_dict = {'a': 1, 'b': 2, 'c': 3}

In [187]: for key in some_dict:
   .....:     print(key)
a
b
c
```

When you write for `key in some_dict`, the Python interpreter first attempts to create an iterator out of `some_dict`:

```
In [188]: dict_iterator = iter(some_dict)

In [189]: dict_iterator
Out[189]: <dict_keyiterator at 0x7f816e037048>
```

An iterator is any object that will yield objects to the Python interpreter when used in a context like a for loop. Most methods expecting a list or list-like object will also accept any iterable object. This includes built-in methods such as `min`, `max`, and `sum`, and type constructors like `list` and `tuple`:

```
In [190]: list(dict_iterator)
Out[190]: ['a', 'b', 'c']
```

A *generator* is a concise way to construct a new iterable object. Whereas normal functions execute and return a single result at a time, generators return a sequence of multiple results lazily, pausing after each one until the next one is requested. To create a generator, use the `yield` keyword instead of `return` in a function:

```
def squares(n=10):
    print('Generating squares from 1 to {0}'.format(n ** 2))
    for i in range(1, n + 1):
        yield i ** 2
```

When you actually call the generator, no code is immediately executed:

```
In [192]: gen = squares()
```

```
In [193]: gen
Out[193]: <generator object squares at 0x7f816e0702b0>
```

It is not until you request elements from the generator that it begins executing its code:

```
In [194]: for x in gen:
   .....:     print(x, end=' ')
Generating squares from 1 to 100
1 4 9 16 25 36 49 64 81 100
```

Generator expresssions

Another even more concise way to make a generator is by using a *generator expression*. This is a generator analogue to list, dict, and set comprehensions; to create one, enclose what would otherwise be a list comprehension within parentheses instead of brackets:

```
In [195]: gen = (x ** 2 for x in range(100))
```

```
In [196]: gen
Out[196]: <generator object <genexpr> at 0x7f816e001e08>
```

This is completely equivalent to the following more verbose generator:

```
def _make_gen():
    for x in range(100):
        yield x ** 2
gen = _make_gen()
```

Generator expressions can be used instead of list comprehensions as function arguments in many cases:

```
In [197]: sum(x ** 2 for x in range(100))
Out[197]: 328350
```

```
In [198]: dict((i, i **2) for i in range(5))
Out[198]: {0: 0, 1: 1, 2: 4, 3: 9, 4: 16}
```

itertools module

The standard library `itertools` module has a collection of generators for many common data algorithms. For example, `groupby` takes any sequence and a function, grouping consecutive elements in the sequence by return value of the function. Here's an example:

```
In [199]: import itertools
```

```
In [200]: first_letter = lambda x: x[0]
```

```
In [201]: names = ['Alan', 'Adam', 'Wes', 'Will', 'Albert', 'Steven']
```

```
In [202]: for letter, names in itertools.groupby(names, first_letter):
```

```
.....:        print(letter, list(names)) # names is a generator
A ['Alan', 'Adam']
W ['Wes', 'Will']
A ['Albert']
S ['Steven']
```

See Table 3-2 for a list of a few other `itertools` functions I've frequently found help-ful. You may like to check out the official Python documentation (*https://docs.python.org/3/library/itertools.html*) for more on this useful built-in utility module.

Table 3-2. Some useful itertools functions

Function	Description
`combinations(iterable, k)`	Generates a sequence of all possible k-tuples of elements in the iterable, ignoring order and without replacement (see also the companion function `combinations_with_replacement`)
`permutations(iterable, k)`	Generates a sequence of all possible k-tuples of elements in the iterable, respecting order
`groupby(iterable[, keyfunc])`	Generates (`key`, `sub-iterator`) for each unique key
`product(*iterables, repeat=1)`	Generates the Cartesian product of the input iterables as tuples, similar to a nested `for` loop

Errors and Exception Handling

Handling Python errors or *exceptions* gracefully is an important part of building robust programs. In data analysis applications, many functions only work on certain kinds of input. As an example, Python's `float` function is capable of casting a string to a floating-point number, but fails with `ValueError` on improper inputs:

```
In [203]: float('1.2345')
Out[203]: 1.2345

In [204]: float('something')
---------------------------------------------------------------------------
ValueError                                Traceback (most recent call last)
<ipython-input-204-439904410854> in <module>()
----> 1 float('something')
ValueError: could not convert string to float: 'something'
```

Suppose we wanted a version of `float` that fails gracefully, returning the input argu-ment. We can do this by writing a function that encloses the call to `float` in a try/except block:

```
def attempt_float(x):
    try:
        return float(x)
    except:
        return x
```

The code in the **except** part of the block will only be executed if `float(x)` raises an exception:

```
In [206]: attempt_float('1.2345')
Out[206]: 1.2345

In [207]: attempt_float('something')
Out[207]: 'something'
```

You might notice that `float` can raise exceptions other than `ValueError`:

```
In [208]: float((1, 2))
---------------------------------------------------------------------------
TypeError                                 Traceback (most recent call last)
<ipython-input-208-842079ebb635> in <module>()
----> 1 float((1, 2))
TypeError: float() argument must be a string or a number, not 'tuple'
```

You might want to only suppress `ValueError`, since a `TypeError` (the input was not a string or numeric value) might indicate a legitimate bug in your program. To do that, write the exception type after `except`:

```
def attempt_float(x):
    try:
        return float(x)
    except ValueError:
        return x
```

We have then:

```
In [210]: attempt_float((1, 2))
---------------------------------------------------------------------------
TypeError                                 Traceback (most recent call last)
<ipython-input-210-9bdfd730cead> in <module>()
----> 1 attempt_float((1, 2))
<ipython-input-209-3e06b8379b6b> in attempt_float(x)
      1 def attempt_float(x):
      2     try:
----> 3         return float(x)
      4     except ValueError:
      5         return x
TypeError: float() argument must be a string or a number, not 'tuple'
```

You can catch multiple exception types by writing a tuple of exception types instead (the parentheses are required):

```
def attempt_float(x):
    try:
        return float(x)
    except (TypeError, ValueError):
        return x
```

In some cases, you may not want to suppress an exception, but you want some code to be executed regardless of whether the code in the try block succeeds or not. To do this, use finally:

```
f = open(path, 'w')

try:
    write_to_file(f)
finally:
    f.close()
```

Here, the file handle f will *always* get closed. Similarly, you can have code that executes only if the try: block succeeds using else:

```
f = open(path, 'w')

try:
    write_to_file(f)
except:
    print('Failed')
else:
    print('Succeeded')
finally:
    f.close()
```

Exceptions in IPython

If an exception is raised while you are %run-ing a script or executing any statement, IPython will by default print a full call stack trace (traceback) with a few lines of context around the position at each point in the stack:

```
In [10]: %run examples/ipython_bug.py
---------------------------------------------------------------------------
AssertionError                            Traceback (most recent call last)
/home/wesm/code/pydata-book/examples/ipython_bug.py in <module>()
     13     throws_an_exception()
     14
---> 15 calling_things()

/home/wesm/code/pydata-book/examples/ipython_bug.py in calling_things()
     11 def calling_things():
     12     works_fine()
---> 13     throws_an_exception()
     14
     15 calling_things()

/home/wesm/code/pydata-book/examples/ipython_bug.py in throws_an_exception()
      7     a = 5
      8     b = 6
----> 9     assert(a + b == 10)
     10
     11 def calling_things():
```

```
AssertionError:
```

Having additional context by itself is a big advantage over the standard Python interpreter (which does not provide any additional context). You can control the amount of context shown using the %xmode magic command, from Plain (same as the standard Python interpreter) to Verbose (which inlines function argument values and more). As you will see later in the chapter, you can step *into the stack* (using the %debug or %pdb magics) after an error has occurred for interactive post-mortem debugging.

3.3 Files and the Operating System

Most of this book uses high-level tools like pandas.read_csv to read data files from disk into Python data structures. However, it's important to understand the basics of how to work with files in Python. Fortunately, it's very simple, which is one reason why Python is so popular for text and file munging.

To open a file for reading or writing, use the built-in open function with either a relative or absolute file path:

```
In [212]: path = 'examples/segismundo.txt'

In [213]: f = open(path)
```

By default, the file is opened in read-only mode 'r'. We can then treat the file handle f like a list and iterate over the lines like so:

```
for line in f:
    pass
```

The lines come out of the file with the end-of-line (EOL) markers intact, so you'll often see code to get an EOL-free list of lines in a file like:

```
In [214]: lines = [x.rstrip() for x in open(path)]

In [215]: lines
Out[215]:
['Sueña el rico en su riqueza,',
 'que más cuidados le ofrece;',
 '',
 'sueña el pobre que padece',
 'su miseria y su pobreza;',
 '',
 'sueña el que a medrar empieza,',
 'sueña el que afana y pretende,',
 'sueña el que agravia y ofende,',
 '',
 'y en el mundo, en conclusión,',
 'todos sueñan lo que son,',
```

```
'aunque ninguno lo entiende.',
'']
```

When you use open to create file objects, it is important to explicitly close the file
when you are finished with it. Closing the file releases its resources back to the operating system:

```
In [216]: f.close()
```

One of the ways to make it easier to clean up open files is to use the with statement:

```
In [217]: with open(path) as f:
    .....:     lines = [x.rstrip() for x in f]
```

This will automatically close the file f when exiting the with block.

If we had typed f = open(path, 'w'), a *new file* at *examples/segismundo.txt* would
have been created (be careful!), overwriting any one in its place. There is also the 'x'
file mode, which creates a writable file but fails if the file path already exists. See
Table 3-3 for a list of all valid file read/write modes.

For readable files, some of the most commonly used methods are read, seek, and
tell. read returns a certain number of characters from the file. What constitutes a
"character" is determined by the file's encoding (e.g., UTF-8) or simply raw bytes if
the file is opened in binary mode:

```
In [218]: f = open(path)

In [219]: f.read(10)
Out[219]: 'Sueña el r'

In [220]: f2 = open(path, 'rb')  # Binary mode

In [221]: f2.read(10)
Out[221]: b'Sue\xc3\xb1a el '
```

The read method advances the file handle's position by the number of bytes read.
tell gives you the current position:

```
In [222]: f.tell()
Out[222]: 11

In [223]: f2.tell()
Out[223]: 10
```

Even though we read 10 characters from the file, the position is 11 because it took
that many bytes to decode 10 characters using the default encoding. You can check
the default encoding in the sys module:

```
In [224]: import sys
```

```
In [225]: sys.getdefaultencoding()
Out[225]: 'utf-8'
```

seek changes the file position to the indicated byte in the file:

```
In [226]: f.seek(3)
Out[226]: 3

In [227]: f.read(1)
Out[227]: 'ñ'
```

Lastly, we remember to close the files:

```
In [228]: f.close()

In [229]: f2.close()
```

Table 3-3. Python file modes

Mode	Description
r	Read-only mode
w	Write-only mode; creates a new file (erasing the data for any file with the same name)
x	Write-only mode; creates a new file, but fails if the file path already exists
a	Append to existing file (create the file if it does not already exist)
r+	Read and write
b	Add to mode for binary files (i.e., 'rb' or 'wb')
t	Text mode for files (automatically decoding bytes to Unicode). This is the default if not specified. Add t to other modes to use this (i.e., 'rt' or 'xt')

To write text to a file, you can use the file's `write` or `writelines` methods. For example, we could create a version of *prof_mod.py* with no blank lines like so:

```
In [230]: with open('tmp.txt', 'w') as handle:
   .....:     handle.writelines(x for x in open(path) if len(x) > 1)

In [231]: with open('tmp.txt') as f:
   .....:     lines = f.readlines()

In [232]: lines
Out[232]:
['Sueña el rico en su riqueza,\n',
 'que más cuidados le ofrece;\n',
 'sueña el pobre que padece\n',
 'su miseria y su pobreza;\n',
 'sueña el que a medrar empieza,\n',
 'sueña el que afana y pretende,\n',
 'sueña el que agravia y ofende,\n',
 'y en el mundo, en conclusión,\n',
 'todos sueñan lo que son,\n',
 'aunque ninguno lo entiende.\n']
```

See Table 3-4 for many of the most commonly used file methods.

Table 3-4. Important Python file methods or attributes

Method	Description
read([size])	Return data from file as a string, with optional size argument indicating the number of bytes to read
readlines([size])	Return list of lines in the file, with optional size argument
write(str)	Write passed string to file
writelines(strings)	Write passed sequence of strings to the file
close()	Close the handle
flush()	Flush the internal I/O buffer to disk
seek(pos)	Move to indicated file position (integer)
tell()	Return current file position as integer
closed	True if the file is closed

Bytes and Unicode with Files

The default behavior for Python files (whether readable or writable) is *text mode*, which means that you intend to work with Python strings (i.e., Unicode). This contrasts with *binary mode*, which you can obtain by appending b onto the file mode. Let's look at the file (which contains non-ASCII characters with UTF-8 encoding) from the previous section:

```
In [235]: with open(path) as f:
   .....:     chars = f.read(10)

In [236]: chars
Out[236]: 'Sueña el r'
```

UTF-8 is a variable-length Unicode encoding, so when I requested some number of characters from the file, Python reads enough bytes (which could be as few as 10 or as many as 40 bytes) from the file to decode that many characters. If I open the file in 'rb' mode instead, read requests exact numbers of bytes:

```
In [237]: with open(path, 'rb') as f:
   .....:     data = f.read(10)

In [238]: data
Out[238]: b'Sue\xc3\xb1a el '
```

Depending on the text encoding, you may be able to decode the bytes to a str object yourself, but only if each of the encoded Unicode characters is fully formed:

```
In [239]: data.decode('utf8')
Out[239]: 'Sueña el '

In [240]: data[:4].decode('utf8')
```

```
--------------------------------------------------------------------
UnicodeDecodeError                         Traceback (most recent call last)
<ipython-input-240-300e0af10bb7> in <module>()
----> 1 data[:4].decode('utf8')
UnicodeDecodeError: 'utf-8' codec can't decode byte 0xc3 in position 3: unexpecte
d end of data
```

Text mode, combined with the encoding option of open, provides a convenient way
to convert from one Unicode encoding to another:

```
In [241]: sink_path = 'sink.txt'

In [242]: with open(path) as source:
    .....:     with open(sink_path, 'xt', encoding='iso-8859-1') as sink:
    .....:         sink.write(source.read())

In [243]: with open(sink_path, encoding='iso-8859-1') as f:
    .....:     print(f.read(10))
Sueña el r
```

Beware using seek when opening files in any mode other than binary. If the file position falls in the middle of the bytes defining a Unicode character, then subsequent
reads will result in an error:

```
In [245]: f = open(path)

In [246]: f.read(5)
Out[246]: 'Sueña'

In [247]: f.seek(4)
Out[247]: 4

In [248]: f.read(1)
-------------------------------------------------------------------
UnicodeDecodeError                         Traceback (most recent call last)
<ipython-input-248-7841103e33f5> in <module>()
----> 1 f.read(1)
/miniconda/envs/book-env/lib/python3.6/codecs.py in decode(self, input, final)
    319         # decode input (taking the buffer into account)
    320         data = self.buffer + input
--> 321         (result, consumed) = self._buffer_decode(data, self.errors, final
)
    322         # keep undecoded input until the next call
    323         self.buffer = data[consumed:]
UnicodeDecodeError: 'utf-8' codec can't decode byte 0xb1 in position 0: invalid s
tart byte

In [249]: f.close()
```

If you find yourself regularly doing data analysis on non-ASCII text data, mastering
Python's Unicode functionality will prove valuable. See Python's online documentation (*https://docs.python.org/*) for much more.

3.4 Conclusion

With some of the basics and the Python environment and language now under our belt, it's time to move on and learn about NumPy and array-oriented computing in Python.

## CHAPTER 4

NumPy Basics: Arrays and Vectorized Computation

NumPy, short for Numerical Python, is one of the most important foundational packages for numerical computing in Python. Most computational packages providing scientific functionality use NumPy's array objects as the *lingua franca* for data exchange.

Here are some of the things you'll find in NumPy:

- ndarray, an efficient multidimensional array providing fast array-oriented arithmetic operations and flexible *broadcasting* capabilities.

- Mathematical functions for fast operations on entire arrays of data without having to write loops.

- Tools for reading/writing array data to disk and working with memory-mapped files.

- Linear algebra, random number generation, and Fourier transform capabilities.

- A C API for connecting NumPy with libraries written in C, C++, or FORTRAN.

Because NumPy provides an easy-to-use C API, it is straightforward to pass data to external libraries written in a low-level language and also for external libraries to return data to Python as NumPy arrays. This feature has made Python a language of choice for wrapping legacy C/C++/Fortran codebases and giving them a dynamic and easy-to-use interface.

While NumPy by itself does not provide modeling or scientific functionality, having an understanding of NumPy arrays and array-oriented computing will help you use tools with array-oriented semantics, like pandas, much more effectively. Since

NumPy is a large topic, I will cover many advanced NumPy features like broadcasting in more depth later (see Appendix A).

For most data analysis applications, the main areas of functionality I'll focus on are:

- Fast vectorized array operations for data munging and cleaning, subsetting and filtering, transformation, and any other kinds of computations
- Common array algorithms like sorting, unique, and set operations
- Efficient descriptive statistics and aggregating/summarizing data
- Data alignment and relational data manipulations for merging and joining together heterogeneous datasets
- Expressing conditional logic as array expressions instead of loops with if-elif-else branches
- Group-wise data manipulations (aggregation, transformation, function application)

While NumPy provides a computational foundation for general numerical data processing, many readers will want to use pandas as the basis for most kinds of statistics or analytics, especially on tabular data. pandas also provides some more domain-specific functionality like time series manipulation, which is not present in NumPy.

Array-oriented computing in Python traces its roots back to 1995, when Jim Hugunin created the Numeric library. Over the next 10 years, many scientific programming communities began doing array programming in Python, but the library ecosystem had become fragmented in the early 2000s. In 2005, Travis Oliphant was able to forge the NumPy project from the then Numeric and Numarray projects to bring the community together around a single array computing framework.

One of the reasons NumPy is so important for numerical computations in Python is because it is designed for efficiency on large arrays of data. There are a number of reasons for this:

- NumPy internally stores data in a contiguous block of memory, independent of other built-in Python objects. NumPy's library of algorithms written in the C language can operate on this memory without any type checking or other overhead. NumPy arrays also use much less memory than built-in Python sequences.
- NumPy operations perform complex computations on entire arrays without the need for Python for loops.

To give you an idea of the performance difference, consider a NumPy array of one million integers, and the equivalent Python list:

```
In [7]: import numpy as np

In [8]: my_arr = np.arange(1000000)

In [9]: my_list = list(range(1000000))
```

Now let's multiply each sequence by 2:

```
In [10]: %time for _ in range(10): my_arr2 = my_arr * 2
CPU times: user 20 ms, sys: 8 ms, total: 28 ms
Wall time: 26.5 ms

In [11]: %time for _ in range(10): my_list2 = [x * 2 for x in my_list]
CPU times: user 408 ms, sys: 64 ms, total: 472 ms
Wall time: 473 ms
```

NumPy-based algorithms are generally 10 to 100 times faster (or more) than their pure Python counterparts and use significantly less memory.

4.1 The NumPy ndarray: A Multidimensional Array Object

One of the key features of NumPy is its N-dimensional array object, or ndarray, which is a fast, flexible container for large datasets in Python. Arrays enable you to perform mathematical operations on whole blocks of data using similar syntax to the equivalent operations between scalar elements.

To give you a flavor of how NumPy enables batch computations with similar syntax to scalar values on built-in Python objects, I first import NumPy and generate a small array of random data:

```
In [12]: import numpy as np

# Generate some random data
In [13]: data = np.random.randn(2, 3)

In [14]: data
Out[14]:
array([[-0.2047,  0.4789, -0.5194],
       [-0.5557,  1.9658,  1.3934]])
```

I then write mathematical operations with data:

```
In [15]: data * 10
Out[15]:
array([[-2.0471,  4.7894, -5.1944],
       [-5.5573, 19.6578, 13.9341]])

In [16]: data + data
Out[16]:
```

```
array([[-0.4094,  0.9579, -1.0389],
       [-1.1115,  3.9316,  2.7868]])
```

In the first example, all of the elements have been multiplied by 10. In the second, the corresponding values in each "cell" in the array have been added to each other.

> In this chapter and throughout the book, I use the standard NumPy convention of always using `import numpy as np`. You are, of course, welcome to put `from numpy import *` in your code to avoid having to write `np.`, but I advise against making a habit of this. The `numpy` namespace is large and contains a number of functions whose names conflict with built-in Python functions (like `min` and `max`).

An ndarray is a generic multidimensional container for homogeneous data; that is, all of the elements must be the same type. Every array has a `shape`, a tuple indicating the size of each dimension, and a `dtype`, an object describing the *data type* of the array:

```
In [17]: data.shape
Out[17]: (2, 3)

In [18]: data.dtype
Out[18]: dtype('float64')
```

This chapter will introduce you to the basics of using NumPy arrays, and should be sufficient for following along with the rest of the book. While it's not necessary to have a deep understanding of NumPy for many data analytical applications, becoming proficient in array-oriented programming and thinking is a key step along the way to becoming a scientific Python guru.

> Whenever you see "array," "NumPy array," or "ndarray" in the text, with few exceptions they all refer to the same thing: the ndarray object.

Creating ndarrays

The easiest way to create an array is to use the `array` function. This accepts any sequence-like object (including other arrays) and produces a new NumPy array containing the passed data. For example, a list is a good candidate for conversion:

```
In [19]: data1 = [6, 7.5, 8, 0, 1]

In [20]: arr1 = np.array(data1)

In [21]: arr1
Out[21]: array([6. , 7.5, 8. , 0. , 1. ])
```

Nested sequences, like a list of equal-length lists, will be converted into a multidimensional array:

```
In [22]: data2 = [[1, 2, 3, 4], [5, 6, 7, 8]]

In [23]: arr2 = np.array(data2)

In [24]: arr2
Out[24]:
array([[1, 2, 3, 4],
       [5, 6, 7, 8]])
```

Since data2 was a list of lists, the NumPy array arr2 has two dimensions with shape inferred from the data. We can confirm this by inspecting the ndim and shape attributes:

```
In [25]: arr2.ndim
Out[25]: 2

In [26]: arr2.shape
Out[26]: (2, 4)
```

Unless explicitly specified (more on this later), np.array tries to infer a good data type for the array that it creates. The data type is stored in a special dtype metadata object; for example, in the previous two examples we have:

```
In [27]: arr1.dtype
Out[27]: dtype('float64')

In [28]: arr2.dtype
Out[28]: dtype('int64')
```

In addition to np.array, there are a number of other functions for creating new arrays. As examples, zeros and ones create arrays of 0s or 1s, respectively, with a given length or shape. empty creates an array without initializing its values to any particular value. To create a higher dimensional array with these methods, pass a tuple for the shape:

```
In [29]: np.zeros(10)
Out[29]: array([0., 0., 0., 0., 0., 0., 0., 0., 0., 0.])

In [30]: np.zeros((3, 6))
Out[30]:
array([[0., 0., 0., 0., 0., 0.],
       [0., 0., 0., 0., 0., 0.],
       [0., 0., 0., 0., 0., 0.]])

In [31]: np.empty((2, 3, 2))
Out[31]:
array([[[0., 0.],
        [0., 0.],
        [0., 0.]],
```

```
    [[0., 0.],
     [0., 0.],
     [0., 0.]]])
```

 It's not safe to assume that np.empty will return an array of all zeros. In some cases, it may return uninitialized "garbage" values.

arange is an array-valued version of the built-in Python range function:

```
In [32]: np.arange(15)
Out[32]: array([ 0,  1,  2,  3,  4,  5,  6,  7,  8,  9, 10, 11, 12, 13, 14])
```

See Table 4-1 for a short list of standard array creation functions. Since NumPy is focused on numerical computing, the data type, if not specified, will in many cases be float64 (floating point).

Table 4-1. Array creation functions

Function	Description
array	Convert input data (list, tuple, array, or other sequence type) to an ndarray either by inferring a dtype or explicitly specifying a dtype; copies the input data by default
asarray	Convert input to ndarray, but do not copy if the input is already an ndarray
arange	Like the built-in range but returns an ndarray instead of a list
ones, ones_like	Produce an array of all 1s with the given shape and dtype; ones_like takes another array and produces a ones array of the same shape and dtype
zeros, zeros_like	Like ones and ones_like but producing arrays of 0s instead
empty, empty_like	Create new arrays by allocating new memory, but do not populate with any values like ones and zeros
full, full_like	Produce an array of the given shape and dtype with all values set to the indicated "fill value" full_like takes another array and produces a filled array of the same shape and dtype
eye, identity	Create a square N × N identity matrix (1s on the diagonal and 0s elsewhere)

Data Types for ndarrays

The *data type* or dtype is a special object containing the information (or *metadata*, data about data) the ndarray needs to interpret a chunk of memory as a particular type of data:

```
In [33]: arr1 = np.array([1, 2, 3], dtype=np.float64)

In [34]: arr2 = np.array([1, 2, 3], dtype=np.int32)

In [35]: arr1.dtype
Out[35]: dtype('float64')
```

```
In [36]: arr2.dtype
Out[36]: dtype('int32')
```

dtypes are a source of NumPy's flexibility for interacting with data coming from other systems. In most cases they provide a mapping directly onto an underlying disk or memory representation, which makes it easy to read and write binary streams of data to disk and also to connect to code written in a low-level language like C or Fortran. The numerical dtypes are named the same way: a type name, like float or int, followed by a number indicating the number of bits per element. A standard double-precision floating-point value (what's used under the hood in Python's float object) takes up 8 bytes or 64 bits. Thus, this type is known in NumPy as float64. See Table 4-2 for a full listing of NumPy's supported data types.

 Don't worry about memorizing the NumPy dtypes, especially if you're a new user. It's often only necessary to care about the general *kind* of data you're dealing with, whether floating point, complex, integer, boolean, string, or general Python object. When you need more control over how data are stored in memory and on disk, especially large datasets, it is good to know that you have control over the storage type.

Table 4-2. NumPy data types

Type	Type code	Description
int8, uint8	i1, u1	Signed and unsigned 8-bit (1 byte) integer types
int16, uint16	i2, u2	Signed and unsigned 16-bit integer types
int32, uint32	i4, u4	Signed and unsigned 32-bit integer types
int64, uint64	i8, u8	Signed and unsigned 64-bit integer types
float16	f2	Half-precision floating point
float32	f4 or f	Standard single-precision floating point; compatible with C float
float64	f8 or d	Standard double-precision floating point; compatible with C double and Python float object
float128	f16 or g	Extended-precision floating point
complex64, complex128, complex256	c8, c16, c32	Complex numbers represented by two 32, 64, or 128 floats, respectively
bool	?	Boolean type storing True and False values
object	O	Python object type; a value can be any Python object
string_	S	Fixed-length ASCII string type (1 byte per character); for example, to create a string dtype with length 10, use 'S10'
unicode_	U	Fixed-length Unicode type (number of bytes platform specific); same specification semantics as string_ (e.g., 'U10')

You can explicitly convert or *cast* an array from one dtype to another using ndarray's astype method:

```
In [37]: arr = np.array([1, 2, 3, 4, 5])

In [38]: arr.dtype
Out[38]: dtype('int64')

In [39]: float_arr = arr.astype(np.float64)

In [40]: float_arr.dtype
Out[40]: dtype('float64')
```

In this example, integers were cast to floating point. If I cast some floating-point numbers to be of integer dtype, the decimal part will be truncated:

```
In [41]: arr = np.array([3.7, -1.2, -2.6, 0.5, 12.9, 10.1])

In [42]: arr
Out[42]: array([ 3.7, -1.2, -2.6,  0.5, 12.9, 10.1])

In [43]: arr.astype(np.int32)
Out[43]: array([ 3, -1, -2,  0, 12, 10], dtype=int32)
```

If you have an array of strings representing numbers, you can use astype to convert them to numeric form:

```
In [44]: numeric_strings = np.array(['1.25', '-9.6', '42'], dtype=np.string_)

In [45]: numeric_strings.astype(float)
Out[45]: array([ 1.25, -9.6 , 42.  ])
```

 It's important to be cautious when using the numpy.string_ type, as string data in NumPy is fixed size and may truncate input without warning. pandas has more intuitive out-of-the-box behavior on non-numeric data.

If casting were to fail for some reason (like a string that cannot be converted to float64), a ValueError will be raised. Here I was a bit lazy and wrote float instead of np.float64; NumPy aliases the Python types to its own equivalent data dtypes.

You can also use another array's dtype attribute:

```
In [46]: int_array = np.arange(10)

In [47]: calibers = np.array([.22, .270, .357, .380, .44, .50], dtype=np.float64)

In [48]: int_array.astype(calibers.dtype)
Out[48]: array([0., 1., 2., 3., 4., 5., 6., 7., 8., 9.])
```

There are shorthand type code strings you can also use to refer to a dtype:

```
In [49]: empty_uint32 = np.empty(8, dtype='u4')
```

```
In [50]: empty_uint32
Out[50]:
array([          0, 1075314688,          0, 1075707904,          0,
       1075838976,          0, 1072693248], dtype=uint32)
```

 Calling astype *always* creates a new array (a copy of the data), even if the new dtype is the same as the old dtype.

Arithmetic with NumPy Arrays

Arrays are important because they enable you to express batch operations on data without writing any for loops. NumPy users call this *vectorization*. Any arithmetic operations between equal-size arrays applies the operation element-wise:

```
In [51]: arr = np.array([[1., 2., 3.], [4., 5., 6.]])
```

```
In [52]: arr
Out[52]:
array([[1., 2., 3.],
       [4., 5., 6.]])
```

```
In [53]: arr * arr
Out[53]:
array([[ 1.,  4.,  9.],
       [16., 25., 36.]])
```

```
In [54]: arr - arr
Out[54]:
array([[0., 0., 0.],
       [0., 0., 0.]])
```

Arithmetic operations with scalars propagate the scalar argument to each element in the array:

```
In [55]: 1 / arr
Out[55]:
array([[1.    , 0.5   , 0.3333],
       [0.25  , 0.2   , 0.1667]])
```

```
In [56]: arr ** 0.5
Out[56]:
array([[1.    , 1.4142, 1.7321],
       [2.    , 2.2361, 2.4495]])
```

Comparisons between arrays of the same size yield boolean arrays:

```
In [57]: arr2 = np.array([[0., 4., 1.], [7., 2., 12.]])

In [58]: arr2
Out[58]:
array([[  0.,   4.,   1.],
       [  7.,   2.,  12.]])

In [59]: arr2 > arr
Out[59]:
array([[False,  True, False],
       [ True, False,  True]])
```

Evaluating operations between differently sized arrays is called *broadcasting* and will be discussed in more detail in Appendix A. Having a deep understanding of broadcasting is not necessary for most of this book.

Basic Indexing and Slicing

NumPy array indexing is a rich topic, as there are many ways you may want to select a subset of your data or individual elements. One-dimensional arrays are simple; on the surface they act similarly to Python lists:

```
In [60]: arr = np.arange(10)

In [61]: arr
Out[61]: array([0, 1, 2, 3, 4, 5, 6, 7, 8, 9])

In [62]: arr[5]
Out[62]: 5

In [63]: arr[5:8]
Out[63]: array([5, 6, 7])

In [64]: arr[5:8] = 12

In [65]: arr
Out[65]: array([ 0,  1,  2,  3,  4, 12, 12, 12,  8,  9])
```

As you can see, if you assign a scalar value to a slice, as in arr[5:8] = 12, the value is propagated (or *broadcasted* henceforth) to the entire selection. An important first distinction from Python's built-in lists is that array slices are *views* on the original array. This means that the data is not copied, and any modifications to the view will be reflected in the source array.

To give an example of this, I first create a slice of arr:

```
In [66]: arr_slice = arr[5:8]

In [67]: arr_slice
Out[67]: array([12, 12, 12])
```

Now, when I change values in `arr_slice`, the mutations are reflected in the original array `arr`:

```
In [68]: arr_slice[1] = 12345

In [69]: arr
Out[69]:
array([   0,    1,    2,    3,    4,   12, 12345,   12,    8,
          9])
```

The "bare" slice [:] will assign to all values in an array:

```
In [70]: arr_slice[:] = 64

In [71]: arr
Out[71]: array([ 0,  1,  2,  3,  4, 64, 64, 64,  8,  9])
```

If you are new to NumPy, you might be surprised by this, especially if you have used other array programming languages that copy data more eagerly. As NumPy has been designed to be able to work with very large arrays, you could imagine performance and memory problems if NumPy insisted on always copying data.

> If you want a copy of a slice of an ndarray instead of a view, you will need to explicitly copy the array—for example, `arr[5:8].copy()`.

With higher dimensional arrays, you have many more options. In a two-dimensional array, the elements at each index are no longer scalars but rather one-dimensional arrays:

```
In [72]: arr2d = np.array([[1, 2, 3], [4, 5, 6], [7, 8, 9]])

In [73]: arr2d[2]
Out[73]: array([7, 8, 9])
```

Thus, individual elements can be accessed recursively. But that is a bit too much work, so you can pass a comma-separated list of indices to select individual elements. So these are equivalent:

```
In [74]: arr2d[0][2]
Out[74]: 3

In [75]: arr2d[0, 2]
Out[75]: 3
```

See Figure 4-1 for an illustration of indexing on a two-dimensional array. I find it helpful to think of axis 0 as the "rows" of the array and axis 1 as the "columns."

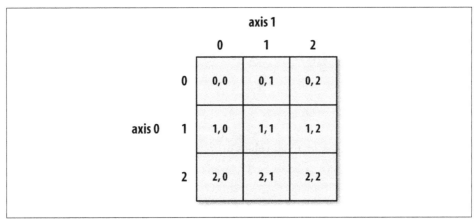

Figure 4-1. Indexing elements in a NumPy array

In multidimensional arrays, if you omit later indices, the returned object will be a lower dimensional ndarray consisting of all the data along the higher dimensions. So in the 2 × 2 × 3 array arr3d:

```
In [76]: arr3d = np.array([[[1, 2, 3], [4, 5, 6]], [[7, 8, 9], [10, 11, 12]]])

In [77]: arr3d
Out[77]:
array([[[ 1,  2,  3],
        [ 4,  5,  6]],
       [[ 7,  8,  9],
        [10, 11, 12]]])
```

arr3d[0] is a 2 × 3 array:

```
In [78]: arr3d[0]
Out[78]:
array([[1, 2, 3],
       [4, 5, 6]])
```

Both scalar values and arrays can be assigned to arr3d[0]:

```
In [79]: old_values = arr3d[0].copy()

In [80]: arr3d[0] = 42

In [81]: arr3d
Out[81]:
array([[[42, 42, 42],
        [42, 42, 42]],
       [[ 7,  8,  9],
        [10, 11, 12]]])

In [82]: arr3d[0] = old_values
```

```
In [83]: arr3d
Out[83]:
array([[[ 1,  2,  3],
        [ 4,  5,  6]],
       [[ 7,  8,  9],
        [10, 11, 12]]])
```

Similarly, `arr3d[1, 0]` gives you all of the values whose indices start with (1, 0), forming a 1-dimensional array:

```
In [84]: arr3d[1, 0]
Out[84]: array([7, 8, 9])
```

This expression is the same as though we had indexed in two steps:

```
In [85]: x = arr3d[1]

In [86]: x
Out[86]:
array([[ 7,  8,  9],
       [10, 11, 12]])

In [87]: x[0]
Out[87]: array([7, 8, 9])
```

Note that in all of these cases where subsections of the array have been selected, the returned arrays are views.

Indexing with slices

Like one-dimensional objects such as Python lists, ndarrays can be sliced with the familiar syntax:

```
In [88]: arr
Out[88]: array([ 0,  1,  2,  3,  4, 64, 64, 64,  8,  9])

In [89]: arr[1:6]
Out[89]: array([ 1,  2,  3,  4, 64])
```

Consider the two-dimensional array from before, `arr2d`. Slicing this array is a bit different:

```
In [90]: arr2d
Out[90]:
array([[1, 2, 3],
       [4, 5, 6],
       [7, 8, 9]])

In [91]: arr2d[:2]
Out[91]:
array([[1, 2, 3],
       [4, 5, 6]])
```

As you can see, it has sliced along axis 0, the first axis. A slice, therefore, selects a range of elements along an axis. It can be helpful to read the expression arr2d[:2] as "select the first two rows of arr2d."

You can pass multiple slices just like you can pass multiple indexes:

```
In [92]: arr2d[:2, 1:]
Out[92]:
array([[2, 3],
       [5, 6]])
```

When slicing like this, you always obtain array views of the same number of dimensions. By mixing integer indexes and slices, you get lower dimensional slices.

For example, I can select the second row but only the first two columns like so:

```
In [93]: arr2d[1, :2]
Out[93]: array([4, 5])
```

Similarly, I can select the third column but only the first two rows like so:

```
In [94]: arr2d[:2, 2]
Out[94]: array([3, 6])
```

See Figure 4-2 for an illustration. Note that a colon by itself means to take the entire axis, so you can slice only higher dimensional axes by doing:

```
In [95]: arr2d[:, :1]
Out[95]:
array([[1],
       [4],
       [7]])
```

Of course, assigning to a slice expression assigns to the whole selection:

```
In [96]: arr2d[:2, 1:] = 0

In [97]: arr2d
Out[97]:
array([[1, 0, 0],
       [4, 0, 0],
       [7, 8, 9]])
```

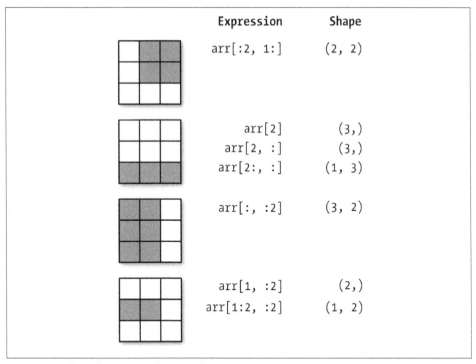

	Expression	Shape
	arr[:2, 1:]	(2, 2)
	arr[2] arr[2, :] arr[2:, :]	(3,) (3,) (1, 3)
	arr[:, :2]	(3, 2)
	arr[1, :2] arr[1:2, :2]	(2,) (1, 2)

Figure 4-2. Two-dimensional array slicing

Boolean Indexing

Let's consider an example where we have some data in an array and an array of names with duplicates. I'm going to use here the randn function in numpy.random to generate some random normally distributed data:

```
In [98]: names = np.array(['Bob', 'Joe', 'Will', 'Bob', 'Will', 'Joe', 'Joe'])

In [99]: data = np.random.randn(7, 4)

In [100]: names
Out[100]: array(['Bob', 'Joe', 'Will', 'Bob', 'Will', 'Joe', 'Joe'], dtype='<U4')

In [101]: data
Out[101]:
array([[ 0.0929,  0.2817,  0.769 ,  1.2464],
       [ 1.0072, -1.2962,  0.275 ,  0.2289],
       [ 1.3529,  0.8864, -2.0016, -0.3718],
       [ 1.669 , -0.4386, -0.5397,  0.477 ],
       [ 3.2489, -1.0212, -0.5771,  0.1241],
       [ 0.3026,  0.5238,  0.0009,  1.3438],
       [-0.7135, -0.8312, -2.3702, -1.8608]])
```

Suppose each name corresponds to a row in the data array and we wanted to select all the rows with corresponding name 'Bob'. Like arithmetic operations, comparisons (such as ==) with arrays are also vectorized. Thus, comparing names with the string 'Bob' yields a boolean array:

```
In [102]: names == 'Bob'
Out[102]: array([ True, False, False,  True, False, False, False])
```

This boolean array can be passed when indexing the array:

```
In [103]: data[names == 'Bob']
Out[103]:
array([[ 0.0929,  0.2817,  0.769 ,  1.2464],
       [ 1.669 , -0.4386, -0.5397,  0.477 ]])
```

The boolean array must be of the same length as the array axis it's indexing. You can even mix and match boolean arrays with slices or integers (or sequences of integers; more on this later).

In these examples, I select from the rows where names == 'Bob' and index the columns, too:

```
In [104]: data[names == 'Bob', 2:]
Out[104]:
array([[ 0.769 ,  1.2464],
       [-0.5397,  0.477 ]])

In [105]: data[names == 'Bob', 3]
Out[105]: array([1.2464, 0.477 ])
```

To select everything but 'Bob', you can either use != or negate the condition using ~:

```
In [106]: names != 'Bob'
Out[106]: array([False,  True,  True, False,  True,  True,  True])

In [107]: data[~(names == 'Bob')]
Out[107]:
array([[ 1.0072, -1.2962,  0.275 ,  0.2289],
       [ 1.3529,  0.8864, -2.0016, -0.3718],
       [ 3.2489, -1.0212, -0.5771,  0.1241],
       [ 0.3026,  0.5238,  0.0009,  1.3438],
       [-0.7135, -0.8312, -2.3702, -1.8608]])
```

The ~ operator can be useful when you want to invert a general condition:

```
In [108]: cond = names == 'Bob'

In [109]: data[~cond]
Out[109]:
array([[ 1.0072, -1.2962,  0.275 ,  0.2289],
       [ 1.3529,  0.8864, -2.0016, -0.3718],
       [ 3.2489, -1.0212, -0.5771,  0.1241],
```

```
         [ 0.3026,  0.5238,  0.0009,  1.3438],
         [-0.7135, -0.8312, -2.3702, -1.8608]])
```

Selecting two of the three names to combine multiple boolean conditions, use boolean arithmetic operators like & (and) and | (or):

```
In [110]: mask = (names == 'Bob') | (names == 'Will')

In [111]: mask
Out[111]: array([ True, False,  True,  True,  True, False, False])

In [112]: data[mask]
Out[112]:
array([[ 0.0929,  0.2817,  0.769 ,  1.2464],
       [ 1.3529,  0.8864, -2.0016, -0.3718],
       [ 1.669 , -0.4386, -0.5397,  0.477 ],
       [ 3.2489, -1.0212, -0.5771,  0.1241]])
```

Selecting data from an array by boolean indexing *always* creates a copy of the data, even if the returned array is unchanged.

The Python keywords and and or do not work with boolean arrays. Use & (and) and | (or) instead.

Setting values with boolean arrays works in a common-sense way. To set all of the negative values in data to 0 we need only do:

```
In [113]: data[data < 0] = 0

In [114]: data
Out[114]:
array([[0.0929, 0.2817, 0.769 , 1.2464],
       [1.0072, 0.    , 0.275 , 0.2289],
       [1.3529, 0.8864, 0.    , 0.    ],
       [1.669 , 0.    , 0.    , 0.477 ],
       [3.2489, 0.    , 0.    , 0.1241],
       [0.3026, 0.5238, 0.0009, 1.3438],
       [0.    , 0.    , 0.    , 0.    ]])
```

Setting whole rows or columns using a one-dimensional boolean array is also easy:

```
In [115]: data[names != 'Joe'] = 7
```

```
In [116]: data
Out[116]:
array([[7.    , 7.    , 7.    , 7.    ],
       [1.0072, 0.    , 0.275 , 0.2289],
       [7.    , 7.    , 7.    , 7.    ],
       [7.    , 7.    , 7.    , 7.    ],
       [7.    , 7.    , 7.    , 7.    ],
       [0.3026, 0.5238, 0.0009, 1.3438],
       [0.    , 0.    , 0.    , 0.    ]])
```

As we will see later, these types of operations on two-dimensional data are convenient to do with pandas.

Fancy Indexing

Fancy indexing is a term adopted by NumPy to describe indexing using integer arrays. Suppose we had an 8 × 4 array:

```
In [117]: arr = np.empty((8, 4))
```

```
In [118]: for i in range(8):
   .....:     arr[i] = i
```

```
In [119]: arr
Out[119]:
array([[0., 0., 0., 0.],
       [1., 1., 1., 1.],
       [2., 2., 2., 2.],
       [3., 3., 3., 3.],
       [4., 4., 4., 4.],
       [5., 5., 5., 5.],
       [6., 6., 6., 6.],
       [7., 7., 7., 7.]])
```

To select out a subset of the rows in a particular order, you can simply pass a list or ndarray of integers specifying the desired order:

```
In [120]: arr[[4, 3, 0, 6]]
Out[120]:
array([[4., 4., 4., 4.],
       [3., 3., 3., 3.],
       [0., 0., 0., 0.],
       [6., 6., 6., 6.]])
```

Hopefully this code did what you expected! Using negative indices selects rows from the end:

```
In [121]: arr[[-3, -5, -7]]
Out[121]:
```

```
array([[5., 5., 5., 5.],
       [3., 3., 3., 3.],
       [1., 1., 1., 1.]])
```

Passing multiple index arrays does something slightly different; it selects a one-dimensional array of elements corresponding to each tuple of indices:

```
In [122]: arr = np.arange(32).reshape((8, 4))
```

```
In [123]: arr
Out[123]:
array([[ 0,  1,  2,  3],
       [ 4,  5,  6,  7],
       [ 8,  9, 10, 11],
       [12, 13, 14, 15],
       [16, 17, 18, 19],
       [20, 21, 22, 23],
       [24, 25, 26, 27],
       [28, 29, 30, 31]])
```

```
In [124]: arr[[1, 5, 7, 2], [0, 3, 1, 2]]
Out[124]: array([ 4, 23, 29, 10])
```

We'll look at the reshape method in more detail in Appendix A.

Here the elements (1, 0), (5, 3), (7, 1), and (2, 2) were selected. Regardless of how many dimensions the array has (here, only 2), the result of fancy indexing with multiple integer arrays is always one-dimensional.

The behavior of fancy indexing in this case is a bit different from what some users might have expected (myself included), which is the rectangular region formed by selecting a subset of the matrix's rows and columns. Here is one way to get that:

```
In [125]: arr[[1, 5, 7, 2]][:, [0, 3, 1, 2]]
Out[125]:
array([[ 4,  7,  5,  6],
       [20, 23, 21, 22],
       [28, 31, 29, 30],
       [ 8, 11,  9, 10]])
```

Keep in mind that fancy indexing, unlike slicing, always copies the data into a new array.

Transposing Arrays and Swapping Axes

Transposing is a special form of reshaping that similarly returns a view on the underlying data without copying anything. Arrays have the transpose method and also the special T attribute:

```
In [126]: arr = np.arange(15).reshape((3, 5))
```

```
In [127]: arr
```

```
Out[127]:
array([[ 0,  1,  2,  3,  4],
       [ 5,  6,  7,  8,  9],
       [10, 11, 12, 13, 14]])

In [128]: arr.T
Out[128]:
array([[ 0,  5, 10],
       [ 1,  6, 11],
       [ 2,  7, 12],
       [ 3,  8, 13],
       [ 4,  9, 14]])
```

When doing matrix computations, you may do this very often—for example, when computing the inner matrix product using np.dot:

```
In [129]: arr = np.random.randn(6, 3)

In [130]: arr
Out[130]:
array([[-0.8608,  0.5601, -1.2659],
       [ 0.1198, -1.0635,  0.3329],
       [-2.3594, -0.1995, -1.542 ],
       [-0.9707, -1.307 ,  0.2863],
       [ 0.378 , -0.7539,  0.3313],
       [ 1.3497,  0.0699,  0.2467]])

In [131]: np.dot(arr.T, arr)
Out[131]:
array([[ 9.2291,  0.9394,  4.948 ],
       [ 0.9394,  3.7662, -1.3622],
       [ 4.948 , -1.3622,  4.3437]])
```

For higher dimensional arrays, transpose will accept a tuple of axis numbers to per-mute the axes (for extra mind bending):

```
In [132]: arr = np.arange(16).reshape((2, 2, 4))

In [133]: arr
Out[133]:
array([[[ 0,  1,  2,  3],
        [ 4,  5,  6,  7]],
       [[ 8,  9, 10, 11],
        [12, 13, 14, 15]]])

In [134]: arr.transpose((1, 0, 2))
Out[134]:
array([[[ 0,  1,  2,  3],
        [ 8,  9, 10, 11]],
       [[ 4,  5,  6,  7],
        [12, 13, 14, 15]]])
```

Here, the axes have been reordered with the second axis first, the first axis second, and the last axis unchanged.

Simple transposing with .T is a special case of swapping axes. ndarray has the method swapaxes, which takes a pair of axis numbers and switches the indicated axes to rearrange the data:

```
In [135]: arr
Out[135]:
array([[[ 0,  1,  2,  3],
        [ 4,  5,  6,  7]],
       [[ 8,  9, 10, 11],
        [12, 13, 14, 15]]])

In [136]: arr.swapaxes(1, 2)
Out[136]:
array([[[ 0,  4],
        [ 1,  5],
        [ 2,  6],
        [ 3,  7]],
       [[ 8, 12],
        [ 9, 13],
        [10, 14],
        [11, 15]]])
```

swapaxes similarly returns a view on the data without making a copy.

4.2 Universal Functions: Fast Element-Wise Array Functions

A universal function, or *ufunc*, is a function that performs element-wise operations on data in ndarrays. You can think of them as fast vectorized wrappers for simple functions that take one or more scalar values and produce one or more scalar results.

Many ufuncs are simple element-wise transformations, like sqrt or exp:

```
In [137]: arr = np.arange(10)

In [138]: arr
Out[138]: array([0, 1, 2, 3, 4, 5, 6, 7, 8, 9])

In [139]: np.sqrt(arr)
Out[139]:
array([0.    , 1.    , 1.4142, 1.7321, 2.    , 2.2361, 2.4495, 2.6458,
       2.8284, 3.    ])

In [140]: np.exp(arr)
Out[140]:
array([   1.    ,    2.7183,    7.3891,   20.0855,   54.5982,  148.4132,
        403.4288, 1096.6332, 2980.958 , 8103.0839])
```

These are referred to as *unary* ufuncs. Others, such as add or maximum, take two arrays (thus, *binary* ufuncs) and return a single array as the result:

```
In [141]: x = np.random.randn(8)

In [142]: y = np.random.randn(8)

In [143]: x
Out[143]:
array([-0.0119,  1.0048,  1.3272, -0.9193, -1.5491,  0.0222,  0.7584,
       -0.6605])

In [144]: y
Out[144]:
array([ 0.8626, -0.01  ,  0.05  ,  0.6702,  0.853 , -0.9559, -0.0235,
       -2.3042])

In [145]: np.maximum(x, y)
Out[145]:
array([ 0.8626,  1.0048,  1.3272,  0.6702,  0.853 ,  0.0222,  0.7584,
       -0.6605])
```

Here, numpy.maximum computed the element-wise maximum of the elements in x and y.

While not common, a ufunc can return multiple arrays. modf is one example, a vectorized version of the built-in Python divmod; it returns the fractional and integral parts of a floating-point array:

```
In [146]: arr = np.random.randn(7) * 5

In [147]: arr
Out[147]: array([-3.2623, -6.0915, -6.663 ,  5.3731,  3.6182,  3.45  ,  5.0077])

In [148]: remainder, whole_part = np.modf(arr)

In [149]: remainder
Out[149]: array([-0.2623, -0.0915, -0.663 ,  0.3731,  0.6182,  0.45  ,  0.0077])

In [150]: whole_part
Out[150]: array([-3., -6., -6.,  5.,  3.,  3.,  5.])
```

Ufuncs accept an optional out argument that allows them to operate in-place on arrays:

```
In [151]: arr
Out[151]: array([-3.2623, -6.0915, -6.663 ,  5.3731,  3.6182,  3.45  ,  5.0077])

In [152]: np.sqrt(arr)
Out[152]: array([   nan,    nan,    nan, 2.318 , 1.9022, 1.8574, 2.2378])

In [153]: np.sqrt(arr, arr)
```

```
Out[153]: array([   nan,    nan,    nan, 2.318 , 1.9022, 1.8574, 2.2378])

In [154]: arr
Out[154]: array([   nan,    nan,    nan, 2.318 , 1.9022, 1.8574, 2.2378])
```

See Tables 4-3 and 4-4 for a listing of available ufuncs.

Table 4-3. Unary ufuncs

Function	Description
abs, fabs	Compute the absolute value element-wise for integer, floating-point, or complex values
sqrt	Compute the square root of each element (equivalent to arr ** 0.5)
square	Compute the square of each element (equivalent to arr ** 2)
exp	Compute the exponent e^x of each element
log, log10, log2, log1p	Natural logarithm (base e), log base 10, log base 2, and log(1 + x), respectively
sign	Compute the sign of each element: 1 (positive), 0 (zero), or −1 (negative)
ceil	Compute the ceiling of each element (i.e., the smallest integer greater than or equal to that number)
floor	Compute the floor of each element (i.e., the largest integer less than or equal to each element)
rint	Round elements to the nearest integer, preserving the dtype
modf	Return fractional and integral parts of array as a separate array
isnan	Return boolean array indicating whether each value is NaN (Not a Number)
isfinite, isinf	Return boolean array indicating whether each element is finite (non-inf, non-NaN) or infinite, respectively
cos, cosh, sin, sinh, tan, tanh	Regular and hyperbolic trigonometric functions
arccos, arccosh, arcsin, arcsinh, arctan, arctanh	Inverse trigonometric functions
logical_not	Compute truth value of not x element-wise (equivalent to ~arr).

Table 4-4. Binary universal functions

Function	Description
add	Add corresponding elements in arrays
subtract	Subtract elements in second array from first array
multiply	Multiply array elements
divide, floor_divide	Divide or floor divide (truncating the remainder)
power	Raise elements in first array to powers indicated in second array
maximum, fmax	Element-wise maximum; fmax ignores NaN
minimum, fmin	Element-wise minimum; fmin ignores NaN
mod	Element-wise modulus (remainder of division)
copysign	Copy sign of values in second argument to values in first argument

Function	Description
greater, greater_equal, less, less_equal, equal, not_equal	Perform element-wise comparison, yielding boolean array (equivalent to infix operators >, >=, <, <=, ==, !=)
logical_and, logical_or, logical_xor	Compute element-wise truth value of logical operation (equivalent to infix operators & |, ^)

4.3 Array-Oriented Programming with Arrays

Using NumPy arrays enables you to express many kinds of data processing tasks as concise array expressions that might otherwise require writing loops. This practice of replacing explicit loops with array expressions is commonly referred to as *vectorization*. In general, vectorized array operations will often be one or two (or more) orders of magnitude faster than their pure Python equivalents, with the biggest impact in any kind of numerical computations. Later, in Appendix A, I explain *broadcasting*, a powerful method for vectorizing computations.

As a simple example, suppose we wished to evaluate the function sqrt(x^2 + y^2) across a regular grid of values. The np.meshgrid function takes two 1D arrays and produces two 2D matrices corresponding to all pairs of (x, y) in the two arrays:

```
In [155]: points = np.arange(-5, 5, 0.01) # 1000 equally spaced points

In [156]: xs, ys = np.meshgrid(points, points)

In [157]: ys
Out[157]:
array([[-5.  , -5.  , -5.  , ..., -5.  , -5.  , -5.  ],
       [-4.99, -4.99, -4.99, ..., -4.99, -4.99, -4.99],
       [-4.98, -4.98, -4.98, ..., -4.98, -4.98, -4.98],
       ...,
       [ 4.97,  4.97,  4.97, ...,  4.97,  4.97,  4.97],
       [ 4.98,  4.98,  4.98, ...,  4.98,  4.98,  4.98],
       [ 4.99,  4.99,  4.99, ...,  4.99,  4.99,  4.99]])
```

Now, evaluating the function is a matter of writing the same expression you would write with two points:

```
In [158]: z = np.sqrt(xs ** 2 + ys ** 2)

In [159]: z
Out[159]:
array([[7.0711, 7.064 , 7.0569, ..., 7.0499, 7.0569, 7.064 ],
       [7.064 , 7.0569, 7.0499, ..., 7.0428, 7.0499, 7.0569],
       [7.0569, 7.0499, 7.0428, ..., 7.0357, 7.0428, 7.0499],
       ...,
       [7.0499, 7.0428, 7.0357, ..., 7.0286, 7.0357, 7.0428],
       [7.0569, 7.0499, 7.0428, ..., 7.0357, 7.0428, 7.0499],
       [7.064 , 7.0569, 7.0499, ..., 7.0428, 7.0499, 7.0569]])
```

As a preview of Chapter 9, I use matplotlib to create visualizations of this two-dimensional array:

```
In [160]: import matplotlib.pyplot as plt

In [161]: plt.imshow(z, cmap=plt.cm.gray); plt.colorbar()
Out[161]: <matplotlib.colorbar.Colorbar at 0x7f8520cd1b38>

In [162]: plt.title("Image plot of $\sqrt{x^2 + y^2}$ for a grid of values")
Out[162]: Text(0.5,1,'Image plot of $\\sqrt{x^2 + y^2}$ for a grid of values')
```

See Figure 4-3. Here I used the matplotlib function imshow to create an image plot from a two-dimensional array of function values.

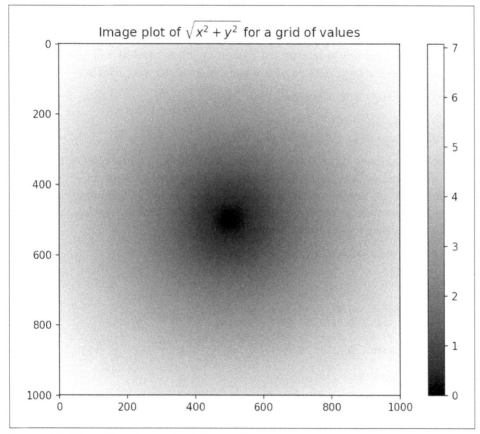

Figure 4-3. Plot of function evaluated on grid

Expressing Conditional Logic as Array Operations

The numpy.where function is a vectorized version of the ternary expression x if condition else y. Suppose we had a boolean array and two arrays of values:

```
In [165]: xarr = np.array([1.1, 1.2, 1.3, 1.4, 1.5])

In [166]: yarr = np.array([2.1, 2.2, 2.3, 2.4, 2.5])

In [167]: cond = np.array([True, False, True, True, False])
```

Suppose we wanted to take a value from xarr whenever the corresponding value in cond is True, and otherwise take the value from yarr. A list comprehension doing this might look like:

```
In [168]: result = [(x if c else y)
   .....:           for x, y, c in zip(xarr, yarr, cond)]

In [169]: result
Out[169]: [1.1, 2.2, 1.3, 1.4, 2.5]
```

This has multiple problems. First, it will not be very fast for large arrays (because all the work is being done in interpreted Python code). Second, it will not work with multidimensional arrays. With np.where you can write this very concisely:

```
In [170]: result = np.where(cond, xarr, yarr)

In [171]: result
Out[171]: array([1.1, 2.2, 1.3, 1.4, 2.5])
```

The second and third arguments to np.where don't need to be arrays; one or both of them can be scalars. A typical use of where in data analysis is to produce a new array of values based on another array. Suppose you had a matrix of randomly generated data and you wanted to replace all positive values with 2 and all negative values with −2. This is very easy to do with np.where:

```
In [172]: arr = np.random.randn(4, 4)

In [173]: arr
Out[173]:
array([[-0.5031, -0.6223, -0.9212, -0.7262],
       [ 0.2229,  0.0513, -1.1577,  0.8167],
       [ 0.4336,  1.0107,  1.8249, -0.9975],
       [ 0.8506, -0.1316,  0.9124,  0.1882]])

In [174]: arr > 0
Out[174]:
array([[False, False, False, False],
       [ True,  True, False,  True],
       [ True,  True,  True, False],
       [ True, False,  True,  True]])

In [175]: np.where(arr > 0, 2, -2)
Out[175]:
array([[-2, -2, -2, -2],
       [ 2,  2, -2,  2],
```

```
       [ 2,  2,  2, -2],
       [ 2, -2,  2,  2]])
```

You can combine scalars and arrays when using np.where. For example, I can replace all positive values in arr with the constant 2 like so:

```
In [176]: np.where(arr > 0, 2, arr) # set only positive values to 2
Out[176]:
array([[-0.5031, -0.6223, -0.9212, -0.7262],
       [ 2.    ,  2.    , -1.1577,  2.    ],
       [ 2.    ,  2.    ,  2.    , -0.9975],
       [ 2.    , -0.1316,  2.    ,  2.    ]])
```

The arrays passed to np.where can be more than just equal-sized arrays or scalars.

Mathematical and Statistical Methods

A set of mathematical functions that compute statistics about an entire array or about the data along an axis are accessible as methods of the array class. You can use aggregations (often called *reductions*) like sum, mean, and std (standard deviation) either by calling the array instance method or using the top-level NumPy function.

Here I generate some normally distributed random data and compute some aggregate statistics:

```
In [177]: arr = np.random.randn(5, 4)

In [178]: arr
Out[178]:
array([[ 2.1695, -0.1149,  2.0037,  0.0296],
       [ 0.7953,  0.1181, -0.7485,  0.585 ],
       [ 0.1527, -1.5657, -0.5625, -0.0327],
       [-0.929 , -0.4826, -0.0363,  1.0954],
       [ 0.9809, -0.5895,  1.5817, -0.5287]])

In [179]: arr.mean()
Out[179]: 0.19607051119998253

In [180]: np.mean(arr)
Out[180]: 0.19607051119998253

In [181]: arr.sum()
Out[181]: 3.9214102239996507
```

Functions like mean and sum take an optional axis argument that computes the statistic over the given axis, resulting in an array with one fewer dimension:

```
In [182]: arr.mean(axis=1)
Out[182]: array([ 1.022 ,  0.1875, -0.502 , -0.0881,  0.3611])

In [183]: arr.sum(axis=0)
Out[183]: array([ 3.1693, -2.6345,  2.2381,  1.1486])
```

Here, `arr.mean(1)` means "compute mean across the columns" where `arr.sum(0)` means "compute sum down the rows."

Other methods like `cumsum` and `cumprod` do not aggregate, instead producing an array of the intermediate results:

```
In [184]: arr = np.array([0, 1, 2, 3, 4, 5, 6, 7])

In [185]: arr.cumsum()
Out[185]: array([ 0,  1,  3,  6, 10, 15, 21, 28])
```

In multidimensional arrays, accumulation functions like `cumsum` return an array of the same size, but with the partial aggregates computed along the indicated axis according to each lower dimensional slice:

```
In [186]: arr = np.array([[0, 1, 2], [3, 4, 5], [6, 7, 8]])

In [187]: arr
Out[187]:
array([[0, 1, 2],
       [3, 4, 5],
       [6, 7, 8]])

In [188]: arr.cumsum(axis=0)
Out[188]:
array([[ 0,  1,  2],
       [ 3,  5,  7],
       [ 9, 12, 15]])

In [189]: arr.cumprod(axis=1)
Out[189]:
array([[  0,   0,   0],
       [  3,  12,  60],
       [  6,  42, 336]])
```

See Table 4-5 for a full listing. We'll see many examples of these methods in action in later chapters.

Table 4-5. Basic array statistical methods

Method	Description
sum	Sum of all the elements in the array or along an axis; zero-length arrays have sum 0
mean	Arithmetic mean; zero-length arrays have NaN mean
std, var	Standard deviation and variance, respectively, with optional degrees of freedom adjustment (default denominator n)
min, max	Minimum and maximum
argmin, argmax	Indices of minimum and maximum elements, respectively
cumsum	Cumulative sum of elements starting from 0
cumprod	Cumulative product of elements starting from 1

Methods for Boolean Arrays

Boolean values are coerced to 1 (True) and 0 (False) in the preceding methods. Thus, sum is often used as a means of counting True values in a boolean array:

```
In [190]: arr = np.random.randn(100)

In [191]: (arr > 0).sum() # Number of positive values
Out[191]: 42
```

There are two additional methods, any and all, useful especially for boolean arrays. any tests whether one or more values in an array is True, while all checks if every value is True:

```
In [192]: bools = np.array([False, False, True, False])

In [193]: bools.any()
Out[193]: True

In [194]: bools.all()
Out[194]: False
```

These methods also work with non-boolean arrays, where non-zero elements evaluate to True.

Sorting

Like Python's built-in list type, NumPy arrays can be sorted in-place with the sort method:

```
In [195]: arr = np.random.randn(6)

In [196]: arr
Out[196]: array([ 0.6095, -0.4938,  1.24  , -0.1357,  1.43  , -0.8469])

In [197]: arr.sort()

In [198]: arr
Out[198]: array([-0.8469, -0.4938, -0.1357,  0.6095,  1.24  ,  1.43  ])
```

You can sort each one-dimensional section of values in a multidimensional array in-place along an axis by passing the axis number to sort:

```
In [199]: arr = np.random.randn(5, 3)

In [200]: arr
Out[200]:
array([[ 0.6033,  1.2636, -0.2555],
       [-0.4457,  0.4684, -0.9616],
       [-1.8245,  0.6254,  1.0229],
       [ 1.1074,  0.0909, -0.3501],
       [ 0.218 , -0.8948, -1.7415]])
```

```
In [201]: arr.sort(1)

In [202]: arr
Out[202]:
array([[-0.2555,  0.6033,  1.2636],
       [-0.9616, -0.4457,  0.4684],
       [-1.8245,  0.6254,  1.0229],
       [-0.3501,  0.0909,  1.1074],
       [-1.7415, -0.8948,  0.218 ]])
```

The top-level method `np.sort` returns a sorted copy of an array instead of modifying the array in-place. A quick-and-dirty way to compute the quantiles of an array is to sort it and select the value at a particular rank:

```
In [203]: large_arr = np.random.randn(1000)

In [204]: large_arr.sort()

In [205]: large_arr[int(0.05 * len(large_arr))] # 5% quantile
Out[205]: -1.5311513550102103
```

For more details on using NumPy's sorting methods, and more advanced techniques like indirect sorts, see Appendix A. Several other kinds of data manipulations related to sorting (e.g., sorting a table of data by one or more columns) can also be found in pandas.

Unique and Other Set Logic

NumPy has some basic set operations for one-dimensional ndarrays. A commonly used one is `np.unique`, which returns the sorted unique values in an array:

```
In [206]: names = np.array(['Bob', 'Joe', 'Will', 'Bob', 'Will', 'Joe', 'Joe'])

In [207]: np.unique(names)
Out[207]: array(['Bob', 'Joe', 'Will'], dtype='<U4')

In [208]: ints = np.array([3, 3, 3, 2, 2, 1, 1, 4, 4])

In [209]: np.unique(ints)
Out[209]: array([1, 2, 3, 4])
```

Contrast `np.unique` with the pure Python alternative:

```
In [210]: sorted(set(names))
Out[210]: ['Bob', 'Joe', 'Will']
```

Another function, `np.in1d`, tests membership of the values in one array in another, returning a boolean array:

```
In [211]: values = np.array([6, 0, 0, 3, 2, 5, 6])
```

```
In [212]: np.in1d(values, [2, 3, 6])
Out[212]: array([ True, False, False,  True,  True, False,  True])
```

See Table 4-6 for a listing of set functions in NumPy.

Table 4-6. Array set operations

Method	Description
unique(x)	Compute the sorted, unique elements in x
intersect1d(x, y)	Compute the sorted, common elements in x and y
union1d(x, y)	Compute the sorted union of elements
in1d(x, y)	Compute a boolean array indicating whether each element of x is contained in y
setdiff1d(x, y)	Set difference, elements in x that are not in y
setxor1d(x, y)	Set symmetric differences; elements that are in either of the arrays, but not both

4.4 File Input and Output with Arrays

NumPy is able to save and load data to and from disk either in text or binary format. In this section I only discuss NumPy's built-in binary format, since most users will prefer pandas and other tools for loading text or tabular data (see Chapter 6 for much more).

np.save and np.load are the two workhorse functions for efficiently saving and loading array data on disk. Arrays are saved by default in an uncompressed raw binary format with file extension *.npy*:

```
In [213]: arr = np.arange(10)

In [214]: np.save('some_array', arr)
```

If the file path does not already end in *.npy*, the extension will be appended. The array on disk can then be loaded with np.load:

```
In [215]: np.load('some_array.npy')
Out[215]: array([0, 1, 2, 3, 4, 5, 6, 7, 8, 9])
```

You save multiple arrays in an uncompressed archive using np.savez and passing the arrays as keyword arguments:

```
In [216]: np.savez('array_archive.npz', a=arr, b=arr)
```

When loading an *.npz* file, you get back a dict-like object that loads the individual arrays lazily:

```
In [217]: arch = np.load('array_archive.npz')

In [218]: arch['b']
Out[218]: array([0, 1, 2, 3, 4, 5, 6, 7, 8, 9])
```

If your data compresses well, you may wish to use numpy.savez_compressed instead:

```
In [219]: np.savez_compressed('arrays_compressed.npz', a=arr, b=arr)
```

4.5 Linear Algebra

Linear algebra, like matrix multiplication, decompositions, determinants, and other square matrix math, is an important part of any array library. Unlike some languages like MATLAB, multiplying two two-dimensional arrays with * is an element-wise product instead of a matrix dot product. Thus, there is a function dot, both an array method and a function in the numpy namespace, for matrix multiplication:

```
In [223]: x = np.array([[1., 2., 3.], [4., 5., 6.]])

In [224]: y = np.array([[6., 23.], [-1, 7], [8, 9]])

In [225]: x
Out[225]:
array([[1., 2., 3.],
       [4., 5., 6.]])

In [226]: y
Out[226]:
array([[ 6., 23.],
       [-1.,  7.],
       [ 8.,  9.]])

In [227]: x.dot(y)
Out[227]:
array([[ 28.,  64.],
       [ 67., 181.]])
```

x.dot(y) is equivalent to np.dot(x, y):

```
In [228]: np.dot(x, y)
Out[228]:
array([[ 28.,  64.],
       [ 67., 181.]])
```

A matrix product between a two-dimensional array and a suitably sized one-dimensional array results in a one-dimensional array:

```
In [229]: np.dot(x, np.ones(3))
Out[229]: array([ 6., 15.])
```

The @ symbol (as of Python 3.5) also works as an infix operator that performs matrix multiplication:

```
In [230]: x @ np.ones(3)
Out[230]: array([ 6., 15.])
```

numpy.linalg has a standard set of matrix decompositions and things like inverse and determinant. These are implemented under the hood via the same industry-standard linear algebra libraries used in other languages like MATLAB and R, such as

BLAS, LAPACK, or possibly (depending on your NumPy build) the proprietary Intel MKL (Math Kernel Library):

```
In [231]: from numpy.linalg import inv, qr

In [232]: X = np.random.randn(5, 5)

In [233]: mat = X.T.dot(X)

In [234]: inv(mat)
Out[234]:
array([[  933.1189,    871.8258, -1417.6902, -1460.4005,  1782.1391],
       [  871.8258,    815.3929, -1325.9965, -1365.9242,  1666.9347],
       [-1417.6902, -1325.9965,  2158.4424,  2222.0191, -2711.6822],
       [-1460.4005, -1365.9242,  2222.0191,  2289.0575, -2793.422 ],
       [ 1782.1391,  1666.9347, -2711.6822, -2793.422 ,  3409.5128]])

In [235]: mat.dot(inv(mat))
Out[235]:
array([[ 1.,  0.,  0.,  0.,  0.],
       [ 0.,  1., -0., -0., -0.],
       [-0., -0.,  1.,  0., -0.],
       [ 0.,  0.,  0.,  1.,  0.],
       [ 0.,  0., -0., -0.,  1.]])

In [236]: q, r = qr(mat)

In [237]: r
Out[237]:
array([[-1.6914,  4.38  ,  0.1757,  0.4075, -0.7838],
       [ 0.    , -2.6436,  0.1939, -3.072 , -1.0702],
       [ 0.    ,  0.    , -0.8138,  1.5414,  0.6155],
       [ 0.    ,  0.    ,  0.    , -2.6445, -2.1669],
       [ 0.    ,  0.    ,  0.    ,  0.    ,  0.0002]])
```

The expression X.T.dot(X) computes the dot product of X with its transpose X.T.

See Table 4-7 for a list of some of the most commonly used linear algebra functions.

Table 4-7. Commonly used numpy.linalg functions

Function	Description
diag	Return the diagonal (or off-diagonal) elements of a square matrix as a 1D array, or convert a 1D array into a square matrix with zeros on the off-diagonal
dot	Matrix multiplication
trace	Compute the sum of the diagonal elements
det	Compute the matrix determinant
eig	Compute the eigenvalues and eigenvectors of a square matrix
inv	Compute the inverse of a square matrix
pinv	Compute the Moore-Penrose pseudo-inverse of a matrix

Function	Description
qr	Compute the QR decomposition
svd	Compute the singular value decomposition (SVD)
solve	Solve the linear system Ax = b for x, where A is a square matrix
lstsq	Compute the least-squares solution to Ax = b

4.6 Pseudorandom Number Generation

The numpy.random module supplements the built-in Python random with functions for efficiently generating whole arrays of sample values from many kinds of probability distributions. For example, you can get a 4 × 4 array of samples from the standard normal distribution using normal:

```
In [238]: samples = np.random.normal(size=(4, 4))
```

```
In [239]: samples
Out[239]:
array([[ 0.5732,  0.1933,  0.4429,  1.2796],
       [ 0.575 ,  0.4339, -0.7658, -1.237 ],
       [-0.5367,  1.8545, -0.92  , -0.1082],
       [ 0.1525,  0.9435, -1.0953, -0.144 ]])
```

Python's built-in random module, by contrast, only samples one value at a time. As you can see from this benchmark, numpy.random is well over an order of magnitude faster for generating very large samples:

```
In [240]: from random import normalvariate
```

```
In [241]: N = 1000000
```

```
In [242]: %timeit samples = [normalvariate(0, 1) for _ in range(N)]
732 ms +- 21.3 ms per loop (mean +- std. dev. of 7 runs, 1 loop each)
```

```
In [243]: %timeit np.random.normal(size=N)
43.7 ms +- 710 us per loop (mean +- std. dev. of 7 runs, 10 loops each)
```

We say that these are *pseudorandom* numbers because they are generated by an algorithm with deterministic behavior based on the *seed* of the random number generator. You can change NumPy's random number generation seed using np.random.seed:

```
In [244]: np.random.seed(1234)
```

The data generation functions in numpy.random use a global random seed. To avoid global state, you can use numpy.random.RandomState to create a random number generator isolated from others:

```
In [245]: rng = np.random.RandomState(1234)
```

```
In [246]: rng.randn(10)
Out[246]:
array([ 0.4714, -1.191 ,  1.4327, -0.3127, -0.7206,  0.8872,  0.8596,
       -0.6365,  0.0157, -2.2427])
```

See Table 4-8 for a partial list of functions available in `numpy.random`. I'll give some examples of leveraging these functions' ability to generate large arrays of samples all at once in the next section.

Table 4-8. Partial list of numpy.random functions

Function	Description
seed	Seed the random number generator
permutation	Return a random permutation of a sequence, or return a permuted range
shuffle	Randomly permute a sequence in-place
rand	Draw samples from a uniform distribution
randint	Draw random integers from a given low-to-high range
randn	Draw samples from a normal distribution with mean 0 and standard deviation 1 (MATLAB-like interface)
binomial	Draw samples from a binomial distribution
normal	Draw samples from a normal (Gaussian) distribution
beta	Draw samples from a beta distribution
chisquare	Draw samples from a chi-square distribution
gamma	Draw samples from a gamma distribution
uniform	Draw samples from a uniform [0, 1) distribution

4.7 Example: Random Walks

The simulation of random walks (*https://en.wikipedia.org/wiki/Random_walk*) provides an illustrative application of utilizing array operations. Let's first consider a simple random walk starting at 0 with steps of 1 and –1 occurring with equal probability.

Here is a pure Python way to implement a single random walk with 1,000 steps using the built-in `random` module:

```
In [247]: import random
   .....: position = 0
   .....: walk = [position]
   .....: steps = 1000
   .....: for i in range(steps):
   .....:     step = 1 if random.randint(0, 1) else -1
   .....:     position += step
   .....:     walk.append(position)
   .....:
```

See Figure 4-4 for an example plot of the first 100 values on one of these random walks:

```
In [249]: plt.plot(walk[:100])
```

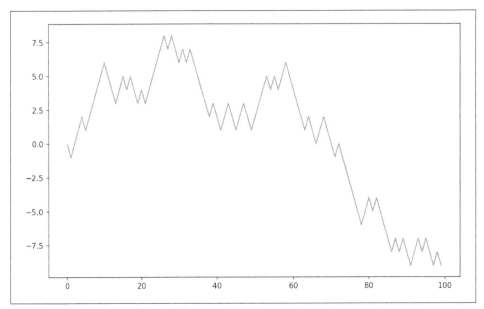

Figure 4-4. A simple random walk

You might make the observation that walk is simply the cumulative sum of the random steps and could be evaluated as an array expression. Thus, I use the np.random module to draw 1,000 coin flips at once, set these to 1 and –1, and compute the cumulative sum:

```
In [251]: nsteps = 1000

In [252]: draws = np.random.randint(0, 2, size=nsteps)

In [253]: steps = np.where(draws > 0, 1, -1)

In [254]: walk = steps.cumsum()
```

From this we can begin to extract statistics like the minimum and maximum value along the walk's trajectory:

```
In [255]: walk.min()
Out[255]: -3

In [256]: walk.max()
Out[256]: 31
```

A more complicated statistic is the *first crossing time*, the step at which the random walk reaches a particular value. Here we might want to know how long it took the random walk to get at least 10 steps away from the origin 0 in either direction. np.abs(walk) >= 10 gives us a boolean array indicating where the walk has reached or exceeded 10, but we want the index of the *first* 10 or –10. Turns out, we can com-

---

pute this using `argmax`, which returns the first index of the maximum value in the boolean array (`True` is the maximum value):

```
In [257]: (np.abs(walk) >= 10).argmax()
Out[257]: 37
```

Note that using `argmax` here is not always efficient because it always makes a full scan of the array. In this special case, once a `True` is observed we know it to be the maximum value.

Simulating Many Random Walks at Once

If your goal was to simulate many random walks, say 5,000 of them, you can generate all of the random walks with minor modifications to the preceding code. If passed a 2-tuple, the `numpy.random` functions will generate a two-dimensional array of draws, and we can compute the cumulative sum across the rows to compute all 5,000 random walks in one shot:

```
In [258]: nwalks = 5000

In [259]: nsteps = 1000

In [260]: draws = np.random.randint(0, 2, size=(nwalks, nsteps)) # 0 or 1

In [261]: steps = np.where(draws > 0, 1, -1)

In [262]: walks = steps.cumsum(1)

In [263]: walks
Out[263]:
array([[  1,   0,   1, ...,   8,   7,   8],
       [  1,   0,  -1, ...,  34,  33,  32],
       [  1,   0,  -1, ...,   4,   5,   4],
       ...,
       [  1,   2,   1, ...,  24,  25,  26],
       [  1,   2,   3, ...,  14,  13,  14],
       [ -1,  -2,  -3, ..., -24, -23, -22]])
```

Now, we can compute the maximum and minimum values obtained over all of the walks:

```
In [264]: walks.max()
Out[264]: 138

In [265]: walks.min()
Out[265]: -133
```

Out of these walks, let's compute the minimum crossing time to 30 or –30. This is slightly tricky because not all 5,000 of them reach 30. We can check this using the any method:

```
In [266]: hits30 = (np.abs(walks) >= 30).any(1)
```

```
In [267]: hits30
Out[267]: array([False,  True, False, ..., False,  True, False])
```

```
In [268]: hits30.sum() # Number that hit 30 or -30
Out[268]: 3410
```

We can use this boolean array to select out the rows of walks that actually cross the
absolute 30 level and call argmax across axis 1 to get the crossing times:

```
In [269]: crossing_times = (np.abs(walks[hits30]) >= 30).argmax(1)
```

```
In [270]: crossing_times
Out[270]: array([735, 409, 253, ..., 327, 453, 447])
```

Lastly, we compute the average minimum crossing time:

```
In [271]: crossing_times.mean()
Out[271]: 498.8897360703812
```

Feel free to experiment with other distributions for the steps other than equal-sized
coin flips. You need only use a different random number generation function, like
normal to generate normally distributed steps with some mean and standard
deviation:

```
In [272]: steps = np.random.normal(loc=0, scale=0.25,
   .....:                          size=(nwalks, nsteps))
```

4.8 Conclusion

While much of the rest of the book will focus on building data wrangling skills with
pandas, we will continue to work in a similar array-based style. In Appendix A, we
will dig deeper into NumPy features to help you further develop your array computing skills.

## CHAPTER 5

Getting Started with pandas

pandas will be a major tool of interest throughout much of the rest of the book. It contains data structures and data manipulation tools designed to make data cleaning and analysis fast and easy in Python. pandas is often used in tandem with numerical computing tools like NumPy and SciPy, analytical libraries like statsmodels and scikit-learn, and data visualization libraries like matplotlib. pandas adopts significant parts of NumPy's idiomatic style of array-based computing, especially array-based functions and a preference for data processing without `for` loops.

While pandas adopts many coding idioms from NumPy, the biggest difference is that pandas is designed for working with tabular or heterogeneous data. NumPy, by contrast, is best suited for working with homogeneous numerical array data.

Since becoming an open source project in 2010, pandas has matured into a quite large library that's applicable in a broad set of real-world use cases. The developer community has grown to over 800 distinct contributors, who've been helping build the project as they've used it to solve their day-to-day data problems.

Throughout the rest of the book, I use the following import convention for pandas:

```
In [1]: import pandas as pd
```

Thus, whenever you see `pd.` in code, it's referring to pandas. You may also find it easier to import Series and DataFrame into the local namespace since they are so frequently used:

```
In [2]: from pandas import Series, DataFrame
```

5.1 Introduction to pandas Data Structures

To get started with pandas, you will need to get comfortable with its two workhorse data structures: *Series* and *DataFrame*. While they are not a universal solution for every problem, they provide a solid, easy-to-use basis for most applications.

Series

A Series is a one-dimensional array-like object containing a sequence of values (of similar types to NumPy types) and an associated array of data labels, called its *index*. The simplest Series is formed from only an array of data:

```
In [13]: obj = pd.Series([4, 7, -5, 3])

In [14]: obj
Out[14]:
0    4
1    7
2   -5
3    3
dtype: int64
```

The string representation of a Series displayed interactively shows the index on the left and the values on the right. Since we did not specify an index for the data, a default one consisting of the integers 0 through N - 1 (where N is the length of the data) is created. You can get the array representation and index object of the Series via its values and index attributes, respectively:

```
In [15]: obj.values
Out[15]: array([ 4,  7, -5,  3])

In [16]: obj.index  # like range(4)
Out[16]: RangeIndex(start=0, stop=4, step=1)
```

Often it will be desirable to create a Series with an index identifying each data point with a label:

```
In [17]: obj2 = pd.Series([4, 7, -5, 3], index=['d', 'b', 'a', 'c'])

In [18]: obj2
Out[18]:
d    4
b    7
a   -5
c    3
dtype: int64

In [19]: obj2.index
Out[19]: Index(['d', 'b', 'a', 'c'], dtype='object')
```

Compared with NumPy arrays, you can use labels in the index when selecting single values or a set of values:

```
In [20]: obj2['a']
Out[20]: -5

In [21]: obj2['d'] = 6

In [22]: obj2[['c', 'a', 'd']]
Out[22]:
c    3
a   -5
d    6
dtype: int64
```

Here `['c', 'a', 'd']` is interpreted as a list of indices, even though it contains strings instead of integers.

Using NumPy functions or NumPy-like operations, such as filtering with a boolean array, scalar multiplication, or applying math functions, will preserve the index-value link:

```
In [23]: obj2[obj2 > 0]
Out[23]:
d    6
b    7
c    3
dtype: int64

In [24]: obj2 * 2
Out[24]:
d    12
b    14
a   -10
c     6
dtype: int64

In [25]: np.exp(obj2)
Out[25]:
d     403.428793
b    1096.633158
a       0.006738
c      20.085537
dtype: float64
```

Another way to think about a Series is as a fixed-length, ordered dict, as it is a mapping of index values to data values. It can be used in many contexts where you might use a dict:

```
In [26]: 'b' in obj2
Out[26]: True
```

```
In [27]: 'e' in obj2
Out[27]: False
```

Should you have data contained in a Python dict, you can create a Series from it by passing the dict:

```
In [28]: sdata = {'Ohio': 35000, 'Texas': 71000, 'Oregon': 16000, 'Utah': 5000}

In [29]: obj3 = pd.Series(sdata)

In [30]: obj3
Out[30]:
Ohio      35000
Texas     71000
Oregon    16000
Utah       5000
dtype: int64
```

When you are only passing a dict, the index in the resulting Series will have the dict's keys in sorted order. You can override this by passing the dict keys in the order you want them to appear in the resulting Series:

```
In [31]: states = ['California', 'Ohio', 'Oregon', 'Texas']

In [32]: obj4 = pd.Series(sdata, index=states)

In [33]: obj4
Out[33]:
California        NaN
Ohio         35000.0
Oregon       16000.0
Texas        71000.0
dtype: float64
```

Here, three values found in sdata were placed in the appropriate locations, but since no value for 'California' was found, it appears as NaN (not a number), which is considered in pandas to mark missing or *NA* values. Since 'Utah' was not included in states, it is excluded from the resulting object.

I will use the terms "missing" or "NA" interchangeably to refer to missing data. The isnull and notnull functions in pandas should be used to detect missing data:

```
In [34]: pd.isnull(obj4)
Out[34]:
California     True
Ohio          False
Oregon        False
Texas         False
dtype: bool

In [35]: pd.notnull(obj4)
Out[35]:
```

```
California    False
Ohio           True
Oregon         True
Texas          True
dtype: bool
```

Series also has these as instance methods:

```
In [36]: obj4.isnull()
Out[36]:
California     True
Ohio          False
Oregon        False
Texas         False
dtype: bool
```

I discuss working with missing data in more detail in Chapter 7.

A useful Series feature for many applications is that it automatically aligns by index label in arithmetic operations:

```
In [37]: obj3
Out[37]:
Ohio       35000
Texas      71000
Oregon     16000
Utah        5000
dtype: int64

In [38]: obj4
Out[38]:
California      NaN
Ohio          35000.0
Oregon        16000.0
Texas         71000.0
dtype: float64

In [39]: obj3 + obj4
Out[39]:
California       NaN
Ohio          70000.0
Oregon        32000.0
Texas        142000.0
Utah             NaN
dtype: float64
```

Data alignment features will be addressed in more detail later. If you have experience with databases, you can think about this as being similar to a join operation.

Both the Series object itself and its index have a name attribute, which integrates with other key areas of pandas functionality:

```
In [40]: obj4.name = 'population'

In [41]: obj4.index.name = 'state'

In [42]: obj4
Out[42]:
state
California        NaN
Ohio          35000.0
Oregon        16000.0
Texas         71000.0
Name: population, dtype: float64
```

A Series's index can be altered in-place by assignment:

```
In [43]: obj
Out[43]:
0    4
1    7
2   -5
3    3
dtype: int64

In [44]: obj.index = ['Bob', 'Steve', 'Jeff', 'Ryan']

In [45]: obj
Out[45]:
Bob       4
Steve     7
Jeff     -5
Ryan      3
dtype: int64
```

DataFrame

A DataFrame represents a rectangular table of data and contains an ordered collection of columns, each of which can be a different value type (numeric, string, boolean, etc.). The DataFrame has both a row and column index; it can be thought of as a dict of Series all sharing the same index. Under the hood, the data is stored as one or more two-dimensional blocks rather than a list, dict, or some other collection of one-dimensional arrays. The exact details of DataFrame's internals are outside the scope of this book.

 While a DataFrame is physically two-dimensional, you can use it to represent higher dimensional data in a tabular format using hierarchical indexing, a subject we will discuss in Chapter 8 and an ingredient in some of the more advanced data-handling features in pandas.

There are many ways to construct a DataFrame, though one of the most common is from a dict of equal-length lists or NumPy arrays:

```
data = {'state': ['Ohio', 'Ohio', 'Ohio', 'Nevada', 'Nevada', 'Nevada'],
        'year': [2000, 2001, 2002, 2001, 2002, 2003],
        'pop': [1.5, 1.7, 3.6, 2.4, 2.9, 3.2]}
frame = pd.DataFrame(data)
```

The resulting DataFrame will have its index assigned automatically as with Series, and the columns are placed in sorted order:

```
In [47]: frame
Out[47]:
    state  year  pop
0    Ohio  2000  1.5
1    Ohio  2001  1.7
2    Ohio  2002  3.6
3  Nevada  2001  2.4
4  Nevada  2002  2.9
5  Nevada  2003  3.2
```

If you are using the Jupyter notebook, pandas DataFrame objects will be displayed as a more browser-friendly HTML table.

For large DataFrames, the head method selects only the first five rows:

```
In [48]: frame.head()
Out[48]:
    state  year  pop
0    Ohio  2000  1.5
1    Ohio  2001  1.7
2    Ohio  2002  3.6
3  Nevada  2001  2.4
4  Nevada  2002  2.9
```

If you specify a sequence of columns, the DataFrame's columns will be arranged in that order:

```
In [49]: pd.DataFrame(data, columns=['year', 'state', 'pop'])
Out[49]:
   year   state  pop
0  2000    Ohio  1.5
1  2001    Ohio  1.7
2  2002    Ohio  3.6
3  2001  Nevada  2.4
4  2002  Nevada  2.9
5  2003  Nevada  3.2
```

If you pass a column that isn't contained in the dict, it will appear with missing values in the result:

```
In [50]: frame2 = pd.DataFrame(data, columns=['year', 'state', 'pop', 'debt'],
   ....:                       index=['one', 'two', 'three', 'four',
   ....:                              'five', 'six'])
```

```
In [51]: frame2
Out[51]:
       year   state  pop debt
one    2000    Ohio  1.5  NaN
two    2001    Ohio  1.7  NaN
three  2002    Ohio  3.6  NaN
four   2001  Nevada  2.4  NaN
five   2002  Nevada  2.9  NaN
six    2003  Nevada  3.2  NaN

In [52]: frame2.columns
Out[52]: Index(['year', 'state', 'pop', 'debt'], dtype='object')
```

A column in a DataFrame can be retrieved as a Series either by dict-like notation or by attribute:

```
In [53]: frame2['state']
Out[53]:
one        Ohio
two        Ohio
three      Ohio
four     Nevada
five     Nevada
six      Nevada
Name: state, dtype: object

In [54]: frame2.year
Out[54]:
one      2000
two      2001
three    2002
four     2001
five     2002
six      2003
Name: year, dtype: int64
```

Attribute-like access (e.g., frame2.year) and tab completion of column names in IPython is provided as a convenience.

frame2[column] works for any column name, but frame2.column only works when the column name is a valid Python variable name.

Note that the returned Series have the same index as the DataFrame, and their name attribute has been appropriately set.

Rows can also be retrieved by position or name with the special loc attribute (much more on this later):

```
In [55]: frame2.loc['three']
Out[55]:
year      2002
state     Ohio
pop        3.6
debt       NaN
Name: three, dtype: object
```

Columns can be modified by assignment. For example, the empty 'debt' column could be assigned a scalar value or an array of values:

```
In [56]: frame2['debt'] = 16.5

In [57]: frame2
Out[57]:
       year   state  pop  debt
one    2000    Ohio  1.5  16.5
two    2001    Ohio  1.7  16.5
three  2002    Ohio  3.6  16.5
four   2001  Nevada  2.4  16.5
five   2002  Nevada  2.9  16.5
six    2003  Nevada  3.2  16.5

In [58]: frame2['debt'] = np.arange(6.)

In [59]: frame2
Out[59]:
       year   state  pop  debt
one    2000    Ohio  1.5   0.0
two    2001    Ohio  1.7   1.0
three  2002    Ohio  3.6   2.0
four   2001  Nevada  2.4   3.0
five   2002  Nevada  2.9   4.0
six    2003  Nevada  3.2   5.0
```

When you are assigning lists or arrays to a column, the value's length must match the length of the DataFrame. If you assign a Series, its labels will be realigned exactly to the DataFrame's index, inserting missing values in any holes:

```
In [60]: val = pd.Series([-1.2, -1.5, -1.7], index=['two', 'four', 'five'])

In [61]: frame2['debt'] = val

In [62]: frame2
Out[62]:
       year   state  pop  debt
one    2000    Ohio  1.5   NaN
two    2001    Ohio  1.7  -1.2
three  2002    Ohio  3.6   NaN
four   2001  Nevada  2.4  -1.5
five   2002  Nevada  2.9  -1.7
six    2003  Nevada  3.2   NaN
```

Assigning a column that doesn't exist will create a new column. The del keyword will delete columns as with a dict.

As an example of del, I first add a new column of boolean values where the state column equals 'Ohio':

```
In [63]: frame2['eastern'] = frame2.state == 'Ohio'
```

```
In [64]: frame2
Out[64]:
       year   state  pop  debt  eastern
one    2000    Ohio  1.5   NaN     True
two    2001    Ohio  1.7  -1.2     True
three  2002    Ohio  3.6   NaN     True
four   2001  Nevada  2.4  -1.5    False
five   2002  Nevada  2.9  -1.7    False
six    2003  Nevada  3.2   NaN    False
```

 New columns cannot be created with the frame2.eastern syntax.

The del method can then be used to remove this column:

```
In [65]: del frame2['eastern']
```

```
In [66]: frame2.columns
Out[66]: Index(['year', 'state', 'pop', 'debt'], dtype='object')
```

 The column returned from indexing a DataFrame is a *view* on the underlying data, not a copy. Thus, any in-place modifications to the Series will be reflected in the DataFrame. The column can be explicitly copied with the Series's copy method.

Another common form of data is a nested dict of dicts:

```
In [67]: pop = {'Nevada': {2001: 2.4, 2002: 2.9},
    ....:        'Ohio': {2000: 1.5, 2001: 1.7, 2002: 3.6}}
```

If the nested dict is passed to the DataFrame, pandas will interpret the outer dict keys as the columns and the inner keys as the row indices:

```
In [68]: frame3 = pd.DataFrame(pop)
```

```
In [69]: frame3
Out[69]:
      Nevada  Ohio
2000     NaN   1.5
```

```
2001     2.4    1.7
2002     2.9    3.6
```

You can transpose the DataFrame (swap rows and columns) with similar syntax to a
NumPy array:

```
In [70]: frame3.T
Out[70]:
        2000  2001  2002
Nevada  NaN   2.4   2.9
Ohio    1.5   1.7   3.6
```

The keys in the inner dicts are combined and sorted to form the index in the result.
This isn't true if an explicit index is specified:

```
In [71]: pd.DataFrame(pop, index=[2001, 2002, 2003])
Out[71]:
      Nevada  Ohio
2001  2.4     1.7
2002  2.9     3.6
2003  NaN     NaN
```

Dicts of Series are treated in much the same way:

```
In [72]: pdata = {'Ohio': frame3['Ohio'][:-1],
   ....:          'Nevada': frame3['Nevada'][:2]}

In [73]: pd.DataFrame(pdata)
Out[73]:
      Ohio  Nevada
2000  1.5   NaN
2001  1.7   2.4
```

For a complete list of things you can pass the DataFrame constructor, see Table 5-1.

If a DataFrame's index and columns have their name attributes set, these will also be
displayed:

```
In [74]: frame3.index.name = 'year'; frame3.columns.name = 'state'

In [75]: frame3
Out[75]:
state  Nevada  Ohio
year
2000   NaN     1.5
2001   2.4     1.7
2002   2.9     3.6
```

As with Series, the values attribute returns the data contained in the DataFrame as a
two-dimensional ndarray:

```
In [76]: frame3.values
Out[76]:
array([[nan, 1.5],
```

```
        [2.4, 1.7],
        [2.9, 3.6]])
```

If the DataFrame's columns are different dtypes, the dtype of the values array will be chosen to accommodate all of the columns:

```
In [77]: frame2.values
Out[77]:
array([[2000, 'Ohio', 1.5, nan],
       [2001, 'Ohio', 1.7, -1.2],
       [2002, 'Ohio', 3.6, nan],
       [2001, 'Nevada', 2.4, -1.5],
       [2002, 'Nevada', 2.9, -1.7],
       [2003, 'Nevada', 3.2, nan]], dtype=object)
```

Table 5-1. Possible data inputs to DataFrame constructor

Type	Notes
2D ndarray	A matrix of data, passing optional row and column labels
dict of arrays, lists, or tuples	Each sequence becomes a column in the DataFrame; all sequences must be the same length
NumPy structured/record array	Treated as the "dict of arrays" case
dict of Series	Each value becomes a column; indexes from each Series are unioned together to form the result's row index if no explicit index is passed
dict of dicts	Each inner dict becomes a column; keys are unioned to form the row index as in the "dict of Series" case
List of dicts or Series	Each item becomes a row in the DataFrame; union of dict keys or Series indexes become the DataFrame's column labels
List of lists or tuples	Treated as the "2D ndarray" case
Another DataFrame	The DataFrame's indexes are used unless different ones are passed
NumPy MaskedArray	Like the "2D ndarray" case except masked values become NA/missing in the DataFrame result

Index Objects

pandas's Index objects are responsible for holding the axis labels and other metadata (like the axis name or names). Any array or other sequence of labels you use when constructing a Series or DataFrame is internally converted to an Index:

```
In [78]: obj = pd.Series(range(3), index=['a', 'b', 'c'])

In [79]: index = obj.index

In [80]: index
Out[80]: Index(['a', 'b', 'c'], dtype='object')

In [81]: index[1:]
Out[81]: Index(['b', 'c'], dtype='object')
```

Index objects are immutable and thus can't be modified by the user:

```
index[1] = 'd'  # TypeError
```

Immutability makes it safer to share Index objects among data structures:

```
In [82]: labels = pd.Index(np.arange(3))

In [83]: labels
Out[83]: Int64Index([0, 1, 2], dtype='int64')

In [84]: obj2 = pd.Series([1.5, -2.5, 0], index=labels)

In [85]: obj2
Out[85]:
0    1.5
1   -2.5
2    0.0
dtype: float64

In [86]: obj2.index is labels
Out[86]: True
```

Some users will not often take advantage of the capabilities provided by indexes, but because some operations will yield results
containing indexed data, it's important to understand how they
work.

In addition to being array-like, an Index also behaves like a fixed-size set:

```
In [87]: frame3
Out[87]:
state  Nevada  Ohio
year
2000     NaN   1.5
2001     2.4   1.7
2002     2.9   3.6

In [88]: frame3.columns
Out[88]: Index(['Nevada', 'Ohio'], dtype='object', name='state')

In [89]: 'Ohio' in frame3.columns
Out[89]: True

In [90]: 2003 in frame3.index
Out[90]: False
```

Unlike Python sets, a pandas Index can contain duplicate labels:

```
In [91]: dup_labels = pd.Index(['foo', 'foo', 'bar', 'bar'])

In [92]: dup_labels
Out[92]: Index(['foo', 'foo', 'bar', 'bar'], dtype='object')
```

Selections with duplicate labels will select all occurrences of that label.

Each Index has a number of methods and properties for set logic, which answer other common questions about the data it contains. Some useful ones are summarized in Table 5-2.

Table 5-2. Some Index methods and properties

Method	Description
append	Concatenate with additional Index objects, producing a new Index
difference	Compute set difference as an Index
intersection	Compute set intersection
union	Compute set union
isin	Compute boolean array indicating whether each value is contained in the passed collection
delete	Compute new Index with element at index i deleted
drop	Compute new Index by deleting passed values
insert	Compute new Index by inserting element at index i
is_monotonic	Returns True if each element is greater than or equal to the previous element
is_unique	Returns True if the Index has no duplicate values
unique	Compute the array of unique values in the Index

5.2 Essential Functionality

This section will walk you through the fundamental mechanics of interacting with the data contained in a Series or DataFrame. In the chapters to come, we will delve more deeply into data analysis and manipulation topics using pandas. This book is not intended to serve as exhaustive documentation for the pandas library; instead, we'll focus on the most important features, leaving the less common (i.e., more esoteric) things for you to explore on your own.

Reindexing

An important method on pandas objects is `reindex`, which means to create a new object with the data *conformed* to a new index. Consider an example:

```
In [93]: obj = pd.Series([4.5, 7.2, -5.3, 3.6], index=['d', 'b', 'a', 'c'])

In [94]: obj
Out[94]:
d    4.5
b    7.2
a   -5.3
c    3.6
dtype: float64
```

Calling `reindex` on this Series rearranges the data according to the new index, introducing missing values if any index values were not already present:

```
In [95]: obj2 = obj.reindex(['a', 'b', 'c', 'd', 'e'])

In [96]: obj2
Out[96]:
a   -5.3
b    7.2
c    3.6
d    4.5
e    NaN
dtype: float64
```

For ordered data like time series, it may be desirable to do some interpolation or filling of values when reindexing. The `method` option allows us to do this, using a method such as `ffill`, which forward-fills the values:

```
In [97]: obj3 = pd.Series(['blue', 'purple', 'yellow'], index=[0, 2, 4])

In [98]: obj3
Out[98]:
0       blue
2     purple
4     yellow
dtype: object

In [99]: obj3.reindex(range(6), method='ffill')
Out[99]:
0       blue
1       blue
2     purple
3     purple
4     yellow
5     yellow
dtype: object
```

With DataFrame, `reindex` can alter either the (row) index, columns, or both. When passed only a sequence, it reindexes the rows in the result:

```
In [100]: frame = pd.DataFrame(np.arange(9).reshape((3, 3)),
   .....:                      index=['a', 'c', 'd'],
   .....:                      columns=['Ohio', 'Texas', 'California'])

In [101]: frame
Out[101]:
   Ohio  Texas  California
a     0      1           2
c     3      4           5
d     6      7           8

In [102]: frame2 = frame.reindex(['a', 'b', 'c', 'd'])
```

```
In [103]: frame2
Out[103]:
   Ohio  Texas  California
a   0.0    1.0         2.0
b   NaN    NaN         NaN
c   3.0    4.0         5.0
d   6.0    7.0         8.0
```

The columns can be reindexed with the `columns` keyword:

```
In [104]: states = ['Texas', 'Utah', 'California']

In [105]: frame.reindex(columns=states)
Out[105]:
   Texas  Utah  California
a      1   NaN           2
c      4   NaN           5
d      7   NaN           8
```

See Table 5-3 for more about the arguments to `reindex`.

As we'll explore in more detail, you can reindex more succinctly by label-indexing with `loc`, and many users prefer to use it exclusively:

```
In [106]: frame.loc[['a', 'b', 'c', 'd'], states]
Out[106]:
   Texas  Utah  California
a    1.0   NaN         2.0
b    NaN   NaN         NaN
c    4.0   NaN         5.0
d    7.0   NaN         8.0
```

Table 5-3. reindex function arguments

Argument	Description
`index`	New sequence to use as index. Can be Index instance or any other sequence-like Python data structure. An Index will be used exactly as is without any copying.
`method`	Interpolation (fill) method; `'ffill'` fills forward, while `'bfill'` fills backward.
`fill_value`	Substitute value to use when introducing missing data by reindexing.
`limit`	When forward- or backfilling, maximum size gap (in number of elements) to fill.
`tolerance`	When forward- or backfilling, maximum size gap (in absolute numeric distance) to fill for inexact matches.
`level`	Match simple Index on level of MultiIndex; otherwise select subset of.
`copy`	If `True`, always copy underlying data even if new index is equivalent to old index; if `False`, do not copy the data when the indexes are equivalent.

Dropping Entries from an Axis

Dropping one or more entries from an axis is easy if you already have an index array or list without those entries. As that can require a bit of munging and set logic, the drop method will return a new object with the indicated value or values deleted from an axis:

```
In [107]: obj = pd.Series(np.arange(5.), index=['a', 'b', 'c', 'd', 'e'])

In [108]: obj
Out[108]:
a    0.0
b    1.0
c    2.0
d    3.0
e    4.0
dtype: float64

In [109]: new_obj = obj.drop('c')

In [110]: new_obj
Out[110]:
a    0.0
b    1.0
d    3.0
e    4.0
dtype: float64

In [111]: obj.drop(['d', 'c'])
Out[111]:
a    0.0
b    1.0
e    4.0
dtype: float64
```

With DataFrame, index values can be deleted from either axis. To illustrate this, we first create an example DataFrame:

```
In [112]: data = pd.DataFrame(np.arange(16).reshape((4, 4)),
   .....:                     index=['Ohio', 'Colorado', 'Utah', 'New York'],
   .....:                     columns=['one', 'two', 'three', 'four'])

In [113]: data
Out[113]:
          one  two  three  four
Ohio        0    1      2     3
Colorado    4    5      6     7
Utah        8    9     10    11
New York   12   13     14    15
```

Calling drop with a sequence of labels will drop values from the row labels (axis 0):

```
In [114]: data.drop(['Colorado', 'Ohio'])
Out[114]:
          one  two  three  four
Utah        8    9     10    11
New York   12   13     14    15
```

You can drop values from the columns by passing `axis=1` or `axis='columns'`:

```
In [115]: data.drop('two', axis=1)
Out[115]:
          one  three  four
Ohio        0      2     3
Colorado    4      6     7
Utah        8     10    11
New York   12     14    15

In [116]: data.drop(['two', 'four'], axis='columns')
Out[116]:
          one  three
Ohio        0      2
Colorado    4      6
Utah        8     10
New York   12     14
```

Many functions, like `drop`, which modify the size or shape of a Series or DataFrame, can manipulate an object *in-place* without returning a new object:

```
In [117]: obj.drop('c', inplace=True)

In [118]: obj
Out[118]:
a    0.0
b    1.0
d    3.0
e    4.0
dtype: float64
```

Be careful with the `inplace`, as it destroys any data that is dropped.

Indexing, Selection, and Filtering

Series indexing (`obj[...]`) works analogously to NumPy array indexing, except you can use the Series's index values instead of only integers. Here are some examples of this:

```
In [119]: obj = pd.Series(np.arange(4.), index=['a', 'b', 'c', 'd'])

In [120]: obj
Out[120]:
a    0.0
b    1.0
c    2.0
d    3.0
dtype: float64

In [121]: obj['b']
Out[121]: 1.0
```

```
In [122]: obj[1]
Out[122]: 1.0

In [123]: obj[2:4]
Out[123]:
c    2.0
d    3.0
dtype: float64

In [124]: obj[['b', 'a', 'd']]
Out[124]:
b    1.0
a    0.0
d    3.0
dtype: float64

In [125]: obj[[1, 3]]
Out[125]:
b    1.0
d    3.0
dtype: float64

In [126]: obj[obj < 2]
Out[126]:
a    0.0
b    1.0
dtype: float64
```

Slicing with labels behaves differently than normal Python slicing in that the endpoint is inclusive:

```
In [127]: obj['b':'c']
Out[127]:
b    1.0
c    2.0
dtype: float64
```

Setting using these methods modifies the corresponding section of the Series:

```
In [128]: obj['b':'c'] = 5

In [129]: obj
Out[129]:
a    0.0
b    5.0
c    5.0
d    3.0
dtype: float64
```

Indexing into a DataFrame is for retrieving one or more columns either with a single value or sequence:

```
In [130]: data = pd.DataFrame(np.arange(16).reshape((4, 4)),
   .....:                      index=['Ohio', 'Colorado', 'Utah', 'New York'],
   .....:                      columns=['one', 'two', 'three', 'four'])

In [131]: data
Out[131]:
          one  two  three  four
Ohio        0    1      2     3
Colorado    4    5      6     7
Utah        8    9     10    11
New York   12   13     14    15

In [132]: data['two']
Out[132]:
Ohio         1
Colorado     5
Utah         9
New York    13
Name: two, dtype: int64

In [133]: data[['three', 'one']]
Out[133]:
          three  one
Ohio          2    0
Colorado      6    4
Utah         10    8
New York     14   12
```

Indexing like this has a few special cases. First, slicing or selecting data with a boolean array:

```
In [134]: data[:2]
Out[134]:
          one  two  three  four
Ohio        0    1      2     3
Colorado    4    5      6     7

In [135]: data[data['three'] > 5]
Out[135]:
          one  two  three  four
Colorado    4    5      6     7
Utah        8    9     10    11
New York   12   13     14    15
```

The row selection syntax `data[:2]` is provided as a convenience. Passing a single element or a list to the [ ] operator selects columns.

Another use case is in indexing with a boolean DataFrame, such as one produced by a scalar comparison:

```
In [136]: data < 5
Out[136]:
             one    two  three   four
Ohio        True   True   True   True
Colorado    True  False  False  False
Utah       False  False  False  False
New York   False  False  False  False

In [137]: data[data < 5] = 0

In [138]: data
Out[138]:
          one  two  three  four
Ohio        0    0      0     0
Colorado    0    5      6     7
Utah        8    9     10    11
New York   12   13     14    15
```

This makes DataFrame syntactically more like a two-dimensional NumPy array in this particular case.

Selection with loc and iloc

For DataFrame label-indexing on the rows, I introduce the special indexing operators loc and iloc. They enable you to select a subset of the rows and columns from a DataFrame with NumPy-like notation using either axis labels (loc) or integers (iloc).

As a preliminary example, let's select a single row and multiple columns by label:

```
In [139]: data.loc['Colorado', ['two', 'three']]
Out[139]:
two      5
three    6
Name: Colorado, dtype: int64
```

We'll then perform some similar selections with integers using iloc:

```
In [140]: data.iloc[2, [3, 0, 1]]
Out[140]:
four    11
one      8
two      9
Name: Utah, dtype: int64

In [141]: data.iloc[2]
Out[141]:
one       8
two       9
three    10
four     11
Name: Utah, dtype: int64
```

```
In [142]: data.iloc[[1, 2], [3, 0, 1]]
Out[142]:
          four  one  two
Colorado     7    0    5
Utah        11    8    9
```

Both indexing functions work with slices in addition to single labels or lists of labels:

```
In [143]: data.loc[:'Utah', 'two']
Out[143]:
Ohio        0
Colorado    5
Utah        9
Name: two, dtype: int64

In [144]: data.iloc[:, :3][data.three > 5]
Out[144]:
           one  two  three
Colorado     0    5      6
Utah         8    9     10
New York    12   13     14
```

So there are many ways to select and rearrange the data contained in a pandas object. For DataFrame, Table 5-4 provides a short summary of many of them. As you'll see later, there are a number of additional options for working with hierarchical indexes.

 When originally designing pandas, I felt that having to type frame[:, col] to select a column was too verbose (and error-prone), since column selection is one of the most common operations. I made the design trade-off to push all of the fancy indexing behavior (both labels and integers) into the ix operator. In practice, this led to many edge cases in data with integer axis labels, so the pandas team decided to create the loc and iloc operators to deal with strictly label-based and integer-based indexing, respectively.

The ix indexing operator still exists, but it is deprecated. I do not recommend using it.

Table 5-4. Indexing options with DataFrame

Type	Notes
df[val]	Select single column or sequence of columns from the DataFrame; special case conveniences: boolean array (filter rows), slice (slice rows), or boolean DataFrame (set values based on some criterion)
df.loc[val]	Selects single row or subset of rows from the DataFrame by label
df.loc[:, val]	Selects single column or subset of columns by label
df.loc[val1, val2]	Select both rows and columns by label
df.iloc[where]	Selects single row or subset of rows from the DataFrame by integer position

Type	Notes
`df.iloc[:, where]`	Selects single column or subset of columns by integer position
`df.iloc[where_i, where_j]`	Select both rows and columns by integer position
`df.at[label_i, label_j]`	Select a single scalar value by row and column label
`df.iat[i, j]`	Select a single scalar value by row and column position (integers)
`reindex` method	Select either rows or columns by labels
`get_value, set_value` methods	Select single value by row and column label

Integer Indexes

Working with pandas objects indexed by integers is something that often trips up new users due to some differences with indexing semantics on built-in Python data structures like lists and tuples. For example, you might not expect the following code to generate an error:

```
ser = pd.Series(np.arange(3.))
ser
ser[-1]
```

In this case, pandas could "fall back" on integer indexing, but it's difficult to do this in general without introducing subtle bugs. Here we have an index containing 0, 1, 2, but inferring what the user wants (label-based indexing or position-based) is difficult:

```
In [146]: ser
Out[146]:
0    0.0
1    1.0
2    2.0
dtype: float64
```

On the other hand, with a non-integer index, there is no potential for ambiguity:

```
In [147]: ser2 = pd.Series(np.arange(3.), index=['a', 'b', 'c'])

In [148]: ser2[-1]
Out[148]: 2.0
```

If you have an axis index containing integers, data selection will always be label-oriented. For more precise handling, use `loc` (for labels) or `iloc` (for integers):

```
In [149]: ser[-1]
---------------------------------------------------------------------
KeyError                                  Traceback (most recent call last)
<ipython-input-149-3cbe0b873a9e> in <module>()
----> 1 ser[-1]
/miniconda/envs/book-env/lib/python3.6/site-packages/pandas/core/series.py in __g
etitem__(self, key)
    777         key = com.apply_if_callable(key, self)
    778         try:
--> 779             result = self.index.get_value(self, key)
```

```
                780
                781             if not is_scalar(result):
/miniconda/envs/book-env/lib/python3.6/site-packages/pandas/core/indexes/base.py
in get_value(self, series, key)
               3138         try:
               3139             return self._engine.get_value(s, k,
        -> 3140                                            tz=getattr(series.dtype, 'tz',
None))
               3141         except KeyError as e1:
               3142             if len(self) > 0 and self.inferred_type in ['integer', 'boole
an']:
pandas/_libs/index.pyx in pandas._libs.index.IndexEngine.get_value()
pandas/_libs/index.pyx in pandas._libs.index.IndexEngine.get_value()
pandas/_libs/index.pyx in pandas._libs.index.IndexEngine.get_loc()
pandas/_libs/hashtable_class_helper.pxi in pandas._libs.hashtable.Int64HashTable.
get_item()
pandas/_libs/hashtable_class_helper.pxi in pandas._libs.hashtable.Int64HashTable.
get_item()
KeyError: -1

In [150]: ser.iloc[-1]
Out[150]: 2.0
```

On the other hand, slicing with integers is always integer-oriented:

```
In [151]: ser[:2]
Out[151]:
0    0.0
1    1.0
dtype: float64
```

Arithmetic and Data Alignment

An important pandas feature for some applications is the behavior of arithmetic between objects with different indexes. When you are adding together objects, if any index pairs are not the same, the respective index in the result will be the union of the index pairs. For users with database experience, this is similar to an automatic outer join on the index labels. Let's look at an example:

```
In [152]: s1 = pd.Series([7.3, -2.5, 3.4, 1.5], index=['a', 'c', 'd', 'e'])

In [153]: s2 = pd.Series([-2.1, 3.6, -1.5, 4, 3.1],
   .....:                 index=['a', 'c', 'e', 'f', 'g'])

In [154]: s1
Out[154]:
a    7.3
c   -2.5
d    3.4
e    1.5
dtype: float64
```

```
In [155]: s2
Out[155]:
a   -2.1
c    3.6
e   -1.5
f    4.0
g    3.1
dtype: float64
```

Adding these together yields:

```
In [156]: s1 + s2
Out[156]:
a    5.2
c    1.1
d    NaN
e    0.0
f    NaN
g    NaN
dtype: float64
```

The internal data alignment introduces missing values in the label locations that don't overlap. Missing values will then propagate in further arithmetic computations.

In the case of DataFrame, alignment is performed on both the rows and the columns:

```
In [157]: df1 = pd.DataFrame(np.arange(9.).reshape((3, 3)), columns=list('bcd'),
   .....:                    index=['Ohio', 'Texas', 'Colorado'])

In [158]: df2 = pd.DataFrame(np.arange(12.).reshape((4, 3)), columns=list('bde'),
   .....:                    index=['Utah', 'Ohio', 'Texas', 'Oregon'])

In [159]: df1
Out[159]:
            b    c    d
Ohio      0.0  1.0  2.0
Texas     3.0  4.0  5.0
Colorado  6.0  7.0  8.0

In [160]: df2
Out[160]:
          b     d     e
Utah    0.0   1.0   2.0
Ohio    3.0   4.0   5.0
Texas   6.0   7.0   8.0
Oregon  9.0  10.0  11.0
```

Adding these together returns a DataFrame whose index and columns are the unions of the ones in each DataFrame:

```
In [161]: df1 + df2
Out[161]:
            b   c    d   e
Colorado  NaN NaN  NaN NaN
```

```
Ohio      3.0 NaN   6.0 NaN
Oregon    NaN NaN   NaN NaN
Texas     9.0 NaN  12.0 NaN
Utah      NaN NaN   NaN NaN
```

Since the `'c'` and `'e'` columns are not found in both DataFrame objects, they appear as all missing in the result. The same holds for the rows whose labels are not common to both objects.

If you add DataFrame objects with no column or row labels in common, the result will contain all nulls:

```
In [162]: df1 = pd.DataFrame({'A': [1, 2]})

In [163]: df2 = pd.DataFrame({'B': [3, 4]})

In [164]: df1
Out[164]:
   A
0  1
1  2

In [165]: df2
Out[165]:
   B
0  3
1  4

In [166]: df1 - df2
Out[166]:
    A    B
0 NaN  NaN
1 NaN  NaN
```

Arithmetic methods with fill values

In arithmetic operations between differently indexed objects, you might want to fill with a special value, like 0, when an axis label is found in one object but not the other:

```
In [167]: df1 = pd.DataFrame(np.arange(12.).reshape((3, 4)),
   .....:                    columns=list('abcd'))

In [168]: df2 = pd.DataFrame(np.arange(20.).reshape((4, 5)),
   .....:                    columns=list('abcde'))

In [169]: df2.loc[1, 'b'] = np.nan

In [170]: df1
Out[170]:
     a    b    c    d
0  0.0  1.0  2.0  3.0
1  4.0  5.0  6.0  7.0
```

```
2  8.0  9.0  10.0  11.0

In [171]: df2
Out[171]:
      a     b     c     d     e
0   0.0   1.0   2.0   3.0   4.0
1   5.0   NaN   7.0   8.0   9.0
2  10.0  11.0  12.0  13.0  14.0
3  15.0  16.0  17.0  18.0  19.0
```

Adding these together results in NA values in the locations that don't overlap:

```
In [172]: df1 + df2
Out[172]:
      a     b     c     d    e
0   0.0   2.0   4.0   6.0  NaN
1   9.0   NaN  13.0  15.0  NaN
2  18.0  20.0  22.0  24.0  NaN
3   NaN   NaN   NaN   NaN  NaN
```

Using the add method on df1, I pass df2 and an argument to fill_value:

```
In [173]: df1.add(df2, fill_value=0)
Out[173]:
      a     b     c     d     e
0   0.0   2.0   4.0   6.0   4.0
1   9.0   5.0  13.0  15.0   9.0
2  18.0  20.0  22.0  24.0  14.0
3  15.0  16.0  17.0  18.0  19.0
```

See Table 5-5 for a listing of Series and DataFrame methods for arithmetic. Each of them has a counterpart, starting with the letter r, that has arguments flipped. So these two statements are equivalent:

```
In [174]: 1 / df1
Out[174]:
          a         b         c         d
0       inf  1.000000  0.500000  0.333333
1  0.250000  0.200000  0.166667  0.142857
2  0.125000  0.111111  0.100000  0.090909

In [175]: df1.rdiv(1)
Out[175]:
          a         b         c         d
0       inf  1.000000  0.500000  0.333333
1  0.250000  0.200000  0.166667  0.142857
2  0.125000  0.111111  0.100000  0.090909
```

Relatedly, when reindexing a Series or DataFrame, you can also specify a different fill value:

```
In [176]: df1.reindex(columns=df2.columns, fill_value=0)
Out[176]:
      a     b     c     d  e
```

```
0   0.0  1.0   2.0   3.0  0
1   4.0  5.0   6.0   7.0  0
2   8.0  9.0  10.0  11.0  0
```

Table 5-5. Flexible arithmetic methods

Method	Description
add, radd	Methods for addition (+)
sub, rsub	Methods for subtraction (-)
div, rdiv	Methods for division (/)
floordiv, rfloordiv	Methods for floor division (//)
mul, rmul	Methods for multiplication (*)
pow, rpow	Methods for exponentiation (**)

Operations between DataFrame and Series

As with NumPy arrays of different dimensions, arithmetic between DataFrame and
Series is also defined. First, as a motivating example, consider the difference between
a two-dimensional array and one of its rows:

```
In [177]: arr = np.arange(12.).reshape((3, 4))

In [178]: arr
Out[178]:
array([[ 0.,  1.,  2.,  3.],
       [ 4.,  5.,  6.,  7.],
       [ 8.,  9., 10., 11.]])

In [179]: arr[0]
Out[179]: array([0., 1., 2., 3.])

In [180]: arr - arr[0]
Out[180]:
array([[0., 0., 0., 0.],
       [4., 4., 4., 4.],
       [8., 8., 8., 8.]])
```

When we subtract arr[0] from arr, the subtraction is performed once for each row.
This is referred to as *broadcasting* and is explained in more detail as it relates to general NumPy arrays in Appendix A. Operations between a DataFrame and a Series are
similar:

```
In [181]: frame = pd.DataFrame(np.arange(12.).reshape((4, 3)),
   .....:                       columns=list('bde'),
   .....:                       index=['Utah', 'Ohio', 'Texas', 'Oregon'])

In [182]: series = frame.iloc[0]

In [183]: frame
Out[183]:
```

```
                b     d      e
Utah     0.0   1.0    2.0
Ohio     3.0   4.0    5.0
Texas    6.0   7.0    8.0
Oregon   9.0  10.0   11.0

In [184]: series
Out[184]:
b    0.0
d    1.0
e    2.0
Name: Utah, dtype: float64
```

By default, arithmetic between DataFrame and Series matches the index of the Series on the DataFrame's columns, broadcasting down the rows:

```
In [185]: frame - series
Out[185]:
            b    d    e
Utah     0.0  0.0  0.0
Ohio     3.0  3.0  3.0
Texas    6.0  6.0  6.0
Oregon   9.0  9.0  9.0
```

If an index value is not found in either the DataFrame's columns or the Series's index, the objects will be reindexed to form the union:

```
In [186]: series2 = pd.Series(range(3), index=['b', 'e', 'f'])

In [187]: frame + series2
Out[187]:
            b    d     e    f
Utah     0.0  NaN   3.0  NaN
Ohio     3.0  NaN   6.0  NaN
Texas    6.0  NaN   9.0  NaN
Oregon   9.0  NaN  12.0  NaN
```

If you want to instead broadcast over the columns, matching on the rows, you have to use one of the arithmetic methods. For example:

```
In [188]: series3 = frame['d']

In [189]: frame
Out[189]:
            b     d      e
Utah     0.0   1.0    2.0
Ohio     3.0   4.0    5.0
Texas    6.0   7.0    8.0
Oregon   9.0  10.0   11.0

In [190]: series3
Out[190]:
Utah        1.0
```

```
Ohio       4.0
Texas      7.0
Oregon    10.0
Name: d, dtype: float64

In [191]: frame.sub(series3, axis='index')
Out[191]:
          b    d    e
Utah   -1.0  0.0  1.0
Ohio   -1.0  0.0  1.0
Texas  -1.0  0.0  1.0
Oregon -1.0  0.0  1.0
```

The axis number that you pass is the *axis to match on*. In this case we mean to match
on the DataFrame's row index (`axis='index'` or `axis=0`) and broadcast across.

Function Application and Mapping

NumPy ufuncs (element-wise array methods) also work with pandas objects:

```
In [192]: frame = pd.DataFrame(np.random.randn(4, 3), columns=list('bde'),
   .....:                       index=['Utah', 'Ohio', 'Texas', 'Oregon'])

In [193]: frame
Out[193]:
              b         d         e
Utah   -0.204708  0.478943 -0.519439
Ohio   -0.555730  1.965781  1.393406
Texas   0.092908  0.281746  0.769023
Oregon  1.246435  1.007189 -1.296221

In [194]: np.abs(frame)
Out[194]:
              b         d         e
Utah    0.204708  0.478943  0.519439
Ohio    0.555730  1.965781  1.393406
Texas   0.092908  0.281746  0.769023
Oregon  1.246435  1.007189  1.296221
```

Another frequent operation is applying a function on one-dimensional arrays to each
column or row. DataFrame's `apply` method does exactly this:

```
In [195]: f = lambda x: x.max() - x.min()

In [196]: frame.apply(f)
Out[196]:
b    1.802165
d    1.684034
e    2.689627
dtype: float64
```

Here the function f, which computes the difference between the maximum and minimum of a Series, is invoked once on each column in `frame`. The result is a Series having the columns of `frame` as its index.

If you pass `axis='columns'` to `apply`, the function will be invoked once per row instead:

```
In [197]: frame.apply(f, axis='columns')
Out[197]:
Utah      0.998382
Ohio      2.521511
Texas     0.676115
Oregon    2.542656
dtype: float64
```

Many of the most common array statistics (like `sum` and `mean`) are DataFrame methods, so using `apply` is not necessary.

The function passed to `apply` need not return a scalar value; it can also return a Series with multiple values:

```
In [198]: def f(x):
   .....:     return pd.Series([x.min(), x.max()], index=['min', 'max'])

In [199]: frame.apply(f)
Out[199]:
            b         d         e
min -0.555730  0.281746 -1.296221
max  1.246435  1.965781  1.393406
```

Element-wise Python functions can be used, too. Suppose you wanted to compute a formatted string from each floating-point value in `frame`. You can do this with `applymap`:

```
In [200]: format = lambda x: '%.2f' % x

In [201]: frame.applymap(format)
Out[201]:
            b     d      e
Utah    -0.20  0.48  -0.52
Ohio    -0.56  1.97   1.39
Texas    0.09  0.28   0.77
Oregon   1.25  1.01  -1.30
```

The reason for the name `applymap` is that Series has a `map` method for applying an element-wise function:

```
In [202]: frame['e'].map(format)
Out[202]:
Utah     -0.52
Ohio      1.39
Texas     0.77
```

```
Oregon    -1.30
Name: e, dtype: object
```

Sorting and Ranking

Sorting a dataset by some criterion is another important built-in operation. To sort lexicographically by row or column index, use the sort_index method, which returns a new, sorted object:

```
In [203]: obj = pd.Series(range(4), index=['d', 'a', 'b', 'c'])

In [204]: obj.sort_index()
Out[204]:
a    1
b    2
c    3
d    0
dtype: int64
```

With a DataFrame, you can sort by index on either axis:

```
In [205]: frame = pd.DataFrame(np.arange(8).reshape((2, 4)),
   .....:                      index=['three', 'one'],
   .....:                      columns=['d', 'a', 'b', 'c'])

In [206]: frame.sort_index()
Out[206]:
       d  a  b  c
one    4  5  6  7
three  0  1  2  3

In [207]: frame.sort_index(axis=1)
Out[207]:
       a  b  c  d
three  1  2  3  0
one    5  6  7  4
```

The data is sorted in ascending order by default, but can be sorted in descending order, too:

```
In [208]: frame.sort_index(axis=1, ascending=False)
Out[208]:
       d  c  b  a
three  0  3  2  1
one    4  7  6  5
```

To sort a Series by its values, use its sort_values method:

```
In [209]: obj = pd.Series([4, 7, -3, 2])

In [210]: obj.sort_values()
Out[210]:
2   -3
```

```
3    2
0    4
1    7
dtype: int64
```

Any missing values are sorted to the end of the Series by default:

```
In [211]: obj = pd.Series([4, np.nan, 7, np.nan, -3, 2])

In [212]: obj.sort_values()
Out[212]:
4    -3.0
5     2.0
0     4.0
2     7.0
1     NaN
3     NaN
dtype: float64
```

When sorting a DataFrame, you can use the data in one or more columns as the sort keys. To do so, pass one or more column names to the by option of sort_values:

```
In [213]: frame = pd.DataFrame({'b': [4, 7, -3, 2], 'a': [0, 1, 0, 1]})

In [214]: frame
Out[214]:
   b  a
0  4  0
1  7  1
2 -3  0
3  2  1

In [215]: frame.sort_values(by='b')
Out[215]:
   b  a
2 -3  0
3  2  1
0  4  0
1  7  1
```

To sort by multiple columns, pass a list of names:

```
In [216]: frame.sort_values(by=['a', 'b'])
Out[216]:
   b  a
2 -3  0
0  4  0
3  2  1
1  7  1
```

Ranking assigns ranks from one through the number of valid data points in an array. The rank methods for Series and DataFrame are the place to look; by default rank breaks ties by assigning each group the mean rank:

```
In [217]: obj = pd.Series([7, -5, 7, 4, 2, 0, 4])

In [218]: obj.rank()
Out[218]:
0    6.5
1    1.0
2    6.5
3    4.5
4    3.0
5    2.0
6    4.5
dtype: float64
```

Ranks can also be assigned according to the order in which they're observed in the data:

```
In [219]: obj.rank(method='first')
Out[219]:
0    6.0
1    1.0
2    7.0
3    4.0
4    3.0
5    2.0
6    5.0
dtype: float64
```

Here, instead of using the average rank 6.5 for the entries 0 and 2, they instead have been set to 6 and 7 because label 0 precedes label 2 in the data.

You can rank in descending order, too:

```
# Assign tie values the maximum rank in the group
In [220]: obj.rank(ascending=False, method='max')
Out[220]:
0    2.0
1    7.0
2    2.0
3    4.0
4    5.0
5    6.0
6    4.0
dtype: float64
```

See Table 5-6 for a list of tie-breaking methods available.

DataFrame can compute ranks over the rows or the columns:

```
In [221]: frame = pd.DataFrame({'b': [4.3, 7, -3, 2], 'a': [0, 1, 0, 1],
   .....:                       'c': [-2, 5, 8, -2.5]})

In [222]: frame
Out[222]:
     b   a    c
```

```
0  4.3  0 -2.0
1  7.0  1  5.0
2 -3.0  0  8.0
3  2.0  1 -2.5

In [223]: frame.rank(axis='columns')
Out[223]:
     b    a    c
0  3.0  2.0  1.0
1  3.0  1.0  2.0
2  1.0  2.0  3.0
3  3.0  2.0  1.0
```

Table 5-6. Tie-breaking methods with rank

Method	Description
'average'	Default: assign the average rank to each entry in the equal group
'min'	Use the minimum rank for the whole group
'max'	Use the maximum rank for the whole group
'first'	Assign ranks in the order the values appear in the data
'dense'	Like method='min', but ranks always increase by 1 in between groups rather than the number of equal elements in a group

Axis Indexes with Duplicate Labels

Up until now all of the examples we've looked at have had unique axis labels (index values). While many pandas functions (like reindex) require that the labels be unique, it's not mandatory. Let's consider a small Series with duplicate indices:

```
In [224]: obj = pd.Series(range(5), index=['a', 'a', 'b', 'b', 'c'])
```

```
In [225]: obj
Out[225]:
a    0
a    1
b    2
b    3
c    4
dtype: int64
```

The index's is_unique property can tell you whether its labels are unique or not:

```
In [226]: obj.index.is_unique
Out[226]: False
```

Data selection is one of the main things that behaves differently with duplicates. Indexing a label with multiple entries returns a Series, while single entries return a scalar value:

```
In [227]: obj['a']
Out[227]:
```

```
a    0
a    1
dtype: int64

In [228]: obj['c']
Out[228]: 4
```

This can make your code more complicated, as the output type from indexing can vary based on whether a label is repeated or not.

The same logic extends to indexing rows in a DataFrame:

```
In [229]: df = pd.DataFrame(np.random.randn(4, 3), index=['a', 'a', 'b', 'b'])

In [230]: df
Out[230]:
          0         1         2
a  0.274992  0.228913  1.352917
a  0.886429 -2.001637 -0.371843
b  1.669025 -0.438570 -0.539741
b  0.476985  3.248944 -1.021228

In [231]: df.loc['b']
Out[231]:
          0         1         2
b  1.669025 -0.438570 -0.539741
b  0.476985  3.248944 -1.021228
```

5.3 Summarizing and Computing Descriptive Statistics

pandas objects are equipped with a set of common mathematical and statistical methods. Most of these fall into the category of *reductions* or *summary statistics*, methods that extract a single value (like the sum or mean) from a Series or a Series of values from the rows or columns of a DataFrame. Compared with the similar methods found on NumPy arrays, they have built-in handling for missing data. Consider a small DataFrame:

```
In [232]: df = pd.DataFrame([[1.4, np.nan], [7.1, -4.5],
   .....:                     [np.nan, np.nan], [0.75, -1.3]],
   .....:                    index=['a', 'b', 'c', 'd'],
   .....:                    columns=['one', 'two'])

In [233]: df
Out[233]:
    one   two
a  1.40   NaN
b  7.10  -4.5
c   NaN   NaN
d  0.75  -1.3
```

Calling DataFrame's sum method returns a Series containing column sums:

```
In [234]: df.sum()
Out[234]:
one    9.25
two   -5.80
dtype: float64
```

Passing `axis='columns'` or `axis=1` sums across the columns instead:

```
In [235]: df.sum(axis='columns')
Out[235]:
a    1.40
b    2.60
c    0.00
d   -0.55
dtype: float64
```

NA values are excluded unless the entire slice (row or column in this case) is NA. This can be disabled with the `skipna` option:

```
In [236]: df.mean(axis='columns', skipna=False)
Out[236]:
a      NaN
b    1.300
c      NaN
d   -0.275
dtype: float64
```

See Table 5-7 for a list of common options for each reduction method.

Table 5-7. Options for reduction methods

Method	Description
axis	Axis to reduce over; 0 for DataFrame's rows and 1 for columns
skipna	Exclude missing values; True by default
level	Reduce grouped by level if the axis is hierarchically indexed (MultiIndex)

Some methods, like `idxmin` and `idxmax`, return indirect statistics like the index value where the minimum or maximum values are attained:

```
In [237]: df.idxmax()
Out[237]:
one    b
two    d
dtype: object
```

Other methods are *accumulations*:

```
In [238]: df.cumsum()
Out[238]:
    one   two
a  1.40   NaN
b  8.50  -4.5
```

```
c   NaN NaN
d   9.25 -5.8
```

Another type of method is neither a reduction nor an accumulation. `describe` is one such example, producing multiple summary statistics in one shot:

```
In [239]: df.describe()
Out[239]:
            one       two
count  3.000000  2.000000
mean   3.083333 -2.900000
std    3.493685  2.262742
min    0.750000 -4.500000
25%    1.075000 -3.700000
50%    1.400000 -2.900000
75%    4.250000 -2.100000
max    7.100000 -1.300000
```

On non-numeric data, `describe` produces alternative summary statistics:

```
In [240]: obj = pd.Series(['a', 'a', 'b', 'c'] * 4)

In [241]: obj.describe()
Out[241]:
count     16
unique     3
top        a
freq       8
dtype: object
```

See Table 5-8 for a full list of summary statistics and related methods.

Table 5-8. Descriptive and summary statistics

Method	Description
count	Number of non-NA values
describe	Compute set of summary statistics for Series or each DataFrame column
min, max	Compute minimum and maximum values
argmin, argmax	Compute index locations (integers) at which minimum or maximum value obtained, respectively
idxmin, idxmax	Compute index labels at which minimum or maximum value obtained, respectively
quantile	Compute sample quantile ranging from 0 to 1
sum	Sum of values
mean	Mean of values
median	Arithmetic median (50% quantile) of values
mad	Mean absolute deviation from mean value
prod	Product of all values
var	Sample variance of values
std	Sample standard deviation of values
skew	Sample skewness (third moment) of values

Method	Description
kurt	Sample kurtosis (fourth moment) of values
cumsum	Cumulative sum of values
cummin, cummax	Cumulative minimum or maximum of values, respectively
cumprod	Cumulative product of values
diff	Compute first arithmetic difference (useful for time series)
pct_change	Compute percent changes

Correlation and Covariance

Some summary statistics, like correlation and covariance, are computed from pairs of arguments. Let's consider some DataFrames of stock prices and volumes obtained from Yahoo! Finance using the add-on pandas-datareader package. If you don't have it installed already, it can be obtained via conda or pip:

```
conda install pandas-datareader
```

I use the pandas_datareader module to download some data for a few stock tickers:

```
import pandas_datareader.data as web
all_data = {ticker: web.get_data_yahoo(ticker)
            for ticker in ['AAPL', 'IBM', 'MSFT', 'GOOG']}

price = pd.DataFrame({ticker: data['Adj Close']
                     for ticker, data in all_data.items()})
volume = pd.DataFrame({ticker: data['Volume']
                      for ticker, data in all_data.items()})
```

 It's possible by the time you are reading this that Yahoo! Finance no longer exists since Yahoo! was acquired by Verizon in 2017. Refer to the pandas-datareader documentation online for the latest functionality.

I now compute percent changes of the prices, a time series operation which will be explored further in Chapter 11:

```
In [244]: returns = price.pct_change()

In [245]: returns.tail()
Out[245]:
                AAPL      GOOG      IBM      MSFT
Date
2016-10-17 -0.000680  0.001837  0.002072 -0.003483
2016-10-18 -0.000681  0.019616 -0.026168  0.007690
2016-10-19 -0.002979  0.007846  0.003583 -0.002255
2016-10-20 -0.000512 -0.005652  0.001719 -0.004867
2016-10-21 -0.003930  0.003011 -0.012474  0.042096
```

The corr method of Series computes the correlation of the overlapping, non-NA, aligned-by-index values in two Series. Relatedly, cov computes the covariance:

```
In [246]: returns['MSFT'].corr(returns['IBM'])
Out[246]: 0.49976361144151144

In [247]: returns['MSFT'].cov(returns['IBM'])
Out[247]: 8.870655479703546e-05
```

Since MSFT is a valid Python attribute, we can also select these columns using more concise syntax:

```
In [248]: returns.MSFT.corr(returns.IBM)
Out[248]: 0.49976361144151144
```

DataFrame's corr and cov methods, on the other hand, return a full correlation or covariance matrix as a DataFrame, respectively:

```
In [249]: returns.corr()
Out[249]:
          AAPL      GOOG       IBM      MSFT
AAPL  1.000000  0.407919  0.386817  0.389695
GOOG  0.407919  1.000000  0.405099  0.465919
IBM   0.386817  0.405099  1.000000  0.499764
MSFT  0.389695  0.465919  0.499764  1.000000

In [250]: returns.cov()
Out[250]:
          AAPL      GOOG       IBM      MSFT
AAPL  0.000277  0.000107  0.000078  0.000095
GOOG  0.000107  0.000251  0.000078  0.000108
IBM   0.000078  0.000078  0.000146  0.000089
MSFT  0.000095  0.000108  0.000089  0.000215
```

Using DataFrame's corrwith method, you can compute pairwise correlations between a DataFrame's columns or rows with another Series or DataFrame. Passing a Series returns a Series with the correlation value computed for each column:

```
In [251]: returns.corrwith(returns.IBM)
Out[251]:
AAPL    0.386817
GOOG    0.405099
IBM     1.000000
MSFT    0.499764
dtype: float64
```

Passing a DataFrame computes the correlations of matching column names. Here I compute correlations of percent changes with volume:

```
In [252]: returns.corrwith(volume)
Out[252]:
AAPL    -0.075565
GOOG    -0.007067
```

```
IBM     -0.204849
MSFT    -0.092950
dtype: float64
```

Passing `axis='columns'` does things row-by-row instead. In all cases, the data points are aligned by label before the correlation is computed.

Unique Values, Value Counts, and Membership

Another class of related methods extracts information about the values contained in a one-dimensional Series. To illustrate these, consider this example:

```
In [253]: obj = pd.Series(['c', 'a', 'd', 'a', 'a', 'b', 'b', 'c', 'c'])
```

The first function is `unique`, which gives you an array of the unique values in a Series:

```
In [254]: uniques = obj.unique()

In [255]: uniques
Out[255]: array(['c', 'a', 'd', 'b'], dtype=object)
```

The unique values are not necessarily returned in sorted order, but could be sorted after the fact if needed (`uniques.sort()`). Relatedly, `value_counts` computes a Series containing value frequencies:

```
In [256]: obj.value_counts()
Out[256]:
a    3
c    3
b    2
d    1
dtype: int64
```

The Series is sorted by value in descending order as a convenience. `value_counts` is also available as a top-level pandas method that can be used with any array or sequence:

```
In [257]: pd.value_counts(obj.values, sort=False)
Out[257]:
c    3
b    2
a    3
d    1
dtype: int64
```

`isin` performs a vectorized set membership check and can be useful in filtering a dataset down to a subset of values in a Series or column in a DataFrame:

```
In [258]: obj
Out[258]:
0    c
1    a
2    d
```

```
3    a
4    a
5    b
6    b
7    c
8    c
dtype: object

In [259]: mask = obj.isin(['b', 'c'])

In [260]: mask
Out[260]:
0     True
1    False
2    False
3    False
4    False
5     True
6     True
7     True
8     True
dtype: bool

In [261]: obj[mask]
Out[261]:
0    c
5    b
6    b
7    c
8    c
dtype: object
```

Related to isin is the Index.get_indexer method, which gives you an index array from an array of possibly non-distinct values into another array of distinct values:

```
In [262]: to_match = pd.Series(['c', 'a', 'b', 'b', 'c', 'a'])

In [263]: unique_vals = pd.Series(['c', 'b', 'a'])

In [264]: pd.Index(unique_vals).get_indexer(to_match)
Out[264]: array([0, 2, 1, 1, 0, 2])
```

See Table 5-9 for a reference on these methods.

Table 5-9. Unique, value counts, and set membership methods

Method	Description
isin	Compute boolean array indicating whether each Series value is contained in the passed sequence of values
get_indexer	Compute integer indices for each value in an array into another array of distinct values; helpful for data alignment and join-type operations
unique	Compute array of unique values in a Series, returned in the order observed

Method	Description
value_counts	Return a Series containing unique values as its index and frequencies as its values, ordered count in descending order

In some cases, you may want to compute a histogram on multiple related columns in a DataFrame. Here's an example:

```
In [265]: data = pd.DataFrame({'Qu1': [1, 3, 4, 3, 4],
   .....:                       'Qu2': [2, 3, 1, 2, 3],
   .....:                       'Qu3': [1, 5, 2, 4, 4]})
```

```
In [266]: data
Out[266]:
   Qu1  Qu2  Qu3
0    1    2    1
1    3    3    5
2    4    1    2
3    3    2    4
4    4    3    4
```

Passing `pandas.value_counts` to this DataFrame's `apply` function gives:

```
In [267]: result = data.apply(pd.value_counts).fillna(0)
```

```
In [268]: result
Out[268]:
   Qu1  Qu2  Qu3
1  1.0  1.0  1.0
2  0.0  2.0  1.0
3  2.0  2.0  0.0
4  2.0  0.0  2.0
5  0.0  0.0  1.0
```

Here, the row labels in the result are the distinct values occurring in all of the columns. The values are the respective counts of these values in each column.

5.4 Conclusion

In the next chapter, we'll discuss tools for reading (or *loading*) and writing datasets with pandas. After that, we'll dig deeper into data cleaning, wrangling, analysis, and visualization tools using pandas.

## CHAPTER 6

Data Loading, Storage, and File Formats

Accessing data is a necessary first step for using most of the tools in this book. I'm going to be focused on data input and output using pandas, though there are numerous tools in other libraries to help with reading and writing data in various formats.

Input and output typically falls into a few main categories: reading text files and other more efficient on-disk formats, loading data from databases, and interacting with network sources like web APIs.

6.1 Reading and Writing Data in Text Format

pandas features a number of functions for reading tabular data as a DataFrame object. Table 6-1 summarizes some of them, though `read_csv` is likely the one you'll use the most.

Table 6-1. Parsing functions in pandas

Function	Description
read_csv	Load delimited data from a file, URL, or file-like object; use comma as default delimiter
read_fwf	Read data in fixed-width column format (i.e., no delimiters)
read_clipboard	Version of read_csv that reads data from the clipboard; useful for converting tables from web pages
read_excel	Read tabular data from an Excel XLS or XLSX file
read_hdf	Read HDF5 files written by pandas
read_html	Read all tables found in the given HTML document
read_json	Read data from a JSON (JavaScript Object Notation) string representation
read_msgpack	Read pandas data encoded using the MessagePack binary format
read_pickle	Read an arbitrary object stored in Python pickle format
read_sas	Read a SAS dataset stored in one of the SAS system's custom storage formats

Function	Description
read_sql	Read the results of a SQL query (using SQLAlchemy) as a pandas DataFrame
read_stata	Read a dataset from Stata file format
read_feather	Read the Feather binary file format

I'll give an overview of the mechanics of these functions, which are meant to convert text data into a DataFrame. The optional arguments for these functions may fall into a few categories:

Indexing
Can treat one or more columns as the returned DataFrame, and whether to get column names from the file, the user, or not at all.

Type inference and data conversion
This includes the user-defined value conversions and custom list of missing value markers.

Datetime parsing
Includes combining capability, including combining date and time information spread over multiple columns into a single column in the result.

Iterating
Support for iterating over chunks of very large files.

Unclean data issues
Skipping rows or a footer, comments, or other minor things like numeric data with thousands separated by commas.

Because of how messy data in the real world can be, some of the data loading functions (especially `read_csv`) have grown very complex in their options over time. It's normal to feel overwhelmed by the number of different parameters (`read_csv` has over 50 as of this writing). The online pandas documentation has many examples about how each of them works, so if you're struggling to read a particular file, there might be a similar enough example to help you find the right parameters.

Some of these functions, like `pandas.read_csv`, perform *type inference*, because the column data types are not part of the data format. That means you don't necessarily have to specify which columns are numeric, integer, boolean, or string. Other data formats, like HDF5, Feather, and msgpack, have the data types stored in the format.

Handling dates and other custom types can require extra effort. Let's start with a small comma-separated (CSV) text file:

```
In [10]: !cat examples/ex1.csv
a,b,c,d,message
1,2,3,4,hello
```

```
5,6,7,8,world
9,10,11,12,foo
```

 Here I used the Unix cat shell command to print the raw contents of the file to the screen. If you're on Windows, you can use type instead of cat to achieve the same effect.

Since this is comma-delimited, we can use read_csv to read it into a DataFrame:

```
In [11]: df = pd.read_csv('examples/ex1.csv')

In [12]: df
Out[12]:
   a   b   c   d message
0  1   2   3   4   hello
1  5   6   7   8   world
2  9  10  11  12     foo
```

A file will not always have a header row. Consider this file:

```
In [13]: !cat examples/ex2.csv
1,2,3,4,hello
5,6,7,8,world
9,10,11,12,foo
```

To read this file, you have a couple of options. You can allow pandas to assign default column names, or you can specify names yourself:

```
In [14]: pd.read_csv('examples/ex2.csv', header=None)
Out[14]:
   0   1   2   3      4
0  1   2   3   4  hello
1  5   6   7   8  world
2  9  10  11  12    foo

In [15]: pd.read_csv('examples/ex2.csv', names=['a', 'b', 'c', 'd', 'message'])
Out[15]:
   a   b   c   d message
0  1   2   3   4   hello
1  5   6   7   8   world
2  9  10  11  12     foo
```

Suppose you wanted the message column to be the index of the returned DataFrame. You can either indicate you want the column at index 4 or named 'message' using the index_col argument:

```
In [16]: names = ['a', 'b', 'c', 'd', 'message']

In [17]: pd.read_csv('examples/ex2.csv', names=names, index_col='message')
Out[17]:
```

```
          a   b   c   d
message
hello     1   2   3   4
world     5   6   7   8
foo       9  10  11  12
```

In the event that you want to form a hierarchical index from multiple columns, pass a list of column numbers or names:

```
In [18]: !cat examples/csv_mindex.csv
key1,key2,value1,value2
one,a,1,2
one,b,3,4
one,c,5,6
one,d,7,8
two,a,9,10
two,b,11,12
two,c,13,14
two,d,15,16

In [19]: parsed = pd.read_csv('examples/csv_mindex.csv',
   ....:                      index_col=['key1', 'key2'])

In [20]: parsed
Out[20]:
           value1  value2
key1 key2
one  a          1       2
     b          3       4
     c          5       6
     d          7       8
two  a          9      10
     b         11      12
     c         13      14
     d         15      16
```

In some cases, a table might not have a fixed delimiter, using whitespace or some other pattern to separate fields. Consider a text file that looks like this:

```
In [21]: list(open('examples/ex3.txt'))
Out[21]:
['            A         B         C\n',
 'aaa -0.264438 -1.026059 -0.619500\n',
 'bbb  0.927272  0.302904 -0.032399\n',
 'ccc -0.264273 -0.386314 -0.217601\n',
 'ddd -0.871858 -0.348382  1.100491\n']
```

While you could do some munging by hand, the fields here are separated by a variable amount of whitespace. In these cases, you can pass a regular expression as a delimiter for read_csv. This can be expressed by the regular expression \s+, so we have then:

```
In [22]: result = pd.read_csv('examples/ex3.txt', sep='\s+')

In [23]: result
Out[23]:
            A         B         C
aaa -0.264438 -1.026059 -0.619500
bbb  0.927272  0.302904 -0.032399
ccc -0.264273 -0.386314 -0.217601
ddd -0.871858 -0.348382  1.100491
```

Because there was one fewer column name than the number of data rows, `read_csv` infers that the first column should be the DataFrame's index in this special case.

The parser functions have many additional arguments to help you handle the wide variety of exception file formats that occur (see a partial listing in Table 6-2). For example, you can skip the first, third, and fourth rows of a file with `skiprows`:

```
In [24]: !cat examples/ex4.csv
# hey!
a,b,c,d,message
# just wanted to make things more difficult for you
# who reads CSV files with computers, anyway?
1,2,3,4,hello
5,6,7,8,world
9,10,11,12,foo
In [25]: pd.read_csv('examples/ex4.csv', skiprows=[0, 2, 3])
Out[25]:
   a   b   c   d message
0  1   2   3   4   hello
1  5   6   7   8   world
2  9  10  11  12     foo
```

Handling missing values is an important and frequently nuanced part of the file parsing process. Missing data is usually either not present (empty string) or marked by some *sentinel* value. By default, pandas uses a set of commonly occurring sentinels, such as NA and NULL:

```
In [26]: !cat examples/ex5.csv
something,a,b,c,d,message
one,1,2,3,4,NA
two,5,6,,8,world
three,9,10,11,12,foo
In [27]: result = pd.read_csv('examples/ex5.csv')

In [28]: result
Out[28]:
  something  a   b     c   d message
0       one  1   2   3.0   4     NaN
1       two  5   6   NaN   8   world
2     three  9  10  11.0  12     foo

In [29]: pd.isnull(result)
```

```
Out[29]:
   something      a      b      c      d  message
0     False  False  False  False  False     True
1     False  False  False   True  False    False
2     False  False  False  False  False    False
```

The `na_values` option can take either a list or set of strings to consider missing values:

```
In [30]: result = pd.read_csv('examples/ex5.csv', na_values=['NULL'])

In [31]: result
Out[31]:
  something  a   b     c   d message
0       one  1   2   3.0   4     NaN
1       two  5   6   NaN   8   world
2     three  9  10  11.0  12     foo
```

Different NA sentinels can be specified for each column in a dict:

```
In [32]: sentinels = {'message': ['foo', 'NA'], 'something': ['two']}

In [33]: pd.read_csv('examples/ex5.csv', na_values=sentinels)
Out[33]:
  something  a   b     c   d message
0       one  1   2   3.0   4     NaN
1       NaN  5   6   NaN   8   world
2     three  9  10  11.0  12     NaN
```

Table 6-2 lists some frequently used options in `pandas.read_csv`.

Table 6-2. Some read_csv function arguments

Argument	Description
path	String indicating filesystem location, URL, or file-like object
sep or delimiter	Character sequence or regular expression to use to split fields in each row
header	Row number to use as column names; defaults to 0 (first row), but should be None if there is no header row
index_col	Column numbers or names to use as the row index in the result; can be a single name/number or a list of them for a hierarchical index
names	List of column names for result, combine with header=None
skiprows	Number of rows at beginning of file to ignore or list of row numbers (starting from 0) to skip.
na_values	Sequence of values to replace with NA.
comment	Character(s) to split comments off the end of lines.
parse_dates	Attempt to parse data to datetime; False by default. If True, will attempt to parse all columns. Otherwise can specify a list of column numbers or name to parse. If element of list is tuple or list, will combine multiple columns together and parse to date (e.g., if date/time split across two columns).
keep_date_col	If joining columns to parse date, keep the joined columns; False by default.
converters	Dict containing column number of name mapping to functions (e.g., {'foo': f} would apply the function f to all values in the 'foo' column).

Argument	Description
dayfirst	When parsing potentially ambiguous dates, treat as international format (e.g., 7/6/2012 -> June 7, 2012); `False` by default.
date_parser	Function to use to parse dates.
nrows	Number of rows to read from beginning of file.
iterator	Return a `TextParser` object for reading file piecemeal.
chunksize	For iteration, size of file chunks.
skip_footer	Number of lines to ignore at end of file.
verbose	Print various parser output information, like the number of missing values placed in non-numeric columns.
encoding	Text encoding for Unicode (e.g., `'utf-8'` for UTF-8 encoded text).
squeeze	If the parsed data only contains one column, return a Series.
thousands	Separator for thousands (e.g., `','` or `'.'`).

Reading Text Files in Pieces

When processing very large files or figuring out the right set of arguments to correctly process a large file, you may only want to read in a small piece of a file or iterate through smaller chunks of the file.

Before we look at a large file, we make the pandas display settings more compact:

```
In [34]: pd.options.display.max_rows = 10
```

Now we have:

```
In [35]: result = pd.read_csv('examples/ex6.csv')

In [36]: result
Out[36]:
           one       two     three      four key
0     0.467976 -0.038649 -0.295344 -1.824726   L
1    -0.358893  1.404453  0.704965 -0.200638   B
2    -0.501840  0.659254 -0.421691 -0.057688   G
3     0.204886  1.074134  1.388361 -0.982404   R
4     0.354628 -0.133116  0.283763 -0.837063   Q
...        ...       ...       ...       ...  ..
9995  2.311896 -0.417070 -1.409599 -0.515821   L
9996 -0.479893 -0.650419  0.745152 -0.646038   E
9997  0.523331  0.787112  0.486066  1.093156   K
9998 -0.362559  0.598894 -1.843201  0.887292   G
9999 -0.096376 -1.012999 -0.657431 -0.573315   0
[10000 rows x 5 columns]
```

If you want to only read a small number of rows (avoiding reading the entire file), specify that with nrows:

```
In [37]: pd.read_csv('examples/ex6.csv', nrows=5)
Out[37]:
        one       two     three      four key
```

```
0   0.467976  -0.038649  -0.295344  -1.824726   L
1  -0.358893   1.404453   0.704965  -0.200638   B
2  -0.501840   0.659254  -0.421691  -0.057688   G
3   0.204886   1.074134   1.388361  -0.982404   R
4   0.354628  -0.133116   0.283763  -0.837063   Q
```

To read a file in pieces, specify a `chunksize` as a number of rows:

```
In [38]: chunker = pd.read_csv('examples/ex6.csv', chunksize=1000)

In [39]: chunker
Out[39]: <pandas.io.parsers.TextFileReader at 0x7f2dfd39e3c8>
```

The `TextFileReader` object returned by `read_csv` allows you to iterate over the parts of the file according to the `chunksize`. For example, we can iterate over `ex6.csv`, aggregating the value counts in the `'key'` column like so:

```
chunker = pd.read_csv('examples/ex6.csv', chunksize=1000)

tot = pd.Series([])
for piece in chunker:
    tot = tot.add(piece['key'].value_counts(), fill_value=0)

tot = tot.sort_values(ascending=False)
```

We have then:

```
In [41]: tot[:10]
Out[41]:
E    368.0
X    364.0
L    346.0
O    343.0
Q    340.0
M    338.0
J    337.0
F    335.0
K    334.0
H    330.0
dtype: float64
```

`TextParser` is also equipped with a `get_chunk` method that enables you to read pieces of an arbitrary size.

Writing Data to Text Format

Data can also be exported to a delimited format. Let's consider one of the CSV files read before:

```
In [42]: data = pd.read_csv('examples/ex5.csv')

In [43]: data
Out[43]:
```

```
   something  a   b     c   d message
0       one  1   2   3.0   4    NaN
1       two  5   6   NaN   8  world
2     three  9  10  11.0  12    foo
```

Using DataFrame's `to_csv` method, we can write the data out to a comma-separated file:

```
In [44]: data.to_csv('examples/out.csv')

In [45]: !cat examples/out.csv
,something,a,b,c,d,message
0,one,1,2,3.0,4,
1,two,5,6,,8,world
2,three,9,10,11.0,12,foo
```

Other delimiters can be used, of course (writing to `sys.stdout` so it prints the text result to the console):

```
In [46]: import sys

In [47]: data.to_csv(sys.stdout, sep='|')
|something|a|b|c|d|message
0|one|1|2|3.0|4|
1|two|5|6||8|world
2|three|9|10|11.0|12|foo
```

Missing values appear as empty strings in the output. You might want to denote them by some other sentinel value:

```
In [48]: data.to_csv(sys.stdout, na_rep='NULL')
,something,a,b,c,d,message
0,one,1,2,3.0,4,NULL
1,two,5,6,NULL,8,world
2,three,9,10,11.0,12,foo
```

With no other options specified, both the row and column labels are written. Both of these can be disabled:

```
In [49]: data.to_csv(sys.stdout, index=False, header=False)
one,1,2,3.0,4,
two,5,6,,8,world
three,9,10,11.0,12,foo
```

You can also write only a subset of the columns, and in an order of your choosing:

```
In [50]: data.to_csv(sys.stdout, index=False, columns=['a', 'b', 'c'])
a,b,c
1,2,3.0
5,6,
9,10,11.0
```

Series also has a `to_csv` method:

```
In [51]: dates = pd.date_range('1/1/2000', periods=7)

In [52]: ts = pd.Series(np.arange(7), index=dates)

In [53]: ts.to_csv('examples/tseries.csv')

In [54]: !cat examples/tseries.csv
2000-01-01,0
2000-01-02,1
2000-01-03,2
2000-01-04,3
2000-01-05,4
2000-01-06,5
2000-01-07,6
```

Working with Delimited Formats

It's possible to load most forms of tabular data from disk using functions like pan
das.read_csv. In some cases, however, some manual processing may be necessary.
It's not uncommon to receive a file with one or more malformed lines that trip up
read_csv. To illustrate the basic tools, consider a small CSV file:

```
In [55]: !cat examples/ex7.csv
"a","b","c"
"1","2","3"
"1","2","3"
```

For any file with a single-character delimiter, you can use Python's built-in csv module. To use it, pass any open file or file-like object to csv.reader:

```
import csv
f = open('examples/ex7.csv')

reader = csv.reader(f)
```

Iterating through the reader like a file yields tuples of values with any quote characters removed:

```
In [57]: for line in reader:
   ....:     print(line)
['a', 'b', 'c']
['1', '2', '3']
['1', '2', '3']
```

From there, it's up to you to do the wrangling necessary to put the data in the form
that you need it. Let's take this step by step. First, we read the file into a list of lines:

```
In [58]: with open('examples/ex7.csv') as f:
   ....:     lines = list(csv.reader(f))
```

Then, we split the lines into the header line and the data lines:

```
In [59]: header, values = lines[0], lines[1:]
```

Then we can create a dictionary of data columns using a dictionary comprehension and the expression zip(*values), which transposes rows to columns:

```
In [60]: data_dict = {h: v for h, v in zip(header, zip(*values))}

In [61]: data_dict
Out[61]: {'a': ('1', '1'), 'b': ('2', '2'), 'c': ('3', '3')}
```

CSV files come in many different flavors. To define a new format with a different delimiter, string quoting convention, or line terminator, we define a simple subclass of csv.Dialect:

```
class my_dialect(csv.Dialect):
    lineterminator = '\n'
    delimiter = ';'
    quotechar = '"'
    quoting = csv.QUOTE_MINIMAL

reader = csv.reader(f, dialect=my_dialect)
```

We can also give individual CSV dialect parameters as keywords to csv.reader without having to define a subclass:

```
reader = csv.reader(f, delimiter='|')
```

The possible options (attributes of csv.Dialect) and what they do can be found in Table 6-3.

Table 6-3. CSV dialect options

Argument	Description
delimiter	One-character string to separate fields; defaults to ','.
lineterminator	Line terminator for writing; defaults to '\r\n'. Reader ignores this and recognizes cross-platform line terminators.
quotechar	Quote character for fields with special characters (like a delimiter); default is '"'.
quoting	Quoting convention. Options include csv.QUOTE_ALL (quote all fields), csv.QUOTE_MINI MAL (only fields with special characters like the delimiter), csv.QUOTE_NONNUMERIC, and csv.QUOTE_NONE (no quoting). See Python's documentation for full details. Defaults to QUOTE_MINIMAL.
skipinitialspace	Ignore whitespace after each delimiter; default is False.
doublequote	How to handle quoting character inside a field; if True, it is doubled (see online documentation for full detail and behavior).
escapechar	String to escape the delimiter if quoting is set to csv.QUOTE_NONE; disabled by default.

 For files with more complicated or fixed multicharacter delimiters, you will not be able to use the csv module. In those cases, you'll have to do the line splitting and other cleanup using string's split method or the regular expression method re.split.

To *write* delimited files manually, you can use `csv.writer`. It accepts an open, writable file object and the same dialect and format options as `csv.reader`:

```
with open('mydata.csv', 'w') as f:
    writer = csv.writer(f, dialect=my_dialect)
    writer.writerow(('one', 'two', 'three'))
    writer.writerow(('1', '2', '3'))
    writer.writerow(('4', '5', '6'))
    writer.writerow(('7', '8', '9'))
```

JSON Data

JSON (short for JavaScript Object Notation) has become one of the standard formats for sending data by HTTP request between web browsers and other applications. It is a much more free-form data format than a tabular text form like CSV. Here is an example:

```
obj = """
{"name": "Wes",
 "places_lived": ["United States", "Spain", "Germany"],
 "pet": null,
 "siblings": [{"name": "Scott", "age": 30, "pets": ["Zeus", "Zuko"]},
              {"name": "Katie", "age": 38,
               "pets": ["Sixes", "Stache", "Cisco"]}]
}
"""
```

JSON is very nearly valid Python code with the exception of its null value `null` and some other nuances (such as disallowing trailing commas at the end of lists). The basic types are objects (dicts), arrays (lists), strings, numbers, booleans, and nulls. All of the keys in an object must be strings. There are several Python libraries for reading and writing JSON data. I'll use `json` here, as it is built into the Python standard library. To convert a JSON string to Python form, use `json.loads`:

```
In [63]: import json

In [64]: result = json.loads(obj)

In [65]: result
Out[65]:
{'name': 'Wes',
 'pet': None,
 'places_lived': ['United States', 'Spain', 'Germany'],
 'siblings': [{'age': 30, 'name': 'Scott', 'pets': ['Zeus', 'Zuko']},
  {'age': 38, 'name': 'Katie', 'pets': ['Sixes', 'Stache', 'Cisco']}]}
```

`json.dumps`, on the other hand, converts a Python object back to JSON:

```
In [66]: asjson = json.dumps(result)
```

How you convert a JSON object or list of objects to a DataFrame or some other data structure for analysis will be up to you. Conveniently, you can pass a list of dicts (which were previously JSON objects) to the DataFrame constructor and select a subset of the data fields:

```
In [67]: siblings = pd.DataFrame(result['siblings'], columns=['name', 'age'])

In [68]: siblings
Out[68]:
    name  age
0  Scott   30
1  Katie   38
```

The `pandas.read_json` can automatically convert JSON datasets in specific arrangements into a Series or DataFrame. For example:

```
In [69]: !cat examples/example.json
[{"a": 1, "b": 2, "c": 3},
 {"a": 4, "b": 5, "c": 6},
 {"a": 7, "b": 8, "c": 9}]
```

The default options for `pandas.read_json` assume that each object in the JSON array is a row in the table:

```
In [70]: data = pd.read_json('examples/example.json')

In [71]: data
Out[71]:
   a  b  c
0  1  2  3
1  4  5  6
2  7  8  9
```

For an extended example of reading and manipulating JSON data (including nested records), see the USDA Food Database example in Chapter 14.

If you need to export data from pandas to JSON, one way is to use the `to_json` methods on Series and DataFrame:

```
In [72]: print(data.to_json())
{"a":{"0":1,"1":4,"2":7},"b":{"0":2,"1":5,"2":8},"c":{"0":3,"1":6,"2":9}}

In [73]: print(data.to_json(orient='records'))
[{"a":1,"b":2,"c":3},{"a":4,"b":5,"c":6},{"a":7,"b":8,"c":9}]
```

XML and HTML: Web Scraping

Python has many libraries for reading and writing data in the ubiquitous HTML and XML formats. Examples include lxml (*http://lxml.de*), Beautiful Soup, and html5lib. While lxml is comparatively much faster in general, the other libraries can better handle malformed HTML or XML files.

---

pandas has a built-in function, read_html, which uses libraries like lxml and Beautiful Soup to automatically parse tables out of HTML files as DataFrame objects. To show how this works, I downloaded an HTML file (used in the pandas documentation) from the United States FDIC government agency showing bank failures.[1] First, you must install some additional libraries used by read_html:

```
conda install lxml
pip install beautifulsoup4 html5lib
```

If you are not using conda, pip install lxml will likely also work.

The pandas.read_html function has a number of options, but by default it searches for and attempts to parse all tabular data contained within <table> tags. The result is a list of DataFrame objects:

```
In [74]: tables = pd.read_html('examples/fdic_failed_bank_list.html')

In [75]: len(tables)
Out[75]: 1

In [76]: failures = tables[0]

In [77]: failures.head()
Out[77]:
                     Bank Name            City  ST   CERT  \
0                   Allied Bank        Mulberry  AR     91
1   The Woodbury Banking Company        Woodbury  GA  11297
2       First CornerStone Bank  King of Prussia  PA  35312
3            Trust Company Bank         Memphis  TN   9956
4     North Milwaukee State Bank       Milwaukee  WI  20364
                   Acquiring Institution        Closing Date       Updated Date
0                           Today's Bank  September 23, 2016  November 17, 2016
1                           United Bank     August 19, 2016  November 17, 2016
2   First-Citizens Bank & Trust Company         May 6, 2016  September 6, 2016
3            The Bank of Fayette County       April 29, 2016  September 6, 2016
4   First-Citizens Bank & Trust Company      March 11, 2016      June 16, 2016
```

Because failures has many columns, pandas inserts a line break character \.

As you will learn in later chapters, from here we could proceed to do some data cleaning and analysis, like computing the number of bank failures by year:

```
In [78]: close_timestamps = pd.to_datetime(failures['Closing Date'])

In [79]: close_timestamps.dt.year.value_counts()
Out[79]:
2010    157
2009    140
```

---

[1] For the full list, see *https://www.fdic.gov/bank/individual/failed/banklist.html*.

```
2011    92
2012    51
2008    25
        ...
2004     4
2001     4
2007     3
2003     3
2000     2
Name: Closing Date, Length: 15, dtype: int64
```

Parsing XML with lxml.objectify

XML (eXtensible Markup Language) is another common structured data format supporting hierarchical, nested data with metadata. The book you are currently reading was actually created from a series of large XML documents.

Earlier, I showed the `pandas.read_html` function, which uses either lxml or Beautiful Soup under the hood to parse data from HTML. XML and HTML are structurally similar, but XML is more general. Here, I will show an example of how to use lxml to parse data from a more general XML format.

The New York Metropolitan Transportation Authority (MTA) publishes a number of data series about its bus and train services (*http://www.mta.info/developers/download.html*). Here we'll look at the performance data, which is contained in a set of XML files. Each train or bus service has a different file (like *Performance_MNR.xml* for the Metro-North Railroad) containing monthly data as a series of XML records that look like this:

```
<INDICATOR>
  <INDICATOR_SEQ>373889</INDICATOR_SEQ>
  <PARENT_SEQ></PARENT_SEQ>
  <AGENCY_NAME>Metro-North Railroad</AGENCY_NAME>
  <INDICATOR_NAME>Escalator Availability</INDICATOR_NAME>
  <DESCRIPTION>Percent of the time that escalators are operational
  systemwide. The availability rate is based on physical observations performed
  the morning of regular business days only. This is a new indicator the agency
  began reporting in 2009.</DESCRIPTION>
  <PERIOD_YEAR>2011</PERIOD_YEAR>
  <PERIOD_MONTH>12</PERIOD_MONTH>
  <CATEGORY>Service Indicators</CATEGORY>
  <FREQUENCY>M</FREQUENCY>
  <DESIRED_CHANGE>U</DESIRED_CHANGE>
  <INDICATOR_UNIT>%</INDICATOR_UNIT>
  <DECIMAL_PLACES>1</DECIMAL_PLACES>
  <YTD_TARGET>97.00</YTD_TARGET>
  <YTD_ACTUAL></YTD_ACTUAL>
  <MONTHLY_TARGET>97.00</MONTHLY_TARGET>
  <MONTHLY_ACTUAL></MONTHLY_ACTUAL>
</INDICATOR>
```

Using lxml.objectify, we parse the file and get a reference to the root node of the XML file with getroot:

```
from lxml import objectify

path = 'datasets/mta_perf/Performance_MNR.xml'
parsed = objectify.parse(open(path))
root = parsed.getroot()
```

root.INDICATOR returns a generator yielding each <INDICATOR> XML element. For each record, we can populate a dict of tag names (like YTD_ACTUAL) to data values (excluding a few tags):

```
data = []

skip_fields = ['PARENT_SEQ', 'INDICATOR_SEQ',
               'DESIRED_CHANGE', 'DECIMAL_PLACES']

for elt in root.INDICATOR:
    el_data = {}
    for child in elt.getchildren():
        if child.tag in skip_fields:
            continue
        el_data[child.tag] = child.pyval
    data.append(el_data)
```

Lastly, convert this list of dicts into a DataFrame:

```
In [82]: perf = pd.DataFrame(data)

In [83]: perf.head()
Out[83]:
                AGENCY_NAME           CATEGORY  \
0  Metro-North Railroad  Service Indicators
1  Metro-North Railroad  Service Indicators
2  Metro-North Railroad  Service Indicators
3  Metro-North Railroad  Service Indicators
4  Metro-North Railroad  Service Indicators

                                                                   DESCRIPTIO
N  \
0  Percent of commuter trains that arrive at their destinations within 5 minute..
.
1  Percent of commuter trains that arrive at their destinations within 5 minute..
.
2  Percent of commuter trains that arrive at their destinations within 5 minute..
.
3  Percent of commuter trains that arrive at their destinations within 5 minute..
.
4  Percent of commuter trains that arrive at their destinations within 5 minute..
.
   FREQUENCY                      INDICATOR_NAME INDICATOR_UNIT  \
0          M  On-Time Performance (West of Hudson)              %
1          M  On-Time Performance (West of Hudson)              %
```

```
2          M  On-Time Performance (West of Hudson)              %
3          M  On-Time Performance (West of Hudson)              %
4          M  On-Time Performance (West of Hudson)              %
  MONTHLY_ACTUAL MONTHLY_TARGET  PERIOD_MONTH  PERIOD_YEAR YTD_ACTUAL  \
0          96.9             95             1         2008       96.9
1            95             95             2         2008         96
2          96.9             95             3         2008       96.3
3          98.3             95             4         2008       96.8
4          95.8             95             5         2008       96.6
  YTD_TARGET
0         95
1         95
2         95
3         95
4         95
```

XML data can get much more complicated than this example. Each tag can have metadata, too. Consider an HTML link tag, which is also valid XML:

```
from io import StringIO
tag = '<a href="http://www.google.com">Google</a>'
root = objectify.parse(StringIO(tag)).getroot()
```

You can now access any of the fields (like href) in the tag or the link text:

```
In [85]: root
Out[85]: <Element a at 0x7f2ddcd62408>

In [86]: root.get('href')
Out[86]: 'http://www.google.com'

In [87]: root.text
Out[87]: 'Google'
```

6.2 Binary Data Formats

One of the easiest ways to store data (also known as *serialization*) efficiently in binary format is using Python's built-in pickle serialization. pandas objects all have a to_pickle method that writes the data to disk in pickle format:

```
In [88]: frame = pd.read_csv('examples/ex1.csv')

In [89]: frame
Out[89]:
   a   b   c   d message
0  1   2   3   4   hello
1  5   6   7   8   world
2  9  10  11  12     foo

In [90]: frame.to_pickle('examples/frame_pickle')
```

You can read any "pickled" object stored in a file by using the built-in `pickle` directly, or even more conveniently using `pandas.read_pickle`:

```
In [91]: pd.read_pickle('examples/frame_pickle')
Out[91]:
   a   b   c   d message
0  1   2   3   4   hello
1  5   6   7   8   world
2  9  10  11  12     foo
```

 `pickle` is only recommended as a short-term storage format. The problem is that it is hard to guarantee that the format will be stable over time; an object pickled today may not unpickle with a later version of a library. We have tried to maintain backward compatibility when possible, but at some point in the future it may be necessary to "break" the pickle format.

pandas has built-in support for two more binary data formats: HDF5 and Message-Pack. I will give some HDF5 examples in the next section, but I encourage you to explore different file formats to see how fast they are and how well they work for your analysis. Some other storage formats for pandas or NumPy data include:

bcolz (http://bcolz.blosc.org/)
   A compressable column-oriented binary format based on the Blosc compression library.

Feather (http://github.com/wesm/feather)
   A cross-language column-oriented file format I designed with the R programming community's Hadley Wickham (*http://hadley.nz/*). Feather uses the Apache Arrow (*http://arrow.apache.org*) columnar memory format.

Using HDF5 Format

HDF5 is a well-regarded file format intended for storing large quantities of scientific array data. It is available as a C library, and it has interfaces available in many other languages, including Java, Julia, MATLAB, and Python. The "HDF" in HDF5 stands for *hierarchical data format*. Each HDF5 file can store multiple datasets and supporting metadata. Compared with simpler formats, HDF5 supports on-the-fly compression with a variety of compression modes, enabling data with repeated patterns to be stored more efficiently. HDF5 can be a good choice for working with very large datasets that don't fit into memory, as you can efficiently read and write small sections of much larger arrays.

While it's possible to directly access HDF5 files using either the PyTables or h5py libraries, pandas provides a high-level interface that simplifies storing Series and

DataFrame object. The HDFStore class works like a dict and handles the low-level details:

```
In [93]: frame = pd.DataFrame({'a': np.random.randn(100)})

In [94]: store = pd.HDFStore('mydata.h5')

In [95]: store['obj1'] = frame

In [96]: store['obj1_col'] = frame['a']

In [97]: store
Out[97]:
<class 'pandas.io.pytables.HDFStore'>
File path: mydata.h5
```

Objects contained in the HDF5 file can then be retrieved with the same dict-like API:

```
In [98]: store['obj1']
Out[98]:
           a
0   -0.204708
1    0.478943
2   -0.519439
3   -0.555730
4    1.965781
..        ...
95   0.795253
96   0.118110
97  -0.748532
98   0.584970
99   0.152677
[100 rows x 1 columns]
```

HDFStore supports two storage schemas, 'fixed' and 'table'. The latter is generally slower, but it supports query operations using a special syntax:

```
In [99]: store.put('obj2', frame, format='table')

In [100]: store.select('obj2', where=['index >= 10 and index <= 15'])
Out[100]:
           a
10   1.007189
11  -1.296221
12   0.274992
13   0.228913
14   1.352917
15   0.886429

In [101]: store.close()
```

The put is an explicit version of the store['obj2'] = frame method but allows us to set other options like the storage format.

The `pandas.read_hdf` function gives you a shortcut to these tools:

```
In [102]: frame.to_hdf('mydata.h5', 'obj3', format='table')

In [103]: pd.read_hdf('mydata.h5', 'obj3', where=['index < 5'])
Out[103]:
          a
0 -0.204708
1  0.478943
2 -0.519439
3 -0.555730
4  1.965781
```

> If you are processing data that is stored on remote servers, like
> Amazon S3 or HDFS, using a different binary format designed for
> distributed storage like Apache Parquet (*http://parquet.apache.org*)
> may be more suitable. Python for Parquet and other such storage
> formats is still developing, so I do not write about them in this
> book.

If you work with large quantities of data locally, I would encourage you to explore
PyTables and h5py to see how they can suit your needs. Since many data analysis
problems are I/O-bound (rather than CPU-bound), using a tool like HDF5 can mas-
sively accelerate your applications.

> HDF5 is *not* a database. It is best suited for write-once, read-many
> datasets. While data can be added to a file at any time, if multiple
> writers do so simultaneously, the file can become corrupted.

Reading Microsoft Excel Files

pandas also supports reading tabular data stored in Excel 2003 (and higher) files
using either the `ExcelFile` class or `pandas.read_excel` function. Internally these
tools use the add-on packages `xlrd` and `openpyxl` to read XLS and XLSX files, respectively. These must be installed separately from pandas using pip or conda.

To use `ExcelFile`, create an instance by passing a path to an `xls` or `xlsx` file:

```
In [105]: xlsx = pd.ExcelFile('examples/ex1.xlsx')
```

Data stored in a sheet can then be read into DataFrame with `parse`:

```
In [106]: pd.read_excel(xlsx, 'Sheet1')
Out[106]:
   a  b  c  d message
0  1  2  3  4   hello
```

```
1   5   6    7   8     world
2   9  10   11  12       foo
```

If you are reading multiple sheets in a file, then it is faster to create the ExcelFile, but you can also simply pass the filename to pandas.read_excel:

```
In [107]: frame = pd.read_excel('examples/ex1.xlsx', 'Sheet1')
```

```
In [108]: frame
Out[108]:
   a   b   c   d message
0  1   2   3   4   hello
1  5   6   7   8   world
2  9  10  11  12     foo
```

To write pandas data to Excel format, you must first create an ExcelWriter, then write data to it using pandas objects' to_excel method:

```
In [109]: writer = pd.ExcelWriter('examples/ex2.xlsx')
```

```
In [110]: frame.to_excel(writer, 'Sheet1')
```

```
In [111]: writer.save()
```

You can also pass a file path to to_excel and avoid the ExcelWriter:

```
In [112]: frame.to_excel('examples/ex2.xlsx')
```

6.3 Interacting with Web APIs

Many websites have public APIs providing data feeds via JSON or some other format. There are a number of ways to access these APIs from Python; one easy-to-use method that I recommend is the requests package (*http://docs.python-requests.org*).

To find the last 30 GitHub issues for pandas on GitHub, we can make a GET HTTP request using the add-on requests library:

```
In [114]: import requests
```

```
In [115]: url = 'https://api.github.com/repos/pandas-dev/pandas/issues'
```

```
In [116]: resp = requests.get(url)
```

```
In [117]: resp
Out[117]: <Response [200]>
```

The Response object's json method will return a dictionary containing JSON parsed into native Python objects:

```
In [118]: data = resp.json()
```

```
In [119]: data[0]['title']
```

```
Out[119]: 'BUG: SparseDataFrame coerces input to dense matrix if string-type inde
x is given'
```

Each element in `data` is a dictionary containing all of the data found on a GitHub issue page (except for the comments). We can pass `data` directly to DataFrame and extract fields of interest:

```
In [120]: issues = pd.DataFrame(data, columns=['number', 'title',
   .....:                                      'labels', 'state'])

In [121]: issues
Out[121]:
    number  \
0    22630
1    22629
2    22628
3    22627
4    22624
..     ...
25   22593
26   22592
27   22591
28   22590
29   22588

                                                                         tit
le  \
0    BUG: SparseDataFrame coerces input to dense matrix if string-type index is g.
..
1    read_excel ignores `sheet_name` parameter in PyInstaller EXE but not in Pyth.
..
2        BUG: Some sas7bdat files with many columns are not parseable by read_s
as
3                   Series.reorder_levels docstring includes extra `axis` argumen
t.
4                                                            Refactor test_sql.
py
..                                                                            .
..
25                                                   Set hypothesis HealthChe
ck
26   Invitation for comments / use: reading large fixed-width datasets efficient
ly
27                                               Inconsistent behaviour in Timestamp.rou
nd
28                                       DataFrame.rolling causes Kernel died, resta
rt
29                   TST: add test to io/formats/test_to_html.py to close GH61
31

                                                                         labe
ls  \
0    []
```

```
1
[]
2    [{'id': 76811, 'node_id': 'MDU6TGFiZWw3NjgxMQ==', 'url': 'https://api.github.
..
3    [{'id': 134699, 'node_id': 'MDU6TGFiZWwxMzQ2OTk=', 'url': 'https://api.githu.
..
4    [{'id': 211029535, 'node_id': 'MDU6TGFiZWwyMTEwMjk1MzU=', 'url': 'https://ap.
..
..
..
25   [{'id': 48070600, 'node_id': 'MDU6TGFiZWw0ODA3MDYwMA==', 'url': 'https://api.
..
26   [{'id': 2301354, 'node_id': 'MDU6TGFiZWwyMzAxMzU0', 'url': 'https://api.gith.
..
27   [{'id': 211840, 'node_id': 'MDU6TGFiZWwyMTE4NDA=', 'url': 'https://api.githu.
..
28   [{'id': 986278782, 'node_id': 'MDU6TGFiZWw5ODYyNzg3ODI=', 'url': 'https://ap.
..
29   [{'id': 57395487, 'node_id': 'MDU6TGFiZWw1NzM5NTQ4Nw==', 'url': 'https://api.
..
     state
0    open
1    open
2    open
3    open
4    open
..    ...
25   open
26   open
27   open
28   open
29   open
[30 rows x 4 columns]
```

With a bit of elbow grease, you can create some higher-level interfaces to common web APIs that return DataFrame objects for easy analysis.

6.4 Interacting with Databases

In a business setting, most data may not be stored in text or Excel files. SQL-based relational databases (such as SQL Server, PostgreSQL, and MySQL) are in wide use, and many alternative databases have become quite popular. The choice of database is usually dependent on the performance, data integrity, and scalability needs of an application.

Loading data from SQL into a DataFrame is fairly straightforward, and pandas has some functions to simplify the process. As an example, I'll create a SQLite database using Python's built-in `sqlite3` driver:

```
In [122]: import sqlite3

In [123]: query = """
   .....: CREATE TABLE test
   .....: (a VARCHAR(20), b VARCHAR(20),
   .....:  c REAL,        d INTEGER
   .....: );"""

In [124]: con = sqlite3.connect('mydata.sqlite')

In [125]: con.execute(query)
Out[125]: <sqlite3.Cursor at 0x7f2dd12c2650>

In [126]: con.commit()
```

Then, insert a few rows of data:

```
In [127]: data = [('Atlanta', 'Georgia', 1.25, 6),
   .....:         ('Tallahassee', 'Florida', 2.6, 3),
   .....:         ('Sacramento', 'California', 1.7, 5)]

In [128]: stmt = "INSERT INTO test VALUES(?, ?, ?, ?)"

In [129]: con.executemany(stmt, data)
Out[129]: <sqlite3.Cursor at 0x7f2dd22535e0>

In [130]: con.commit()
```

Most Python SQL drivers (PyODBC, psycopg2, MySQLdb, pymssql, etc.) return a list of tuples when selecting data from a table:

```
In [131]: cursor = con.execute('select * from test')

In [132]: rows = cursor.fetchall()

In [133]: rows
Out[133]:
[('Atlanta', 'Georgia', 1.25, 6),
 ('Tallahassee', 'Florida', 2.6, 3),
 ('Sacramento', 'California', 1.7, 5)]
```

You can pass the list of tuples to the DataFrame constructor, but you also need the column names, contained in the cursor's `description` attribute:

```
In [134]: cursor.description
Out[134]:
(('a', None, None, None, None, None, None),
 ('b', None, None, None, None, None, None),
 ('c', None, None, None, None, None, None),
 ('d', None, None, None, None, None, None))

In [135]: pd.DataFrame(rows, columns=[x[0] for x in cursor.description])
Out[135]:
            a          b     c  d
```

```
0      Atlanta      Georgia  1.25  6
1   Tallahassee     Florida  2.60  3
2   Sacramento   California  1.70  5
```

This is quite a bit of munging that you'd rather not repeat each time you query the database. The SQLAlchemy project (*http://www.sqlalchemy.org/*) is a popular Python SQL toolkit that abstracts away many of the common differences between SQL databases. pandas has a `read_sql` function that enables you to read data easily from a general SQLAlchemy connection. Here, we'll connect to the same SQLite database with SQLAlchemy and read data from the table created before:

```
In [136]: import sqlalchemy as sqla

In [137]: db = sqla.create_engine('sqlite:///mydata.sqlite')

In [138]: pd.read_sql('select * from test', db)
Out[138]:
            a           b     c  d
0      Atlanta      Georgia  1.25  6
1   Tallahassee     Florida  2.60  3
2   Sacramento   California  1.70  5
```

6.5 Conclusion

Getting access to data is frequently the first step in the data analysis process. We have looked at a number of useful tools in this chapter that should help you get started. In the upcoming chapters we will dig deeper into data wrangling, data visualization, time series analysis, and other topics.

Data Cleaning and Preparation

During the course of doing data analysis and modeling, a significant amount of time is spent on data preparation: loading, cleaning, transforming, and rearranging. Such tasks are often reported to take up 80% or more of an analyst's time. Sometimes the way that data is stored in files or databases is not in the right format for a particular task. Many researchers choose to do ad hoc processing of data from one form to another using a general-purpose programming language, like Python, Perl, R, or Java, or Unix text-processing tools like sed or awk. Fortunately, pandas, along with the built-in Python language features, provides you with a high-level, flexible, and fast set of tools to enable you to manipulate data into the right form.

If you identify a type of data manipulation that isn't anywhere in this book or elsewhere in the pandas library, feel free to share your use case on one of the Python mailing lists or on the pandas GitHub site. Indeed, much of the design and implementation of pandas has been driven by the needs of real-world applications.

In this chapter I discuss tools for missing data, duplicate data, string manipulation, and some other analytical data transformations. In the next chapter, I focus on combining and rearranging datasets in various ways.

7.1 Handling Missing Data

Missing data occurs commonly in many data analysis applications. One of the goals of pandas is to make working with missing data as painless as possible. For example, all of the descriptive statistics on pandas objects exclude missing data by default.

The way that missing data is represented in pandas objects is somewhat imperfect, but it is functional for a lot of users. For numeric data, pandas uses the floating-point value NaN (Not a Number) to represent missing data. We call this a *sentinel value* that can be easily detected:

```
In [12]: string_data = pd.Series(['aardvark', 'artichoke', np.nan, 'avocado'])

In [13]: string_data
Out[13]:
0     aardvark
1     artichoke
2          NaN
3      avocado
dtype: object

In [14]: string_data.isnull()
Out[14]:
0    False
1    False
2     True
3    False
dtype: bool
```

In pandas, we've adopted a convention used in the R programming language by referring to missing data as NA, which stands for *not available*. In statistics applications,
NA data may either be data that does not exist or that exists but was not observed
(through problems with data collection, for example). When cleaning up data for
analysis, it is often important to do analysis on the missing data itself to identify data
collection problems or potential biases in the data caused by missing data.

The built-in Python None value is also treated as NA in object arrays:

```
In [15]: string_data[0] = None

In [16]: string_data.isnull()
Out[16]:
0     True
1    False
2     True
3    False
dtype: bool
```

There is work ongoing in the pandas project to improve the internal details of how
missing data is handled, but the user API functions, like pandas.isnull, abstract
away many of the annoying details. See Table 7-1 for a list of some functions related
to missing data handling.

Table 7-1. NA handling methods

Argument	Description
dropna	Filter axis labels based on whether values for each label have missing data, with varying thresholds for how much missing data to tolerate.
fillna	Fill in missing data with some value or using an interpolation method such as 'ffill' or 'bfill'.
isnull	Return boolean values indicating which values are missing/NA.
notnull	Negation of isnull.

Filtering Out Missing Data

There are a few ways to filter out missing data. While you always have the option to do it by hand using `pandas.isnull` and boolean indexing, the `dropna` can be helpful. On a Series, it returns the Series with only the non-null data and index values:

```
In [17]: from numpy import nan as NA

In [18]: data = pd.Series([1, NA, 3.5, NA, 7])

In [19]: data.dropna()
Out[19]:
0    1.0
2    3.5
4    7.0
dtype: float64
```

This is equivalent to:

```
In [20]: data[data.notnull()]
Out[20]:
0    1.0
2    3.5
4    7.0
dtype: float64
```

With DataFrame objects, things are a bit more complex. You may want to drop rows or columns that are all NA or only those containing any NAs. `dropna` by default drops any row containing a missing value:

```
In [21]: data = pd.DataFrame([[1., 6.5, 3.], [1., NA, NA],
   ....:                       [NA, NA, NA], [NA, 6.5, 3.]])

In [22]: cleaned = data.dropna()

In [23]: data
Out[23]:
     0    1    2
0  1.0  6.5  3.0
1  1.0  NaN  NaN
2  NaN  NaN  NaN
3  NaN  6.5  3.0

In [24]: cleaned
Out[24]:
     0    1    2
0  1.0  6.5  3.0
```

Passing `how='all'` will only drop rows that are all NA:

```
In [25]: data.dropna(how='all')
Out[25]:
     0    1    2
```

```
0  1.0  6.5  3.0
1  1.0  NaN  NaN
3  NaN  6.5  3.0
```

To drop columns in the same way, pass `axis=1`:

```
In [26]: data[4] = NA

In [27]: data
Out[27]:
     0    1    2    4
0  1.0  6.5  3.0  NaN
1  1.0  NaN  NaN  NaN
2  NaN  NaN  NaN  NaN
3  NaN  6.5  3.0  NaN

In [28]: data.dropna(axis=1, how='all')
Out[28]:
     0    1    2
0  1.0  6.5  3.0
1  1.0  NaN  NaN
2  NaN  NaN  NaN
3  NaN  6.5  3.0
```

A related way to filter out DataFrame rows tends to concern time series data. Suppose you want to keep only rows containing a certain number of observations. You can indicate this with the `thresh` argument:

```
In [29]: df = pd.DataFrame(np.random.randn(7, 3))

In [30]: df.iloc[:4, 1] = NA

In [31]: df.iloc[:2, 2] = NA

In [32]: df
Out[32]:
          0         1         2
0 -0.204708       NaN       NaN
1 -0.555730       NaN       NaN
2  0.092908       NaN  0.769023
3  1.246435       NaN -1.296221
4  0.274992  0.228913  1.352917
5  0.886429 -2.001637 -0.371843
6  1.669025 -0.438570 -0.539741

In [33]: df.dropna()
Out[33]:
          0         1         2
4  0.274992  0.228913  1.352917
5  0.886429 -2.001637 -0.371843
6  1.669025 -0.438570 -0.539741

In [34]: df.dropna(thresh=2)
```

```
Out[34]:
          0        1         2
2  0.092908      NaN  0.769023
3  1.246435      NaN -1.296221
4  0.274992  0.228913  1.352917
5  0.886429 -2.001637 -0.371843
6  1.669025 -0.438570 -0.539741
```

Filling In Missing Data

Rather than filtering out missing data (and potentially discarding other data along with it), you may want to fill in the "holes" in any number of ways. For most purposes, the fillna method is the workhorse function to use. Calling fillna with a constant replaces missing values with that value:

```
In [35]: df.fillna(0)
Out[35]:
          0        1         2
0 -0.204708  0.000000  0.000000
1 -0.555730  0.000000  0.000000
2  0.092908  0.000000  0.769023
3  1.246435  0.000000 -1.296221
4  0.274992  0.228913  1.352917
5  0.886429 -2.001637 -0.371843
6  1.669025 -0.438570 -0.539741
```

Calling fillna with a dict, you can use a different fill value for each column:

```
In [36]: df.fillna({1: 0.5, 2: 0})
Out[36]:
          0        1         2
0 -0.204708  0.500000  0.000000
1 -0.555730  0.500000  0.000000
2  0.092908  0.500000  0.769023
3  1.246435  0.500000 -1.296221
4  0.274992  0.228913  1.352917
5  0.886429 -2.001637 -0.371843
6  1.669025 -0.438570 -0.539741
```

fillna returns a new object, but you can modify the existing object in-place:

```
In [37]: _ = df.fillna(0, inplace=True)

In [38]: df
Out[38]:
          0        1         2
0 -0.204708  0.000000  0.000000
1 -0.555730  0.000000  0.000000
2  0.092908  0.000000  0.769023
3  1.246435  0.000000 -1.296221
4  0.274992  0.228913  1.352917
5  0.886429 -2.001637 -0.371843
6  1.669025 -0.438570 -0.539741
```

The same interpolation methods available for reindexing can be used with `fillna`:

```
In [39]: df = pd.DataFrame(np.random.randn(6, 3))

In [40]: df.iloc[2:, 1] = NA

In [41]: df.iloc[4:, 2] = NA

In [42]: df
Out[42]:
          0         1         2
0  0.476985  3.248944 -1.021228
1 -0.577087  0.124121  0.302614
2  0.523772       NaN  1.343810
3 -0.713544       NaN -2.370232
4 -1.860761       NaN       NaN
5 -1.265934       NaN       NaN

In [43]: df.fillna(method='ffill')
Out[43]:
          0         1         2
0  0.476985  3.248944 -1.021228
1 -0.577087  0.124121  0.302614
2  0.523772  0.124121  1.343810
3 -0.713544  0.124121 -2.370232
4 -1.860761  0.124121 -2.370232
5 -1.265934  0.124121 -2.370232

In [44]: df.fillna(method='ffill', limit=2)
Out[44]:
          0         1         2
0  0.476985  3.248944 -1.021228
1 -0.577087  0.124121  0.302614
2  0.523772  0.124121  1.343810
3 -0.713544  0.124121 -2.370232
4 -1.860761       NaN -2.370232
5 -1.265934       NaN -2.370232
```

With `fillna` you can do lots of other things with a little creativity. For example, you might pass the mean or median value of a Series:

```
In [45]: data = pd.Series([1., NA, 3.5, NA, 7])

In [46]: data.fillna(data.mean())
Out[46]:
0    1.000000
1    3.833333
2    3.500000
3    3.833333
4    7.000000
dtype: float64
```

See Table 7-2 for a reference on `fillna`.

Table 7-2. fillna function arguments

Argument	Description
value	Scalar value or dict-like object to use to fill missing values
method	Interpolation; by default `'ffill'` if function called with no other arguments
axis	Axis to fill on; default `axis=0`
inplace	Modify the calling object without producing a copy
limit	For forward and backward filling, maximum number of consecutive periods to fill

7.2 Data Transformation

So far in this chapter we've been concerned with rearranging data. Filtering, cleaning, and other transformations are another class of important operations.

Removing Duplicates

Duplicate rows may be found in a DataFrame for any number of reasons. Here is an example:

```
In [47]: data = pd.DataFrame({'k1': ['one', 'two'] * 3 + ['two'],
   ....:                       'k2': [1, 1, 2, 3, 3, 4, 4]})

In [48]: data
Out[48]:
    k1  k2
0  one   1
1  two   1
2  one   2
3  two   3
4  one   3
5  two   4
6  two   4
```

The DataFrame method `duplicated` returns a boolean Series indicating whether each row is a duplicate (has been observed in a previous row) or not:

```
In [49]: data.duplicated()
Out[49]:
0    False
1    False
2    False
3    False
4    False
5    False
6     True
dtype: bool
```

Relatedly, `drop_duplicates` returns a DataFrame where the `duplicated` array is `False`:

```
In [50]: data.drop_duplicates()
Out[50]:
    k1 k2
0  one  1
1  two  1
2  one  2
3  two  3
4  one  3
5  two  4
```

Both of these methods by default consider all of the columns; alternatively, you can specify any subset of them to detect duplicates. Suppose we had an additional column of values and wanted to filter duplicates only based on the 'k1' column:

```
In [51]: data['v1'] = range(7)

In [52]: data.drop_duplicates(['k1'])
Out[52]:
    k1 k2 v1
0  one  1  0
1  two  1  1
```

duplicated and drop_duplicates by default keep the first observed value combination. Passing keep='last' will return the last one:

```
In [53]: data.drop_duplicates(['k1', 'k2'], keep='last')
Out[53]:
    k1 k2 v1
0  one  1  0
1  two  1  1
2  one  2  2
3  two  3  3
4  one  3  4
6  two  4  6
```

Transforming Data Using a Function or Mapping

For many datasets, you may wish to perform some transformation based on the values in an array, Series, or column in a DataFrame. Consider the following hypothetical data collected about various kinds of meat:

```
In [54]: data = pd.DataFrame({'food': ['bacon', 'pulled pork', 'bacon',
   ....:                               'Pastrami', 'corned beef', 'Bacon',
   ....:                               'pastrami', 'honey ham', 'nova lox'],
   ....:                      'ounces': [4, 3, 12, 6, 7.5, 8, 3, 5, 6]})

In [55]: data
Out[55]:
          food  ounces
0        bacon     4.0
1  pulled pork     3.0
2        bacon    12.0
```

```
3       Pastrami     6.0
4    corned beef     7.5
5          Bacon     8.0
6       pastrami     3.0
7      honey ham     5.0
8       nova lox     6.0
```

Suppose you wanted to add a column indicating the type of animal that each food came from. Let's write down a mapping of each distinct meat type to the kind of animal:

```
meat_to_animal = {
  'bacon': 'pig',
  'pulled pork': 'pig',
  'pastrami': 'cow',
  'corned beef': 'cow',
  'honey ham': 'pig',
  'nova lox': 'salmon'
}
```

The map method on a Series accepts a function or dict-like object containing a mapping, but here we have a small problem in that some of the meats are capitalized and others are not. Thus, we need to convert each value to lowercase using the str.lower Series method:

```
In [57]: lowercased = data['food'].str.lower()

In [58]: lowercased
Out[58]:
0           bacon
1     pulled pork
2           bacon
3        pastrami
4     corned beef
5           bacon
6        pastrami
7       honey ham
8        nova lox
Name: food, dtype: object

In [59]: data['animal'] = lowercased.map(meat_to_animal)

In [60]: data
Out[60]:
          food  ounces  animal
0        bacon     4.0     pig
1  pulled pork     3.0     pig
2        bacon    12.0     pig
3     Pastrami     6.0     cow
4  corned beef     7.5     cow
5        Bacon     8.0     pig
6     pastrami     3.0     cow
```

```
7    honey ham    5.0     pig
8     nova lox    6.0  salmon
```

We could also have passed a function that does all the work:

```
In [61]: data['food'].map(lambda x: meat_to_animal[x.lower()])
Out[61]:
0       pig
1       pig
2       pig
3       cow
4       cow
5       pig
6       cow
7       pig
8    salmon
Name: food, dtype: object
```

Using map is a convenient way to perform element-wise transformations and other data cleaning–related operations.

Replacing Values

Filling in missing data with the fillna method is a special case of more general value replacement. As you've already seen, map can be used to modify a subset of values in an object but replace provides a simpler and more flexible way to do so. Let's consider this Series:

```
In [62]: data = pd.Series([1., -999., 2., -999., -1000., 3.])

In [63]: data
Out[63]:
0       1.0
1    -999.0
2       2.0
3    -999.0
4   -1000.0
5       3.0
dtype: float64
```

The -999 values might be sentinel values for missing data. To replace these with NA values that pandas understands, we can use replace, producing a new Series (unless you pass inplace=True):

```
In [64]: data.replace(-999, np.nan)
Out[64]:
0       1.0
1       NaN
2       2.0
3       NaN
4   -1000.0
```

```
5      3.0
dtype: float64
```

If you want to replace multiple values at once, you instead pass a list and then the substitute value:

```
In [65]: data.replace([-999, -1000], np.nan)
Out[65]:
0    1.0
1    NaN
2    2.0
3    NaN
4    NaN
5    3.0
dtype: float64
```

To use a different replacement for each value, pass a list of substitutes:

```
In [66]: data.replace([-999, -1000], [np.nan, 0])
Out[66]:
0    1.0
1    NaN
2    2.0
3    NaN
4    0.0
5    3.0
dtype: float64
```

The argument passed can also be a dict:

```
In [67]: data.replace({-999: np.nan, -1000: 0})
Out[67]:
0    1.0
1    NaN
2    2.0
3    NaN
4    0.0
5    3.0
dtype: float64
```

> The data.replace method is distinct from data.str.replace, which performs string substitution element-wise. We look at these string methods on Series later in the chapter.

Renaming Axis Indexes

Like values in a Series, axis labels can be similarly transformed by a function or mapping of some form to produce new, differently labeled objects. You can also modify the axes in-place without creating a new data structure. Here's a simple example:

```
In [68]: data = pd.DataFrame(np.arange(12).reshape((3, 4)),
   ....:                     index=['Ohio', 'Colorado', 'New York'],
   ....:                     columns=['one', 'two', 'three', 'four'])
```

Like a Series, the axis indexes have a map method:

```
In [69]: transform = lambda x: x[:4].upper()
```

```
In [70]: data.index.map(transform)
Out[70]: Index(['OHIO', 'COLO', 'NEW '], dtype='object')
```

You can assign to index, modifying the DataFrame in-place:

```
In [71]: data.index = data.index.map(transform)
```

```
In [72]: data
Out[72]:
      one  two  three  four
OHIO    0    1      2     3
COLO    4    5      6     7
NEW     8    9     10    11
```

If you want to create a transformed version of a dataset without modifying the original, a useful method is rename:

```
In [73]: data.rename(index=str.title, columns=str.upper)
Out[73]:
      ONE  TWO  THREE  FOUR
Ohio    0    1      2     3
Colo    4    5      6     7
New     8    9     10    11
```

Notably, rename can be used in conjunction with a dict-like object providing new values for a subset of the axis labels:

```
In [74]: data.rename(index={'OHIO': 'INDIANA'},
   ....:             columns={'three': 'peekaboo'})
Out[74]:
         one  two  peekaboo  four
INDIANA    0    1         2     3
COLO       4    5         6     7
NEW        8    9        10    11
```

rename saves you from the chore of copying the DataFrame manually and assigning to its index and columns attributes. Should you wish to modify a dataset in-place, pass inplace=True:

```
In [75]: data.rename(index={'OHIO': 'INDIANA'}, inplace=True)
```

```
In [76]: data
Out[76]:
         one  two  three  four
INDIANA    0    1      2     3
```

```
COLO        4    5    6    7
NEW         8    9    10   11
```

Discretization and Binning

Continuous data is often discretized or otherwise separated into "bins" for analysis. Suppose you have data about a group of people in a study, and you want to group them into discrete age buckets:

```
In [77]: ages = [20, 22, 25, 27, 21, 23, 37, 31, 61, 45, 41, 32]
```

Let's divide these into bins of 18 to 25, 26 to 35, 36 to 60, and finally 61 and older. To do so, you have to use cut, a function in pandas:

```
In [78]: bins = [18, 25, 35, 60, 100]

In [79]: cats = pd.cut(ages, bins)

In [80]: cats
Out[80]:
[(18, 25], (18, 25], (18, 25], (25, 35], (18, 25], ..., (25, 35], (60, 100], (35,
60], (35, 60], (25, 35]]
Length: 12
Categories (4, interval[int64]): [(18, 25] < (25, 35] < (35, 60] < (60, 100]]
```

The object pandas returns is a special Categorical object. The output you see describes the bins computed by pandas.cut. You can treat it like an array of strings indicating the bin name; internally it contains a categories array specifying the distinct category names along with a labeling for the ages data in the codes attribute:

```
In [81]: cats.codes
Out[81]: array([0, 0, 0, 1, 0, 0, 2, 1, 3, 2, 2, 1], dtype=int8)

In [82]: cats.categories
Out[82]:
IntervalIndex([(18, 25], (25, 35], (35, 60], (60, 100]],
              closed='right',
              dtype='interval[int64]')

In [83]: pd.value_counts(cats)
Out[83]:
(18, 25]     5
(35, 60]     3
(25, 35]     3
(60, 100]    1
dtype: int64
```

Note that pd.value_counts(cats) are the bin counts for the result of pandas.cut.

Consistent with mathematical notation for intervals, a parenthesis means that the side is *open*, while the square bracket means it is *closed* (inclusive). You can change which side is closed by passing right=False:

```
In [84]: pd.cut(ages, [18, 26, 36, 61, 100], right=False)
Out[84]:
[[18, 26), [18, 26), [18, 26), [26, 36), [18, 26), ..., [26, 36), [61, 100), [36,
 61), [36, 61), [26, 36)]
Length: 12
Categories (4, interval[int64]): [[18, 26) < [26, 36) < [36, 61) < [61, 100)]
```

You can also pass your own bin names by passing a list or array to the labels option:

```
In [85]: group_names = ['Youth', 'YoungAdult', 'MiddleAged', 'Senior']

In [86]: pd.cut(ages, bins, labels=group_names)
Out[86]:
[Youth, Youth, Youth, YoungAdult, Youth, ..., YoungAdult, Senior, MiddleAged, Mid
dleAged, YoungAdult]
Length: 12
Categories (4, object): [Youth < YoungAdult < MiddleAged < Senior]
```

If you pass an integer number of bins to cut instead of explicit bin edges, it will compute equal-length bins based on the minimum and maximum values in the data.
Consider the case of some uniformly distributed data chopped into fourths:

```
In [87]: data = np.random.rand(20)

In [88]: pd.cut(data, 4, precision=2)
Out[88]:
[(0.34, 0.55], (0.34, 0.55], (0.76, 0.97], (0.76, 0.97], (0.34, 0.55], ..., (0.34
, 0.55], (0.34, 0.55], (0.55, 0.76], (0.34, 0.55], (0.12, 0.34]]
Length: 20
Categories (4, interval[float64]): [(0.12, 0.34] < (0.34, 0.55] < (0.55, 0.76] <
(0.76, 0.97]]
```

The precision=2 option limits the decimal precision to two digits.

A closely related function, qcut, bins the data based on sample quantiles. Depending
on the distribution of the data, using cut will not usually result in each bin having the
same number of data points. Since qcut uses sample quantiles instead, by definition
you will obtain roughly equal-size bins:

```
In [89]: data = np.random.randn(1000)  # Normally distributed

In [90]: cats = pd.qcut(data, 4)  # Cut into quartiles

In [91]: cats
Out[91]:
[(-0.0265, 0.62], (0.62, 3.928], (-0.68, -0.0265], (0.62, 3.928], (-0.0265, 0.62]
, ..., (-0.68, -0.0265], (-0.68, -0.0265], (-2.9499999999999997, -0.68], (0.62, 3
.928], (-0.68, -0.0265]]
Length: 1000
Categories (4, interval[float64]): [(-2.9499999999999997, -0.68] < (-0.68, -0.026
5] < (-0.0265, 0.62] <
                                    (0.62, 3.928]]
```

```
In [92]: pd.value_counts(cats)
Out[92]:
(0.62, 3.928]                      250
(-0.0265, 0.62]                    250
(-0.68, -0.0265]                   250
(-2.9499999999999997, -0.68]       250
dtype: int64
```

Similar to cut you can pass your own quantiles (numbers between 0 and 1, inclusive):

```
In [93]: pd.qcut(data, [0, 0.1, 0.5, 0.9, 1.])
Out[93]:
[(-0.0265, 1.286], (-0.0265, 1.286], (-1.187, -0.0265], (-0.0265, 1.286], (-0.026
5, 1.286], ..., (-1.187, -0.0265], (-1.187, -0.0265], (-2.9499999999999997, -1.18
7], (-0.0265, 1.286], (-1.187, -0.0265]]
Length: 1000
Categories (4, interval[float64]): [(-2.9499999999999997, -1.187] < (-1.187, -0.0
265] < (-0.0265, 1.286] <
                              (1.286, 3.928]]
```

We'll return to cut and qcut later in the chapter during our discussion of aggregation and group operations, as these discretization functions are especially useful for quantile and group analysis.

Detecting and Filtering Outliers

Filtering or transforming outliers is largely a matter of applying array operations. Consider a DataFrame with some normally distributed data:

```
In [94]: data = pd.DataFrame(np.random.randn(1000, 4))

In [95]: data.describe()
Out[95]:
                 0            1            2            3
count  1000.000000  1000.000000  1000.000000  1000.000000
mean      0.049091     0.026112    -0.002544    -0.051827
std       0.996947     1.007458     0.995232     0.998311
min      -3.645860    -3.184377    -3.745356    -3.428254
25%      -0.599807    -0.612162    -0.687373    -0.747478
50%       0.047101    -0.013609    -0.022158    -0.088274
75%       0.756646     0.695298     0.699046     0.623331
max       2.653656     3.525865     2.735527     3.366626
```

Suppose you wanted to find values in one of the columns exceeding 3 in absolute value:

```
In [96]: col = data[2]

In [97]: col[np.abs(col) > 3]
Out[97]:
41     -3.399312
136    -3.745356
Name: 2, dtype: float64
```

To select all rows having a value exceeding 3 or –3, you can use the any method on a boolean DataFrame:

```
In [98]: data[(np.abs(data) > 3).any(1)]
Out[98]:
            0         1         2         3
41   0.457246 -0.025907 -3.399312 -0.974657
60   1.951312  3.260383  0.963301  1.201206
136  0.508391 -0.196713 -3.745356 -1.520113
235 -0.242459 -3.056990  1.918403 -0.578828
258  0.682841  0.326045  0.425384 -3.428254
322  1.179227 -3.184377  1.369891 -1.074833
544 -3.548824  1.553205 -2.186301  1.277104
635 -0.578093  0.193299  1.397822  3.366626
782 -0.207434  3.525865  0.283070  0.544635
803 -3.645860  0.255475 -0.549574 -1.907459
```

Values can be set based on these criteria. Here is code to cap values outside the interval –3 to 3:

```
In [99]: data[np.abs(data) > 3] = np.sign(data) * 3

In [100]: data.describe()
Out[100]:
                 0            1            2            3
count  1000.000000  1000.000000  1000.000000  1000.000000
mean      0.050286     0.025567    -0.001399    -0.051765
std       0.992920     1.004214     0.991414     0.995761
min      -3.000000    -3.000000    -3.000000    -3.000000
25%      -0.599807    -0.612162    -0.687373    -0.747478
50%       0.047101    -0.013609    -0.022158    -0.088274
75%       0.756646     0.695298     0.699046     0.623331
max       2.653656     3.000000     2.735527     3.000000
```

The statement np.sign(data) produces 1 and –1 values based on whether the values in data are positive or negative:

```
In [101]: np.sign(data).head()
Out[101]:
     0    1    2    3
0 -1.0  1.0 -1.0  1.0
1  1.0 -1.0  1.0 -1.0
2  1.0  1.0  1.0 -1.0
3 -1.0 -1.0  1.0 -1.0
4 -1.0  1.0 -1.0 -1.0
```

Permutation and Random Sampling

Permuting (randomly reordering) a Series or the rows in a DataFrame is easy to do using the numpy.random.permutation function. Calling permutation with the length of the axis you want to permute produces an array of integers indicating the new ordering:

```
In [102]: df = pd.DataFrame(np.arange(5 * 4).reshape((5, 4)))

In [103]: sampler = np.random.permutation(5)

In [104]: sampler
Out[104]: array([3, 1, 4, 2, 0])
```

That array can then be used in `iloc`-based indexing or the equivalent `take` function:

```
In [105]: df
Out[105]:
    0   1   2   3
0   0   1   2   3
1   4   5   6   7
2   8   9  10  11
3  12  13  14  15
4  16  17  18  19

In [106]: df.take(sampler)
Out[106]:
    0   1   2   3
3  12  13  14  15
1   4   5   6   7
4  16  17  18  19
2   8   9  10  11
0   0   1   2   3
```

To select a random subset without replacement, you can use the `sample` method on Series and DataFrame:

```
In [107]: df.sample(n=3)
Out[107]:
    0   1   2   3
3  12  13  14  15
4  16  17  18  19
2   8   9  10  11
```

To generate a sample *with* replacement (to allow repeat choices), pass `replace=True` to `sample`:

```
In [108]: choices = pd.Series([5, 7, -1, 6, 4])

In [109]: draws = choices.sample(n=10, replace=True)

In [110]: draws
Out[110]:
4   4
1   7
4   4
2  -1
0   5
3   6
1   7
```

```
4    4
0    5
4    4
dtype: int64
```

Computing Indicator/Dummy Variables

Another type of transformation for statistical modeling or machine learning applications is converting a categorical variable into a "dummy" or "indicator" matrix. If a column in a DataFrame has k distinct values, you would derive a matrix or DataFrame with k columns containing all 1s and 0s. pandas has a `get_dummies` function for doing this, though devising one yourself is not difficult. Let's consider an example DataFrame:

```
In [111]: df = pd.DataFrame({'key': ['b', 'b', 'a', 'c', 'a', 'b'],
   .....:                     'data1': range(6)})

In [112]: pd.get_dummies(df['key'])
Out[112]:
   a  b  c
0  0  1  0
1  0  1  0
2  1  0  0
3  0  0  1
4  1  0  0
5  0  1  0
```

In some cases, you may want to add a prefix to the columns in the indicator DataFrame, which can then be merged with the other data. `get_dummies` has a prefix argument for doing this:

```
In [113]: dummies = pd.get_dummies(df['key'], prefix='key')

In [114]: df_with_dummy = df[['data1']].join(dummies)

In [115]: df_with_dummy
Out[115]:
   data1  key_a  key_b  key_c
0      0      0      1      0
1      1      0      1      0
2      2      1      0      0
3      3      0      0      1
4      4      1      0      0
5      5      0      1      0
```

If a row in a DataFrame belongs to multiple categories, things are a bit more complicated. Let's look at the MovieLens 1M dataset, which is investigated in more detail in Chapter 14:

```
In [116]: mnames = ['movie_id', 'title', 'genres']

In [117]: movies = pd.read_table('datasets/movielens/movies.dat', sep='::',
   .....:                         header=None, names=mnames)

In [118]: movies[:10]
Out[118]:
   movie_id                               title                        genres
0         1                    Toy Story (1995)   Animation|Children's|Comedy
1         2                      Jumanji (1995)  Adventure|Children's|Fantasy
2         3             Grumpier Old Men (1995)                Comedy|Romance
3         4            Waiting to Exhale (1995)                  Comedy|Drama
4         5  Father of the Bride Part II (1995)                        Comedy
5         6                         Heat (1995)         Action|Crime|Thriller
6         7                      Sabrina (1995)                Comedy|Romance
7         8                 Tom and Huck (1995)            Adventure|Children's
8         9                 Sudden Death (1995)                        Action
9        10                    GoldenEye (1995)     Action|Adventure|Thriller
```

Adding indicator variables for each genre requires a little bit of wrangling. First, we extract the list of unique genres in the dataset:

```
In [119]: all_genres = []

In [120]: for x in movies.genres:
   .....:     all_genres.extend(x.split('|'))

In [121]: genres = pd.unique(all_genres)
```

Now we have:

```
In [122]: genres
Out[122]:
array(['Animation', "Children's", 'Comedy', 'Adventure', 'Fantasy',
       'Romance', 'Drama', 'Action', 'Crime', 'Thriller', 'Horror',
       'Sci-Fi', 'Documentary', 'War', 'Musical', 'Mystery', 'Film-Noir',
       'Western'], dtype=object)
```

One way to construct the indicator DataFrame is to start with a DataFrame of all zeros:

```
In [123]: zero_matrix = np.zeros((len(movies), len(genres)))

In [124]: dummies = pd.DataFrame(zero_matrix, columns=genres)
```

Now, iterate through each movie and set entries in each row of dummies to 1. To do this, we use the dummies.columns to compute the column indices for each genre:

```
In [125]: gen = movies.genres[0]

In [126]: gen.split('|')
Out[126]: ['Animation', "Children's", 'Comedy']

In [127]: dummies.columns.get_indexer(gen.split('|'))
Out[127]: array([0, 1, 2])
```

Then, we can use .iloc to set values based on these indices:

```
In [128]: for i, gen in enumerate(movies.genres):
    .....:     indices = dummies.columns.get_indexer(gen.split('|'))
    .....:     dummies.iloc[i, indices] = 1
    .....:
```

Then, as before, you can combine this with movies:

```
In [129]: movies_windic = movies.join(dummies.add_prefix('Genre_'))

In [130]: movies_windic.iloc[0]
Out[130]:
movie_id                                     1
title                          Toy Story (1995)
genres              Animation|Children's|Comedy
Genre_Animation                              1
Genre_Children's                             1
Genre_Comedy                                 1
Genre_Adventure                              0
Genre_Fantasy                                0
Genre_Romance                                0
Genre_Drama                                  0
                              ...
Genre_Crime                                  0
Genre_Thriller                               0
Genre_Horror                                 0
Genre_Sci-Fi                                 0
Genre_Documentary                            0
Genre_War                                    0
Genre_Musical                                0
Genre_Mystery                                0
Genre_Film-Noir                              0
Genre_Western                                0
Name: 0, Length: 21, dtype: object
```

> For much larger data, this method of constructing indicator variables with multiple membership is not especially speedy. It would be better to write a lower-level function that writes directly to a NumPy array, and then wrap the result in a DataFrame.

A useful recipe for statistical applications is to combine get_dummies with a discretization function like cut:

```
In [131]: np.random.seed(12345)

In [132]: values = np.random.rand(10)

In [133]: values
Out[133]:
array([0.9296, 0.3164, 0.1839, 0.2046, 0.5677, 0.5955, 0.9645, 0.6532,
       0.7489, 0.6536])

In [134]: bins = [0, 0.2, 0.4, 0.6, 0.8, 1]

In [135]: pd.get_dummies(pd.cut(values, bins))
Out[135]:
   (0.0, 0.2]  (0.2, 0.4]  (0.4, 0.6]  (0.6, 0.8]  (0.8, 1.0]
0           0           0           0           0           1
1           0           1           0           0           0
2           1           0           0           0           0
3           0           1           0           0           0
4           0           0           1           0           0
5           0           0           1           0           0
6           0           0           0           0           1
7           0           0           0           1           0
8           0           0           0           1           0
9           0           0           0           1           0
```

We set the random seed with `numpy.random.seed` to make the example deterministic. We will look again at `pandas.get_dummies` later in the book.

7.3 String Manipulation

Python has long been a popular raw data manipulation language in part due to its ease of use for string and text processing. Most text operations are made simple with the string object's built-in methods. For more complex pattern matching and text manipulations, regular expressions may be needed. pandas adds to the mix by enabling you to apply string and regular expressions concisely on whole arrays of data, additionally handling the annoyance of missing data.

String Object Methods

In many string munging and scripting applications, built-in string methods are sufficient. As an example, a comma-separated string can be broken into pieces with `split`:

```
In [136]: val = 'a,b,  guido'

In [137]: val.split(',')
Out[137]: ['a', 'b', '  guido']
```

`split` is often combined with `strip` to trim whitespace (including line breaks):

```
In [138]: pieces = [x.strip() for x in val.split(',')]

In [139]: pieces
Out[139]: ['a', 'b', 'guido']
```

These substrings could be concatenated together with a two-colon delimiter using addition:

```
In [140]: first, second, third = pieces

In [141]: first + '::' + second + '::' + third
Out[141]: 'a::b::guido'
```

But this isn't a practical generic method. A faster and more Pythonic way is to pass a list or tuple to the join method on the string '::':

```
In [142]: '::'.join(pieces)
Out[142]: 'a::b::guido'
```

Other methods are concerned with locating substrings. Using Python's in keyword is the best way to detect a substring, though index and find can also be used:

```
In [143]: 'guido' in val
Out[143]: True

In [144]: val.index(',')
Out[144]: 1

In [145]: val.find(':')
Out[145]: -1
```

Note the difference between find and index is that index raises an exception if the string isn't found (versus returning –1):

```
In [146]: val.index(':')
---------------------------------------------------------------------------
ValueError                                Traceback (most recent call last)
<ipython-input-146-280f8b2856ce> in <module>()
----> 1 val.index(':')
ValueError: substring not found
```

Relatedly, count returns the number of occurrences of a particular substring:

```
In [147]: val.count(',')
Out[147]: 2
```

replace will substitute occurrences of one pattern for another. It is commonly used to delete patterns, too, by passing an empty string:

```
In [148]: val.replace(',', '::')
Out[148]: 'a::b::  guido'

In [149]: val.replace(',', '')
Out[149]: 'ab  guido'
```

See Table 7-3 for a listing of some of Python's string methods.

Regular expressions can also be used with many of these operations, as you'll see.

Table 7-3. Python built-in string methods

Method	Description
count	Return the number of non-overlapping occurrences of substring in the string.
endswith	Returns True if string ends with suffix.
startswith	Returns True if string starts with prefix.
join	Use string as delimiter for concatenating a sequence of other strings.
index	Return position of first character in substring if found in the string; raises ValueError if not found.
find	Return position of first character of *first* occurrence of substring in the string; like index, but returns −1 if not found.
rfind	Return position of first character of *last* occurrence of substring in the string; returns −1 if not found.
replace	Replace occurrences of string with another string.
strip, rstrip, lstrip	Trim whitespace, including newlines; equivalent to x.strip() (and rstrip, lstrip, respectively) for each element.
split	Break string into list of substrings using passed delimiter.
lower	Convert alphabet characters to lowercase.
upper	Convert alphabet characters to uppercase.
casefold	Convert characters to lowercase, and convert any region-specific variable character combinations to a common comparable form.
ljust, rjust	Left justify or right justify, respectively; pad opposite side of string with spaces (or some other fill character) to return a string with a minimum width.

Regular Expressions

Regular expressions provide a flexible way to search or match (often more complex) string patterns in text. A single expression, commonly called a *regex*, is a string formed according to the regular expression language. Python's built-in re module is responsible for applying regular expressions to strings; I'll give a number of examples of its use here.

> The art of writing regular expressions could be a chapter of its own and thus is outside the book's scope. There are many excellent tutorials and references available on the internet and in other books.

The re module functions fall into three categories: pattern matching, substitution, and splitting. Naturally these are all related; a regex describes a pattern to locate in the text, which can then be used for many purposes. Let's look at a simple example:

suppose we wanted to split a string with a variable number of whitespace characters (tabs, spaces, and newlines). The regex describing one or more whitespace characters is \s+:

```
In [150]: import re

In [151]: text = "foo    bar\t baz  \tqux"

In [152]: re.split('\s+', text)
Out[152]: ['foo', 'bar', 'baz', 'qux']
```

When you call re.split('\s+', text), the regular expression is first *compiled*, and then its split method is called on the passed text. You can compile the regex yourself with re.compile, forming a reusable regex object:

```
In [153]: regex = re.compile('\s+')

In [154]: regex.split(text)
Out[154]: ['foo', 'bar', 'baz', 'qux']
```

If, instead, you wanted to get a list of all patterns matching the regex, you can use the findall method:

```
In [155]: regex.findall(text)
Out[155]: ['    ', '\t ', ' \t']
```

> To avoid unwanted escaping with \ in a regular expression, use *raw* string literals like r'C:\x' instead of the equivalent 'C:\\x'.

Creating a regex object with re.compile is highly recommended if you intend to apply the same expression to many strings; doing so will save CPU cycles.

match and search are closely related to findall. While findall returns all matches in a string, search returns only the first match. More rigidly, match *only* matches at the beginning of the string. As a less trivial example, let's consider a block of text and a regular expression capable of identifying most email addresses:

```
text = """Dave dave@google.com
Steve steve@gmail.com
Rob rob@gmail.com
Ryan ryan@yahoo.com
"""
pattern = r'[A-Z0-9._%+-]+@[A-Z0-9.-]+\.[A-Z]{2,4}'

# re.IGNORECASE makes the regex case-insensitive
regex = re.compile(pattern, flags=re.IGNORECASE)
```

Using findall on the text produces a list of the email addresses:

```
In [157]: regex.findall(text)
Out[157]:
['dave@google.com',
 'steve@gmail.com',
 'rob@gmail.com',
 'ryan@yahoo.com']
```

search returns a special match object for the first email address in the text. For the preceding regex, the match object can only tell us the start and end position of the pattern in the string:

```
In [158]: m = regex.search(text)
```

```
In [159]: m
Out[159]: <_sre.SRE_Match object; span=(5, 20), match='dave@google.com'>
```

```
In [160]: text[m.start():m.end()]
Out[160]: 'dave@google.com'
```

regex.match returns None, as it only will match if the pattern occurs at the start of the string:

```
In [161]: print(regex.match(text))
None
```

Relatedly, sub will return a new string with occurrences of the pattern replaced by the a new string:

```
In [162]: print(regex.sub('REDACTED', text))
Dave REDACTED
Steve REDACTED
Rob REDACTED
Ryan REDACTED
```

Suppose you wanted to find email addresses and simultaneously segment each address into its three components: username, domain name, and domain suffix. To do this, put parentheses around the parts of the pattern to segment:

```
In [163]: pattern = r'([A-Z0-9._%+-]+)@([A-Z0-9.-]+)\.([A-Z]{2,4})'
```

```
In [164]: regex = re.compile(pattern, flags=re.IGNORECASE)
```

A match object produced by this modified regex returns a tuple of the pattern components with its groups method:

```
In [165]: m = regex.match('wesm@bright.net')
```

```
In [166]: m.groups()
Out[166]: ('wesm', 'bright', 'net')
```

findall returns a list of tuples when the pattern has groups:

```
In [167]: regex.findall(text)
Out[167]:
```

```
[('dave', 'google', 'com'),
 ('steve', 'gmail', 'com'),
 ('rob', 'gmail', 'com'),
 ('ryan', 'yahoo', 'com')]
```

sub also has access to groups in each match using special symbols like \1 and \2. The symbol \1 corresponds to the first matched group, \2 corresponds to the second, and so forth:

```
In [168]: print(regex.sub(r'Username: \1, Domain: \2, Suffix: \3', text))
Dave Username: dave, Domain: google, Suffix: com
Steve Username: steve, Domain: gmail, Suffix: com
Rob Username: rob, Domain: gmail, Suffix: com
Ryan Username: ryan, Domain: yahoo, Suffix: com
```

There is much more to regular expressions in Python, most of which is outside the book's scope. Table 7-4 provides a brief summary.

Table 7-4. Regular expression methods

Method	Description
findall	Return all non-overlapping matching patterns in a string as a list
finditer	Like findall, but returns an iterator
match	Match pattern at start of string and optionally segment pattern components into groups; if the pattern matches, returns a match object, and otherwise None
search	Scan string for match to pattern; returning a match object if so; unlike match, the match can be anywhere in the string as opposed to only at the beginning
split	Break string into pieces at each occurrence of pattern
sub, subn	Replace all (sub) or first n occurrences (subn) of pattern in string with replacement expression; use symbols \1, \2, ... to refer to match group elements in the replacement string

Vectorized String Functions in pandas

Cleaning up a messy dataset for analysis often requires a lot of string munging and regularization. To complicate matters, a column containing strings will sometimes have missing data:

```
In [169]: data = {'Dave': 'dave@google.com', 'Steve': 'steve@gmail.com',
   .....:          'Rob': 'rob@gmail.com', 'Wes': np.nan}

In [170]: data = pd.Series(data)

In [171]: data
Out[171]:
Dave      dave@google.com
Steve     steve@gmail.com
Rob         rob@gmail.com
Wes                   NaN
dtype: object
```

```
In [172]: data.isnull()
Out[172]:
Dave      False
Steve     False
Rob       False
Wes        True
dtype: bool
```

You can apply string and regular expression methods can be applied (passing a `lambda` or other function) to each value using `data.map`, but it will fail on the NA (null) values. To cope with this, Series has array-oriented methods for string operations that skip NA values. These are accessed through Series's `str` attribute; for example, we could check whether each email address has `'gmail'` in it with `str.contains`:

```
In [173]: data.str.contains('gmail')
Out[173]:
Dave      False
Steve      True
Rob        True
Wes         NaN
dtype: object
```

Regular expressions can be used, too, along with any `re` options like IGNORECASE:

```
In [174]: pattern = r'([A-Z0-9._%+-]+)@([A-Z0-9.-]+)\.([A-Z]{2,4})'
```

```
In [175]: data.str.findall(pattern, flags=re.IGNORECASE)
Out[175]:
Dave      [(dave, google, com)]
Steve     [(steve, gmail, com)]
Rob         [(rob, gmail, com)]
Wes                         NaN
dtype: object
```

There are a couple of ways to do vectorized element retrieval. Either use `str.get` or index into the `str` attribute:

```
In [176]: matches = data.str.findall(pattern, flags=re.IGNORECASE).str[0]
```

```
In [177]: matches
Out[177]:
Dave      (dave, google, com)
Steve     (steve, gmail, com)
Rob         (rob, gmail, com)
Wes                       NaN
dtype: object
```

```
In [178]: matches.str.get(1)
Out[178]:
Dave      google
Steve      gmail
Rob        gmail
```

```
Wes         NaN
dtype: object
```

You can similarly slice strings using this syntax:

```
In [179]: data.str[:5]
Out[179]:
Dave     dave@
Steve    steve
Rob      rob@g
Wes        NaN
dtype: object
```

The `extract` method will return the captured groups of a regular expression as a DataFrame:

```
In [180]: data.str.extract(pattern, flags=re.IGNORECASE)
Out[180]:
             0       1    2
Dave      dave  google  com
Steve    steve   gmail  com
Rob        rob   gmail  com
Wes        NaN     NaN  NaN
```

See Table 7-5 for more pandas string methods.

Table 7-5. Partial listing of vectorized string methods

Method	Description
`cat`	Concatenate strings element-wise with optional delimiter
`contains`	Return boolean array if each string contains pattern/regex
`count`	Count occurrences of pattern
`extract`	Use a regular expression with groups to extract one or more strings from a Series of strings; the result will be a DataFrame with one column per group
`endswith`	Equivalent to `x.endswith(pattern)` for each element
`startswith`	Equivalent to `x.startswith(pattern)` for each element
`findall`	Compute list of all occurrences of pattern/regex for each string
`get`	Index into each element (retrieve *i*-th element)
`isalnum`	Equivalent to built-in `str.alnum`
`isalpha`	Equivalent to built-in `str.isalpha`
`isdecimal`	Equivalent to built-in `str.isdecimal`
`isdigit`	Equivalent to built-in `str.isdigit`
`islower`	Equivalent to built-in `str.islower`
`isnumeric`	Equivalent to built-in `str.isnumeric`
`isupper`	Equivalent to built-in `str.isupper`
`join`	Join strings in each element of the Series with passed separator
`len`	Compute length of each string
`lower, upper`	Convert cases; equivalent to `x.lower()` or `x.upper()` for each element

Method	Description
match	Use re.match with the passed regular expression on each element, returning True or False whether it matches.
extract	Extract captured group element (if any) by index from each string
pad	Add whitespace to left, right, or both sides of strings
center	Equivalent to pad(side='both')
repeat	Duplicate values (e.g., s.str.repeat(3) is equivalent to x * 3 for each string)
replace	Replace occurrences of pattern/regex with some other string
slice	Slice each string in the Series
split	Split strings on delimiter or regular expression
strip	Trim whitespace from both sides, including newlines
rstrip	Trim whitespace on right side
lstrip	Trim whitespace on left side

7.4 Conclusion

Effective data preparation can significantly improve productivity by enabling you to spend more time analyzing data and less time getting it ready for analysis. We have explored a number of tools in this chapter, but the coverage here is by no means comprehensive. In the next chapter, we will explore pandas's joining and grouping functionality.

Data Wrangling: Join, Combine, and Reshape

In many applications, data may be spread across a number of files or databases or be arranged in a form that is not easy to analyze. This chapter focuses on tools to help combine, join, and rearrange data.

First, I introduce the concept of *hierarchical indexing* in pandas, which is used extensively in some of these operations. I then dig into the particular data manipulations. You can see various applied usages of these tools in Chapter 14.

8.1 Hierarchical Indexing

Hierarchical indexing is an important feature of pandas that enables you to have multiple (two or more) index *levels* on an axis. Somewhat abstractly, it provides a way for you to work with higher dimensional data in a lower dimensional form. Let's start with a simple example; create a Series with a list of lists (or arrays) as the index:

```
In [11]: data = pd.Series(np.random.randn(9),
   ....:                   index=[['a', 'a', 'a', 'b', 'b', 'c', 'c', 'd', 'd'],
   ....:                          [1, 2, 3, 1, 3, 1, 2, 2, 3]])

In [12]: data
Out[12]:
a  1   -0.204708
   2    0.478943
   3   -0.519439
b  1   -0.555730
   3    1.965781
c  1    1.393406
   2    0.092908
d  2    0.281746
```

```
3    0.769023
dtype: float64
```

What you're seeing is a prettified view of a Series with a MultiIndex as its index. The "gaps" in the index display mean "use the label directly above":

```
In [13]: data.index
Out[13]:
MultiIndex(levels=[['a', 'b', 'c', 'd'], [1, 2, 3]],
           labels=[[0, 0, 0, 1, 1, 2, 2, 3, 3], [0, 1, 2, 0, 2, 0, 1, 1, 2]])
```

With a hierarchically indexed object, so-called *partial* indexing is possible, enabling you to concisely select subsets of the data:

```
In [14]: data['b']
Out[14]:
1   -0.555730
3    1.965781
dtype: float64

In [15]: data['b':'c']
Out[15]:
b  1   -0.555730
   3    1.965781
c  1    1.393406
   2    0.092908
dtype: float64

In [16]: data.loc[['b', 'd']]
Out[16]:
b  1   -0.555730
   3    1.965781
d  2    0.281746
   3    0.769023
dtype: float64
```

Selection is even possible from an "inner" level:

```
In [17]: data.loc[:, 2]
Out[17]:
a    0.478943
c    0.092908
d    0.281746
dtype: float64
```

Hierarchical indexing plays an important role in reshaping data and group-based operations like forming a pivot table. For example, you could rearrange the data into a DataFrame using its unstack method:

```
In [18]: data.unstack()
Out[18]:
          1         2         3
a -0.204708  0.478943 -0.519439
b -0.555730       NaN  1.965781
```

```
c  1.393406  0.092908       NaN
d       NaN  0.281746  0.769023
```

The inverse operation of unstack is stack:

```
In [19]: data.unstack().stack()
Out[19]:
a  1    -0.204708
   2     0.478943
   3    -0.519439
b  1    -0.555730
   3     1.965781
c  1     1.393406
   2     0.092908
d  2     0.281746
   3     0.769023
dtype: float64
```

stack and unstack will be explored in more detail later in this chapter.

With a DataFrame, either axis can have a hierarchical index:

```
In [20]: frame = pd.DataFrame(np.arange(12).reshape((4, 3)),
   ....:                      index=[['a', 'a', 'b', 'b'], [1, 2, 1, 2]],
   ....:                      columns=[['Ohio', 'Ohio', 'Colorado'],
   ....:                               ['Green', 'Red', 'Green']])

In [21]: frame
Out[21]:
     Ohio     Colorado
     Green Red    Green
a 1     0   1        2
  2     3   4        5
b 1     6   7        8
  2     9  10       11
```

The hierarchical levels can have names (as strings or any Python objects). If so, these will show up in the console output:

```
In [22]: frame.index.names = ['key1', 'key2']

In [23]: frame.columns.names = ['state', 'color']

In [24]: frame
Out[24]:
state      Ohio     Colorado
color      Green Red    Green
key1 key2
a    1        0   1        2
     2        3   4        5
b    1        6   7        8
     2        9  10       11
```

Be careful to distinguish the index names `'state'` and `'color'` from the row labels.

With partial column indexing you can similarly select groups of columns:

```
In [25]: frame['Ohio']
Out[25]:
color        Green  Red
key1 key2
a    1           0    1
     2           3    4
b    1           6    7
     2           9   10
```

A MultiIndex can be created by itself and then reused; the columns in the preceding DataFrame with level names could be created like this:

```
pd.MultiIndex.from_arrays([['Ohio', 'Ohio', 'Colorado'],
                           ['Green', 'Red', 'Green']],
                          names=['state', 'color'])
```

Reordering and Sorting Levels

At times you will need to rearrange the order of the levels on an axis or sort the data by the values in one specific level. The `swaplevel` takes two level numbers or names and returns a new object with the levels interchanged (but the data is otherwise unaltered):

```
In [26]: frame.swaplevel('key1', 'key2')
Out[26]:
state        Ohio       Colorado
color        Green Red     Green
key2 key1
1    a           0   1         2
2    a           3   4         5
1    b           6   7         8
2    b           9  10        11
```

`sort_index`, on the other hand, sorts the data using only the values in a single level. When swapping levels, it's not uncommon to also use `sort_index` so that the result is lexicographically sorted by the indicated level:

```
In [27]: frame.sort_index(level=1)
Out[27]:
state        Ohio       Colorado
color        Green Red     Green
key1 key2
a    1           0   1         2
b    1           6   7         8
```

```
a    2        3   4        5
b    2        9  10       11

In [28]: frame.swaplevel(0, 1).sort_index(level=0)
Out[28]:
state        Ohio        Colorado
color       Green Red     Green
key2 key1
1    a         0   1        2
     b         6   7        8
2    a         3   4        5
     b         9  10       11
```

 Data selection performance is much better on hierarchically indexed objects if the index is lexicographically sorted starting with the outermost level—that is, the result of calling `sort_index(level=0)` or `sort_index()`.

Summary Statistics by Level

Many descriptive and summary statistics on DataFrame and Series have a `level` option in which you can specify the level you want to aggregate by on a particular axis. Consider the above DataFrame; we can aggregate by level on either the rows or columns like so:

```
In [29]: frame.sum(level='key2')
Out[29]:
state Ohio        Colorado
color Green Red     Green
key2
1        6   8        10
2       12  14        16

In [30]: frame.sum(level='color', axis=1)
Out[30]:
color        Green  Red
key1 key2
a    1          2    1
     2          8    4
b    1         14    7
     2         20   10
```

Under the hood, this utilizes pandas's groupby machinery, which will be discussed in more detail later in the book.

Indexing with a DataFrame's columns

It's not unusual to want to use one or more columns from a DataFrame as the row index; alternatively, you may wish to move the row index into the DataFrame's columns. Here's an example DataFrame:

```
In [31]: frame = pd.DataFrame({'a': range(7), 'b': range(7, 0, -1),
   ....:                       'c': ['one', 'one', 'one', 'two', 'two',
   ....:                             'two', 'two'],
   ....:                       'd': [0, 1, 2, 0, 1, 2, 3]})

In [32]: frame
Out[32]:
   a  b    c  d
0  0  7  one  0
1  1  6  one  1
2  2  5  one  2
3  3  4  two  0
4  4  3  two  1
5  5  2  two  2
6  6  1  two  3
```

DataFrame's `set_index` function will create a new DataFrame using one or more of its columns as the index:

```
In [33]: frame2 = frame.set_index(['c', 'd'])

In [34]: frame2
Out[34]:
       a  b
c   d
one 0  0  7
    1  1  6
    2  2  5
two 0  3  4
    1  4  3
    2  5  2
    3  6  1
```

By default the columns are removed from the DataFrame, though you can leave them in:

```
In [35]: frame.set_index(['c', 'd'], drop=False)
Out[35]:
       a  b    c  d
c   d
one 0  0  7  one  0
    1  1  6  one  1
    2  2  5  one  2
two 0  3  4  two  0
    1  4  3  two  1
    2  5  2  two  2
    3  6  1  two  3
```

reset_index, on the other hand, does the opposite of set_index; the hierarchical index levels are moved into the columns:

```
In [36]: frame2.reset_index()
Out[36]:
     c  d  a  b
0  one  0  0  7
1  one  1  1  6
2  one  2  2  5
3  two  0  3  4
4  two  1  4  3
5  two  2  5  2
6  two  3  6  1
```

8.2 Combining and Merging Datasets

Data contained in pandas objects can be combined together in a number of ways:

- pandas.merge connects rows in DataFrames based on one or more keys. This will be familiar to users of SQL or other relational databases, as it implements database *join* operations.
- pandas.concat concatenates or "stacks" together objects along an axis.
- The combine_first instance method enables splicing together overlapping data to fill in missing values in one object with values from another.

I will address each of these and give a number of examples. They'll be utilized in examples throughout the rest of the book.

Database-Style DataFrame Joins

Merge or *join* operations combine datasets by linking rows using one or more *keys*. These operations are central to relational databases (e.g., SQL-based). The merge function in pandas is the main entry point for using these algorithms on your data.

Let's start with a simple example:

```
In [37]: df1 = pd.DataFrame({'key': ['b', 'b', 'a', 'c', 'a', 'a', 'b'],
   ....:                      'data1': range(7)})

In [38]: df2 = pd.DataFrame({'key': ['a', 'b', 'd'],
   ....:                      'data2': range(3)})

In [39]: df1
Out[39]:
  key  data1
0   b      0
1   b      1
2   a      2
```

```
3  c     3
4  a     4
5  a     5
6  b     6

In [40]: df2
Out[40]:
  key  data2
0   a      0
1   b      1
2   d      2
```

This is an example of a *many-to-one* join; the data in df1 has multiple rows labeled a
and b, whereas df2 has only one row for each value in the key column. Calling merge
with these objects we obtain:

```
In [41]: pd.merge(df1, df2)
Out[41]:
  key  data1  data2
0   b      0      1
1   b      1      1
2   b      6      1
3   a      2      0
4   a      4      0
5   a      5      0
```

Note that I didn't specify which column to join on. If that information is not specified, merge uses the overlapping column names as the keys. It's a good practice to
specify explicitly, though:

```
In [42]: pd.merge(df1, df2, on='key')
Out[42]:
  key  data1  data2
0   b      0      1
1   b      1      1
2   b      6      1
3   a      2      0
4   a      4      0
5   a      5      0
```

If the column names are different in each object, you can specify them separately:

```
In [43]: df3 = pd.DataFrame({'lkey': ['b', 'b', 'a', 'c', 'a', 'a', 'b'],
   ....:                     'data1': range(7)})

In [44]: df4 = pd.DataFrame({'rkey': ['a', 'b', 'd'],
   ....:                     'data2': range(3)})

In [45]: pd.merge(df3, df4, left_on='lkey', right_on='rkey')
Out[45]:
  lkey  data1 rkey  data2
0    b      0    b      1
1    b      1    b      1
```

```
2   b   6   b   1
3   a   2   a   0
4   a   4   a   0
5   a   5   a   0
```

You may notice that the 'c' and 'd' values and associated data are missing from the result. By default merge does an 'inner' join; the keys in the result are the intersection, or the common set found in both tables. Other possible options are 'left', 'right', and 'outer'. The outer join takes the union of the keys, combining the effect of applying both left and right joins:

```
In [46]: pd.merge(df1, df2, how='outer')
Out[46]:
  key  data1  data2
0   b    0.0    1.0
1   b    1.0    1.0
2   b    6.0    1.0
3   a    2.0    0.0
4   a    4.0    0.0
5   a    5.0    0.0
6   c    3.0    NaN
7   d    NaN    2.0
```

See Table 8-1 for a summary of the options for how.

Table 8-1. Different join types with how argument

Option	Behavior
'inner'	Use only the key combinations observed in both tables
'left'	Use all key combinations found in the left table
'right'	Use all key combinations found in the right table
'outer'	Use all key combinations observed in both tables together

Many-to-many merges have well-defined, though not necessarily intuitive, behavior. Here's an example:

```
In [47]: df1 = pd.DataFrame({'key': ['b', 'b', 'a', 'c', 'a', 'b'],
   ....:                     'data1': range(6)})

In [48]: df2 = pd.DataFrame({'key': ['a', 'b', 'a', 'b', 'd'],
   ....:                     'data2': range(5)})

In [49]: df1
Out[49]:
  key  data1
0   b      0
1   b      1
2   a      2
3   c      3
4   a      4
```

```
 5   b       5

In [50]: df2
Out[50]:
   key  data2
0   a      0
1   b      1
2   a      2
3   b      3
4   d      4

In [51]: pd.merge(df1, df2, on='key', how='left')
Out[51]:
    key  data1  data2
0    b      0    1.0
1    b      0    3.0
2    b      1    1.0
3    b      1    3.0
4    a      2    0.0
5    a      2    2.0
6    c      3    NaN
7    a      4    0.0
8    a      4    2.0
9    b      5    1.0
10   b      5    3.0
```

Many-to-many joins form the Cartesian product of the rows. Since there were three 'b' rows in the left DataFrame and two in the right one, there are six 'b' rows in the result. The join method only affects the distinct key values appearing in the result:

```
In [52]: pd.merge(df1, df2, how='inner')
Out[52]:
   key  data1  data2
0   b      0      1
1   b      0      3
2   b      1      1
3   b      1      3
4   b      5      1
5   b      5      3
6   a      2      0
7   a      2      2
8   a      4      0
9   a      4      2
```

To merge with multiple keys, pass a list of column names:

```
In [53]: left = pd.DataFrame({'key1': ['foo', 'foo', 'bar'],
   ....:                      'key2': ['one', 'two', 'one'],
   ....:                      'lval': [1, 2, 3]})

In [54]: right = pd.DataFrame({'key1': ['foo', 'foo', 'bar', 'bar'],
   ....:                       'key2': ['one', 'one', 'one', 'two'],
   ....:                       'rval': [4, 5, 6, 7]})
```

```
In [55]: pd.merge(left, right, on=['key1', 'key2'], how='outer')
Out[55]:
  key1 key2  lval  rval
0  foo  one   1.0   4.0
1  foo  one   1.0   5.0
2  foo  two   2.0   NaN
3  bar  one   3.0   6.0
4  bar  two   NaN   7.0
```

To determine which key combinations will appear in the result depending on the choice of merge method, think of the multiple keys as forming an array of tuples to be used as a single join key (even though it's not actually implemented that way).

 When you're joining columns-on-columns, the indexes on the passed DataFrame objects are discarded.

A last issue to consider in merge operations is the treatment of overlapping column names. While you can address the overlap manually (see the earlier section on renaming axis labels), merge has a suffixes option for specifying strings to append to overlapping names in the left and right DataFrame objects:

```
In [56]: pd.merge(left, right, on='key1')
Out[56]:
  key1 key2_x  lval key2_y  rval
0  foo    one     1    one     4
1  foo    one     1    one     5
2  foo    two     2    one     4
3  foo    two     2    one     5
4  bar    one     3    one     6
5  bar    one     3    two     7

In [57]: pd.merge(left, right, on='key1', suffixes=('_left', '_right'))
Out[57]:
  key1 key2_left  lval key2_right  rval
0  foo       one     1        one     4
1  foo       one     1        one     5
2  foo       two     2        one     4
3  foo       two     2        one     5
4  bar       one     3        one     6
5  bar       one     3        two     7
```

See Table 8-2 for an argument reference on merge. Joining using the DataFrame's row index is the subject of the next section.

Table 8-2. merge function arguments

Argument	Description
left	DataFrame to be merged on the left side.
right	DataFrame to be merged on the right side.
how	One of 'inner', 'outer', 'left', or 'right'; defaults to 'inner'.
on	Column names to join on. Must be found in both DataFrame objects. If not specified and no other join keys given, will use the intersection of the column names in left and right as the join keys.
left_on	Columns in left DataFrame to use as join keys.
right_on	Analogous to left_on for left DataFrame.
left_index	Use row index in left as its join key (or keys, if a MultiIndex).
right_index	Analogous to left_index.
sort	Sort merged data lexicographically by join keys; True by default (disable to get better performance in some cases on large datasets).
suffixes	Tuple of string values to append to column names in case of overlap; defaults to ('_x', '_y') (e.g., if 'data' in both DataFrame objects, would appear as 'data_x' and 'data_y' in result).
copy	If False, avoid copying data into resulting data structure in some exceptional cases; by default always copies.
indicator	Adds a special column _merge that indicates the source of each row; values will be 'left_only', 'right_only', or 'both' based on the origin of the joined data in each row.

Merging on Index

In some cases, the merge key(s) in a DataFrame will be found in its index. In this case, you can pass left_index=True or right_index=True (or both) to indicate that the index should be used as the merge key:

```
In [58]: left1 = pd.DataFrame({'key': ['a', 'b', 'a', 'a', 'b', 'c'],
   ....:                        'value': range(6)})

In [59]: right1 = pd.DataFrame({'group_val': [3.5, 7]}, index=['a', 'b'])

In [60]: left1
Out[60]:
  key  value
0   a      0
1   b      1
2   a      2
3   a      3
4   b      4
5   c      5

In [61]: right1
Out[61]:
   group_val
a        3.5
b        7.0
```

```
In [62]: pd.merge(left1, right1, left_on='key', right_index=True)
Out[62]:
  key  value  group_val
0   a      0        3.5
2   a      2        3.5
3   a      3        3.5
1   b      1        7.0
4   b      4        7.0
```

Since the default merge method is to intersect the join keys, you can instead form the union of them with an outer join:

```
In [63]: pd.merge(left1, right1, left_on='key', right_index=True, how='outer')
Out[63]:
  key  value  group_val
0   a      0        3.5
2   a      2        3.5
3   a      3        3.5
1   b      1        7.0
4   b      4        7.0
5   c      5        NaN
```

With hierarchically indexed data, things are more complicated, as joining on index is implicitly a multiple-key merge:

```
In [64]: lefth = pd.DataFrame({'key1': ['Ohio', 'Ohio', 'Ohio',
   ....:                                 'Nevada', 'Nevada'],
   ....:                        'key2': [2000, 2001, 2002, 2001, 2002],
   ....:                        'data': np.arange(5.)})

In [65]: righth = pd.DataFrame(np.arange(12).reshape((6, 2)),
   ....:                        index=[['Nevada', 'Nevada', 'Ohio', 'Ohio',
   ....:                                'Ohio', 'Ohio'],
   ....:                               [2001, 2000, 2000, 2000, 2001, 2002]],
   ....:                        columns=['event1', 'event2'])

In [66]: lefth
Out[66]:
     key1  key2  data
0    Ohio  2000   0.0
1    Ohio  2001   1.0
2    Ohio  2002   2.0
3  Nevada  2001   3.0
4  Nevada  2002   4.0

In [67]: righth
Out[67]:
             event1  event2
Nevada 2001       0       1
       2000       2       3
Ohio   2000       4       5
       2000       6       7
```

```
      2001      8      9
      2002     10     11
```

In this case, you have to indicate multiple columns to merge on as a list (note the handling of duplicate index values with how='outer'):

```
In [68]: pd.merge(lefth, righth, left_on=['key1', 'key2'], right_index=True)
Out[68]:
    key1  key2  data  event1  event2
0   Ohio  2000   0.0       4       5
0   Ohio  2000   0.0       6       7
1   Ohio  2001   1.0       8       9
2   Ohio  2002   2.0      10      11
3 Nevada  2001   3.0       0       1

In [69]: pd.merge(lefth, righth, left_on=['key1', 'key2'],
   ....:          right_index=True, how='outer')
Out[69]:
    key1  key2  data  event1  event2
0   Ohio  2000   0.0     4.0     5.0
0   Ohio  2000   0.0     6.0     7.0
1   Ohio  2001   1.0     8.0     9.0
2   Ohio  2002   2.0    10.0    11.0
3 Nevada  2001   3.0     0.0     1.0
4 Nevada  2002   4.0     NaN     NaN
4 Nevada  2000   NaN     2.0     3.0
```

Using the indexes of both sides of the merge is also possible:

```
In [70]: left2 = pd.DataFrame([[1., 2.], [3., 4.], [5., 6.]],
   ....:                       index=['a', 'c', 'e'],
   ....:                       columns=['Ohio', 'Nevada'])

In [71]: right2 = pd.DataFrame([[7., 8.], [9., 10.], [11., 12.], [13, 14]],
   ....:                        index=['b', 'c', 'd', 'e'],
   ....:                        columns=['Missouri', 'Alabama'])

In [72]: left2
Out[72]:
   Ohio  Nevada
a   1.0     2.0
c   3.0     4.0
e   5.0     6.0

In [73]: right2
Out[73]:
   Missouri  Alabama
b       7.0      8.0
c       9.0     10.0
d      11.0     12.0
e      13.0     14.0

In [74]: pd.merge(left2, right2, how='outer', left_index=True, right_index=True)
```

```
     Ohio  Nevada  Missouri  Alabama
a    1.0     2.0       NaN      NaN
b    NaN     NaN       7.0      8.0
c    3.0     4.0       9.0     10.0
d    NaN     NaN      11.0     12.0
e    5.0     6.0      13.0     14.0
```

DataFrame has a convenient `join` instance for merging by index. It can also be used to combine together many DataFrame objects having the same or similar indexes but non-overlapping columns. In the prior example, we could have written:

```
In [75]: left2.join(right2, how='outer')
Out[75]:
     Ohio  Nevada  Missouri  Alabama
a    1.0     2.0       NaN      NaN
b    NaN     NaN       7.0      8.0
c    3.0     4.0       9.0     10.0
d    NaN     NaN      11.0     12.0
e    5.0     6.0      13.0     14.0
```

In part for legacy reasons (i.e., much earlier versions of pandas), DataFrame's `join` method performs a left join on the join keys, exactly preserving the left frame's row index. It also supports joining the index of the passed DataFrame on one of the columns of the calling DataFrame:

```
In [76]: left1.join(right1, on='key')
Out[76]:
  key  value  group_val
0   a      0        3.5
1   b      1        7.0
2   a      2        3.5
3   a      3        3.5
4   b      4        7.0
5   c      5        NaN
```

Lastly, for simple index-on-index merges, you can pass a list of DataFrames to `join` as an alternative to using the more general `concat` function described in the next section:

```
In [77]: another = pd.DataFrame([[7., 8.], [9., 10.], [11., 12.], [16., 17.]],
   ....:                        index=['a', 'c', 'e', 'f'],
   ....:                        columns=['New York', 'Oregon'])

In [78]: another
Out[78]:
     New York  Oregon
a         7.0     8.0
c         9.0    10.0
e        11.0    12.0
f        16.0    17.0
```

```
In [79]: left2.join([right2, another])
Out[79]:
    Ohio  Nevada  Missouri  Alabama  New York  Oregon
a    1.0     2.0       NaN      NaN       7.0     8.0
c    3.0     4.0       9.0     10.0       9.0    10.0
e    5.0     6.0      13.0     14.0      11.0    12.0

In [80]: left2.join([right2, another], how='outer')
Out[80]:
    Ohio  Nevada  Missouri  Alabama  New York  Oregon
a    1.0     2.0       NaN      NaN       7.0     8.0
b    NaN     NaN       7.0      8.0       NaN     NaN
c    3.0     4.0       9.0     10.0       9.0    10.0
d    NaN     NaN      11.0     12.0       NaN     NaN
e    5.0     6.0      13.0     14.0      11.0    12.0
f    NaN     NaN       NaN      NaN      16.0    17.0
```

Concatenating Along an Axis

Another kind of data combination operation is referred to interchangeably as concatenation, binding, or stacking. NumPy's `concatenate` function can do this with NumPy arrays:

```
In [81]: arr = np.arange(12).reshape((3, 4))

In [82]: arr
Out[82]:
array([[ 0,  1,  2,  3],
       [ 4,  5,  6,  7],
       [ 8,  9, 10, 11]])

In [83]: np.concatenate([arr, arr], axis=1)
Out[83]:
array([[ 0,  1,  2,  3,  0,  1,  2,  3],
       [ 4,  5,  6,  7,  4,  5,  6,  7],
       [ 8,  9, 10, 11,  8,  9, 10, 11]])
```

In the context of pandas objects such as Series and DataFrame, having labeled axes enable you to further generalize array concatenation. In particular, you have a number of additional things to think about:

- If the objects are indexed differently on the other axes, should we combine the distinct elements in these axes or use only the shared values (the intersection)?

- Do the concatenated chunks of data need to be identifiable in the resulting object?

- Does the "concatenation axis" contain data that needs to be preserved? In many cases, the default integer labels in a DataFrame are best discarded during concatenation.

The concat function in pandas provides a consistent way to address each of these concerns. I'll give a number of examples to illustrate how it works. Suppose we have three Series with no index overlap:

```
In [84]: s1 = pd.Series([0, 1], index=['a', 'b'])

In [85]: s2 = pd.Series([2, 3, 4], index=['c', 'd', 'e'])

In [86]: s3 = pd.Series([5, 6], index=['f', 'g'])
```

Calling concat with these objects in a list glues together the values and indexes:

```
In [87]: pd.concat([s1, s2, s3])
Out[87]:
a    0
b    1
c    2
d    3
e    4
f    5
g    6
dtype: int64
```

By default concat works along axis=0, producing another Series. If you pass axis=1, the result will instead be a DataFrame (axis=1 is the columns):

```
In [88]: pd.concat([s1, s2, s3], axis=1)
Out[88]:
     0    1    2
a  0.0  NaN  NaN
b  1.0  NaN  NaN
c  NaN  2.0  NaN
d  NaN  3.0  NaN
e  NaN  4.0  NaN
f  NaN  NaN  5.0
g  NaN  NaN  6.0
```

In this case there is no overlap on the other axis, which as you can see is the sorted union (the 'outer' join) of the indexes. You can instead intersect them by passing join='inner':

```
In [89]: s4 = pd.concat([s1, s3])

In [90]: s4
Out[90]:
a    0
b    1
f    5
g    6
dtype: int64

In [91]: pd.concat([s1, s4], axis=1)
Out[91]:
```

```
     0  1
a  0.0  0
b  1.0  1
f  NaN  5
g  NaN  6

In [92]: pd.concat([s1, s4], axis=1, join='inner')
Out[92]:
   0  1
a  0  0
b  1  1
```

In this last example, the 'f' and 'g' labels disappeared because of the join='inner' option.

You can even specify the axes to be used on the other axes with join_axes:

```
In [93]: pd.concat([s1, s4], axis=1, join_axes=[['a', 'c', 'b', 'e']])
Out[93]:
     0    1
a  0.0  0.0
c  NaN  NaN
b  1.0  1.0
e  NaN  NaN
```

A potential issue is that the concatenated pieces are not identifiable in the result. Suppose instead you wanted to create a hierarchical index on the concatenation axis. To do this, use the keys argument:

```
In [94]: result = pd.concat([s1, s1, s3], keys=['one', 'two', 'three'])

In [95]: result
Out[95]:
one    a    0
       b    1
two    a    0
       b    1
three  f    5
       g    6
dtype: int64

In [96]: result.unstack()
Out[96]:
         a    b    f    g
one    0.0  1.0  NaN  NaN
two    0.0  1.0  NaN  NaN
three  NaN  NaN  5.0  6.0
```

In the case of combining Series along axis=1, the keys become the DataFrame column headers:

```
In [97]: pd.concat([s1, s2, s3], axis=1, keys=['one', 'two', 'three'])
Out[97]:
```

```
      one  two  three
a     0.0  NaN    NaN
b     1.0  NaN    NaN
c     NaN  2.0    NaN
d     NaN  3.0    NaN
e     NaN  4.0    NaN
f     NaN  NaN    5.0
g     NaN  NaN    6.0
```

The same logic extends to DataFrame objects:

```
In [98]: df1 = pd.DataFrame(np.arange(6).reshape(3, 2), index=['a', 'b', 'c'],
   ....:                     columns=['one', 'two'])

In [99]: df2 = pd.DataFrame(5 + np.arange(4).reshape(2, 2), index=['a', 'c'],
   ....:                     columns=['three', 'four'])

In [100]: df1
Out[100]:
   one  two
a    0    1
b    2    3
c    4    5

In [101]: df2
Out[101]:
   three  four
a      5     6
c      7     8

In [102]: pd.concat([df1, df2], axis=1, keys=['level1', 'level2'])
Out[102]:
  level1      level2
     one two  three four
a      0   1    5.0  6.0
b      2   3    NaN  NaN
c      4   5    7.0  8.0
```

If you pass a dict of objects instead of a list, the dict's keys will be used for the keys option:

```
In [103]: pd.concat({'level1': df1, 'level2': df2}, axis=1)
Out[103]:
  level1      level2
     one two  three four
a      0   1    5.0  6.0
b      2   3    NaN  NaN
c      4   5    7.0  8.0
```

There are additional arguments governing how the hierarchical index is created (see Table 8-3). For example, we can name the created axis levels with the names argument:

```
In [104]: pd.concat([df1, df2], axis=1, keys=['level1', 'level2'],
   .....:                names=['upper', 'lower'])
Out[104]:
upper level1     level2
lower    one two  three four
a          0   1    5.0  6.0
b          2   3    NaN  NaN
c          4   5    7.0  8.0
```

A last consideration concerns DataFrames in which the row index does not contain
any relevant data:

```
In [105]: df1 = pd.DataFrame(np.random.randn(3, 4), columns=['a', 'b', 'c', 'd'])

In [106]: df2 = pd.DataFrame(np.random.randn(2, 3), columns=['b', 'd', 'a'])

In [107]: df1
Out[107]:
          a         b         c         d
0  1.246435  1.007189 -1.296221  0.274992
1  0.228913  1.352917  0.886429 -2.001637
2 -0.371843  1.669025 -0.438570 -0.539741

In [108]: df2
Out[108]:
          b         d         a
0  0.476985  3.248944 -1.021228
1 -0.577087  0.124121  0.302614
```

In this case, you can pass `ignore_index=True`:

```
In [109]: pd.concat([df1, df2], ignore_index=True)
Out[109]:
          a         b         c         d
0  1.246435  1.007189 -1.296221  0.274992
1  0.228913  1.352917  0.886429 -2.001637
2 -0.371843  1.669025 -0.438570 -0.539741
3 -1.021228  0.476985       NaN  3.248944
4  0.302614 -0.577087       NaN  0.124121
```

Table 8-3. concat function arguments

Argument	Description
objs	List or dict of pandas objects to be concatenated; this is the only required argument
axis	Axis to concatenate along; defaults to 0 (along rows)
join	Either 'inner' or 'outer' ('outer' by default); whether to intersection (inner) or union (outer) together indexes along the other axes
join_axes	Specific indexes to use for the other $n-1$ axes instead of performing union/intersection logic
keys	Values to associate with objects being concatenated, forming a hierarchical index along the concatenation axis; can either be a list or array of arbitrary values, an array of tuples, or a list of arrays (if multiple-level arrays passed in levels)

Argument	Description
levels	Specific indexes to use as hierarchical index level or levels if keys passed
names	Names for created hierarchical levels if keys and/or levels passed
verify_integrity	Check new axis in concatenated object for duplicates and raise exception if so; by default (False) allows duplicates
ignore_index	Do not preserve indexes along concatenation axis, instead producing a new range(total_length) index

Combining Data with Overlap

There is another data combination situation that can't be expressed as either a merge or concatenation operation. You may have two datasets whose indexes overlap in full or part. As a motivating example, consider NumPy's where function, which performs the array-oriented equivalent of an if-else expression:

```
In [110]: a = pd.Series([np.nan, 2.5, 0.0, 3.5, 4.5, np.nan],
   .....:               index=['f', 'e', 'd', 'c', 'b', 'a'])

In [111]: b = pd.Series([0., np.nan, 2., np.nan, np.nan, 5.],
   .....:               index=['a', 'b', 'c', 'd', 'e', 'f'])

In [112]: a
Out[112]:
f    NaN
e    2.5
d    0.0
c    3.5
b    4.5
a    NaN
dtype: float64

In [113]: b
Out[113]:
a    0.0
b    NaN
c    2.0
d    NaN
e    NaN
f    5.0
dtype: float64

In [114]: np.where(pd.isnull(a), b, a)
Out[114]: array([0. , 2.5, 0. , 3.5, 4.5, 5. ])
```

Series has a combine_first method, which performs the equivalent of this operation along with pandas's usual data alignment logic:

```
In [115]: b.combine_first(a)
Out[115]:
a    0.0
```

```
b    4.5
c    2.0
d    0.0
e    2.5
f    5.0
dtype: float64
```

With DataFrames, `combine_first` does the same thing column by column, so you can think of it as "patching" missing data in the calling object with data from the object you pass:

```
In [116]: df1 = pd.DataFrame({'a': [1., np.nan, 5., np.nan],
   .....:                     'b': [np.nan, 2., np.nan, 6.],
   .....:                     'c': range(2, 18, 4)})

In [117]: df2 = pd.DataFrame({'a': [5., 4., np.nan, 3., 7.],
   .....:                     'b': [np.nan, 3., 4., 6., 8.]})

In [118]: df1
Out[118]:
     a    b   c
0  1.0  NaN   2
1  NaN  2.0   6
2  5.0  NaN  10
3  NaN  6.0  14

In [119]: df2
Out[119]:
     a    b
0  5.0  NaN
1  4.0  3.0
2  NaN  4.0
3  3.0  6.0
4  7.0  8.0

In [120]: df1.combine_first(df2)
Out[120]:
     a    b     c
0  1.0  NaN   2.0
1  4.0  2.0   6.0
2  5.0  4.0  10.0
3  3.0  6.0  14.0
4  7.0  8.0   NaN
```

8.3 Reshaping and Pivoting

There are a number of basic operations for rearranging tabular data. These are alternatingly referred to as *reshape* or *pivot* operations.

Reshaping with Hierarchical Indexing

Hierarchical indexing provides a consistent way to rearrange data in a DataFrame. There are two primary actions:

stack
> This "rotates" or pivots from the columns in the data to the rows

unstack
> This pivots from the rows into the columns

I'll illustrate these operations through a series of examples. Consider a small Data-Frame with string arrays as row and column indexes:

```
In [121]: data = pd.DataFrame(np.arange(6).reshape((2, 3)),
   .....:                     index=pd.Index(['Ohio', 'Colorado'], name='state'),
   .....:                     columns=pd.Index(['one', 'two', 'three'],
   .....:                     name='number'))

In [122]: data
Out[122]:
number    one  two  three
state
Ohio        0    1      2
Colorado    3    4      5
```

Using the stack method on this data pivots the columns into the rows, producing a Series:

```
In [123]: result = data.stack()

In [124]: result
Out[124]:
state     number
Ohio      one       0
          two       1
          three     2
Colorado  one       3
          two       4
          three     5
dtype: int64
```

From a hierarchically indexed Series, you can rearrange the data back into a Data-Frame with unstack:

```
In [125]: result.unstack()
Out[125]:
number    one  two  three
state
Ohio        0    1      2
Colorado    3    4      5
```

By default the innermost level is unstacked (same with `stack`). You can unstack a different level by passing a level number or name:

```
In [126]: result.unstack(0)
Out[126]:
state   Ohio  Colorado
number
one        0         3
two        1         4
three      2         5

In [127]: result.unstack('state')
Out[127]:
state   Ohio  Colorado
number
one        0         3
two        1         4
three      2         5
```

Unstacking might introduce missing data if all of the values in the level aren't found in each of the subgroups:

```
In [128]: s1 = pd.Series([0, 1, 2, 3], index=['a', 'b', 'c', 'd'])

In [129]: s2 = pd.Series([4, 5, 6], index=['c', 'd', 'e'])

In [130]: data2 = pd.concat([s1, s2], keys=['one', 'two'])

In [131]: data2
Out[131]:
one  a    0
     b    1
     c    2
     d    3
two  c    4
     d    5
     e    6
dtype: int64

In [132]: data2.unstack()
Out[132]:
       a    b    c    d    e
one  0.0  1.0  2.0  3.0  NaN
two  NaN  NaN  4.0  5.0  6.0
```

Stacking filters out missing data by default, so the operation is more easily invertible:

```
In [133]: data2.unstack()
Out[133]:
       a    b    c    d    e
one  0.0  1.0  2.0  3.0  NaN
two  NaN  NaN  4.0  5.0  6.0
```

```
In [134]: data2.unstack().stack()
Out[134]:
one  a    0.0
     b    1.0
     c    2.0
     d    3.0
two  c    4.0
     d    5.0
     e    6.0
dtype: float64

In [135]: data2.unstack().stack(dropna=False)
Out[135]:
one  a    0.0
     b    1.0
     c    2.0
     d    3.0
     e    NaN
two  a    NaN
     b    NaN
     c    4.0
     d    5.0
     e    6.0
dtype: float64
```

When you unstack in a DataFrame, the level unstacked becomes the lowest level in the result:

```
In [136]: df = pd.DataFrame({'left': result, 'right': result + 5},
   .....:                   columns=pd.Index(['left', 'right'], name='side'))

In [137]: df
Out[137]:
side              left  right
state    number
Ohio     one         0      5
         two         1      6
         three       2      7
Colorado one         3      8
         two         4      9
         three       5     10

In [138]: df.unstack('state')
Out[138]:
side    left          right
state   Ohio Colorado  Ohio Colorado
number
one        0        3     5        8
two        1        4     6        9
three      2        5     7       10
```

When calling stack, we can indicate the name of the axis to stack:

```
In [139]: df.unstack('state').stack('side')
Out[139]:
state          Colorado  Ohio
number side
one    left           3     0
       right          8     5
two    left           4     1
       right          9     6
three  left           5     2
       right         10     7
```

Pivoting "Long" to "Wide" Format

A common way to store multiple time series in databases and CSV is in so-called *long* or *stacked* format. Let's load some example data and do a small amount of time series wrangling and other data cleaning:

```
In [140]: data = pd.read_csv('examples/macrodata.csv')

In [141]: data.head()
Out[141]:
     year  quarter   realgdp  realcons  realinv  realgovt  realdpi    cpi  \
0  1959.0      1.0  2710.349    1707.4  286.898   470.045   1886.9  28.98
1  1959.0      2.0  2778.801    1733.7  310.859   481.301   1919.7  29.15
2  1959.0      3.0  2775.488    1751.8  289.226   491.260   1916.4  29.35
3  1959.0      4.0  2785.204    1753.7  299.356   484.052   1931.3  29.37
4  1960.0      1.0  2847.699    1770.5  331.722   462.199   1955.5  29.54
      m1  tbilrate  unemp      pop  infl  realint
0  139.7      2.82    5.8  177.146  0.00     0.00
1  141.7      3.08    5.1  177.830  2.34     0.74
2  140.5      3.82    5.3  178.657  2.74     1.09
3  140.0      4.33    5.6  179.386  0.27     4.06
4  139.6      3.50    5.2  180.007  2.31     1.19

In [142]: periods = pd.PeriodIndex(year=data.year, quarter=data.quarter,
   .....:                          name='date')

In [143]: columns = pd.Index(['realgdp', 'infl', 'unemp'], name='item')

In [144]: data = data.reindex(columns=columns)

In [145]: data.index = periods.to_timestamp('D', 'end')

In [146]: ldata = data.stack().reset_index().rename(columns={0: 'value'})
```

We will look at PeriodIndex a bit more closely in Chapter 11. In short, it combines the year and quarter columns to create a kind of time interval type.

Now, ldata looks like:

```
In [147]: ldata[:10]
Out[147]:
```

```
                          date       item      value
0 1959-03-31 23:59:59.999999999   realgdp   2710.349
1 1959-03-31 23:59:59.999999999      infl      0.000
2 1959-03-31 23:59:59.999999999     unemp      5.800
3 1959-06-30 23:59:59.999999999   realgdp   2778.801
4 1959-06-30 23:59:59.999999999      infl      2.340
5 1959-06-30 23:59:59.999999999     unemp      5.100
6 1959-09-30 23:59:59.999999999   realgdp   2775.488
7 1959-09-30 23:59:59.999999999      infl      2.740
8 1959-09-30 23:59:59.999999999     unemp      5.300
9 1959-12-31 23:59:59.999999999   realgdp   2785.204
```

This is the so-called *long* format for multiple time series, or other observational data with two or more keys (here, our keys are date and item). Each row in the table represents a single observation.

Data is frequently stored this way in relational databases like MySQL, as a fixed schema (column names and data types) allows the number of distinct values in the item column to change as data is added to the table. In the previous example, date and item would usually be the primary keys (in relational database parlance), offering both relational integrity and easier joins. In some cases, the data may be more difficult to work with in this format; you might prefer to have a DataFrame containing one column per distinct item value indexed by timestamps in the date column. Data-Frame's pivot method performs exactly this transformation:

```
In [148]: pivoted = ldata.pivot('date', 'item', 'value')

In [149]: pivoted
Out[149]:
item                              infl    realgdp   unemp
date
1959-03-31 23:59:59.999999999     0.00   2710.349     5.8
1959-06-30 23:59:59.999999999     2.34   2778.801     5.1
1959-09-30 23:59:59.999999999     2.74   2775.488     5.3
1959-12-31 23:59:59.999999999     0.27   2785.204     5.6
1960-03-31 23:59:59.999999999     2.31   2847.699     5.2
1960-06-30 23:59:59.999999999     0.14   2834.390     5.2
1960-09-30 23:59:59.999999999     2.70   2839.022     5.6
1960-12-31 23:59:59.999999999     1.21   2802.616     6.3
1961-03-31 23:59:59.999999999    -0.40   2819.264     6.8
1961-06-30 23:59:59.999999999     1.47   2872.005     7.0
...                                ...        ...     ...
2007-06-30 23:59:59.999999999     2.75  13203.977     4.5
2007-09-30 23:59:59.999999999     3.45  13321.109     4.7
2007-12-31 23:59:59.999999999     6.38  13391.249     4.8
2008-03-31 23:59:59.999999999     2.82  13366.865     4.9
2008-06-30 23:59:59.999999999     8.53  13415.266     5.4
2008-09-30 23:59:59.999999999    -3.16  13324.600     6.0
2008-12-31 23:59:59.999999999    -8.79  13141.920     6.9
2009-03-31 23:59:59.999999999     0.94  12925.410     8.1
2009-06-30 23:59:59.999999999     3.37  12901.504     9.2
```

```
2009-09-30 23:59:59.999999999  3.56  12990.341  9.6
[203 rows x 3 columns]
```

The first two values passed are the columns to be used respectively as the row and column index, then finally an optional value column to fill the DataFrame. Suppose you had two value columns that you wanted to reshape simultaneously:

```
In [150]: ldata['value2'] = np.random.randn(len(ldata))

In [151]: ldata[:10]
Out[151]:
                        date     item     value      value2
0 1959-03-31 23:59:59.999999999  realgdp  2710.349   0.523772
1 1959-03-31 23:59:59.999999999     infl     0.000   0.000940
2 1959-03-31 23:59:59.999999999    unemp     5.800   1.343810
3 1959-06-30 23:59:59.999999999  realgdp  2778.801  -0.713544
4 1959-06-30 23:59:59.999999999     infl     2.340  -0.831154
5 1959-06-30 23:59:59.999999999    unemp     5.100  -2.370232
6 1959-09-30 23:59:59.999999999  realgdp  2775.488  -1.860761
7 1959-09-30 23:59:59.999999999     infl     2.740  -0.860757
8 1959-09-30 23:59:59.999999999    unemp     5.300   0.560145
9 1959-12-31 23:59:59.999999999  realgdp  2785.204  -1.265934
```

By omitting the last argument, you obtain a DataFrame with hierarchical columns:

```
In [152]: pivoted = ldata.pivot('date', 'item')

In [153]: pivoted[:5]
Out[153]:
                               value                        value2            \
item                            infl   realgdp unemp       infl    realgdp
date
1959-03-31 23:59:59.999999999   0.00  2710.349   5.8   0.000940   0.523772
1959-06-30 23:59:59.999999999   2.34  2778.801   5.1  -0.831154  -0.713544
1959-09-30 23:59:59.999999999   2.74  2775.488   5.3  -0.860757  -1.860761
1959-12-31 23:59:59.999999999   0.27  2785.204   5.6   0.119827  -1.265934
1960-03-31 23:59:59.999999999   2.31  2847.699   5.2  -2.359419   0.332883

item                                  unemp
date
1959-03-31 23:59:59.999999999       1.343810
1959-06-30 23:59:59.999999999      -2.370232
1959-09-30 23:59:59.999999999       0.560145
1959-12-31 23:59:59.999999999      -1.063512
1960-03-31 23:59:59.999999999      -0.199543

In [154]: pivoted['value'][:5]
Out[154]:
item                            infl   realgdp unemp
date
1959-03-31 23:59:59.999999999   0.00  2710.349   5.8
1959-06-30 23:59:59.999999999   2.34  2778.801   5.1
1959-09-30 23:59:59.999999999   2.74  2775.488   5.3
```

```
1959-12-31 23:59:59.999999999  0.27  2785.204    5.6
1960-03-31 23:59:59.999999999  2.31  2847.699    5.2
```

Note that `pivot` is equivalent to creating a hierarchical index using `set_index` followed by a call to `unstack`:

```
In [155]: unstacked = ldata.set_index(['date', 'item']).unstack('item')

In [156]: unstacked[:7]
Out[156]:
                                   value                     value2             \
item                                infl   realgdp unemp      infl   realgdp
date
1959-03-31 23:59:59.999999999       0.00  2710.349   5.8  0.000940  0.523772
1959-06-30 23:59:59.999999999       2.34  2778.801   5.1 -0.831154 -0.713544
1959-09-30 23:59:59.999999999       2.74  2775.488   5.3 -0.860757 -1.860761
1959-12-31 23:59:59.999999999       0.27  2785.204   5.6  0.119827 -1.265934
1960-03-31 23:59:59.999999999       2.31  2847.699   5.2 -2.359419  0.332883
1960-06-30 23:59:59.999999999       0.14  2834.390   5.2 -0.970736 -1.541996
1960-09-30 23:59:59.999999999       2.70  2839.022   5.6  0.377984  0.286350

item                                 unemp
date
1959-03-31 23:59:59.999999999     1.343810
1959-06-30 23:59:59.999999999    -2.370232
1959-09-30 23:59:59.999999999     0.560145
1959-12-31 23:59:59.999999999    -1.063512
1960-03-31 23:59:59.999999999    -0.199543
1960-06-30 23:59:59.999999999    -1.307030
1960-09-30 23:59:59.999999999    -0.753887
```

Pivoting "Wide" to "Long" Format

An inverse operation to `pivot` for DataFrames is `pandas.melt`. Rather than transforming one column into many in a new DataFrame, it merges multiple columns into one, producing a DataFrame that is longer than the input. Let's look at an example:

```
In [158]: df = pd.DataFrame({'key': ['foo', 'bar', 'baz'],
   .....:                    'A': [1, 2, 3],
   .....:                    'B': [4, 5, 6],
   .....:                    'C': [7, 8, 9]})

In [159]: df
Out[159]:
   key  A  B  C
0  foo  1  4  7
1  bar  2  5  8
2  baz  3  6  9
```

The `'key'` column may be a group indicator, and the other columns are data values. When using `pandas.melt`, we must indicate which columns (if any) are group indicators. Let's use `'key'` as the only group indicator here:

```
In [160]: melted = pd.melt(df, ['key'])
```

```
In [161]: melted
Out[161]:
   key variable  value
0  foo        A      1
1  bar        A      2
2  baz        A      3
3  foo        B      4
4  bar        B      5
5  baz        B      6
6  foo        C      7
7  bar        C      8
8  baz        C      9
```

Using pivot, we can reshape back to the original layout:

```
In [162]: reshaped = melted.pivot('key', 'variable', 'value')
```

```
In [163]: reshaped
Out[163]:
variable  A  B  C
key
bar       2  5  8
baz       3  6  9
foo       1  4  7
```

Since the result of pivot creates an index from the column used as the row labels, we may want to use reset_index to move the data back into a column:

```
In [164]: reshaped.reset_index()
Out[164]:
variable  key  A  B  C
0         bar  2  5  8
1         baz  3  6  9
2         foo  1  4  7
```

You can also specify a subset of columns to use as value columns:

```
In [165]: pd.melt(df, id_vars=['key'], value_vars=['A', 'B'])
Out[165]:
   key variable  value
0  foo        A      1
1  bar        A      2
2  baz        A      3
3  foo        B      4
4  bar        B      5
5  baz        B      6
```

pandas.melt can be used without any group identifiers, too:

```
In [166]: pd.melt(df, value_vars=['A', 'B', 'C'])
Out[166]:
  variable  value
```

```
0        A        1
1        A        2
2        A        3
3        B        4
4        B        5
5        B        6
6        C        7
7        C        8
8        C        9

In [167]: pd.melt(df, value_vars=['key', 'A', 'B'])
Out[167]:
  variable value
0      key   foo
1      key   bar
2      key   baz
3        A     1
4        A     2
5        A     3
6        B     4
7        B     5
8        B     6
```

8.4 Conclusion

Now that you have some pandas basics for data import, cleaning, and reorganization under your belt, we are ready to move on to data visualization with matplotlib. We will return to pandas later in the book when we discuss more advanced analytics.

Plotting and Visualization

Making informative visualizations (sometimes called *plots*) is one of the most important tasks in data analysis. It may be a part of the exploratory process—for example, to help identify outliers or needed data transformations, or as a way of generating ideas for models. For others, building an interactive visualization for the web may be the end goal. Python has many add-on libraries for making static or dynamic visualizations, but I'll be mainly focused on matplotlib (*http://matplotlib.sourceforge.net*) and libraries that build on top of it.

matplotlib is a desktop plotting package designed for creating (mostly two-dimensional) publication-quality plots. The project was started by John Hunter in 2002 to enable a MATLAB-like plotting interface in Python. The matplotlib and IPython communities have collaborated to simplify interactive plotting from the IPython shell (and now, Jupyter notebook). matplotlib supports various GUI backends on all operating systems and additionally can export visualizations to all of the common vector and raster graphics formats (PDF, SVG, JPG, PNG, BMP, GIF, etc.). With the exception of a few diagrams, nearly all of the graphics in this book were produced using matplotlib.

Over time, matplotlib has spawned a number of add-on toolkits for data visualization that use matplotlib for their underlying plotting. One of these is seaborn (*http://seaborn.pydata.org*), which we explore later in this chapter.

The simplest way to follow the code examples in the chapter is to use interactive plotting in the Jupyter notebook. To set this up, execute the following statement in a Jupyter notebook:

```
%matplotlib notebook
```

9.1 A Brief matplotlib API Primer

With matplotlib, we use the following import convention:

```
In [13]: import matplotlib.pyplot as plt
```

After running %matplotlib notebook in Jupyter (or simply %matplotlib in IPython), we can try creating a simple plot. If everything is set up right, a line plot like Figure 9-1 should appear:

```
In [14]: import numpy as np

In [15]: data = np.arange(10)

In [16]: data
Out[16]: array([0, 1, 2, 3, 4, 5, 6, 7, 8, 9])

In [17]: plt.plot(data)
```

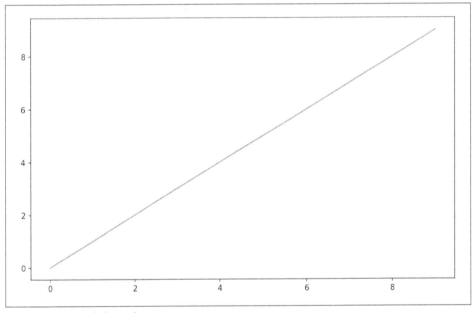

Figure 9-1. Simple line plot

While libraries like seaborn and pandas's built-in plotting functions will deal with many of the mundane details of making plots, should you wish to customize them beyond the function options provided, you will need to learn a bit about the matplotlib API.

There is not enough room in the book to give a comprehensive treatment to the breadth and depth of functionality in matplotlib. It should be enough to teach you the ropes to get up and running. The matplotlib gallery and documentation are the best resource for learning advanced features.

Figures and Subplots

Plots in matplotlib reside within a `Figure` object. You can create a new figure with `plt.figure`:

```
In [18]: fig = plt.figure()
```

In IPython, an empty plot window will appear, but in Jupyter nothing will be shown until we use a few more commands. `plt.figure` has a number of options; notably, `figsize` will guarantee the figure has a certain size and aspect ratio if saved to disk.

You can't make a plot with a blank figure. You have to create one or more `subplots` using `add_subplot`:

```
In [19]: ax1 = fig.add_subplot(2, 2, 1)
```

This means that the figure should be 2 × 2 (so up to four plots in total), and we're selecting the first of four subplots (numbered from 1). If you create the next two subplots, you'll end up with a visualization that looks like Figure 9-2:

```
In [20]: ax2 = fig.add_subplot(2, 2, 2)
```

```
In [21]: ax3 = fig.add_subplot(2, 2, 3)
```

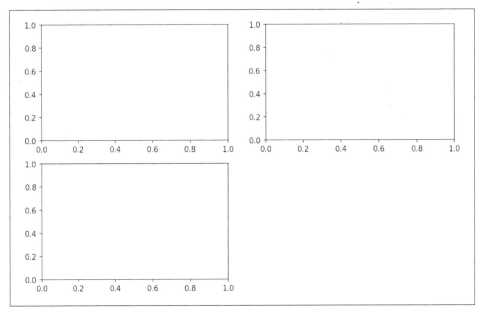

Figure 9-2. An empty matplotlib figure with three subplots

 One nuance of using Jupyter notebooks is that plots are reset after each cell is evaluated, so for more complex plots you must put all of the plotting commands in a single notebook cell.

Here we run all of these commands in the same cell:

```
fig = plt.figure()
ax1 = fig.add_subplot(2, 2, 1)
ax2 = fig.add_subplot(2, 2, 2)
ax3 = fig.add_subplot(2, 2, 3)
```

When you issue a plotting command like plt.plot([1.5, 3.5, -2, 1.6]), matplotlib draws on the last figure and subplot used (creating one if necessary), thus hiding the figure and subplot creation. So if we add the following command, you'll get something like Figure 9-3:

```
In [22]: plt.plot(np.random.randn(50).cumsum(), 'k--')
```

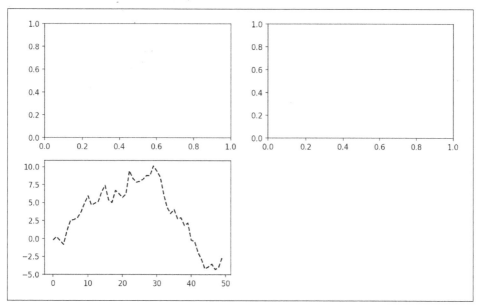

Figure 9-3. Data visualization after single plot

The 'k--' is a *style* option instructing matplotlib to plot a black dashed line. The objects returned by fig.add_subplot here are AxesSubplot objects, on which you can directly plot on the other empty subplots by calling each one's instance method (see Figure 9-4):

```
In [23]: _ = ax1.hist(np.random.randn(100), bins=20, color='k', alpha=0.3)

In [24]: ax2.scatter(np.arange(30), np.arange(30) + 3 * np.random.randn(30))
```

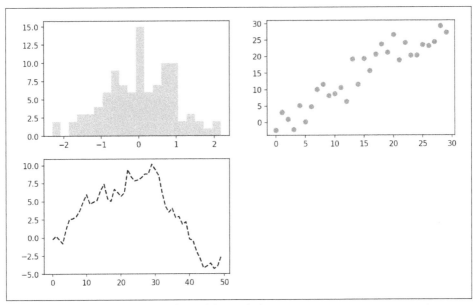

Figure 9-4. Data visualization after additional plots

You can find a comprehensive catalog of plot types in the matplotlib documentation (*http://matplotlib.sourceforge.net*).

Creating a figure with a grid of subplots is a very common task, so matplotlib includes a convenience method, `plt.subplots`, that creates a new figure and returns a NumPy array containing the created subplot objects:

```
In [26]: fig, axes = plt.subplots(2, 3)

In [27]: axes
Out[27]:
array([[<matplotlib.axes._subplots.AxesSubplot object at 0x7f8c6e3e1ac8>,
        <matplotlib.axes._subplots.AxesSubplot object at 0x7f8c6e371f28>,
        <matplotlib.axes._subplots.AxesSubplot object at 0x7f8c6e3245f8>],
       [<matplotlib.axes._subplots.AxesSubplot object at 0x7f8c6e34ac88>,
        <matplotlib.axes._subplots.AxesSubplot object at 0x7f8c6e2fa390>,
        <matplotlib.axes._subplots.AxesSubplot object at 0x7f8c6e2a19e8>]],
      dtype=object)
```

This is very useful, as the `axes` array can be easily indexed like a two-dimensional array; for example, `axes[0, 1]`. You can also indicate that subplots should have the same x- or y-axis using `sharex` and `sharey`, respectively. This is especially useful when you're comparing data on the same scale; otherwise, matplotlib autoscales plot limits independently. See Table 9-1 for more on this method.

Table 9-1. pyplot.subplots options

Argument	Description
nrows	Number of rows of subplots
ncols	Number of columns of subplots
sharex	All subplots should use the same x-axis ticks (adjusting the xlim will affect all subplots)
sharey	All subplots should use the same y-axis ticks (adjusting the ylim will affect all subplots)
subplot_kw	Dict of keywords passed to add_subplot call used to create each subplot
**fig_kw	Additional keywords to subplots are used when creating the figure, such as plt.subplots(2, 2, figsize=(8, 6))

Adjusting the spacing around subplots

By default matplotlib leaves a certain amount of padding around the outside of the subplots and spacing between subplots. This spacing is all specified relative to the height and width of the plot, so that if you resize the plot either programmatically or manually using the GUI window, the plot will dynamically adjust itself. You can change the spacing using the subplots_adjust method on Figure objects, also available as a top-level function:

```
subplots_adjust(left=None, bottom=None, right=None, top=None,
                wspace=None, hspace=None)
```

wspace and hspace controls the percent of the figure width and figure height, respectively, to use as spacing between subplots. Here is a small example where I shrink the spacing all the way to zero (see Figure 9-5):

```
fig, axes = plt.subplots(2, 2, sharex=True, sharey=True)
for i in range(2):
    for j in range(2):
        axes[i, j].hist(np.random.randn(500), bins=50, color='k', alpha=0.5)
plt.subplots_adjust(wspace=0, hspace=0)
```

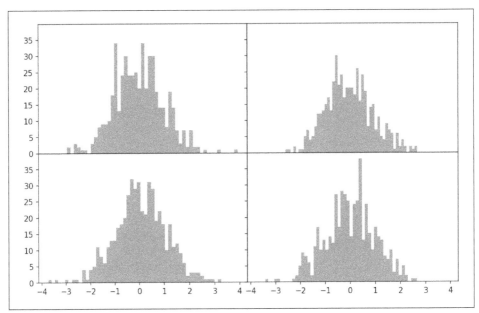

Figure 9-5. Data visualization with no inter-subplot spacing

You may notice that the axis labels overlap. matplotlib doesn't check whether the labels overlap, so in a case like this you would need to fix the labels yourself by specifying explicit tick locations and tick labels (we'll look at how to do this in the following sections).

Colors, Markers, and Line Styles

Matplotlib's main plot function accepts arrays of x and y coordinates and optionally a string abbreviation indicating color and line style. For example, to plot x versus y with green dashes, you would execute:

```
ax.plot(x, y, 'g--')
```

This way of specifying both color and line style in a string is provided as a convenience; in practice if you were creating plots programmatically you might prefer not to have to munge strings together to create plots with the desired style. The same plot could also have been expressed more explicitly as:

```
ax.plot(x, y, linestyle='--', color='g')
```

There are a number of color abbreviations provided for commonly used colors, but you can use any color on the spectrum by specifying its hex code (e.g., '#CECECE'). You can see the full set of line styles by looking at the docstring for plot (use plot? in IPython or Jupyter).

Line plots can additionally have *markers* to highlight the actual data points. Since matplotlib creates a continuous line plot, interpolating between points, it can occasionally be unclear where the points lie. The marker can be part of the style string, which must have color followed by marker type and line style (see Figure 9-6):

```
In [32]: from numpy.random import randn
```

```
In [33]: plt.plot(randn(30).cumsum(), 'ko--')
```

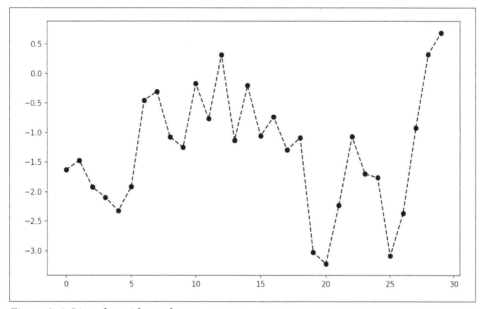

Figure 9-6. Line plot with markers

This could also have been written more explicitly as:

```
plot(randn(30).cumsum(), color='k', linestyle='dashed', marker='o')
```

For line plots, you will notice that subsequent points are linearly interpolated by default. This can be altered with the `drawstyle` option (Figure 9-7):

```
In [35]: data = np.random.randn(30).cumsum()
```

```
In [36]: plt.plot(data, 'k--', label='Default')
Out[36]: [<matplotlib.lines.Line2D at 0x7f8c59dca3c8>]
```

```
In [37]: plt.plot(data, 'k-', drawstyle='steps-post', label='steps-post')
Out[37]: [<matplotlib.lines.Line2D at 0x7f8c59dca898>]
```

```
In [38]: plt.legend(loc='best')
```

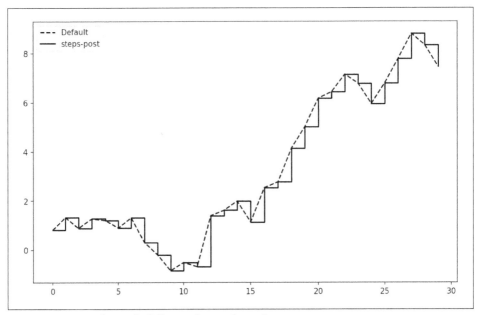

Figure 9-7. Line plot with different drawstyle options

You may notice output like `<matplotlib.lines.Line2D at ...>` when you run this. matplotlib returns objects that reference the plot subcomponent that was just added. A lot of the time you can safely ignore this output. Here, since we passed the `label` arguments to `plot`, we are able to create a plot legend to identify each line using `plt.legend`.

> You must call `plt.legend` (or `ax.legend`, if you have a reference to the axes) to create the legend, whether or not you passed the `label` options when plotting the data.

Ticks, Labels, and Legends

For most kinds of plot decorations, there are two main ways to do things: using the procedural `pyplot` interface (i.e., `matplotlib.pyplot`) and the more object-oriented native matplotlib API.

The `pyplot` interface, designed for interactive use, consists of methods like `xlim`, `xticks`, and `xticklabels`. These control the plot range, tick locations, and tick labels, respectively. They can be used in two ways:

- Called with no arguments returns the current parameter value (e.g., `plt.xlim()` returns the current x-axis plotting range)
- Called with parameters sets the parameter value (e.g., `plt.xlim([0, 10])`, sets the x-axis range to 0 to 10)

All such methods act on the active or most recently created `AxesSubplot`. Each of them corresponds to two methods on the subplot object itself; in the case of `xlim` these are `ax.get_xlim` and `ax.set_xlim`. I prefer to use the subplot instance methods myself in the interest of being explicit (and especially when working with multiple subplots), but you can certainly use whichever you find more convenient.

Setting the title, axis labels, ticks, and ticklabels

To illustrate customizing the axes, I'll create a simple figure and plot of a random walk (see Figure 9-8):

```
In [39]: fig = plt.figure()

In [40]: ax = fig.add_subplot(1, 1, 1)

In [41]: ax.plot(np.random.randn(1000).cumsum())
```

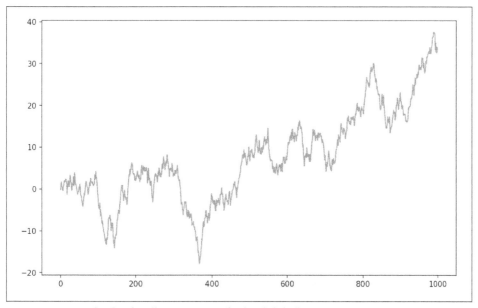

Figure 9-8. Simple plot for illustrating xticks (with label)

To change the x-axis ticks, it's easiest to use `set_xticks` and `set_xticklabels`. The former instructs matplotlib where to place the ticks along the data range; by default these locations will also be the labels. But we can set any other values as the labels using set_xticklabels:

```
In [42]: ticks = ax.set_xticks([0, 250, 500, 750, 1000])
```

```
In [43]: labels = ax.set_xticklabels(['one', 'two', 'three', 'four', 'five'],
   ....:                             rotation=30, fontsize='small')
```

The rotation option sets the x tick labels at a 30-degree rotation. Lastly, set_xlabel gives a name to the x-axis and set_title the subplot title (see Figure 9-9 for the resulting figure):

```
In [44]: ax.set_title('My first matplotlib plot')
Out[44]: Text(0.5,1,'My first matplotlib plot')
```

```
In [45]: ax.set_xlabel('Stages')
```

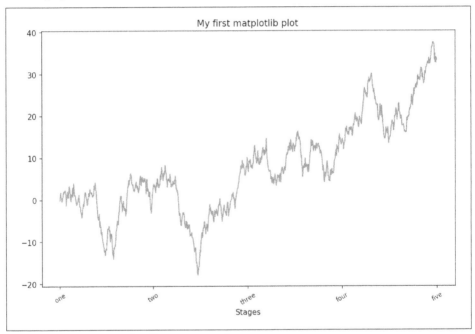

Figure 9-9. Simple plot for illustrating xticks

Modifying the y-axis consists of the same process, substituting y for x in the above. The axes class has a set method that allows batch setting of plot properties. From the prior example, we could also have written:

```
props = {
    'title': 'My first matplotlib plot',
    'xlabel': 'Stages'
}
ax.set(**props)
```

Adding legends

Legends are another critical element for identifying plot elements. There are a couple of ways to add one. The easiest is to pass the `label` argument when adding each piece of the plot:

```
In [46]: from numpy.random import randn

In [47]: fig = plt.figure(); ax = fig.add_subplot(1, 1, 1)

In [48]: ax.plot(randn(1000).cumsum(), 'k', label='one')
Out[48]: [<matplotlib.lines.Line2D at 0x7f8c4c439940>]

In [49]: ax.plot(randn(1000).cumsum(), 'k--', label='two')
Out[49]: [<matplotlib.lines.Line2D at 0x7f8c4c454f60>]

In [50]: ax.plot(randn(1000).cumsum(), 'k.', label='three')
Out[50]: [<matplotlib.lines.Line2D at 0x7f8c4c460438>]
```

Once you've done this, you can either call `ax.legend()` or `plt.legend()` to automatically create a legend. The resulting plot is in Figure 9-10:

```
In [51]: ax.legend(loc='best')
```

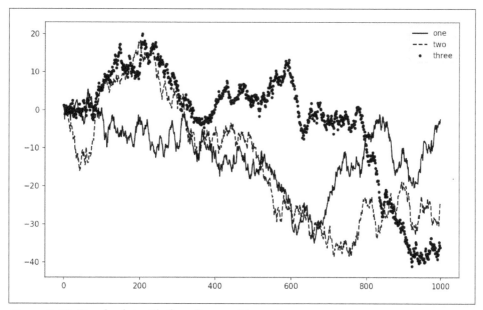

Figure 9-10. Simple plot with three lines and legend

The `legend` method has several other choices for the location `loc` argument. See the docstring (with `ax.legend?`) for more information.

The loc tells matplotlib where to place the plot. If you aren't picky, 'best' is a good option, as it will choose a location that is most out of the way. To exclude one or more elements from the legend, pass no label or label='_nolegend_'.

Annotations and Drawing on a Subplot

In addition to the standard plot types, you may wish to draw your own plot annotations, which could consist of text, arrows, or other shapes. You can add annotations and text using the text, arrow, and annotate functions. text draws text at given coordinates (x, y) on the plot with optional custom styling:

```
ax.text(x, y, 'Hello world!',
        family='monospace', fontsize=10)
```

Annotations can draw both text and arrows arranged appropriately. As an example, let's plot the closing S&P 500 index price since 2007 (obtained from Yahoo! Finance) and annotate it with some of the important dates from the 2008–2009 financial crisis. You can most easily reproduce this code example in a single cell in a Jupyter notebook. See Figure 9-11 for the result:

```
from datetime import datetime

fig = plt.figure()
ax = fig.add_subplot(1, 1, 1)

data = pd.read_csv('examples/spx.csv', index_col=0, parse_dates=True)
spx = data['SPX']

spx.plot(ax=ax, style='k-')

crisis_data = [
    (datetime(2007, 10, 11), 'Peak of bull market'),
    (datetime(2008, 3, 12), 'Bear Stearns Fails'),
    (datetime(2008, 9, 15), 'Lehman Bankruptcy')
]

for date, label in crisis_data:
    ax.annotate(label, xy=(date, spx.asof(date) + 75),
                xytext=(date, spx.asof(date) + 225),
                arrowprops=dict(facecolor='black', headwidth=4, width=2,
                                headlength=4),
                horizontalalignment='left', verticalalignment='top')

# Zoom in on 2007-2010
ax.set_xlim(['1/1/2007', '1/1/2011'])
ax.set_ylim([600, 1800])

ax.set_title('Important dates in the 2008-2009 financial crisis')
```

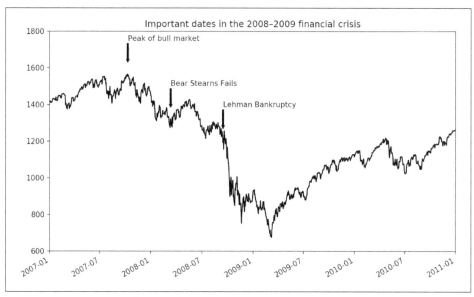

Figure 9-11. Important dates in the 2008–2009 financial crisis

There are a couple of important points to highlight in this plot: the ax.annotate method can draw labels at the indicated x and y coordinates. We use the set_xlim and set_ylim methods to manually set the start and end boundaries for the plot rather than using matplotlib's default. Lastly, ax.set_title adds a main title to the plot.

See the online matplotlib gallery for many more annotation examples to learn from.

Drawing shapes requires some more care. matplotlib has objects that represent many common shapes, referred to as *patches*. Some of these, like Rectangle and Circle, are found in matplotlib.pyplot, but the full set is located in matplotlib.patches.

To add a shape to a plot, you create the patch object shp and add it to a subplot by calling ax.add_patch(shp) (see Figure 9-12):

```
fig = plt.figure()
ax = fig.add_subplot(1, 1, 1)

rect = plt.Rectangle((0.2, 0.75), 0.4, 0.15, color='k', alpha=0.3)
circ = plt.Circle((0.7, 0.2), 0.15, color='b', alpha=0.3)
pgon = plt.Polygon([[0.15, 0.15], [0.35, 0.4], [0.2, 0.6]],
                   color='g', alpha=0.5)

ax.add_patch(rect)
ax.add_patch(circ)
ax.add_patch(pgon)
```

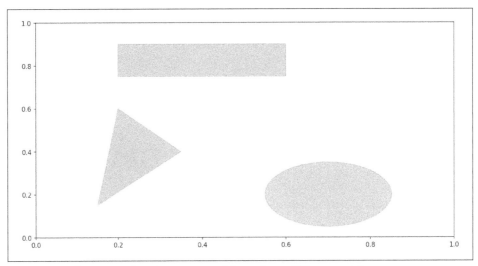

Figure 9-12. Data visualization composed from three different patches

If you look at the implementation of many familiar plot types, you will see that they are assembled from patches.

Saving Plots to File

You can save the active figure to file using `plt.savefig`. This method is equivalent to the figure object's `savefig` instance method. For example, to save an SVG version of a figure, you need only type:

```
plt.savefig('figpath.svg')
```

The file type is inferred from the file extension. So if you used `.pdf` instead, you would get a PDF. There are a couple of important options that I use frequently for publishing graphics: `dpi`, which controls the dots-per-inch resolution, and `bbox_inches`, which can trim the whitespace around the actual figure. To get the same plot as a PNG with minimal whitespace around the plot and at 400 DPI, you would do:

```
plt.savefig('figpath.png', dpi=400, bbox_inches='tight')
```

`savefig` doesn't have to write to disk; it can also write to any file-like object, such as a `BytesIO`:

```
from io import BytesIO
buffer = BytesIO()
plt.savefig(buffer)
plot_data = buffer.getvalue()
```

See Table 9-2 for a list of some other options for `savefig`.

Table 9-2. Figure.savefig options

Argument	Description
fname	String containing a filepath or a Python file-like object. The figure format is inferred from the file extension (e.g., `.pdf` for PDF or `.png` for PNG)
dpi	The figure resolution in dots per inch; defaults to 100 out of the box but can be configured
facecolor, edgecolor	The color of the figure background outside of the subplots; `'w'` (white), by default
format	The explicit file format to use (`'png'`, `'pdf'`, `'svg'`, `'ps'`, `'eps'`, ...)
bbox_inches	The portion of the figure to save; if `'tight'` is passed, will attempt to trim the empty space around the figure

matplotlib Configuration

matplotlib comes configured with color schemes and defaults that are geared primarily toward preparing figures for publication. Fortunately, nearly all of the default behavior can be customized via an extensive set of global parameters governing figure size, subplot spacing, colors, font sizes, grid styles, and so on. One way to modify the configuration programmatically from Python is to use the rc method; for example, to set the global default figure size to be 10 × 10, you could enter:

```
plt.rc('figure', figsize=(10, 10))
```

The first argument to rc is the component you wish to customize, such as `'figure'`, `'axes'`, `'xtick'`, `'ytick'`, `'grid'`, `'legend'`, or many others. After that can follow a sequence of keyword arguments indicating the new parameters. An easy way to write down the options in your program is as a dict:

```
font_options = {'family' : 'monospace',
                'weight' : 'bold',
                'size'   : 'small'}
plt.rc('font', **font_options)
```

For more extensive customization and to see a list of all the options, matplotlib comes with a configuration file *matplotlibrc* in the *matplotlib/mpl-data* directory. If you customize this file and place it in your home directory titled *.matplotlibrc*, it will be loaded each time you use matplotlib.

As we'll see in the next section, the seaborn package has several built-in plot themes or *styles* that use matplotlib's configuration system internally.

9.2 Plotting with pandas and seaborn

matplotlib can be a fairly low-level tool. You assemble a plot from its base components: the data display (i.e., the type of plot: line, bar, box, scatter, contour, etc.), legend, title, tick labels, and other annotations.

In pandas we may have multiple columns of data, along with row and column labels. pandas itself has built-in methods that simplify creating visualizations from Data-Frame and Series objects. Another library is seaborn (*https://seaborn.pydata.org/*), a statistical graphics library created by Michael Waskom. Seaborn simplifies creating many common visualization types.

 Importing seaborn modifies the default matplotlib color schemes and plot styles to improve readability and aesthetics. Even if you do not use the seaborn API, you may prefer to import seaborn as a simple way to improve the visual aesthetics of general matplotlib plots.

Line Plots

Series and DataFrame each have a plot attribute for making some basic plot types. By default, plot() makes line plots (see Figure 9-13):

```
In [62]: s = pd.Series(np.random.randn(10).cumsum(), index=np.arange(0, 100, 10))

In [63]: s.plot()
```

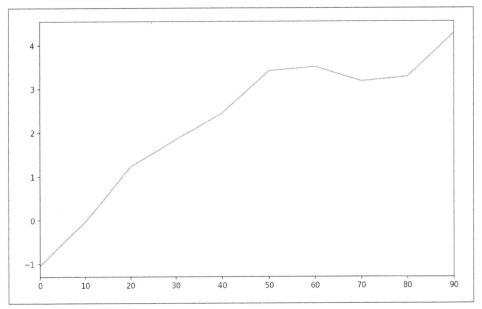

Figure 9-13. Simple Series plot

The Series object's index is passed to matplotlib for plotting on the x-axis, though you can disable this by passing use_index=False. The x-axis ticks and limits can be adjusted with the xticks and xlim options, and y-axis respectively with yticks and ylim. See Table 9-3 for a full listing of plot options. I'll comment on a few more of them throughout this section and leave the rest to you to explore.

Most of pandas's plotting methods accept an optional ax parameter, which can be a matplotlib subplot object. This gives you more flexible placement of subplots in a grid layout.

DataFrame's plot method plots each of its columns as a different line on the same subplot, creating a legend automatically (see Figure 9-14):

```
In [64]: df = pd.DataFrame(np.random.randn(10, 4).cumsum(0),
   ....:                    columns=['A', 'B', 'C', 'D'],
   ....:                    index=np.arange(0, 100, 10))

In [65]: df.plot()
```

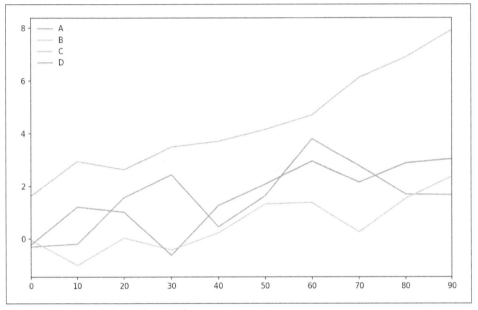

Figure 9-14. Simple DataFrame plot

The plot attribute contains a "family" of methods for different plot types. For example, df.plot() is equivalent to df.plot.line(). We'll explore some of these methods next.

Additional keyword arguments to plot are passed through to the respective matplotlib plotting function, so you can further customize these plots by learning more about the matplotlib API.

Table 9-3. Series.plot method arguments

Argument	Description
label	Label for plot legend
ax	matplotlib subplot object to plot on; if nothing passed, uses active matplotlib subplot
style	Style string, like 'ko--', to be passed to matplotlib
alpha	The plot fill opacity (from 0 to 1)
kind	Can be 'area', 'bar', 'barh', 'density', 'hist', 'kde', 'line', 'pie'
logy	Use logarithmic scaling on the y-axis
use_index	Use the object index for tick labels
rot	Rotation of tick labels (0 through 360)
xticks	Values to use for x-axis ticks
yticks	Values to use for y-axis ticks
xlim	x-axis limits (e.g., [0, 10])
ylim	y-axis limits
grid	Display axis grid (on by default)

DataFrame has a number of options allowing some flexibility with how the columns are handled; for example, whether to plot them all on the same subplot or to create separate subplots. See Table 9-4 for more on these.

Table 9-4. DataFrame-specific plot arguments

Argument	Description
subplots	Plot each DataFrame column in a separate subplot
sharex	If subplots=True, share the same x-axis, linking ticks and limits
sharey	If subplots=True, share the same y-axis
figsize	Size of figure to create as tuple
title	Plot title as string
legend	Add a subplot legend (True by default)
sort_columns	Plot columns in alphabetical order; by default uses existing column order

 For time series plotting, see Chapter 11.

Bar Plots

The `plot.bar()` and `plot.barh()` make vertical and horizontal bar plots, respectively. In this case, the Series or DataFrame index will be used as the x (`bar`) or y (`barh`) ticks (see Figure 9-15):

```
In [66]: fig, axes = plt.subplots(2, 1)

In [67]: data = pd.Series(np.random.rand(16), index=list('abcdefghijklmnop'))

In [68]: data.plot.bar(ax=axes[0], color='k', alpha=0.7)
Out[68]: <matplotlib.axes._subplots.AxesSubplot at 0x7f8c4c1b9b00>

In [69]: data.plot.barh(ax=axes[1], color='k', alpha=0.7)
```

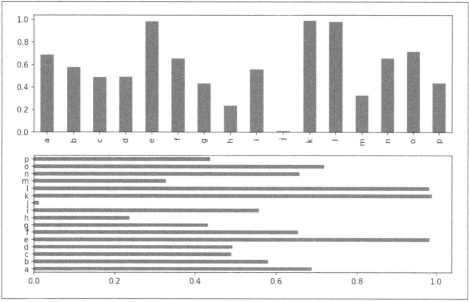

Figure 9-15. Horizonal and vertical bar plot

The options `color='k'` and `alpha=0.7` set the color of the plots to black and use partial transparency on the filling.

With a DataFrame, bar plots group the values in each row together in a group in bars, side by side, for each value. See Figure 9-16:

```
In [71]: df = pd.DataFrame(np.random.rand(6, 4),
   ....:                    index=['one', 'two', 'three', 'four', 'five', 'six'],
   ....:                    columns=pd.Index(['A', 'B', 'C', 'D'], name='Genus'))

In [72]: df
Out[72]:
Genus         A         B         C         D
one    0.370670  0.602792  0.229159  0.486744
two    0.420082  0.571653  0.049024  0.880592
three  0.814568  0.277160  0.880316  0.431326
four   0.374020  0.899420  0.460304  0.100843
five   0.433270  0.125107  0.494675  0.961825
six    0.601648  0.478576  0.205690  0.560547

In [73]: df.plot.bar()
```

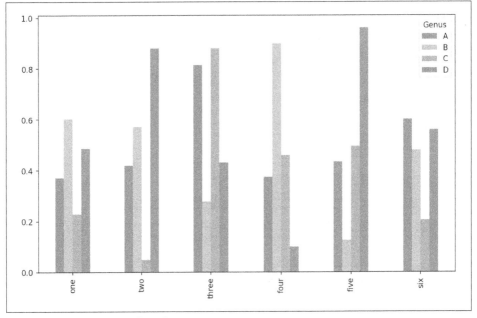

Figure 9-16. DataFrame bar plot

Note that the name "Genus" on the DataFrame's columns is used to title the legend.

We create stacked bar plots from a DataFrame by passing `stacked=True`, resulting in the value in each row being stacked together (see Figure 9-17):

```
In [75]: df.plot.barh(stacked=True, alpha=0.5)
```

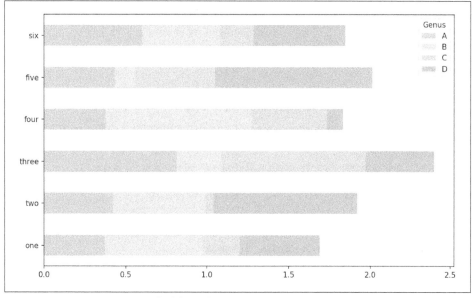

Figure 9-17. DataFrame stacked bar plot

 A useful recipe for bar plots is to visualize a Series's value frequency using `value_counts`: `s.value_counts().plot.bar()`.

Let's have a look at an example dataset about restaurant tipping, and suppose we wanted to make a stacked bar plot showing the percentage of data points for each party size on each day. I load the data using `read_csv` and make a cross-tabulation by day and party size:

```
In [77]: tips = pd.read_csv('examples/tips.csv')

In [78]: tips.head()
Out[78]:
   total_bill   tip smoker  day    time  size
0       16.99  1.01     No  Sun  Dinner     2
1       10.34  1.66     No  Sun  Dinner     3
2       21.01  3.50     No  Sun  Dinner     3
3       23.68  3.31     No  Sun  Dinner     2
4       24.59  3.61     No  Sun  Dinner     4
```

```
In [79]: party_counts = pd.crosstab(tips['day'], tips['size'])

In [80]: party_counts
Out[80]:
size  1   2   3   4  5  6
day
Fri   1  16   1   1  0  0
Sat   2  53  18  13  1  0
Sun   0  39  15  18  3  1
Thur  1  48   4   5  1  3

# Not many 1- and 6-person parties
In [81]: party_counts = party_counts.loc[:, 2:5]
```

Then, normalize so that each row sums to 1 and make the plot (see Figure 9-18):

```
# Normalize to sum to 1
In [82]: party_pcts = party_counts.div(party_counts.sum(1), axis=0)

In [83]: party_pcts
Out[83]:
size         2         3         4         5
day
Fri   0.888889  0.055556  0.055556  0.000000
Sat   0.623529  0.211765  0.152941  0.011765
Sun   0.520000  0.200000  0.240000  0.040000
Thur  0.827586  0.068966  0.086207  0.017241

In [84]: party_pcts.plot.bar()
```

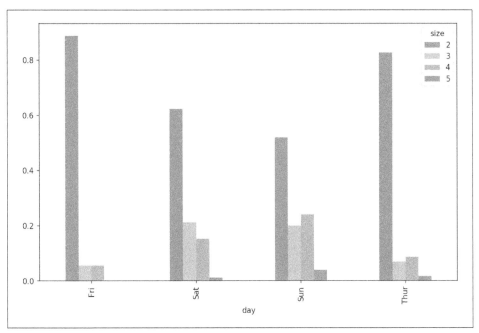

Figure 9-18. Fraction of parties by size on each day

So you can see that party sizes appear to increase on the weekend in this dataset.

With data that requires aggregation or summarization before making a plot, using the seaborn package can make things much simpler. Let's look now at the tipping percentage by day with seaborn (see Figure 9-19 for the resulting plot):

```
In [86]: import seaborn as sns

In [87]: tips['tip_pct'] = tips['tip'] / (tips['total_bill'] - tips['tip'])

In [88]: tips.head()
Out[88]:
   total_bill   tip smoker  day    time  size    tip_pct
0       16.99  1.01     No  Sun  Dinner     2   0.063204
1       10.34  1.66     No  Sun  Dinner     3   0.191244
2       21.01  3.50     No  Sun  Dinner     3   0.199886
3       23.68  3.31     No  Sun  Dinner     2   0.162494
4       24.59  3.61     No  Sun  Dinner     4   0.172069

In [89]: sns.barplot(x='tip_pct', y='day', data=tips, orient='h')
```

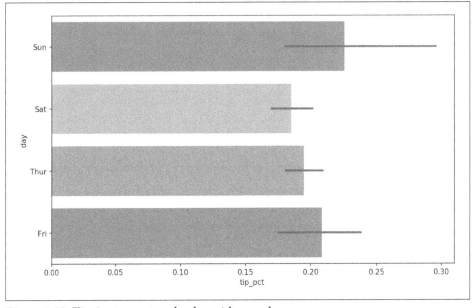

Figure 9-19. Tipping percentage by day with error bars

Plotting functions in seaborn take a data argument, which can be a pandas Data-Frame. The other arguments refer to column names. Because there are multiple observations for each value in the day, the bars are the average value of tip_pct. The black lines drawn on the bars represent the 95% confidence interval (this can be configured through optional arguments).

seaborn.barplot has a hue option that enables us to split by an additional categorical value (Figure 9-20):

```
In [91]: sns.barplot(x='tip_pct', y='day', hue='time', data=tips, orient='h')
```

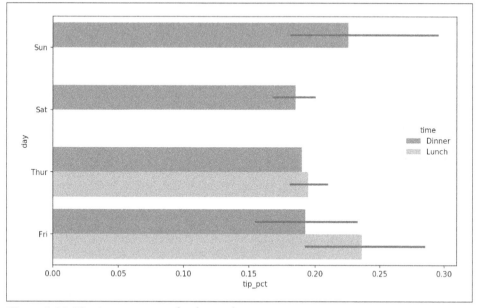

Figure 9-20. Tipping percentage by day and time

Notice that seaborn has automatically changed the aesthetics of plots: the default color palette, plot background, and grid line colors. You can switch between different plot appearances using seaborn.set:

```
In [93]: sns.set(style="whitegrid")
```

Histograms and Density Plots

A histogram is a kind of bar plot that gives a discretized display of value frequency. The data points are split into discrete, evenly spaced bins, and the number of data points in each bin is plotted. Using the tipping data from before, we can make a histogram of tip percentages of the total bill using the plot.hist method on the Series (see Figure 9-21):

```
In [95]: tips['tip_pct'].plot.hist(bins=50)
```

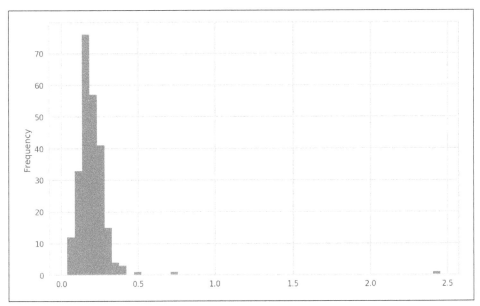

Figure 9-21. Histogram of tip percentages

A related plot type is a *density plot*, which is formed by computing an estimate of a continuous probability distribution that might have generated the observed data. The usual procedure is to approximate this distribution as a mixture of "kernels"—that is, simpler distributions like the normal distribution. Thus, density plots are also known as kernel density estimate (KDE) plots. Using `plot.kde` makes a density plot using the conventional mixture-of-normals estimate (see Figure 9-22):

```
In [97]: tips['tip_pct'].plot.density()
```

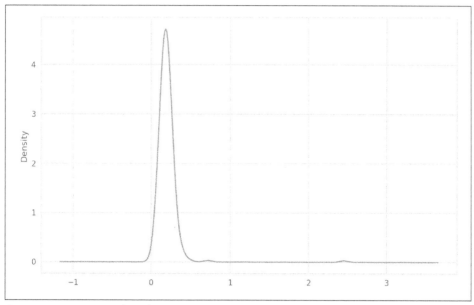

Figure 9-22. Density plot of tip percentages

Seaborn makes histograms and density plots even easier through its `distplot` method, which can plot both a histogram and a continuous density estimate simultaneously. As an example, consider a bimodal distribution consisting of draws from two different standard normal distributions (see Figure 9-23):

```
In [99]: comp1 = np.random.normal(0, 1, size=200)

In [100]: comp2 = np.random.normal(10, 2, size=200)

In [101]: values = pd.Series(np.concatenate([comp1, comp2]))

In [102]: sns.distplot(values, bins=100, color='k')
```

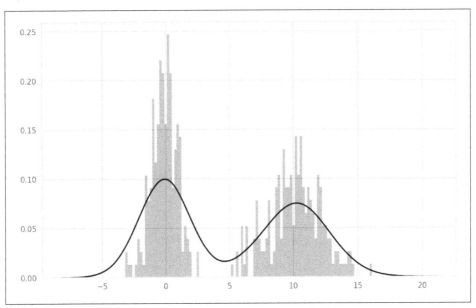

Figure 9-23. Normalized histogram of normal mixture with density estimate

Scatter or Point Plots

Point plots or scatter plots can be a useful way of examining the relationship between two one-dimensional data series. For example, here we load the `macrodata` dataset from the statsmodels project, select a few variables, then compute log differences:

```
In [103]: macro = pd.read_csv('examples/macrodata.csv')

In [104]: data = macro[['cpi', 'm1', 'tbilrate', 'unemp']]

In [105]: trans_data = np.log(data).diff().dropna()

In [106]: trans_data[-5:]
Out[106]:
           cpi        m1  tbilrate      unemp
198  -0.007904  0.045361 -0.396881  0.105361
199  -0.021979  0.066753 -2.277267  0.139762
200   0.002340  0.010286  0.606136  0.160343
201   0.008419  0.037461 -0.200671  0.127339
202   0.008894  0.012202 -0.405465  0.042560
```

We can then use seaborn's `regplot` method, which makes a scatter plot and fits a linear regression line (see Figure 9-24):

```
In [108]: sns.regplot('m1', 'unemp', data=trans_data)
Out[108]: <matplotlib.axes._subplots.AxesSubplot at 0x7f8c66961978>

In [109]: plt.title('Changes in log %s versus log %s' % ('m1', 'unemp'))
```

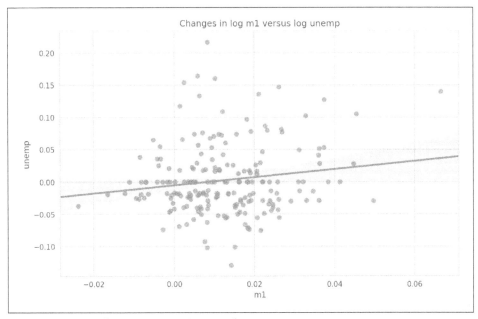

Figure 9-24. A seaborn regression/scatter plot

In exploratory data analysis it's helpful to be able to look at all the scatter plots among
a group of variables; this is known as a *pairs* plot or *scatter plot matrix*. Making such a
plot from scratch is a bit of work, so seaborn has a convenient `pairplot` function,
which supports placing histograms or density estimates of each variable along the
diagonal (see Figure 9-25 for the resulting plot):

```
In [110]: sns.pairplot(trans_data, diag_kind='kde', plot_kws={'alpha': 0.2})
```

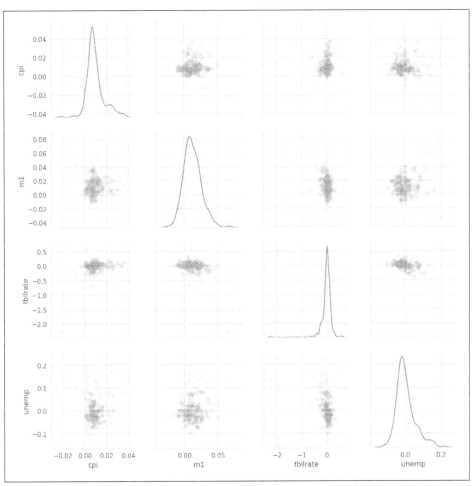

Figure 9-25. Pair plot matrix of statsmodels macro data

You may notice the `plot_kws` argument. This enables us to pass down configuration options to the individual plotting calls on the off-diagonal elements. Check out the `seaborn.pairplot` docstring for more granular configuration options.

Facet Grids and Categorical Data

What about datasets where we have additional grouping dimensions? One way to visualize data with many categorical variables is to use a *facet grid*. Seaborn has a useful built-in function `factorplot` that simplifies making many kinds of faceted plots (see Figure 9-26 for the resulting plot):

```
In [111]: sns.factorplot(x='day', y='tip_pct', hue='time', col='smoker',
     .....:               kind='bar', data=tips[tips.tip_pct < 1])
```

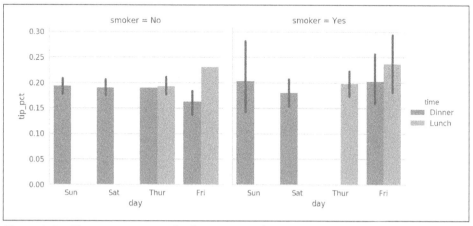

Figure 9-26. Tipping percentage by day/time/smoker

Instead of grouping by `'time'` by different bar colors within a facet, we can also expand the facet grid by adding one row per `time` value (Figure 9-27):

```
In [112]: sns.factorplot(x='day', y='tip_pct', row='time',
     .....:               col='smoker',
     .....:               kind='bar', data=tips[tips.tip_pct < 1])
```

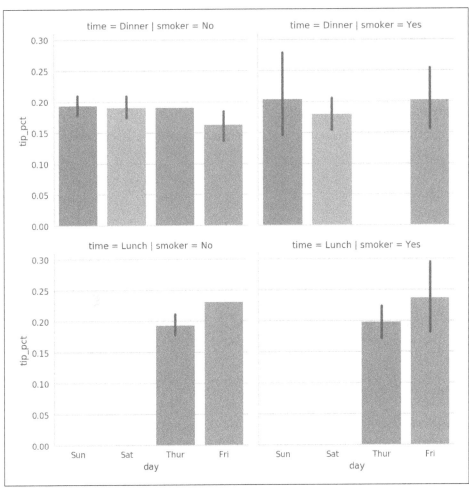

Figure 9-27. tip_pct by day; facet by time/smoker

`factorplot` supports other plot types that may be useful depending on what you are trying to display. For example, box plots (which show the median, quartiles, and outliers) can be an effective visualization type (Figure 9-28):

```
In [113]: sns.factorplot(x='tip_pct', y='day', kind='box',
   .....:                 data=tips[tips.tip_pct < 0.5])
```

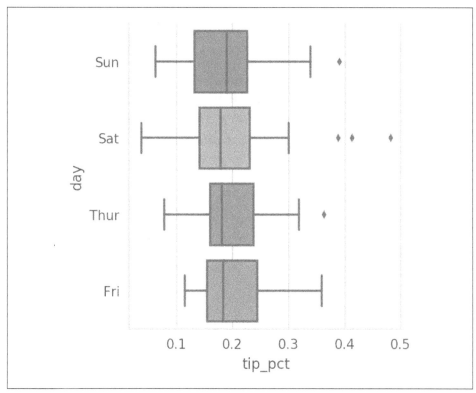

Figure 9-28. Box plot of tip_pct by day

You can create your own facet grid plots using the more general `seaborn.FacetGrid` class. See the seaborn documentation (*https://seaborn.pydata.org/*) for more.

9.3 Other Python Visualization Tools

As is common with open source, there are a plethora of options for creating graphics in Python (too many to list). Since 2010, much development effort has been focused on creating interactive graphics for publication on the web. With tools like Bokeh (*http://bokeh.pydata.org/*) and Plotly (*https://github.com/plotly/plotly.py*), it's now possible to specify dynamic, interactive graphics in Python that are destined for a web browser.

For creating static graphics for print or web, I recommend defaulting to matplotlib and add-on libraries like pandas and seaborn for your needs. For other data visualization requirements, it may be useful to learn one of the other available tools out there. I encourage you to explore the ecosystem as it continues to involve and innovate into the future.

9.4 Conclusion

The goal of this chapter was to get your feet wet with some basic data visualization using pandas, matplotlib, and seaborn. If visually communicating the results of data analysis is important in your work, I encourage you to seek out resources to learn more about effective data visualization. It is an active field of research and you can practice with many excellent learning resources available online and in print form.

In the next chapter, we turn our attention to data aggregation and group operations with pandas.

Data Aggregation and Group Operations

Categorizing a dataset and applying a function to each group, whether an aggregation or transformation, is often a critical component of a data analysis workflow. After loading, merging, and preparing a dataset, you may need to compute group statistics or possibly *pivot tables* for reporting or visualization purposes. pandas provides a flexible groupby interface, enabling you to slice, dice, and summarize datasets in a natural way.

One reason for the popularity of relational databases and SQL (which stands for "structured query language") is the ease with which data can be joined, filtered, transformed, and aggregated. However, query languages like SQL are somewhat constrained in the kinds of group operations that can be performed. As you will see, with the expressiveness of Python and pandas, we can perform quite complex group operations by utilizing any function that accepts a pandas object or NumPy array. In this chapter, you will learn how to:

- Split a pandas object into pieces using one or more keys (in the form of functions, arrays, or DataFrame column names)

- Calculate group summary statistics, like count, mean, or standard deviation, or a user-defined function

- Apply within-group transformations or other manipulations, like normalization, linear regression, rank, or subset selection

- Compute pivot tables and cross-tabulations

- Perform quantile analysis and other statistical group analyses

Aggregation of time series data, a special use case of `groupby`, is referred to as *resampling* in this book and will receive separate treatment in Chapter 11.

10.1 GroupBy Mechanics

Hadley Wickham, an author of many popular packages for the R programming language, coined the term *split-apply-combine* for describing group operations. In the first stage of the process, data contained in a pandas object, whether a Series, DataFrame, or otherwise, is *split* into groups based on one or more *keys* that you provide. The splitting is performed on a particular axis of an object. For example, a DataFrame can be grouped on its rows (`axis=0`) or its columns (`axis=1`). Once this is done, a function is *applied* to each group, producing a new value. Finally, the results of all those function applications are *combined* into a result object. The form of the resulting object will usually depend on what's being done to the data. See Figure 10-1 for a mockup of a simple group aggregation.

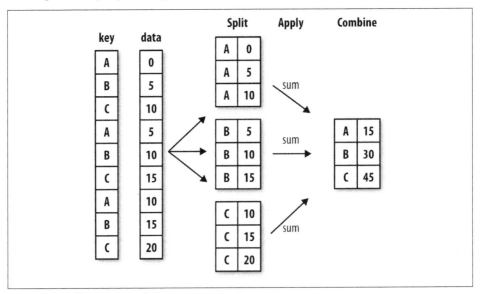

Figure 10-1. Illustration of a group aggregation

Each grouping key can take many forms, and the keys do not have to be all of the same type:

- A list or array of values that is the same length as the axis being grouped
- A value indicating a column name in a DataFrame

- A dict or Series giving a correspondence between the values on the axis being grouped and the group names
- A function to be invoked on the axis index or the individual labels in the index

Note that the latter three methods are shortcuts for producing an array of values to be used to split up the object. Don't worry if this all seems abstract. Throughout this chapter, I will give many examples of all these methods. To get started, here is a small tabular dataset as a DataFrame:

```
In [12]: df = pd.DataFrame({'key1' : ['a', 'a', 'b', 'b', 'a'],
   ....:                    'key2' : ['one', 'two', 'one', 'two', 'one'],
   ....:                    'data1' : np.random.randn(5),
   ....:                    'data2' : np.random.randn(5)})

In [13]: df
Out[13]:
  key1 key2    data1     data2
0    a  one -0.204708  1.393406
1    a  two  0.478943  0.092908
2    b  one -0.519439  0.281746
3    b  two -0.555730  0.769023
4    a  one  1.965781  1.246435
```

Suppose you wanted to compute the mean of the data1 column using the labels from key1. There are a number of ways to do this. One is to access data1 and call groupby with the column (a Series) at key1:

```
In [14]: grouped = df['data1'].groupby(df['key1'])

In [15]: grouped
Out[15]: <pandas.core.groupby.generic.SeriesGroupBy object at 0x7f345f628588>
```

This grouped variable is now a *GroupBy* object. It has not actually computed anything yet except for some intermediate data about the group key df['key1']. The idea is that this object has all of the information needed to then apply some operation to each of the groups. For example, to compute group means we can call the GroupBy's mean method:

```
In [16]: grouped.mean()
Out[16]:
key1
a     0.746672
b    -0.537585
Name: data1, dtype: float64
```

Later, I'll explain more about what happens when you call .mean(). The important thing here is that the data (a Series) has been aggregated according to the group key, producing a new Series that is now indexed by the unique values in the key1 column.

The result index has the name 'key1' because the DataFrame column df['key1'] did.

If instead we had passed multiple arrays as a list, we'd get something different:

```
In [17]: means = df['data1'].groupby([df['key1'], df['key2']]).mean()

In [18]: means
Out[18]:
key1  key2
a     one      0.880536
      two      0.478943
b     one     -0.519439
      two     -0.555730
Name: data1, dtype: float64
```

Here we grouped the data using two keys, and the resulting Series now has a hierarchical index consisting of the unique pairs of keys observed:

```
In [19]: means.unstack()
Out[19]:
key2        one        two
key1
a      0.880536   0.478943
b     -0.519439  -0.555730
```

In this example, the group keys are all Series, though they could be any arrays of the right length:

```
In [20]: states = np.array(['Ohio', 'California', 'California', 'Ohio', 'Ohio'])

In [21]: years = np.array([2005, 2005, 2006, 2005, 2006])

In [22]: df['data1'].groupby([states, years]).mean()
Out[22]:
California  2005     0.478943
           2006    -0.519439
Ohio       2005    -0.380219
           2006     1.965781
Name: data1, dtype: float64
```

Frequently the grouping information is found in the same DataFrame as the data you want to work on. In that case, you can pass column names (whether those are strings, numbers, or other Python objects) as the group keys:

```
In [23]: df.groupby('key1').mean()
Out[23]:
         data1     data2
key1
a      0.746672  0.910916
b     -0.537585  0.525384

In [24]: df.groupby(['key1', 'key2']).mean()
```

```
Out[24]:
                data1       data2
key1  key2
a     one    0.880536    1.319920
      two    0.478943    0.092908
b     one   -0.519439    0.281746
      two   -0.555730    0.769023
```

You may have noticed in the first case `df.groupby('key1').mean()` that there is no key2 column in the result. Because `df['key2']` is not numeric data, it is said to be a *nuisance column*, which is therefore excluded from the result. By default, all of the numeric columns are aggregated, though it is possible to filter down to a subset, as you'll see soon.

Regardless of the objective in using `groupby`, a generally useful GroupBy method is `size`, which returns a Series containing group sizes:

```
In [25]: df.groupby(['key1', 'key2']).size()
Out[25]:
key1  key2
a     one     2
      two     1
b     one     1
      two     1
dtype: int64
```

Take note that any missing values in a group key will be excluded from the result.

Iterating Over Groups

The GroupBy object supports iteration, generating a sequence of 2-tuples containing the group name along with the chunk of data. Consider the following:

```
In [26]: for name, group in df.groupby('key1'):
   ....:     print(name)
   ....:     print(group)
   ....:
a
  key1 key2     data1      data2
0    a  one -0.204708   1.393406
1    a  two  0.478943   0.092908
4    a  one  1.965781   1.246435
b
  key1 key2     data1      data2
2    b  one -0.519439   0.281746
3    b  two -0.555730   0.769023
```

In the case of multiple keys, the first element in the tuple will be a tuple of key values:

```
In [27]: for (k1, k2), group in df.groupby(['key1', 'key2']):
   ....:     print((k1, k2))
   ....:     print(group)
```

```
  ....:
('a', 'one')
  key1 key2      data1     data2
0    a  one -0.204708  1.393406
4    a  one  1.965781  1.246435
('a', 'two')
  key1 key2      data1     data2
1    a  two  0.478943  0.092908
('b', 'one')
  key1 key2      data1     data2
2    b  one -0.519439  0.281746
('b', 'two')
  key1 key2     data1     data2
3    b  two -0.55573  0.769023
```

Of course, you can choose to do whatever you want with the pieces of data. A recipe
you may find useful is computing a dict of the data pieces as a one-liner:

```
In [28]: pieces = dict(list(df.groupby('key1')))

In [29]: pieces['b']
Out[29]:
  key1 key2      data1     data2
2    b  one -0.519439  0.281746
3    b  two -0.555730  0.769023
```

By default groupby groups on axis=0, but you can group on any of the other axes.
For example, we could group the columns of our example df here by dtype like so:

```
In [30]: df.dtypes
Out[30]:
key1      object
key2      object
data1    float64
data2    float64
dtype: object

In [31]: grouped = df.groupby(df.dtypes, axis=1)
```

We can print out the groups like so:

```
In [32]: for dtype, group in grouped:
    ....:     print(dtype)
    ....:     print(group)
    ....:
float64
      data1     data2
0 -0.204708  1.393406
1  0.478943  0.092908
2 -0.519439  0.281746
3 -0.555730  0.769023
4  1.965781  1.246435
object
  key1 key2
```

```
0    a    one
1    a    two
2    b    one
3    b    two
4    a    one
```

Selecting a Column or Subset of Columns

Indexing a GroupBy object created from a DataFrame with a column name or array of column names has the effect of column subsetting for aggregation. This means that:

```
df.groupby('key1')['data1']
df.groupby('key1')[['data2']]
```

are syntactic sugar for:

```
df['data1'].groupby(df['key1'])
df[['data2']].groupby(df['key1'])
```

Especially for large datasets, it may be desirable to aggregate only a few columns. For example, in the preceding dataset, to compute means for just the data2 column and get the result as a DataFrame, we could write:

```
In [33]: df.groupby(['key1', 'key2'])[['data2']].mean()
Out[33]:
                data2
key1 key2
a    one     1.319920
     two     0.092908
b    one     0.281746
     two     0.769023
```

The object returned by this indexing operation is a grouped DataFrame if a list or array is passed or a grouped Series if only a single column name is passed as a scalar:

```
In [34]: s_grouped = df.groupby(['key1', 'key2'])['data2']

In [35]: s_grouped
Out[35]: <pandas.core.groupby.generic.SeriesGroupBy object at 0x7f345f5e43c8>

In [36]: s_grouped.mean()
Out[36]:
key1  key2
a     one     1.319920
      two     0.092908
b     one     0.281746
      two     0.769023
Name: data2, dtype: float64
```

Grouping with Dicts and Series

Grouping information may exist in a form other than an array. Let's consider another example DataFrame:

```
In [37]: people = pd.DataFrame(np.random.randn(5, 5),
   ....:                       columns=['a', 'b', 'c', 'd', 'e'],
   ....:                       index=['Joe', 'Steve', 'Wes', 'Jim', 'Travis'])

In [38]: people.iloc[2:3, [1, 2]] = np.nan # Add a few NA values

In [39]: people
Out[39]:
               a         b         c         d         e
Joe     1.007189 -1.296221  0.274992  0.228913  1.352917
Steve   0.886429 -2.001637 -0.371843  1.669025 -0.438570
Wes    -0.539741       NaN       NaN -1.021228 -0.577087
Jim     0.124121  0.302614  0.523772  0.000940  1.343810
Travis -0.713544 -0.831154 -2.370232 -1.860761 -0.860757
```

Now, suppose I have a group correspondence for the columns and want to sum together the columns by group:

```
In [40]: mapping = {'a': 'red', 'b': 'red', 'c': 'blue',
   ....:            'd': 'blue', 'e': 'red', 'f' : 'orange'}
```

Now, you could construct an array from this dict to pass to groupby, but instead we can just pass the dict (I included the key 'f' to highlight that unused grouping keys are OK):

```
In [41]: by_column = people.groupby(mapping, axis=1)

In [42]: by_column.sum()
Out[42]:
            blue       red
Joe     0.503905  1.063885
Steve   1.297183 -1.553778
Wes    -1.021228 -1.116829
Jim     0.524712  1.770545
Travis -4.230992 -2.405455
```

The same functionality holds for Series, which can be viewed as a fixed-size mapping:

```
In [43]: map_series = pd.Series(mapping)

In [44]: map_series
Out[44]:
a       red
b       red
c      blue
d      blue
e       red
f    orange
```

```
dtype: object

In [45]: people.groupby(map_series, axis=1).count()
Out[45]:
        blue  red
Joe        2    3
Steve      2    3
Wes        1    2
Jim        2    3
Travis     2    3
```

Grouping with Functions

Using Python functions is a more generic way of defining a group mapping compared with a dict or Series. Any function passed as a group key will be called once per index value, with the return values being used as the group names. More concretely, consider the example DataFrame from the previous section, which has people's first names as index values. Suppose you wanted to group by the length of the names; while you could compute an array of string lengths, it's simpler to just pass the len function:

```
In [46]: people.groupby(len).sum()
Out[46]:
          a         b         c         d         e
3  0.591569 -0.993608  0.798764 -0.791374  2.119639
5  0.886429 -2.001637 -0.371843  1.669025 -0.438570
6 -0.713544 -0.831154 -2.370232 -1.860761 -0.860757
```

Mixing functions with arrays, dicts, or Series is not a problem as everything gets converted to arrays internally:

```
In [47]: key_list = ['one', 'one', 'one', 'two', 'two']

In [48]: people.groupby([len, key_list]).min()
Out[48]:
              a         b         c         d         e
3 one -0.539741 -1.296221  0.274992 -1.021228 -0.577087
  two  0.124121  0.302614  0.523772  0.000940  1.343810
5 one  0.886429 -2.001637 -0.371843  1.669025 -0.438570
6 two -0.713544 -0.831154 -2.370232 -1.860761 -0.860757
```

Grouping by Index Levels

A final convenience for hierarchically indexed datasets is the ability to aggregate using one of the levels of an axis index. Let's look at an example:

```
In [49]: columns = pd.MultiIndex.from_arrays([['US', 'US', 'US', 'JP', 'JP'],
   ....:                                      [1, 3, 5, 1, 3]],
   ....:                                      names=['cty', 'tenor'])

In [50]: hier_df = pd.DataFrame(np.random.randn(4, 5), columns=columns)
```

```
In [51]: hier_df
Out[51]:
cty          US                           JP
tenor         1         3         5         1         3
0      0.560145 -1.265934  0.119827 -1.063512  0.332883
1     -2.359419 -0.199543 -1.541996 -0.970736 -1.307030
2      0.286350  0.377984 -0.753887  0.331286  1.349742
3      0.069877  0.246674 -0.011862  1.004812  1.327195
```

To group by level, pass the level number or name using the `level` keyword:

```
In [52]: hier_df.groupby(level='cty', axis=1).count()
Out[52]:
cty  JP  US
0     2   3
1     2   3
2     2   3
3     2   3
```

10.2 Data Aggregation

Aggregations refer to any data transformation that produces scalar values from arrays. The preceding examples have used several of them, including `mean`, `count`, `min`, and `sum`. You may wonder what is going on when you invoke `mean()` on a GroupBy object. Many common aggregations, such as those found in Table 10-1, have optimized implementations. However, you are not limited to only this set of methods.

Table 10-1. Optimized groupby methods

Function name	Description
count	Number of non-NA values in the group
sum	Sum of non-NA values
mean	Mean of non-NA values
median	Arithmetic median of non-NA values
std, var	Unbiased (n − 1 denominator) standard deviation and variance
min, max	Minimum and maximum of non-NA values
prod	Product of non-NA values
first, last	First and last non-NA values

You can use aggregations of your own devising and additionally call any method that is also defined on the grouped object. For example, you might recall that `quantile` computes sample quantiles of a Series or a DataFrame's columns.

While `quantile` is not explicitly implemented for GroupBy, it is a Series method and thus available for use. Internally, GroupBy efficiently slices up the Series, calls piece.quantile(0.9) for each piece, and then assembles those results together into the result object:

```
In [53]: df
Out[53]:
  key1 key2     data1     data2
0    a  one -0.204708  1.393406
1    a  two  0.478943  0.092908
2    b  one -0.519439  0.281746
3    b  two -0.555730  0.769023
4    a  one  1.965781  1.246435

In [54]: grouped = df.groupby('key1')

In [55]: grouped['data1'].quantile(0.9)
Out[55]:
key1
a    1.668413
b   -0.523068
Name: data1, dtype: float64
```

To use your own aggregation functions, pass any function that aggregates an array to the aggregate or agg method:

```
In [56]: def peak_to_peak(arr):
   ....:     return arr.max() - arr.min()

In [57]: grouped.agg(peak_to_peak)
Out[57]:
         data1     data2
key1
a     2.170488  1.300498
b     0.036292  0.487276
```

You may notice that some methods like describe also work, even though they are not aggregations, strictly speaking:

```
In [58]: grouped.describe()
Out[58]:
     data1                                                              \
     count      mean       std       min       25%       50%       75%
key1
a      3.0  0.746672  1.109736 -0.204708  0.137118  0.478943  1.222362
b      2.0 -0.537585  0.025662 -0.555730 -0.546657 -0.537585 -0.528512
                    data2                                               \
         max count      mean       std       min       25%       50%
key1
a   1.965781   3.0  0.910916  0.712217  0.092908  0.669671  1.246435
b  -0.519439   2.0  0.525384  0.344556  0.281746  0.403565  0.525384

         75%       max
key1
```

```
a     1.319920   1.393406
b     0.647203   0.769023
```

I will explain in more detail what has happened here in Section 10.3, "Apply: General split-apply-combine," on page 308.

 Custom aggregation functions are generally much slower than the optimized functions found in Table 10-1. This is because there is some extra overhead (function calls, data rearrangement) in constructing the intermediate group data chunks.

Column-Wise and Multiple Function Application

Let's return to the tipping dataset used in the last chapter. After loading it with `read_csv`, we add a tipping percentage column `tip_pct`:

```
In [59]: tips = pd.read_csv('examples/tips.csv')

# Add tip percentage of total bill
In [60]: tips['tip_pct'] = tips['tip'] / tips['total_bill']

In [61]: tips[:6]
Out[61]:
   total_bill   tip smoker  day    time  size    tip_pct
0       16.99  1.01     No  Sun  Dinner     2   0.059447
1       10.34  1.66     No  Sun  Dinner     3   0.160542
2       21.01  3.50     No  Sun  Dinner     3   0.166587
3       23.68  3.31     No  Sun  Dinner     2   0.139780
4       24.59  3.61     No  Sun  Dinner     4   0.146808
5       25.29  4.71     No  Sun  Dinner     4   0.186240
```

As you've already seen, aggregating a Series or all of the columns of a DataFrame is a matter of using `aggregate` with the desired function or calling a method like `mean` or `std`. However, you may want to aggregate using a different function depending on the column, or multiple functions at once. Fortunately, this is possible to do, which I'll illustrate through a number of examples. First, I'll group the `tips` by `day` and `smoker`:

```
In [62]: grouped = tips.groupby(['day', 'smoker'])
```

Note that for descriptive statistics like those in Table 10-1, you can pass the name of the function as a string:

```
In [63]: grouped_pct = grouped['tip_pct']

In [64]: grouped_pct.agg('mean')
Out[64]:
day   smoker
Fri   No        0.151650
      Yes       0.174783
Sat   No        0.158048
```

```
        Yes      0.147906
Sun  No       0.160113
        Yes      0.187250
Thur No       0.160298
        Yes      0.163863
Name: tip_pct, dtype: float64
```

If you pass a list of functions or function names instead, you get back a DataFrame with column names taken from the functions:

```
In [65]: grouped_pct.agg(['mean', 'std', peak_to_peak])
Out[65]:
                mean       std  peak_to_peak
day  smoker
Fri  No       0.151650  0.028123      0.067349
     Yes      0.174783  0.051293      0.159925
Sat  No       0.158048  0.039767      0.235193
     Yes      0.147906  0.061375      0.290095
Sun  No       0.160113  0.042347      0.193226
     Yes      0.187250  0.154134      0.644685
Thur No       0.160298  0.038774      0.193350
     Yes      0.163863  0.039389      0.151240
```

Here we passed a list of aggregation functions to agg to evaluate indepedently on the data groups.

You don't need to accept the names that GroupBy gives to the columns; notably, lambda functions have the name '<lambda>', which makes them hard to identify (you can see for yourself by looking at a function's __name__ attribute). Thus, if you pass a list of (name, function) tuples, the first element of each tuple will be used as the DataFrame column names (you can think of a list of 2-tuples as an ordered mapping):

```
In [66]: grouped_pct.agg([('foo', 'mean'), ('bar', np.std)])
Out[66]:
                foo       bar
day  smoker
Fri  No       0.151650  0.028123
     Yes      0.174783  0.051293
Sat  No       0.158048  0.039767
     Yes      0.147906  0.061375
Sun  No       0.160113  0.042347
     Yes      0.187250  0.154134
Thur No       0.160298  0.038774
     Yes      0.163863  0.039389
```

With a DataFrame you have more options, as you can specify a list of functions to apply to all of the columns or different functions per column. To start, suppose we wanted to compute the same three statistics for the tip_pct and total_bill columns:

```
In [67]: functions = ['count', 'mean', 'max']

In [68]: result = grouped['tip_pct', 'total_bill'].agg(functions)

In [69]: result
Out[69]:
            tip_pct                       total_bill
            count    mean      max        count    mean       max
day  smoker
Fri  No         4  0.151650  0.187735         4  18.420000  22.75
     Yes       15  0.174783  0.263480        15  16.813333  40.17
Sat  No        45  0.158048  0.291990        45  19.661778  48.33
     Yes       42  0.147906  0.325733        42  21.276667  50.81
Sun  No        57  0.160113  0.252672        57  20.506667  48.17
     Yes       19  0.187250  0.710345        19  24.120000  45.35
Thur No        45  0.160298  0.266312        45  17.113111  41.19
     Yes       17  0.163863  0.241255        17  19.190588  43.11
```

As you can see, the resulting DataFrame has hierarchical columns, the same as you would get aggregating each column separately and using concat to glue the results together using the column names as the keys argument:

```
In [70]: result['tip_pct']
Out[70]:
            count    mean      max
day  smoker
Fri  No         4  0.151650  0.187735
     Yes       15  0.174783  0.263480
Sat  No        45  0.158048  0.291990
     Yes       42  0.147906  0.325733
Sun  No        57  0.160113  0.252672
     Yes       19  0.187250  0.710345
Thur No        45  0.160298  0.266312
     Yes       17  0.163863  0.241255
```

As before, a list of tuples with custom names can be passed:

```
In [71]: ftuples = [('Durchschnitt', 'mean'), ('Abweichung', np.var)]

In [72]: grouped['tip_pct', 'total_bill'].agg(ftuples)
Out[72]:
                  tip_pct                  total_bill
            Durchschnitt Abweichung Durchschnitt  Abweichung
day  smoker
Fri  No         0.151650   0.000791    18.420000   25.596333
     Yes        0.174783   0.002631    16.813333   82.562438
Sat  No         0.158048   0.001581    19.661778   79.908965
     Yes        0.147906   0.003767    21.276667  101.387535
Sun  No         0.160113   0.001793    20.506667   66.099980
     Yes        0.187250   0.023757    24.120000  109.046044
Thur No         0.160298   0.001503    17.113111   59.625081
     Yes        0.163863   0.001551    19.190588   69.808518
```

Now, suppose you wanted to apply potentially different functions to one or more of the columns. To do this, pass a dict to agg that contains a mapping of column names to any of the function specifications listed so far:

```
In [73]: grouped.agg({'tip' : np.max, 'size' : 'sum'})
Out[73]:
                tip  size
day  smoker
Fri  No        3.50     9
     Yes       4.73    31
Sat  No        9.00   115
     Yes      10.00   104
Sun  No        6.00   167
     Yes       6.50    49
Thur No        6.70   112
     Yes       5.00    40

In [74]: grouped.agg({'tip_pct' : ['min', 'max', 'mean', 'std'],
   ....:             'size' : 'sum'})
Out[74]:
                tip_pct                                   size
                    min       max      mean       std     sum
day  smoker
Fri  No        0.120385  0.187735  0.151650  0.028123       9
     Yes       0.103555  0.263480  0.174783  0.051293      31
Sat  No        0.056797  0.291990  0.158048  0.039767     115
     Yes       0.035638  0.325733  0.147906  0.061375     104
Sun  No        0.059447  0.252672  0.160113  0.042347     167
     Yes       0.065660  0.710345  0.187250  0.154134      49
Thur No        0.072961  0.266312  0.160298  0.038774     112
     Yes       0.090014  0.241255  0.163863  0.039389      40
```

A DataFrame will have hierarchical columns only if multiple functions are applied to at least one column.

Returning Aggregated Data Without Row Indexes

In all of the examples up until now, the aggregated data comes back with an index, potentially hierarchical, composed from the unique group key combinations. Since this isn't always desirable, you can disable this behavior in most cases by passing as_index=False to groupby:

```
In [75]: tips.groupby(['day', 'smoker'], as_index=False).mean()
Out[75]:
   day smoker  total_bill       tip      size   tip_pct
0  Fri     No   18.420000  2.812500  2.250000  0.151650
1  Fri    Yes   16.813333  2.714000  2.066667  0.174783
2  Sat     No   19.661778  3.102889  2.555556  0.158048
3  Sat    Yes   21.276667  2.875476  2.476190  0.147906
4  Sun     No   20.506667  3.167895  2.929825  0.160113
5  Sun    Yes   24.120000  3.516842  2.578947  0.187250
```

```
6   Thur    No   17.113111  2.673778  2.488889  0.160298
7   Thur    Yes  19.190588  3.030000  2.352941  0.163863
```

Of course, it's always possible to obtain the result in this format by calling
`reset_index` on the result. Using the `as_index=False` method avoids some unneces‐
sary computations.

10.3 Apply: General split-apply-combine

The most general-purpose GroupBy method is `apply`, which is the subject of the rest
of this section. As illustrated in Figure 10-2, `apply` splits the object being manipulated
into pieces, invokes the passed function on each piece, and then attempts to concate‐
nate the pieces together.

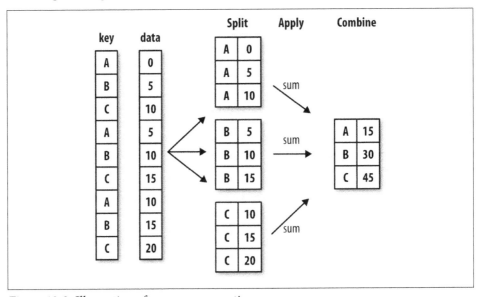

Figure 10-2. Illustration of a group aggregation

Returning to the tipping dataset from before, suppose you wanted to select the top
five `tip_pct` values by group. First, write a function that selects the rows with the
largest values in a particular column:

```
In [76]: def top(df, n=5, column='tip_pct'):
   ....:     return df.sort_values(by=column)[-n:]

In [77]: top(tips, n=6)
Out[77]:
     total_bill   tip smoker  day    time  size   tip_pct
109       14.31  4.00    Yes  Sat  Dinner     2  0.279525
183       23.17  6.50    Yes  Sun  Dinner     4  0.280535
232       11.61  3.39     No  Sat  Dinner     2  0.291990
```

```
67              3.07   1.00   Yes  Sat  Dinner     1   0.325733
178             9.60   4.00   Yes  Sun  Dinner     2   0.416667
172             7.25   5.15   Yes  Sun  Dinner     2   0.710345
```

Now, if we group by smoker, say, and call apply with this function, we get the following:

```
In [78]: tips.groupby('smoker').apply(top)
Out[78]:
             total_bill   tip smoker   day    time  size   tip_pct
smoker
No      88        24.71  5.85     No  Thur   Lunch     2  0.236746
        185       20.69  5.00     No   Sun  Dinner     5  0.241663
        51        10.29  2.60     No   Sun  Dinner     2  0.252672
        149        7.51  2.00     No  Thur   Lunch     2  0.266312
        232       11.61  3.39     No   Sat  Dinner     2  0.291990
Yes     109       14.31  4.00    Yes   Sat  Dinner     2  0.279525
        183       23.17  6.50    Yes   Sun  Dinner     4  0.280535
        67         3.07  1.00    Yes   Sat  Dinner     1  0.325733
        178        9.60  4.00    Yes   Sun  Dinner     2  0.416667
        172        7.25  5.15    Yes   Sun  Dinner     2  0.710345
```

What has happened here? The top function is called on each row group from the DataFrame, and then the results are glued together using pandas.concat, labeling the pieces with the group names. The result therefore has a hierarchical index whose inner level contains index values from the original DataFrame.

If you pass a function to apply that takes other arguments or keywords, you can pass these after the function:

```
In [79]: tips.groupby(['smoker', 'day']).apply(top, n=1, column='total_bill')
Out[79]:
                  total_bill    tip smoker   day    time  size   tip_pct
smoker day
No     Fri   94        22.75   3.25     No   Fri  Dinner     2  0.142857
       Sat   212       48.33   9.00     No   Sat  Dinner     4  0.186220
       Sun   156       48.17   5.00     No   Sun  Dinner     6  0.103799
       Thur  142       41.19   5.00     No  Thur   Lunch     5  0.121389
Yes    Fri   95        40.17   4.73    Yes   Fri  Dinner     4  0.117750
       Sat   170       50.81  10.00    Yes   Sat  Dinner     3  0.196812
       Sun   182       45.35   3.50    Yes   Sun  Dinner     3  0.077178
       Thur  197       43.11   5.00    Yes  Thur   Lunch     4  0.115982
```

 Beyond these basic usage mechanics, getting the most out of apply may require some creativity. What occurs inside the function passed is up to you; it only needs to return a pandas object or a scalar value. The rest of this chapter will mainly consist of examples showing you how to solve various problems using groupby.

You may recall that I earlier called `describe` on a GroupBy object:

```
In [80]: result = tips.groupby('smoker')['tip_pct'].describe()

In [81]: result
Out[81]:
        count      mean       std       min       25%       50%       75%  \
smoker
No      151.0  0.159328  0.039910  0.056797  0.136906  0.155625  0.185014
Yes      93.0  0.163196  0.085119  0.035638  0.106771  0.153846  0.195059

             max
smoker
No      0.291990
Yes     0.710345

In [82]: result.unstack('smoker')
Out[82]:
       smoker
count  No      151.000000
       Yes      93.000000
mean   No        0.159328
       Yes       0.163196
std    No        0.039910
       Yes       0.085119
min    No        0.056797
       Yes       0.035638
25%    No        0.136906
       Yes       0.106771
50%    No        0.155625
       Yes       0.153846
75%    No        0.185014
       Yes       0.195059
max    No        0.291990
       Yes       0.710345
dtype: float64
```

Inside GroupBy, when you invoke a method like `describe`, it is actually just a short-cut for:

```
f = lambda x: x.describe()
grouped.apply(f)
```

Suppressing the Group Keys

In the preceding examples, you see that the resulting object has a hierarchical index formed from the group keys along with the indexes of each piece of the original object. You can disable this by passing `group_keys=False` to groupby:

```
In [83]: tips.groupby('smoker', group_keys=False).apply(top)
Out[83]:
     total_bill   tip smoker   day    time  size   tip_pct
88        24.71  5.85     No  Thur   Lunch     2  0.236746
185       20.69  5.00     No   Sun  Dinner     5  0.241663
51        10.29  2.60     No   Sun  Dinner     2  0.252672
149        7.51  2.00     No  Thur   Lunch     2  0.266312
232       11.61  3.39     No   Sat  Dinner     2  0.291990
109       14.31  4.00    Yes   Sat  Dinner     2  0.279525
183       23.17  6.50    Yes   Sun  Dinner     4  0.280535
67         3.07  1.00    Yes   Sat  Dinner     1  0.325733
178        9.60  4.00    Yes   Sun  Dinner     2  0.416667
172        7.25  5.15    Yes   Sun  Dinner     2  0.710345
```

Quantile and Bucket Analysis

As you may recall from Chapter 8, pandas has some tools, in particular cut and qcut, for slicing data up into buckets with bins of your choosing or by sample quantiles. Combining these functions with groupby makes it convenient to perform bucket or quantile analysis on a dataset. Consider a simple random dataset and an equal-length bucket categorization using cut:

```
In [84]: frame = pd.DataFrame({'data1': np.random.randn(1000),
   ....:                       'data2': np.random.randn(1000)})

In [85]: quartiles = pd.cut(frame.data1, 4)

In [86]: quartiles[:10]
Out[86]:
0      (-1.23, 0.489]
1     (-2.956, -1.23]
2      (-1.23, 0.489]
3      (0.489, 2.208]
4      (-1.23, 0.489]
5      (0.489, 2.208]
6      (-1.23, 0.489]
7      (-1.23, 0.489]
8      (0.489, 2.208]
9      (0.489, 2.208]
Name: data1, dtype: category
Categories (4, interval[float64]): [(-2.956, -1.23] < (-1.23, 0.489] < (0.489, 2.
208] < (2.208, 3.928]]
```

The Categorical object returned by cut can be passed directly to groupby. So we could compute a set of statistics for the data2 column like so:

```
In [87]: def get_stats(group):
   ....:     return {'min': group.min(), 'max': group.max(),
   ....:             'count': group.count(), 'mean': group.mean()}

In [88]: grouped = frame.data2.groupby(quartiles)
```

```
In [89]: grouped.apply(get_stats).unstack()
Out[89]:
                  count      max      mean      min
data1
(-2.956, -1.23]    95.0  1.670835 -0.039521 -3.399312
(-1.23, 0.489]    598.0  3.260383 -0.002051 -2.989741
(0.489, 2.208]    297.0  2.954439  0.081822 -3.745356
(2.208, 3.928]     10.0  1.765640  0.024750 -1.929776
```

These were equal-length buckets; to compute equal-size buckets based on sample quantiles, use qcut. I'll pass labels=False to just get quantile numbers:

```
# Return quantile numbers
In [90]: grouping = pd.qcut(frame.data1, 10, labels=False)

In [91]: grouped = frame.data2.groupby(grouping)

In [92]: grouped.apply(get_stats).unstack()
Out[92]:
       count      max      mean      min
data1
0      100.0  1.670835 -0.049902 -3.399312
1      100.0  2.628441  0.030989 -1.950098
2      100.0  2.527939 -0.067179 -2.925113
3      100.0  3.260383  0.065713 -2.315555
4      100.0  2.074345 -0.111653 -2.047939
5      100.0  2.184810  0.052130 -2.989741
6      100.0  2.458842 -0.021489 -2.223506
7      100.0  2.954439 -0.026459 -3.056990
8      100.0  2.735527  0.103406 -3.745356
9      100.0  2.377020  0.220122 -2.064111
```

We will take a closer look at pandas's Categorical type in Chapter 12.

Example: Filling Missing Values with Group-Specific Values

When cleaning up missing data, in some cases you will replace data observations using dropna, but in others you may want to impute (fill in) the null (NA) values using a fixed value or some value derived from the data. fillna is the right tool to use; for example, here I fill in NA values with the mean:

```
In [93]: s = pd.Series(np.random.randn(6))

In [94]: s[::2] = np.nan

In [95]: s
Out[95]:
0         NaN
1   -0.125921
2         NaN
3   -0.884475
```

```
4          NaN
5     0.227290
dtype: float64

In [96]: s.fillna(s.mean())
Out[96]:
0    -0.261035
1    -0.125921
2    -0.261035
3    -0.884475
4    -0.261035
5     0.227290
dtype: float64
```

Suppose you need the fill value to vary by group. One way to do this is to group the data and use apply with a function that calls fillna on each data chunk. Here is some sample data on US states divided into eastern and western regions:

```
In [97]: states = ['Ohio', 'New York', 'Vermont', 'Florida',
   ....:           'Oregon', 'Nevada', 'California', 'Idaho']

In [98]: group_key = ['East'] * 4 + ['West'] * 4

In [99]: data = pd.Series(np.random.randn(8), index=states)

In [100]: data
Out[100]:
Ohio           0.922264
New York      -2.153545
Vermont       -0.365757
Florida       -0.375842
Oregon         0.329939
Nevada         0.981994
California      1.105913
Idaho         -1.613716
dtype: float64
```

Note that the syntax ['East'] * 4 produces a list containing four copies of the elements in ['East']. Adding lists together concatenates them.

Let's set some values in the data to be missing:

```
In [101]: data[['Vermont', 'Nevada', 'Idaho']] = np.nan

In [102]: data
Out[102]:
Ohio           0.922264
New York      -2.153545
Vermont             NaN
Florida       -0.375842
Oregon         0.329939
Nevada              NaN
California      1.105913
```

```
Idaho            NaN
dtype: float64

In [103]: data.groupby(group_key).mean()
Out[103]:
East    -0.535707
West     0.717926
dtype: float64
```

We can fill the NA values using the group means like so:

```
In [104]: fill_mean = lambda g: g.fillna(g.mean())

In [105]: data.groupby(group_key).apply(fill_mean)
Out[105]:
Ohio           0.922264
New York      -2.153545
Vermont       -0.535707
Florida       -0.375842
Oregon         0.329939
Nevada         0.717926
California     1.105913
Idaho          0.717926
dtype: float64
```

In another case, you might have predefined fill values in your code that vary by group. Since the groups have a name attribute set internally, we can use that:

```
In [106]: fill_values = {'East': 0.5, 'West': -1}

In [107]: fill_func = lambda g: g.fillna(fill_values[g.name])

In [108]: data.groupby(group_key).apply(fill_func)
Out[108]:
Ohio           0.922264
New York      -2.153545
Vermont        0.500000
Florida       -0.375842
Oregon         0.329939
Nevada        -1.000000
California     1.105913
Idaho         -1.000000
dtype: float64
```

Example: Random Sampling and Permutation

Suppose you wanted to draw a random sample (with or without replacement) from a large dataset for Monte Carlo simulation purposes or some other application. There are a number of ways to perform the "draws"; here we use the sample method for Series.

To demonstrate, here's a way to construct a deck of English-style playing cards:

```
# Hearts, Spades, Clubs, Diamonds
suits = ['H', 'S', 'C', 'D']
card_val = (list(range(1, 11)) + [10] * 3) * 4
base_names = ['A'] + list(range(2, 11)) + ['J', 'K', 'Q']
cards = []
for suit in ['H', 'S', 'C', 'D']:
    cards.extend(str(num) + suit for num in base_names)

deck = pd.Series(card_val, index=cards)
```

So now we have a Series of length 52 whose index contains card names and values are the ones used in Blackjack and other games (to keep things simple, I just let the ace 'A' be 1):

```
In [110]: deck[:13]
Out[110]:
AH      1
2H      2
3H      3
4H      4
5H      5
6H      6
7H      7
8H      8
9H      9
10H    10
JH     10
KH     10
QH     10
dtype: int64
```

Now, based on what I said before, drawing a hand of five cards from the deck could be written as:

```
In [111]: def draw(deck, n=5):
    .....:     return deck.sample(n)

In [112]: draw(deck)
Out[112]:
AD      1
8C      8
5H      5
KC     10
2C      2
dtype: int64
```

Suppose you wanted two random cards from each suit. Because the suit is the last character of each card name, we can group based on this and use apply:

```
In [113]: get_suit = lambda card: card[-1] # last letter is suit

In [114]: deck.groupby(get_suit).apply(draw, n=2)
Out[114]:
```

```
C   2C    2
    3C    3
D   KD   10
    8D    8
H   KH   10
    3H    3
S   2S    2
    4S    4
dtype: int64
```

Alternatively, we could write:

```
In [115]: deck.groupby(get_suit, group_keys=False).apply(draw, n=2)
Out[115]:
KC   10
JC   10
AD    1
5D    5
5H    5
6H    6
7S    7
KS   10
dtype: int64
```

Example: Group Weighted Average and Correlation

Under the split-apply-combine paradigm of groupby, operations between columns in a DataFrame or two Series, such as a group weighted average, are possible. As an example, take this dataset containing group keys, values, and some weights:

```
In [116]: df = pd.DataFrame({'category': ['a', 'a', 'a', 'a',
   .....:                                 'b', 'b', 'b', 'b'],
   .....:                    'data': np.random.randn(8),
   .....:                    'weights': np.random.rand(8)})

In [117]: df
Out[117]:
  category      data   weights
0        a  1.561587  0.957515
1        a  1.219984  0.347267
2        a -0.482239  0.581362
3        a  0.315667  0.217091
4        b -0.047852  0.894406
5        b -0.454145  0.918564
6        b -0.556774  0.277825
7        b  0.253321  0.955905
```

The group weighted average by category would then be:

```
In [118]: grouped = df.groupby('category')

In [119]: get_wavg = lambda g: np.average(g['data'], weights=g['weights'])
```

```
In [120]: grouped.apply(get_wavg)
Out[120]:
category
a     0.811643
b    -0.122262
dtype: float64
```

As another example, consider a financial dataset originally obtained from Yahoo! Finance containing end-of-day prices for a few stocks and the S&P 500 index (the SPX symbol):

```
In [121]: close_px = pd.read_csv('examples/stock_px_2.csv', parse_dates=True,
   .....:                          index_col=0)

In [122]: close_px.info()
<class 'pandas.core.frame.DataFrame'>
DatetimeIndex: 2214 entries, 2003-01-02 to 2011-10-14
Data columns (total 4 columns):
AAPL    2214 non-null float64
MSFT    2214 non-null float64
XOM     2214 non-null float64
SPX     2214 non-null float64
dtypes: float64(4)
memory usage: 86.5 KB

In [123]: close_px[-4:]
Out[123]:
              AAPL    MSFT    XOM      SPX
2011-10-11  400.29   27.00  76.27  1195.54
2011-10-12  402.19   26.96  77.16  1207.25
2011-10-13  408.43   27.18  76.37  1203.66
2011-10-14  422.00   27.27  78.11  1224.58
```

One task of interest might be to compute a DataFrame consisting of the yearly correlations of daily returns (computed from percent changes) with SPX. As one way to do this, we first create a function that computes the pairwise correlation of each column with the 'SPX' column:

```
In [124]: spx_corr = lambda x: x.corrwith(x['SPX'])
```

Next, we compute percent change on close_px using pct_change:

```
In [125]: rets = close_px.pct_change().dropna()
```

Lastly, we group these percent changes by year, which can be extracted from each row label with a one-line function that returns the year attribute of each datetime label:

```
In [126]: get_year = lambda x: x.year

In [127]: by_year = rets.groupby(get_year)

In [128]: by_year.apply(spx_corr)
Out[128]:
```

```
          AAPL      MSFT      XOM   SPX
2003  0.541124  0.745174  0.661265  1.0
2004  0.374283  0.588531  0.557742  1.0
2005  0.467540  0.562374  0.631010  1.0
2006  0.428267  0.406126  0.518514  1.0
2007  0.508118  0.658770  0.786264  1.0
2008  0.681434  0.804626  0.828303  1.0
2009  0.707103  0.654902  0.797921  1.0
2010  0.710105  0.730118  0.839057  1.0
2011  0.691931  0.800996  0.859975  1.0
```

You could also compute inter-column correlations. Here we compute the annual correlation between Apple and Microsoft:

```
In [129]: by_year.apply(lambda g: g['AAPL'].corr(g['MSFT']))
Out[129]:
2003    0.480868
2004    0.259024
2005    0.300093
2006    0.161735
2007    0.417738
2008    0.611901
2009    0.432738
2010    0.571946
2011    0.581987
dtype: float64
```

Example: Group-Wise Linear Regression

In the same theme as the previous example, you can use groupby to perform more complex group-wise statistical analysis, as long as the function returns a pandas object or scalar value. For example, I can define the following regress function (using the statsmodels econometrics library), which executes an ordinary least squares (OLS) regression on each chunk of data:

```
import statsmodels.api as sm
def regress(data, yvar, xvars):
    Y = data[yvar]
    X = data[xvars]
    X['intercept'] = 1.
    result = sm.OLS(Y, X).fit()
    return result.params
```

Now, to run a yearly linear regression of AAPL on SPX returns, execute:

```
In [131]: by_year.apply(regress, 'AAPL', ['SPX'])
Out[131]:
           SPX  intercept
2003  1.195406   0.000710
2004  1.363463   0.004201
2005  1.766415   0.003246
2006  1.645496   0.000080
```

```
2007  1.198761   0.003438
2008  0.968016  -0.001110
2009  0.879103   0.002954
2010  1.052608   0.001261
2011  0.806605   0.001514
```

10.4 Pivot Tables and Cross-Tabulation

A *pivot table* is a data summarization tool frequently found in spreadsheet programs and other data analysis software. It aggregates a table of data by one or more keys, arranging the data in a rectangle with some of the group keys along the rows and some along the columns. Pivot tables in Python with pandas are made possible through the groupby facility described in this chapter combined with reshape operations utilizing hierarchical indexing. DataFrame has a pivot_table method, and there is also a top-level pandas.pivot_table function. In addition to providing a convenience interface to groupby, pivot_table can add partial totals, also known as *margins*.

Returning to the tipping dataset, suppose you wanted to compute a table of group means (the default pivot_table aggregation type) arranged by day and smoker on the rows:

```
In [132]: tips.pivot_table(index=['day', 'smoker'])
Out[132]:
                 size       tip   tip_pct  total_bill
day  smoker
Fri  No      2.250000  2.812500  0.151650   18.420000
     Yes     2.066667  2.714000  0.174783   16.813333
Sat  No      2.555556  3.102889  0.158048   19.661778
     Yes     2.476190  2.875476  0.147906   21.276667
Sun  No      2.929825  3.167895  0.160113   20.506667
     Yes     2.578947  3.516842  0.187250   24.120000
Thur No      2.488889  2.673778  0.160298   17.113111
     Yes     2.352941  3.030000  0.163863   19.190588
```

This could have been produced with groupby directly. Now, suppose we want to aggregate only tip_pct and size, and additionally group by time. I'll put smoker in the table columns and day in the rows:

```
In [133]: tips.pivot_table(['tip_pct', 'size'], index=['time', 'day'],
   .....:                   columns='smoker')
Out[133]:
                 size               tip_pct
smoker             No       Yes         No       Yes
time   day
Dinner Fri   2.000000  2.222222   0.139622  0.165347
       Sat   2.555556  2.476190   0.158048  0.147906
       Sun   2.929825  2.578947   0.160113  0.187250
       Thur  2.000000       NaN   0.159744       NaN
```

```
Lunch  Fri    3.000000  1.833333  0.187735  0.188937
       Thur   2.500000  2.352941  0.160311  0.163863
```

We could augment this table to include partial totals by passing margins=True. This has the effect of adding All row and column labels, with corresponding values being the group statistics for all the data within a single tier:

```
In [134]: tips.pivot_table(['tip_pct', 'size'], index=['time', 'day'],
   .....:                    columns='smoker', margins=True)
Out[134]:
                    size                        tip_pct
smoker                No       Yes       All        No       Yes       All
time    day
Dinner  Fri     2.000000  2.222222  2.166667  0.139622  0.165347  0.158916
        Sat     2.555556  2.476190  2.517241  0.158048  0.147906  0.153152
        Sun     2.929825  2.578947  2.842105  0.160113  0.187250  0.166897
        Thur    2.000000       NaN  2.000000  0.159744       NaN  0.159744
Lunch   Fri     3.000000  1.833333  2.000000  0.187735  0.188937  0.188765
        Thur    2.500000  2.352941  2.459016  0.160311  0.163863  0.161301
All             2.668874  2.408602  2.569672  0.159328  0.163196  0.160803
```

Here, the All values are means without taking into account smoker versus non-smoker (the All columns) or any of the two levels of grouping on the rows (the All row).

To use a different aggregation function, pass it to aggfunc. For example, 'count' or len will give you a cross-tabulation (count or frequency) of group sizes:

```
In [135]: tips.pivot_table('tip_pct', index=['time', 'smoker'], columns='day',
   .....:                    aggfunc=len, margins=True)
Out[135]:
day            Fri   Sat   Sun  Thur    All
time    smoker
Dinner  No     3.0  45.0  57.0   1.0  106.0
        Yes    9.0  42.0  19.0   NaN   70.0
Lunch   No     1.0   NaN   NaN  44.0   45.0
        Yes    6.0   NaN   NaN  17.0   23.0
All           19.0  87.0  76.0  62.0  244.0
```

If some combinations are empty (or otherwise NA), you may wish to pass a fill_value:

```
In [136]: tips.pivot_table('tip_pct', index=['time', 'size', 'smoker'],
   .....:                    columns='day', aggfunc='mean', fill_value=0)
Out[136]:
day                         Fri       Sat       Sun      Thur
time    size smoker
Dinner  1    No        0.000000  0.137931  0.000000  0.000000
             Yes       0.000000  0.325733  0.000000  0.000000
        2    No        0.139622  0.162705  0.168859  0.159744
             Yes       0.171297  0.148668  0.207893  0.000000
        3    No        0.000000  0.154661  0.152663  0.000000
```

```
          Yes    0.000000  0.144995  0.152660  0.000000
     4    No     0.000000  0.150096  0.148143  0.000000
          Yes    0.117750  0.124515  0.193370  0.000000
     5    No     0.000000  0.000000  0.206928  0.000000
          Yes    0.000000  0.106572  0.065660  0.000000
...             ...       ...       ...       ...
Lunch 1    No     0.000000  0.000000  0.000000  0.181728
          Yes    0.223776  0.000000  0.000000  0.000000
     2    No     0.000000  0.000000  0.000000  0.166005
          Yes    0.181969  0.000000  0.000000  0.158843
     3    No     0.187735  0.000000  0.000000  0.084246
          Yes    0.000000  0.000000  0.000000  0.204952
     4    No     0.000000  0.000000  0.000000  0.138919
          Yes    0.000000  0.000000  0.000000  0.155410
     5    No     0.000000  0.000000  0.000000  0.121389
     6    No     0.000000  0.000000  0.000000  0.173706
[21 rows x 4 columns]
```

See Table 10-2 for a summary of `pivot_table` methods.

Table 10-2. pivot_table options

Function name	Description
values	Column name or names to aggregate; by default aggregates all numeric columns
index	Column names or other group keys to group on the rows of the resulting pivot table
columns	Column names or other group keys to group on the columns of the resulting pivot table
aggfunc	Aggregation function or list of functions ('mean' by default); can be any function valid in a groupby context
fill_value	Replace missing values in result table
dropna	If True, do not include columns whose entries are all NA
margins	Add row/column subtotals and grand total (False by default)

Cross-Tabulations: Crosstab

A cross-tabulation (or *crosstab* for short) is a special case of a pivot table that computes group frequencies. Here is an example:

```
In [140]: data
Out[140]:
    Sample Nationality   Handedness
0     1          USA  Right-handed
1     2        Japan   Left-handed
2     3          USA  Right-handed
3     4        Japan  Right-handed
4     5        Japan   Left-handed
5     6        Japan  Right-handed
6     7          USA  Right-handed
7     8          USA   Left-handed
8     9        Japan  Right-handed
9    10          USA  Right-handed
```

As part of some survey analysis, we might want to summarize this data by nationality and handedness. You could use `pivot_table` to do this, but the `pandas.crosstab` function can be more convenient:

```
In [141]: pd.crosstab(data.Nationality, data.Handedness, margins=True)
Out[141]:
Handedness   Left-handed  Right-handed  All
Nationality
Japan                  2             3    5
USA                    1             4    5
All                    3             7   10
```

The first two arguments to `crosstab` can each either be an array or Series or a list of arrays. As in the tips data:

```
In [142]: pd.crosstab([tips.time, tips.day], tips.smoker, margins=True)
Out[142]:
smoker        No  Yes  All
time   day
Dinner Fri     3    9   12
       Sat    45   42   87
       Sun    57   19   76
       Thur    1    0    1
Lunch  Fri     1    6    7
       Thur   44   17   61
All          151   93  244
```

10.5 Conclusion

Mastering pandas's data grouping tools can help both with data cleaning as well as modeling or statistical analysis work. In Chapter 14 we will look at several more example use cases for `groupby` on real data.

In the next chapter, we turn our attention to time series data.

Time Series

Time series data is an important form of structured data in many different fields, such as finance, economics, ecology, neuroscience, and physics. Anything that is observed or measured at many points in time forms a time series. Many time series are *fixed frequency*, which is to say that data points occur at regular intervals according to some rule, such as every 15 seconds, every 5 minutes, or once per month. Time series can also be *irregular* without a fixed unit of time or offset between units. How you mark and refer to time series data depends on the application, and you may have one of the following:

- *Timestamps*, specific instants in time
- Fixed *periods*, such as the month January 2007 or the full year 2010
- *Intervals* of time, indicated by a start and end timestamp. Periods can be thought of as special cases of intervals
- Experiment or elapsed time; each timestamp is a measure of time relative to a particular start time (e.g., the diameter of a cookie baking each second since being placed in the oven)

In this chapter, I am mainly concerned with time series in the first three categories, though many of the techniques can be applied to experimental time series where the index may be an integer or floating-point number indicating elapsed time from the start of the experiment. The simplest and most widely used kind of time series are those indexed by timestamp.

pandas also supports indexes based on timedeltas, which can be a useful way of representing experiment or elapsed time. We do not explore timedelta indexes in this book, but you can learn more in the pandas documentation (*http://pandas.pydata.org*).

pandas provides many built-in time series tools and data algorithms. You can efficiently work with very large time series and easily slice and dice, aggregate, and resample irregular- and fixed-frequency time series. Some of these tools are especially useful for financial and economics applications, but you could certainly use them to analyze server log data, too.

11.1 Date and Time Data Types and Tools

The Python standard library includes data types for date and time data, as well as calendar-related functionality. The datetime, time, and calendar modules are the main places to start. The datetime.datetime type, or simply datetime, is widely used:

```
In [12]: from datetime import datetime

In [13]: now = datetime.now()

In [14]: now
Out[14]: datetime.datetime(2018, 9, 7, 19, 46, 54, 557479)

In [15]: now.year, now.month, now.day
Out[15]: (2018, 9, 7)
```

datetime stores both the date and time down to the microsecond. timedelta represents the temporal difference between two datetime objects:

```
In [16]: delta = datetime(2011, 1, 7) - datetime(2008, 6, 24, 8, 15)

In [17]: delta
Out[17]: datetime.timedelta(926, 56700)

In [18]: delta.days
Out[18]: 926

In [19]: delta.seconds
Out[19]: 56700
```

You can add (or subtract) a timedelta or multiple thereof to a datetime object to yield a new shifted object:

```
In [20]: from datetime import timedelta

In [21]: start = datetime(2011, 1, 7)
```

```
In [22]: start + timedelta(12)
Out[22]: datetime.datetime(2011, 1, 19, 0, 0)

In [23]: start - 2 * timedelta(12)
Out[23]: datetime.datetime(2010, 12, 14, 0, 0)
```

Table 11-1 summarizes the data types in the datetime module. While this chapter is mainly concerned with the data types in pandas and higher-level time series manipulation, you may encounter the datetime-based types in many other places in Python in the wild.

Table 11-1. Types in datetime module

Type	Description
date	Store calendar date (year, month, day) using the Gregorian calendar
time	Store time of day as hours, minutes, seconds, and microseconds
datetime	Stores both date and time
timedelta	Represents the difference between two datetime values (as days, seconds, and microseconds)
tzinfo	Base type for storing time zone information

Converting Between String and Datetime

You can format datetime objects and pandas Timestamp objects, which I'll introduce later, as strings using str or the strftime method, passing a format specification:

```
In [24]: stamp = datetime(2011, 1, 3)

In [25]: str(stamp)
Out[25]: '2011-01-03 00:00:00'

In [26]: stamp.strftime('%Y-%m-%d')
Out[26]: '2011-01-03'
```

See Table 11-2 for a complete list of the format codes (reproduced from Chapter 2).

Table 11-2. Datetime format specification (ISO C89 compatible)

Type	Description
%Y	Four-digit year
%y	Two-digit year
%m	Two-digit month [01, 12]
%d	Two-digit day [01, 31]
%H	Hour (24-hour clock) [00, 23]
%I	Hour (12-hour clock) [01, 12]
%M	Two-digit minute [00, 59]
%S	Second [00, 61] (seconds 60, 61 account for leap seconds)
%w	Weekday as integer [0 (Sunday), 6]

Type	Description
%U	Week number of the year [00, 53]; Sunday is considered the first day of the week, and days before the first Sunday of the year are "week 0"
%W	Week number of the year [00, 53]; Monday is considered the first day of the week, and days before the first Monday of the year are "week 0"
%z	UTC time zone offset as +HHMM or -HHMM; empty if time zone naive
%F	Shortcut for %Y-%m-%d (e.g., 2012-4-18)
%D	Shortcut for %m/%d/%y (e.g., 04/18/12)

You can use many of the same format codes to convert strings to dates using `date time.strptime` (some codes, like %F, cannot be used):

```
In [27]: value = '2011-01-03'

In [28]: datetime.strptime(value, '%Y-%m-%d')
Out[28]: datetime.datetime(2011, 1, 3, 0, 0)

In [29]: datestrs = ['7/6/2011', '8/6/2011']

In [30]: [datetime.strptime(x, '%m/%d/%Y') for x in datestrs]
Out[30]:
[datetime.datetime(2011, 7, 6, 0, 0),
 datetime.datetime(2011, 8, 6, 0, 0)]
```

`datetime.strptime` is a good way to parse a date with a known format. However, it can be a bit annoying to have to write a format spec each time, especially for common date formats. In this case, you can use the `parser.parse` method in the third-party `dateutil` package (this is installed automatically when you install pandas):

```
In [31]: from dateutil.parser import parse
```

```
In [32]: parse('2011-01-03')
Out[32]: datetime.datetime(2011, 1, 3, 0, 0)
```

`dateutil` is capable of parsing most human-intelligible date representations:

```
In [33]: parse('Jan 31, 1997 10:45 PM')
Out[33]: datetime.datetime(1997, 1, 31, 22, 45)
```

In international locales, day appearing before month is very common, so you can pass `dayfirst=True` to indicate this:

```
In [34]: parse('6/12/2011', dayfirst=True)
Out[34]: datetime.datetime(2011, 12, 6, 0, 0)
```

pandas is generally oriented toward working with arrays of dates, whether used as an axis index or a column in a DataFrame. The `to_datetime` method parses many different kinds of date representations. Standard date formats like ISO 8601 can be parsed very quickly:

```
In [35]: datestrs = ['2011-07-06 12:00:00', '2011-08-06 00:00:00']

In [36]: pd.to_datetime(datestrs)
Out[36]: DatetimeIndex(['2011-07-06 12:00:00', '2011-08-06 00:00:00'], dtype='dat
etime64[ns]', freq=None)
```

It also handles values that should be considered missing (None, empty string, etc.):

```
In [37]: idx = pd.to_datetime(datestrs + [None])

In [38]: idx
Out[38]: DatetimeIndex(['2011-07-06 12:00:00', '2011-08-06 00:00:00', 'NaT'], dty
pe='datetime64[ns]', freq=None)

In [39]: idx[2]
Out[39]: NaT

In [40]: pd.isnull(idx)
Out[40]: array([False, False,  True])
```

NaT (Not a Time) is pandas's null value for timestamp data.

> dateutil.parser is a useful but imperfect tool. Notably, it will rec-
> ognize some strings as dates that you might prefer that it didn't—
> for example, '42' will be parsed as the year 2042 with today's cal-
> endar date.

datetime objects also have a number of locale-specific formatting options for systems in other countries or languages. For example, the abbreviated month names will be different on German or French systems compared with English systems. See Table 11-3 for a listing.

Table 11-3. Locale-specific date formatting

Type	Description
%a	Abbreviated weekday name
%A	Full weekday name
%b	Abbreviated month name
%B	Full month name
%c	Full date and time (e.g., 'Tue 01 May 2012 04:20:57 PM')
%p	Locale equivalent of AM or PM
%x	Locale-appropriate formatted date (e.g., in the United States, May 1, 2012 yields '05/01/2012')
%X	Locale-appropriate time (e.g., '04:24:12 PM')

11.2 Time Series Basics

A basic kind of time series object in pandas is a Series indexed by timestamps, which is often represented external to pandas as Python strings or datetime objects:

```
In [41]: from datetime import datetime

In [42]: dates = [datetime(2011, 1, 2), datetime(2011, 1, 5),
   ....:          datetime(2011, 1, 7), datetime(2011, 1, 8),
   ....:          datetime(2011, 1, 10), datetime(2011, 1, 12)]

In [43]: ts = pd.Series(np.random.randn(6), index=dates)

In [44]: ts
Out[44]:
2011-01-02   -0.204708
2011-01-05    0.478943
2011-01-07   -0.519439
2011-01-08   -0.555730
2011-01-10    1.965781
2011-01-12    1.393406
dtype: float64
```

Under the hood, these datetime objects have been put in a DatetimeIndex:

```
In [45]: ts.index
Out[45]:
DatetimeIndex(['2011-01-02', '2011-01-05', '2011-01-07', '2011-01-08',
               '2011-01-10', '2011-01-12'],
              dtype='datetime64[ns]', freq=None)
```

Like other Series, arithmetic operations between differently indexed time series automatically align on the dates:

```
In [46]: ts + ts[::2]
Out[46]:
2011-01-02   -0.409415
2011-01-05         NaN
2011-01-07   -1.038877
2011-01-08         NaN
2011-01-10    3.931561
2011-01-12         NaN
dtype: float64
```

Recall that ts[::2] selects every second element in ts.

pandas stores timestamps using NumPy's datetime64 data type at the nanosecond resolution:

```
In [47]: ts.index.dtype
Out[47]: dtype('<M8[ns]')
```

Scalar values from a DatetimeIndex are pandas Timestamp objects:

```
In [48]: stamp = ts.index[0]

In [49]: stamp
Out[49]: Timestamp('2011-01-02 00:00:00')
```

A `Timestamp` can be substituted anywhere you would use a `datetime` object. Additionally, it can store frequency information (if any) and understands how to do time zone conversions and other kinds of manipulations. More on both of these things later.

Indexing, Selection, Subsetting

Time series behaves like any other `pandas.Series` when you are indexing and selecting data based on label:

```
In [50]: stamp = ts.index[2]

In [51]: ts[stamp]
Out[51]: -0.5194387150567381
```

As a convenience, you can also pass a string that is interpretable as a date:

```
In [52]: ts['1/10/2011']
Out[52]: 1.9657805725027142

In [53]: ts['20110110']
Out[53]: 1.9657805725027142
```

For longer time series, a year or only a year and month can be passed to easily select slices of data:

```
In [54]: longer_ts = pd.Series(np.random.randn(1000),
   ....:                       index=pd.date_range('1/1/2000', periods=1000))

In [55]: longer_ts
Out[55]:
2000-01-01    0.092908
2000-01-02    0.281746
2000-01-03    0.769023
2000-01-04    1.246435
2000-01-05    1.007189
2000-01-06   -1.296221
2000-01-07    0.274992
2000-01-08    0.228913
2000-01-09    1.352917
2000-01-10    0.886429
                ...
2002-09-17   -0.139298
2002-09-18   -1.159926
2002-09-19    0.618965
2002-09-20    1.373890
2002-09-21   -0.983505
```

```
2002-09-22    0.930944
2002-09-23   -0.811676
2002-09-24   -1.830156
2002-09-25   -0.138730
2002-09-26    0.334088
Freq: D, Length: 1000, dtype: float64

In [56]: longer_ts['2001']
Out[56]:
2001-01-01    1.599534
2001-01-02    0.474071
2001-01-03    0.151326
2001-01-04   -0.542173
2001-01-05   -0.475496
2001-01-06    0.106403
2001-01-07   -1.308228
2001-01-08    2.173185
2001-01-09    0.564561
2001-01-10   -0.190481
                ...
2001-12-22    0.000369
2001-12-23    0.900885
2001-12-24   -0.454869
2001-12-25   -0.864547
2001-12-26    1.129120
2001-12-27    0.057874
2001-12-28   -0.433739
2001-12-29    0.092698
2001-12-30   -1.397820
2001-12-31    1.457823
Freq: D, Length: 365, dtype: float64
```

Here, the string '2001' is interpreted as a year and selects that time period. This also works if you specify the month:

```
In [57]: longer_ts['2001-05']
Out[57]:
2001-05-01   -0.622547
2001-05-02    0.936289
2001-05-03    0.750018
2001-05-04   -0.056715
2001-05-05    2.300675
2001-05-06    0.569497
2001-05-07    1.489410
2001-05-08    1.264250
2001-05-09   -0.761837
2001-05-10   -0.331617
                ...
2001-05-22    0.503699
2001-05-23   -1.387874
2001-05-24    0.204851
2001-05-25    0.603705
2001-05-26    0.545680
```

```
2001-05-27     0.235477
2001-05-28     0.111835
2001-05-29    -1.251504
2001-05-30    -2.949343
2001-05-31     0.634634
Freq: D, Length: 31, dtype: float64
```

Slicing with datetime objects works as well:

```
In [58]: ts[datetime(2011, 1, 7):]
Out[58]:
2011-01-07    -0.519439
2011-01-08    -0.555730
2011-01-10     1.965781
2011-01-12     1.393406
dtype: float64
```

Because most time series data is ordered chronologically, you can slice with timestamps not contained in a time series to perform a range query:

```
In [59]: ts
Out[59]:
2011-01-02    -0.204708
2011-01-05     0.478943
2011-01-07    -0.519439
2011-01-08    -0.555730
2011-01-10     1.965781
2011-01-12     1.393406
dtype: float64

In [60]: ts['1/6/2011':'1/11/2011']
Out[60]:
2011-01-07    -0.519439
2011-01-08    -0.555730
2011-01-10     1.965781
dtype: float64
```

As before, you can pass either a string date, datetime, or timestamp. Remember that slicing in this manner produces views on the source time series like slicing NumPy arrays. This means that no data is copied and modifications on the slice will be reflected in the original data.

There is an equivalent instance method, truncate, that slices a Series between two dates:

```
In [61]: ts.truncate(after='1/9/2011')
Out[61]:
2011-01-02    -0.204708
2011-01-05     0.478943
2011-01-07    -0.519439
2011-01-08    -0.555730
dtype: float64
```

All of this holds true for DataFrame as well, indexing on its rows:

```
In [62]: dates = pd.date_range('1/1/2000', periods=100, freq='W-WED')

In [63]: long_df = pd.DataFrame(np.random.randn(100, 4),
   ....:                        index=dates,
   ....:                        columns=['Colorado', 'Texas',
   ....:                                 'New York', 'Ohio'])

In [64]: long_df.loc['5-2001']
Out[64]:
            Colorado     Texas  New York      Ohio
2001-05-02 -0.006045  0.490094 -0.277186 -0.707213
2001-05-09 -0.560107  2.735527  0.927335  1.513906
2001-05-16  0.538600  1.273768  0.667876 -0.969206
2001-05-23  1.676091 -0.817649  0.050188  1.951312
2001-05-30  3.260383  0.963301  1.201206 -1.852001
```

Time Series with Duplicate Indices

In some applications, there may be multiple data observations falling on a particular timestamp. Here is an example:

```
In [65]: dates = pd.DatetimeIndex(['1/1/2000', '1/2/2000', '1/2/2000',
   ....:                           '1/2/2000', '1/3/2000'])

In [66]: dup_ts = pd.Series(np.arange(5), index=dates)

In [67]: dup_ts
Out[67]:
2000-01-01    0
2000-01-02    1
2000-01-02    2
2000-01-02    3
2000-01-03    4
dtype: int64
```

We can tell that the index is not unique by checking its is_unique property:

```
In [68]: dup_ts.index.is_unique
Out[68]: False
```

Indexing into this time series will now either produce scalar values or slices depending on whether a timestamp is duplicated:

```
In [69]: dup_ts['1/3/2000']  # not duplicated
Out[69]: 4

In [70]: dup_ts['1/2/2000']  # duplicated
Out[70]:
2000-01-02    1
2000-01-02    2
```

```
2000-01-02    3
dtype: int64
```

Suppose you wanted to aggregate the data having non-unique timestamps. One way to do this is to use groupby and pass level=0:

```
In [71]: grouped = dup_ts.groupby(level=0)

In [72]: grouped.mean()
Out[72]:
2000-01-01    0
2000-01-02    2
2000-01-03    4
dtype: int64

In [73]: grouped.count()
Out[73]:
2000-01-01    1
2000-01-02    3
2000-01-03    1
dtype: int64
```

11.3 Date Ranges, Frequencies, and Shifting

Generic time series in pandas are assumed to be irregular; that is, they have no fixed frequency. For many applications this is sufficient. However, it's often desirable to work relative to a fixed frequency, such as daily, monthly, or every 15 minutes, even if that means introducing missing values into a time series. Fortunately pandas has a full suite of standard time series frequencies and tools for resampling, inferring frequencies, and generating fixed-frequency date ranges. For example, you can convert the sample time series to be fixed daily frequency by calling resample:

```
In [74]: ts
Out[74]:
2011-01-02   -0.204708
2011-01-05    0.478943
2011-01-07   -0.519439
2011-01-08   -0.555730
2011-01-10    1.965781
2011-01-12    1.393406
dtype: float64

In [75]: resampler = ts.resample('D')
```

The string 'D' is interpreted as daily frequency.

Conversion between frequencies or *resampling* is a big enough topic to have its own section later (Section 11.6, "Resampling and Frequency Conversion," on page 354). Here I'll show you how to use the base frequencies and multiples thereof.

Generating Date Ranges

While I used it previously without explanation, `pandas.date_range` is responsible for generating a `DatetimeIndex` with an indicated length according to a particular frequency:

```
In [76]: index = pd.date_range('2012-04-01', '2012-06-01')

In [77]: index
Out[77]:
DatetimeIndex(['2012-04-01', '2012-04-02', '2012-04-03', '2012-04-04',
               '2012-04-05', '2012-04-06', '2012-04-07', '2012-04-08',
               '2012-04-09', '2012-04-10', '2012-04-11', '2012-04-12',
               '2012-04-13', '2012-04-14', '2012-04-15', '2012-04-16',
               '2012-04-17', '2012-04-18', '2012-04-19', '2012-04-20',
               '2012-04-21', '2012-04-22', '2012-04-23', '2012-04-24',
               '2012-04-25', '2012-04-26', '2012-04-27', '2012-04-28',
               '2012-04-29', '2012-04-30', '2012-05-01', '2012-05-02',
               '2012-05-03', '2012-05-04', '2012-05-05', '2012-05-06',
               '2012-05-07', '2012-05-08', '2012-05-09', '2012-05-10',
               '2012-05-11', '2012-05-12', '2012-05-13', '2012-05-14',
               '2012-05-15', '2012-05-16', '2012-05-17', '2012-05-18',
               '2012-05-19', '2012-05-20', '2012-05-21', '2012-05-22',
               '2012-05-23', '2012-05-24', '2012-05-25', '2012-05-26',
               '2012-05-27', '2012-05-28', '2012-05-29', '2012-05-30',
               '2012-05-31', '2012-06-01'],
              dtype='datetime64[ns]', freq='D')
```

By default, `date_range` generates daily timestamps. If you pass only a start or end date, you must pass a number of periods to generate:

```
In [78]: pd.date_range(start='2012-04-01', periods=20)
Out[78]:
DatetimeIndex(['2012-04-01', '2012-04-02', '2012-04-03', '2012-04-04',
               '2012-04-05', '2012-04-06', '2012-04-07', '2012-04-08',
               '2012-04-09', '2012-04-10', '2012-04-11', '2012-04-12',
               '2012-04-13', '2012-04-14', '2012-04-15', '2012-04-16',
               '2012-04-17', '2012-04-18', '2012-04-19', '2012-04-20'],
              dtype='datetime64[ns]', freq='D')

In [79]: pd.date_range(end='2012-06-01', periods=20)
Out[79]:
DatetimeIndex(['2012-05-13', '2012-05-14', '2012-05-15', '2012-05-16',
               '2012-05-17', '2012-05-18', '2012-05-19', '2012-05-20',
               '2012-05-21', '2012-05-22', '2012-05-23', '2012-05-24',
               '2012-05-25', '2012-05-26', '2012-05-27', '2012-05-28',
               '2012-05-29', '2012-05-30', '2012-05-31', '2012-06-01'],
              dtype='datetime64[ns]', freq='D')
```

The start and end dates define strict boundaries for the generated date index. For example, if you wanted a date index containing the last business day of each month, you would pass the `'BM'` frequency (business end of month; see more complete listing of frequencies in Table 11-4) and only dates falling on or inside the date interval will be included:

```
In [80]: pd.date_range('2000-01-01', '2000-12-01', freq='BM')
Out[80]:
DatetimeIndex(['2000-01-31', '2000-02-29', '2000-03-31', '2000-04-28',
               '2000-05-31', '2000-06-30', '2000-07-31', '2000-08-31',
               '2000-09-29', '2000-10-31', '2000-11-30'],
              dtype='datetime64[ns]', freq='BM')
```

Table 11-4. Base time series frequencies (not comprehensive)

Alias	Offset type	Description
D	Day	Calendar daily
B	BusinessDay	Business daily
H	Hour	Hourly
T or min	Minute	Minutely
S	Second	Secondly
L or ms	Milli	Millisecond (1/1,000 of 1 second)
U	Micro	Microsecond (1/1,000,000 of 1 second)
M	MonthEnd	Last calendar day of month
BM	BusinessMonthEnd	Last business day (weekday) of month
MS	MonthBegin	First calendar day of month
BMS	BusinessMonthBegin	First weekday of month
W-MON, W-TUE, ...	Week	Weekly on given day of week (MON, TUE, WED, THU, FRI, SAT, or SUN)
WOM-1MON, WOM-2MON, ...	WeekOfMonth	Generate weekly dates in the first, second, third, or fourth week of the month (e.g., WOM-3FRI for the third Friday of each month)
Q-JAN, Q-FEB, ...	QuarterEnd	Quarterly dates anchored on last calendar day of each month, for year ending in indicated month (JAN, FEB, MAR, APR, MAY, JUN, JUL, AUG, SEP, OCT, NOV, or DEC)
BQ-JAN, BQ-FEB, ...	BusinessQuarterEnd	Quarterly dates anchored on last weekday day of each month, for year ending in indicated month
QS-JAN, QS-FEB, ...	QuarterBegin	Quarterly dates anchored on first calendar day of each month, for year ending in indicated month
BQS-JAN, BQS-FEB, ...	BusinessQuarterBegin	Quarterly dates anchored on first weekday day of each month, for year ending in indicated month
A-JAN, A-FEB, ...	YearEnd	Annual dates anchored on last calendar day of given month (JAN, FEB, MAR, APR, MAY, JUN, JUL, AUG, SEP, OCT, NOV, or DEC)
BA-JAN, BA-FEB, ...	BusinessYearEnd	Annual dates anchored on last weekday of given month
AS-JAN, AS-FEB, ...	YearBegin	Annual dates anchored on first day of given month
BAS-JAN, BAS-FEB, ...	BusinessYearBegin	Annual dates anchored on first weekday of given month

date_range by default preserves the time (if any) of the start or end timestamp:

```
In [81]: pd.date_range('2012-05-02 12:56:31', periods=5)
Out[81]:
DatetimeIndex(['2012-05-02 12:56:31', '2012-05-03 12:56:31',
               '2012-05-04 12:56:31', '2012-05-05 12:56:31',
               '2012-05-06 12:56:31'],
              dtype='datetime64[ns]', freq='D')
```

Sometimes you will have start or end dates with time information but want to generate a set of timestamps *normalized* to midnight as a convention. To do this, there is a normalize option:

```
In [82]: pd.date_range('2012-05-02 12:56:31', periods=5, normalize=True)
Out[82]:
DatetimeIndex(['2012-05-02', '2012-05-03', '2012-05-04', '2012-05-05',
               '2012-05-06'],
              dtype='datetime64[ns]', freq='D')
```

Frequencies and Date Offsets

Frequencies in pandas are composed of a *base frequency* and a multiplier. Base frequencies are typically referred to by a string alias, like 'M' for monthly or 'H' for hourly. For each base frequency, there is an object defined generally referred to as a *date offset*. For example, hourly frequency can be represented with the Hour class:

```
In [83]: from pandas.tseries.offsets import Hour, Minute
```

```
In [84]: hour = Hour()
```

```
In [85]: hour
Out[85]: <Hour>
```

You can define a multiple of an offset by passing an integer:

```
In [86]: four_hours = Hour(4)
```

```
In [87]: four_hours
Out[87]: <4 * Hours>
```

In most applications, you would never need to explicitly create one of these objects, instead using a string alias like 'H' or '4H'. Putting an integer before the base frequency creates a multiple:

```
In [88]: pd.date_range('2000-01-01', '2000-01-03 23:59', freq='4h')
Out[88]:
DatetimeIndex(['2000-01-01 00:00:00', '2000-01-01 04:00:00',
               '2000-01-01 08:00:00', '2000-01-01 12:00:00',
               '2000-01-01 16:00:00', '2000-01-01 20:00:00',
               '2000-01-02 00:00:00', '2000-01-02 04:00:00',
               '2000-01-02 08:00:00', '2000-01-02 12:00:00',
               '2000-01-02 16:00:00', '2000-01-02 20:00:00',
```

```
                    '2000-01-03 00:00:00', '2000-01-03 04:00:00',
                    '2000-01-03 08:00:00', '2000-01-03 12:00:00',
                    '2000-01-03 16:00:00', '2000-01-03 20:00:00'],
                  dtype='datetime64[ns]', freq='4H')
```

Many offsets can be combined together by addition:

```
In [89]: Hour(2) + Minute(30)
Out[89]: <150 * Minutes>
```

Similarly, you can pass frequency strings, like `'1h30min'`, that will effectively be parsed to the same expression:

```
In [90]: pd.date_range('2000-01-01', periods=10, freq='1h30min')
Out[90]:
DatetimeIndex(['2000-01-01 00:00:00', '2000-01-01 01:30:00',
               '2000-01-01 03:00:00', '2000-01-01 04:30:00',
               '2000-01-01 06:00:00', '2000-01-01 07:30:00',
               '2000-01-01 09:00:00', '2000-01-01 10:30:00',
               '2000-01-01 12:00:00', '2000-01-01 13:30:00'],
              dtype='datetime64[ns]', freq='90T')
```

Some frequencies describe points in time that are not evenly spaced. For example, `'M'` (calendar month end) and `'BM'` (last business/weekday of month) depend on the number of days in a month and, in the latter case, whether the month ends on a weekend or not. We refer to these as *anchored* offsets.

Refer back to Table 11-4 for a listing of frequency codes and date offset classes available in pandas.

> Users can define their own custom frequency classes to provide date logic not available in pandas, though the full details of that are outside the scope of this book.

Week of month dates

One useful frequency class is "week of month," starting with WOM. This enables you to get dates like the third Friday of each month:

```
In [91]: rng = pd.date_range('2012-01-01', '2012-09-01', freq='WOM-3FRI')

In [92]: list(rng)
Out[92]:
[Timestamp('2012-01-20 00:00:00', freq='WOM-3FRI'),
 Timestamp('2012-02-17 00:00:00', freq='WOM-3FRI'),
 Timestamp('2012-03-16 00:00:00', freq='WOM-3FRI'),
 Timestamp('2012-04-20 00:00:00', freq='WOM-3FRI'),
 Timestamp('2012-05-18 00:00:00', freq='WOM-3FRI'),
 Timestamp('2012-06-15 00:00:00', freq='WOM-3FRI'),
```

```
        Timestamp('2012-07-20 00:00:00', freq='WOM-3FRI'),
        Timestamp('2012-08-17 00:00:00', freq='WOM-3FRI')]
```

Shifting (Leading and Lagging) Data

"Shifting" refers to moving data backward and forward through time. Both Series and
DataFrame have a `shift` method for doing naive shifts forward or backward, leaving
the index unmodified:

```
In [93]: ts = pd.Series(np.random.randn(4),
    ....:               index=pd.date_range('1/1/2000', periods=4, freq='M'))

In [94]: ts
Out[94]:
2000-01-31    -0.066748
2000-02-29     0.838639
2000-03-31    -0.117388
2000-04-30    -0.517795
Freq: M, dtype: float64

In [95]: ts.shift(2)
Out[95]:
2000-01-31          NaN
2000-02-29          NaN
2000-03-31    -0.066748
2000-04-30     0.838639
Freq: M, dtype: float64

In [96]: ts.shift(-2)
Out[96]:
2000-01-31    -0.117388
2000-02-29    -0.517795
2000-03-31          NaN
2000-04-30          NaN
Freq: M, dtype: float64
```

When we shift like this, missing data is introduced either at the start or the end of the
time series.

A common use of `shift` is computing percent changes in a time series or multiple
time series as DataFrame columns. This is expressed as:

```
ts / ts.shift(1) - 1
```

Because naive shifts leave the index unmodified, some data is discarded. Thus if the
frequency is known, it can be passed to `shift` to advance the timestamps instead of
simply the data:

```
In [97]: ts.shift(2, freq='M')
Out[97]:
2000-03-31    -0.066748
2000-04-30     0.838639
```

```
2000-05-31    -0.117388
2000-06-30    -0.517795
Freq: M, dtype: float64
```

Other frequencies can be passed, too, giving you some flexibility in how to lead and lag the data:

```
In [98]: ts.shift(3, freq='D')
Out[98]:
2000-02-03    -0.066748
2000-03-03     0.838639
2000-04-03    -0.117388
2000-05-03    -0.517795
dtype: float64

In [99]: ts.shift(1, freq='90T')
Out[99]:
2000-01-31 01:30:00    -0.066748
2000-02-29 01:30:00     0.838639
2000-03-31 01:30:00    -0.117388
2000-04-30 01:30:00    -0.517795
Freq: M, dtype: float64
```

The T here stands for minutes. Note that the freq parameter here indicates the offset to apply to the timestamps, but it does not change the underlying frequency of the data, if any.

Shifting dates with offsets

The pandas date offsets can also be used with datetime or Timestamp objects:

```
In [100]: from pandas.tseries.offsets import Day, MonthEnd

In [101]: now = datetime(2011, 11, 17)

In [102]: now + 3 * Day()
Out[102]: Timestamp('2011-11-20 00:00:00')
```

If you add an anchored offset like MonthEnd, the first increment will "roll forward" a date to the next date according to the frequency rule:

```
In [103]: now + MonthEnd()
Out[103]: Timestamp('2011-11-30 00:00:00')

In [104]: now + MonthEnd(2)
Out[104]: Timestamp('2011-12-31 00:00:00')
```

Anchored offsets can explicitly "roll" dates forward or backward by simply using their rollforward and rollback methods, respectively:

```
In [105]: offset = MonthEnd()

In [106]: offset.rollforward(now)
```

```
Out[106]: Timestamp('2011-11-30 00:00:00')

In [107]: offset.rollback(now)
Out[107]: Timestamp('2011-10-31 00:00:00')
```

A creative use of date offsets is to use these methods with groupby:

```
In [108]: ts = pd.Series(np.random.randn(20),
   .....:                index=pd.date_range('1/15/2000', periods=20, freq='4d'))

In [109]: ts
Out[109]:
2000-01-15   -0.116696
2000-01-19    2.389645
2000-01-23   -0.932454
2000-01-27   -0.229331
2000-01-31   -1.140330
2000-02-04    0.439920
2000-02-08   -0.823758
2000-02-12   -0.520930
2000-02-16    0.350282
2000-02-20    0.204395
2000-02-24    0.133445
2000-02-28    0.327905
2000-03-03    0.072153
2000-03-07    0.131678
2000-03-11   -1.297459
2000-03-15    0.997747
2000-03-19    0.870955
2000-03-23   -0.991253
2000-03-27    0.151699
2000-03-31    1.266151
Freq: 4D, dtype: float64

In [110]: ts.groupby(offset.rollforward).mean()
Out[110]:
2000-01-31   -0.005833
2000-02-29    0.015894
2000-03-31    0.150209
dtype: float64
```

Of course, an easier and faster way to do this is using `resample` (we'll discuss this in much more depth in Section 11.6, "Resampling and Frequency Conversion," on page 354):

```
In [111]: ts.resample('M').mean()
Out[111]:
2000-01-31   -0.005833
2000-02-29    0.015894
2000-03-31    0.150209
Freq: M, dtype: float64
```

11.4 Time Zone Handling

Working with time zones is generally considered one of the most unpleasant parts of time series manipulation. As a result, many time series users choose to work with time series in *coordinated universal time* or *UTC*, which is the successor to Greenwich Mean Time and is the current international standard. Time zones are expressed as offsets from UTC; for example, New York is four hours behind UTC during daylight saving time and five hours behind the rest of the year.

In Python, time zone information comes from the third-party pytz library (installable with pip or conda), which exposes the *Olson database*, a compilation of world time zone information. This is especially important for historical data because the daylight saving time (DST) transition dates (and even UTC offsets) have been changed numerous times depending on the whims of local governments. In the United States, the DST transition times have been changed many times since 1900!

For detailed information about the pytz library, you'll need to look at that library's documentation. As far as this book is concerned, pandas wraps pytz's functionality so you can ignore its API outside of the time zone names. Time zone names can be found interactively and in the docs:

```
In [112]: import pytz

In [113]: pytz.common_timezones[-5:]
Out[113]: ['US/Eastern', 'US/Hawaii', 'US/Mountain', 'US/Pacific', 'UTC']
```

To get a time zone object from pytz, use pytz.timezone:

```
In [114]: tz = pytz.timezone('America/New_York')

In [115]: tz
Out[115]: <DstTzInfo 'America/New_York' LMT-1 day, 19:04:00 STD>
```

Methods in pandas will accept either time zone names or these objects.

Time Zone Localization and Conversion

By default, time series in pandas are *time zone naive*. For example, consider the following time series:

```
In [116]: rng = pd.date_range('3/9/2012 9:30', periods=6, freq='D')

In [117]: ts = pd.Series(np.random.randn(len(rng)), index=rng)

In [118]: ts
Out[118]:
2012-03-09 09:30:00   -0.202469
2012-03-10 09:30:00    0.050718
2012-03-11 09:30:00    0.639869
2012-03-12 09:30:00    0.597594
```

```
2012-03-13 09:30:00    -0.797246
2012-03-14 09:30:00     0.472879
Freq: D, dtype: float64
```

The index's tz field is None:

```
In [119]: print(ts.index.tz)
None
```

Date ranges can be generated with a time zone set:

```
In [120]: pd.date_range('3/9/2012 9:30', periods=10, freq='D', tz='UTC')
Out[120]:
DatetimeIndex(['2012-03-09 09:30:00+00:00', '2012-03-10 09:30:00+00:00',
               '2012-03-11 09:30:00+00:00', '2012-03-12 09:30:00+00:00',
               '2012-03-13 09:30:00+00:00', '2012-03-14 09:30:00+00:00',
               '2012-03-15 09:30:00+00:00', '2012-03-16 09:30:00+00:00',
               '2012-03-17 09:30:00+00:00', '2012-03-18 09:30:00+00:00'],
              dtype='datetime64[ns, UTC]', freq='D')
```

Conversion from naive to *localized* is handled by the tz_localize method:

```
In [121]: ts
Out[121]:
2012-03-09 09:30:00    -0.202469
2012-03-10 09:30:00     0.050718
2012-03-11 09:30:00     0.639869
2012-03-12 09:30:00     0.597594
2012-03-13 09:30:00    -0.797246
2012-03-14 09:30:00     0.472879
Freq: D, dtype: float64

In [122]: ts_utc = ts.tz_localize('UTC')

In [123]: ts_utc
Out[123]:
2012-03-09 09:30:00+00:00    -0.202469
2012-03-10 09:30:00+00:00     0.050718
2012-03-11 09:30:00+00:00     0.639869
2012-03-12 09:30:00+00:00     0.597594
2012-03-13 09:30:00+00:00    -0.797246
2012-03-14 09:30:00+00:00     0.472879
Freq: D, dtype: float64

In [124]: ts_utc.index
Out[124]:
DatetimeIndex(['2012-03-09 09:30:00+00:00', '2012-03-10 09:30:00+00:00',
               '2012-03-11 09:30:00+00:00', '2012-03-12 09:30:00+00:00',
               '2012-03-13 09:30:00+00:00', '2012-03-14 09:30:00+00:00'],
              dtype='datetime64[ns, UTC]', freq='D')
```

Once a time series has been localized to a particular time zone, it can be converted to another time zone with tz_convert:

```
In [125]: ts_utc.tz_convert('America/New_York')
Out[125]:
2012-03-09 04:30:00-05:00    -0.202469
2012-03-10 04:30:00-05:00     0.050718
2012-03-11 05:30:00-04:00     0.639869
2012-03-12 05:30:00-04:00     0.597594
2012-03-13 05:30:00-04:00    -0.797246
2012-03-14 05:30:00-04:00     0.472879
Freq: D, dtype: float64
```

In the case of the preceding time series, which straddles a DST transition in the America/New_York time zone, we could localize to EST and convert to, say, UTC or Berlin time:

```
In [126]: ts_eastern = ts.tz_localize('America/New_York')

In [127]: ts_eastern.tz_convert('UTC')
Out[127]:
2012-03-09 14:30:00+00:00    -0.202469
2012-03-10 14:30:00+00:00     0.050718
2012-03-11 13:30:00+00:00     0.639869
2012-03-12 13:30:00+00:00     0.597594
2012-03-13 13:30:00+00:00    -0.797246
2012-03-14 13:30:00+00:00     0.472879
Freq: D, dtype: float64

In [128]: ts_eastern.tz_convert('Europe/Berlin')
Out[128]:
2012-03-09 15:30:00+01:00    -0.202469
2012-03-10 15:30:00+01:00     0.050718
2012-03-11 14:30:00+01:00     0.639869
2012-03-12 14:30:00+01:00     0.597594
2012-03-13 14:30:00+01:00    -0.797246
2012-03-14 14:30:00+01:00     0.472879
Freq: D, dtype: float64
```

tz_localize and tz_convert are also instance methods on DatetimeIndex:

```
In [129]: ts.index.tz_localize('Asia/Shanghai')
Out[129]:
DatetimeIndex(['2012-03-09 09:30:00+08:00', '2012-03-10 09:30:00+08:00',
               '2012-03-11 09:30:00+08:00', '2012-03-12 09:30:00+08:00',
               '2012-03-13 09:30:00+08:00', '2012-03-14 09:30:00+08:00'],
              dtype='datetime64[ns, Asia/Shanghai]', freq='D')
```

Localizing naive timestamps also checks for ambiguous or non-existent times around daylight saving time transitions.

Operations with Time Zone—Aware Timestamp Objects

Similar to time series and date ranges, individual `Timestamp` objects similarly can be localized from naive to time zone–aware and converted from one time zone to another:

```
In [130]: stamp = pd.Timestamp('2011-03-12 04:00')

In [131]: stamp_utc = stamp.tz_localize('utc')

In [132]: stamp_utc.tz_convert('America/New_York')
Out[132]: Timestamp('2011-03-11 23:00:00-0500', tz='America/New_York')
```

You can also pass a time zone when creating the `Timestamp`:

```
In [133]: stamp_moscow = pd.Timestamp('2011-03-12 04:00', tz='Europe/Moscow')

In [134]: stamp_moscow
Out[134]: Timestamp('2011-03-12 04:00:00+0300', tz='Europe/Moscow')
```

Time zone–aware `Timestamp` objects internally store a UTC timestamp value as nanoseconds since the Unix epoch (January 1, 1970); this UTC value is invariant between time zone conversions:

```
In [135]: stamp_utc.value
Out[135]: 1299902400000000000

In [136]: stamp_utc.tz_convert('America/New_York').value
Out[136]: 1299902400000000000
```

When performing time arithmetic using pandas's `DateOffset` objects, pandas respects daylight saving time transitions where possible. Here we construct timestamps that occur right before DST transitions (forward and backward). First, 30 minutes before transitioning to DST:

```
In [137]: from pandas.tseries.offsets import Hour

In [138]: stamp = pd.Timestamp('2012-03-11 01:30', tz='US/Eastern')

In [139]: stamp
Out[139]: Timestamp('2012-03-11 01:30:00-0500', tz='US/Eastern')

In [140]: stamp + Hour()
Out[140]: Timestamp('2012-03-11 03:30:00-0400', tz='US/Eastern')
```

Then, 90 minutes before transitioning out of DST:

```
In [141]: stamp = pd.Timestamp('2012-11-04 00:30', tz='US/Eastern')

In [142]: stamp
Out[142]: Timestamp('2012-11-04 00:30:00-0400', tz='US/Eastern')
```

```
In [143]: stamp + 2 * Hour()
Out[143]: Timestamp('2012-11-04 01:30:00-0500', tz='US/Eastern')
```

Operations Between Different Time Zones

If two time series with different time zones are combined, the result will be UTC.
Since the timestamps are stored under the hood in UTC, this is a straightforward
operation and requires no conversion to happen:

```
In [144]: rng = pd.date_range('3/7/2012 9:30', periods=10, freq='B')
```

```
In [145]: ts = pd.Series(np.random.randn(len(rng)), index=rng)
```

```
In [146]: ts
Out[146]:
2012-03-07 09:30:00     0.522356
2012-03-08 09:30:00    -0.546348
2012-03-09 09:30:00    -0.733537
2012-03-12 09:30:00     1.302736
2012-03-13 09:30:00     0.022199
2012-03-14 09:30:00     0.364287
2012-03-15 09:30:00    -0.922839
2012-03-16 09:30:00     0.312656
2012-03-19 09:30:00    -1.128497
2012-03-20 09:30:00    -0.333488
Freq: B, dtype: float64
```

```
In [147]: ts1 = ts[:7].tz_localize('Europe/London')
```

```
In [148]: ts2 = ts1[2:].tz_convert('Europe/Moscow')
```

```
In [149]: result = ts1 + ts2
```

```
In [150]: result.index
Out[150]:
DatetimeIndex(['2012-03-07 09:30:00+00:00', '2012-03-08 09:30:00+00:00',
               '2012-03-09 09:30:00+00:00', '2012-03-12 09:30:00+00:00',
               '2012-03-13 09:30:00+00:00', '2012-03-14 09:30:00+00:00',
               '2012-03-15 09:30:00+00:00'],
              dtype='datetime64[ns, UTC]', freq='B')
```

11.5 Periods and Period Arithmetic

Periods represent timespans, like days, months, quarters, or years. The `Period` class
represents this data type, requiring a string or integer and a frequency from
Table 11-4:

```
In [151]: p = pd.Period(2007, freq='A-DEC')
```

```
In [152]: p
Out[152]: Period('2007', 'A-DEC')
```

In this case, the `Period` object represents the full timespan from January 1, 2007, to December 31, 2007, inclusive. Conveniently, adding and subtracting integers from periods has the effect of shifting by their frequency:

```
In [153]: p + 5
Out[153]: Period('2012', 'A-DEC')

In [154]: p - 2
Out[154]: Period('2005', 'A-DEC')
```

If two periods have the same frequency, their difference is the number of units between them:

```
In [155]: pd.Period('2014', freq='A-DEC') - p
Out[155]: <7 * YearEnds: month=12>
```

Regular ranges of periods can be constructed with the `period_range` function:

```
In [156]: rng = pd.period_range('2000-01-01', '2000-06-30', freq='M')

In [157]: rng
Out[157]: PeriodIndex(['2000-01', '2000-02', '2000-03', '2000-04', '2000-05', '20
00-06'], dtype='period[M]', freq='M')
```

The `PeriodIndex` class stores a sequence of periods and can serve as an axis index in any pandas data structure:

```
In [158]: pd.Series(np.random.randn(6), index=rng)
Out[158]:
2000-01   -0.514551
2000-02   -0.559782
2000-03   -0.783408
2000-04   -1.797685
2000-05   -0.172670
2000-06    0.680215
Freq: M, dtype: float64
```

If you have an array of strings, you can also use the `PeriodIndex` class:

```
In [159]: values = ['2001Q3', '2002Q2', '2003Q1']

In [160]: index = pd.PeriodIndex(values, freq='Q-DEC')

In [161]: index
Out[161]: PeriodIndex(['2001Q3', '2002Q2', '2003Q1'], dtype='period[Q-DEC]', freq
='Q-DEC')
```

Period Frequency Conversion

Periods and `PeriodIndex` objects can be converted to another frequency with their `asfreq` method. As an example, suppose we had an annual period and wanted to convert it into a monthly period either at the start or end of the year. This is fairly straightforward:

```
In [162]: p = pd.Period('2007', freq='A-DEC')

In [163]: p
Out[163]: Period('2007', 'A-DEC')

In [164]: p.asfreq('M', how='start')
Out[164]: Period('2007-01', 'M')

In [165]: p.asfreq('M', how='end')
Out[165]: Period('2007-12', 'M')
```

You can think of Period('2007', 'A-DEC') as being a sort of cursor pointing to a span of time, subdivided by monthly periods. See Figure 11-1 for an illustration of this. For a *fiscal year* ending on a month other than December, the corresponding monthly subperiods are different:

```
In [166]: p = pd.Period('2007', freq='A-JUN')

In [167]: p
Out[167]: Period('2007', 'A-JUN')

In [168]: p.asfreq('M', 'start')
Out[168]: Period('2006-07', 'M')

In [169]: p.asfreq('M', 'end')
Out[169]: Period('2007-06', 'M')
```

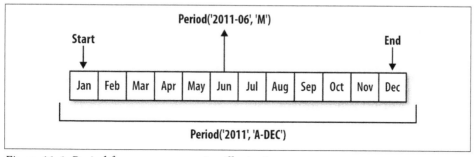

Figure 11-1. Period frequency conversion illustration

When you are converting from high to low frequency, pandas determines the superperiod depending on where the subperiod "belongs." For example, in A-JUN frequency, the month Aug-2007 is actually part of the 2008 period:

```
In [170]: p = pd.Period('Aug-2007', 'M')

In [171]: p.asfreq('A-JUN')
Out[171]: Period('2008', 'A-JUN')
```

Whole `PeriodIndex` objects or time series can be similarly converted with the same semantics:

```
In [172]: rng = pd.period_range('2006', '2009', freq='A-DEC')

In [173]: ts = pd.Series(np.random.randn(len(rng)), index=rng)

In [174]: ts
Out[174]:
2006    1.607578
2007    0.200381
2008   -0.834068
2009   -0.302988
Freq: A-DEC, dtype: float64

In [175]: ts.asfreq('M', how='start')
Out[175]:
2006-01    1.607578
2007-01    0.200381
2008-01   -0.834068
2009-01   -0.302988
Freq: M, dtype: float64
```

Here, the annual periods are replaced with monthly periods corresponding to the first month falling within each annual period. If we instead wanted the last business day of each year, we can use the `'B'` frequency and indicate that we want the end of the period:

```
In [176]: ts.asfreq('B', how='end')
Out[176]:
2006-12-29    1.607578
2007-12-31    0.200381
2008-12-31   -0.834068
2009-12-31   -0.302988
Freq: B, dtype: float64
```

Quarterly Period Frequencies

Quarterly data is standard in accounting, finance, and other fields. Much quarterly data is reported relative to a *fiscal year end*, typically the last calendar or business day of one of the 12 months of the year. Thus, the period 2012Q4 has a different meaning depending on fiscal year end. pandas supports all 12 possible quarterly frequencies as Q-JAN through Q-DEC:

```
In [177]: p = pd.Period('2012Q4', freq='Q-JAN')

In [178]: p
Out[178]: Period('2012Q4', 'Q-JAN')
```

In the case of fiscal year ending in January, 2012Q4 runs from November through January, which you can check by converting to daily frequency. See Figure 11-2 for an illustration.

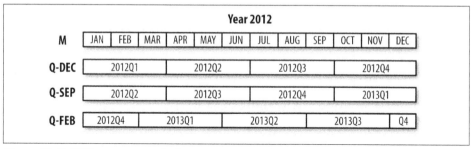

Figure 11-2. Different quarterly frequency conventions

```
In [179]: p.asfreq('D', 'start')
Out[179]: Period('2011-11-01', 'D')

In [180]: p.asfreq('D', 'end')
Out[180]: Period('2012-01-31', 'D')
```

Thus, it's possible to do easy period arithmetic; for example, to get the timestamp at 4 PM on the second-to-last business day of the quarter, you could do:

```
In [181]: p4pm = (p.asfreq('B', 'e') - 1).asfreq('T', 's') + 16 * 60

In [182]: p4pm
Out[182]: Period('2012-01-30 16:00', 'T')

In [183]: p4pm.to_timestamp()
Out[183]: Timestamp('2012-01-30 16:00:00')
```

You can generate quarterly ranges using `period_range`. Arithmetic is identical, too:

```
In [184]: rng = pd.period_range('2011Q3', '2012Q4', freq='Q-JAN')

In [185]: ts = pd.Series(np.arange(len(rng)), index=rng)

In [186]: ts
Out[186]:
2011Q3    0
2011Q4    1
2012Q1    2
2012Q2    3
2012Q3    4
2012Q4    5
Freq: Q-JAN, dtype: int64

In [187]: new_rng = (rng.asfreq('B', 'e') - 1).asfreq('T', 's') + 16 * 60

In [188]: ts.index = new_rng.to_timestamp()
```

```
In [189]: ts
Out[189]:
2010-10-28 16:00:00    0
2011-01-28 16:00:00    1
2011-04-28 16:00:00    2
2011-07-28 16:00:00    3
2011-10-28 16:00:00    4
2012-01-30 16:00:00    5
dtype: int64
```

Converting Timestamps to Periods (and Back)

Series and DataFrame objects indexed by timestamps can be converted to periods
with the to_period method:

```
In [190]: rng = pd.date_range('2000-01-01', periods=3, freq='M')

In [191]: ts = pd.Series(np.random.randn(3), index=rng)

In [192]: ts
Out[192]:
2000-01-31     1.663261
2000-02-29    -0.996206
2000-03-31     1.521760
Freq: M, dtype: float64

In [193]: pts = ts.to_period()

In [194]: pts
Out[194]:
2000-01     1.663261
2000-02    -0.996206
2000-03     1.521760
Freq: M, dtype: float64
```

Since periods refer to non-overlapping timespans, a timestamp can only belong to a
single period for a given frequency. While the frequency of the new PeriodIndex is
inferred from the timestamps by default, you can specify any frequency you want.
There is also no problem with having duplicate periods in the result:

```
In [195]: rng = pd.date_range('1/29/2000', periods=6, freq='D')

In [196]: ts2 = pd.Series(np.random.randn(6), index=rng)

In [197]: ts2
Out[197]:
2000-01-29     0.244175
2000-01-30     0.423331
2000-01-31    -0.654040
2000-02-01     2.089154
2000-02-02    -0.060220
```

```
2000-02-03    -0.167933
Freq: D, dtype: float64

In [198]: ts2.to_period('M')
Out[198]:
2000-01     0.244175
2000-01     0.423331
2000-01    -0.654040
2000-02     2.089154
2000-02    -0.060220
2000-02    -0.167933
Freq: M, dtype: float64
```

To convert back to timestamps, use to_timestamp:

```
In [199]: pts = ts2.to_period()

In [200]: pts
Out[200]:
2000-01-29     0.244175
2000-01-30     0.423331
2000-01-31    -0.654040
2000-02-01     2.089154
2000-02-02    -0.060220
2000-02-03    -0.167933
Freq: D, dtype: float64

In [201]: pts.to_timestamp(how='end')
Out[201]:
2000-01-29 23:59:59.999999999     0.244175
2000-01-30 23:59:59.999999999     0.423331
2000-01-31 23:59:59.999999999    -0.654040
2000-02-01 23:59:59.999999999     2.089154
2000-02-02 23:59:59.999999999    -0.060220
2000-02-03 23:59:59.999999999    -0.167933
Freq: D, dtype: float64
```

Creating a PeriodIndex from Arrays

Fixed frequency datasets are sometimes stored with timespan information spread across multiple columns. For example, in this macroeconomic dataset, the year and quarter are in different columns:

```
In [202]: data = pd.read_csv('examples/macrodata.csv')

In [203]: data.head(5)
Out[203]:
     year  quarter   realgdp  realcons  realinv  realgovt  realdpi    cpi  \
0  1959.0      1.0  2710.349    1707.4  286.898   470.045   1886.9  28.98
1  1959.0      2.0  2778.801    1733.7  310.859   481.301   1919.7  29.15
2  1959.0      3.0  2775.488    1751.8  289.226   491.260   1916.4  29.35
3  1959.0      4.0  2785.204    1753.7  299.356   484.052   1931.3  29.37
```

```
4  1960.0     1.0  2847.699    1770.5 331.722    462.199   1955.5 29.54
      m1  tbilrate  unemp      pop  infl  realint
0  139.7     2.82    5.8  177.146  0.00     0.00
1  141.7     3.08    5.1  177.830  2.34     0.74
2  140.5     3.82    5.3  178.657  2.74     1.09
3  140.0     4.33    5.6  179.386  0.27     4.06
4  139.6     3.50    5.2  180.007  2.31     1.19

In [204]: data.year
Out[204]:
0       1959.0
1       1959.0
2       1959.0
3       1959.0
4       1960.0
5       1960.0
6       1960.0
7       1960.0
8       1961.0
9       1961.0
         ...
193     2007.0
194     2007.0
195     2007.0
196     2008.0
197     2008.0
198     2008.0
199     2008.0
200     2009.0
201     2009.0
202     2009.0
Name: year, Length: 203, dtype: float64

In [205]: data.quarter
Out[205]:
0       1.0
1       2.0
2       3.0
3       4.0
4       1.0
5       2.0
6       3.0
7       4.0
8       1.0
9       2.0
         ...
193     2.0
194     3.0
195     4.0
196     1.0
197     2.0
198     3.0
```

```
199    4.0
200    1.0
201    2.0
202    3.0
Name: quarter, Length: 203, dtype: float64
```

By passing these arrays to `PeriodIndex` with a frequency, you can combine them to form an index for the DataFrame:

```
In [206]: index = pd.PeriodIndex(year=data.year, quarter=data.quarter,
   .....:                         freq='Q-DEC')

In [207]: index
Out[207]:
PeriodIndex(['1959Q1', '1959Q2', '1959Q3', '1959Q4', '1960Q1', '1960Q2',
             '1960Q3', '1960Q4', '1961Q1', '1961Q2',
             ...
             '2007Q2', '2007Q3', '2007Q4', '2008Q1', '2008Q2', '2008Q3',
             '2008Q4', '2009Q1', '2009Q2', '2009Q3'],
            dtype='period[Q-DEC]', length=203, freq='Q-DEC')

In [208]: data.index = index

In [209]: data.infl
Out[209]:
1959Q1    0.00
1959Q2    2.34
1959Q3    2.74
1959Q4    0.27
1960Q1    2.31
1960Q2    0.14
1960Q3    2.70
1960Q4    1.21
1961Q1   -0.40
1961Q2    1.47
           ...
2007Q2    2.75
2007Q3    3.45
2007Q4    6.38
2008Q1    2.82
2008Q2    8.53
2008Q3   -3.16
2008Q4   -8.79
2009Q1    0.94
2009Q2    3.37
2009Q3    3.56
Freq: Q-DEC, Name: infl, Length: 203, dtype: float64
```

11.6 Resampling and Frequency Conversion

Resampling refers to the process of converting a time series from one frequency to another. Aggregating higher frequency data to lower frequency is called *downsampling*, while converting lower frequency to higher frequency is called *upsampling*. Not all resampling falls into either of these categories; for example, converting W-WED (weekly on Wednesday) to W-FRI is neither upsampling nor downsampling.

pandas objects are equipped with a `resample` method, which is the workhorse function for all frequency conversion. `resample` has a similar API to `groupby`; you call `resample` to group the data, then call an aggregation function:

```
In [210]: rng = pd.date_range('2000-01-01', periods=100, freq='D')

In [211]: ts = pd.Series(np.random.randn(len(rng)), index=rng)

In [212]: ts
Out[212]:
2000-01-01    0.631634
2000-01-02   -1.594313
2000-01-03   -1.519937
2000-01-04    1.108752
2000-01-05    1.255853
2000-01-06   -0.024330
2000-01-07   -2.047939
2000-01-08   -0.272657
2000-01-09   -1.692615
2000-01-10    1.423830
                ...
2000-03-31   -0.007852
2000-04-01   -1.638806
2000-04-02    1.401227
2000-04-03    1.758539
2000-04-04    0.628932
2000-04-05   -0.423776
2000-04-06    0.789740
2000-04-07    0.937568
2000-04-08   -2.253294
2000-04-09   -1.772919
Freq: D, Length: 100, dtype: float64

In [213]: ts.resample('M').mean()
Out[213]:
2000-01-31   -0.165893
2000-02-29    0.078606
2000-03-31    0.223811
2000-04-30   -0.063643
Freq: M, dtype: float64

In [214]: ts.resample('M', kind='period').mean()
Out[214]:
```

```
2000-01   -0.165893
2000-02    0.078606
2000-03    0.223811
2000-04   -0.063643
Freq: M, dtype: float64
```

resample is a flexible and high-performance method that can be used to process very large time series. The examples in the following sections illustrate its semantics and use. Table 11-5 summarizes some of its options.

Table 11-5. Resample method arguments

Argument	Description
freq	String or DateOffset indicating desired resampled frequency (e.g., 'M', '5min', or Second(15))
axis	Axis to resample on; default axis=0
fill_method	How to interpolate when upsampling, as in 'ffill' or 'bfill'; by default does no interpolation
closed	In downsampling, which end of each interval is closed (inclusive), 'right' or 'left'
label	In downsampling, how to label the aggregated result, with the 'right' or 'left' bin edge (e.g., the 9:30 to 9:35 five-minute interval could be labeled 9:30 or 9:35)
loffset	Time adjustment to the bin labels, such as '-1s' / Second(-1) to shift the aggregate labels one second earlier
limit	When forward or backward filling, the maximum number of periods to fill
kind	Aggregate to periods ('period') or timestamps ('timestamp'); defaults to the type of index the time series has
convention	When resampling periods, the convention ('start' or 'end') for converting the low-frequency period to high frequency; defaults to 'start'

Downsampling

Aggregating data to a regular, lower frequency is a pretty normal time series task. The data you're aggregating doesn't need to be fixed frequently; the desired frequency defines *bin edges* that are used to slice the time series into pieces to aggregate. For example, to convert to monthly, 'M' or 'BM', you need to chop up the data into one-month intervals. Each interval is said to be *half-open*; a data point can only belong to one interval, and the union of the intervals must make up the whole time frame. There are a couple things to think about when using resample to downsample data:

- Which side of each interval is *closed*
- How to label each aggregated bin, either with the start of the interval or the end

To illustrate, let's look at some one-minute data:

```
In [215]: rng = pd.date_range('2000-01-01', periods=12, freq='T')

In [216]: ts = pd.Series(np.arange(12), index=rng)
```

```
In [217]: ts
Out[217]:
2000-01-01 00:00:00     0
2000-01-01 00:01:00     1
2000-01-01 00:02:00     2
2000-01-01 00:03:00     3
2000-01-01 00:04:00     4
2000-01-01 00:05:00     5
2000-01-01 00:06:00     6
2000-01-01 00:07:00     7
2000-01-01 00:08:00     8
2000-01-01 00:09:00     9
2000-01-01 00:10:00    10
2000-01-01 00:11:00    11
Freq: T, dtype: int64
```

Suppose you wanted to aggregate this data into five-minute chunks or *bars* by taking the sum of each group:

```
In [218]: ts.resample('5min', closed='right').sum()
Out[218]:
1999-12-31 23:55:00     0
2000-01-01 00:00:00    15
2000-01-01 00:05:00    40
2000-01-01 00:10:00    11
Freq: 5T, dtype: int64
```

The frequency you pass defines bin edges in five-minute increments. By default, the *left* bin edge is inclusive, so the 00:00 value is included in the 00:00 to 00:05 interval.[1] Passing closed='right' changes the interval to be closed on the right:

```
In [219]: ts.resample('5min', closed='right').sum()
Out[219]:
1999-12-31 23:55:00     0
2000-01-01 00:00:00    15
2000-01-01 00:05:00    40
2000-01-01 00:10:00    11
Freq: 5T, dtype: int64
```

The resulting time series is labeled by the timestamps from the left side of each bin. By passing label='right' you can label them with the right bin edge:

```
In [220]: ts.resample('5min', closed='right', label='right').sum()
Out[220]:
2000-01-01 00:00:00     0
2000-01-01 00:05:00    15
```

---

1 The choice of the default values for closed and label might seem a bit odd to some users. In practice the choice is somewhat arbitrary; for some target frequencies, closed='left' is preferable, while for others closed='right' makes more sense. The important thing is that you keep in mind exactly how you are segmenting the data.

```
2000-01-01 00:10:00    40
2000-01-01 00:15:00    11
Freq: 5T, dtype: int64
```

See Figure 11-3 for an illustration of minute frequency data being resampled to five-minute frequency.

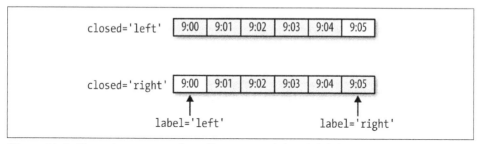

Figure 11-3. Five-minute resampling illustration of closed, label conventions

Lastly, you might want to shift the result index by some amount, say subtracting one second from the right edge to make it more clear which interval the timestamp refers to. To do this, pass a string or date offset to `loffset`:

```
In [221]: ts.resample('5min', closed='right',
   .....:              label='right', loffset='-1s').sum()
Out[221]:
1999-12-31 23:59:59     0
2000-01-01 00:04:59    15
2000-01-01 00:09:59    40
2000-01-01 00:14:59    11
Freq: 5T, dtype: int64
```

You also could have accomplished the effect of `loffset` by calling the `shift` method on the result without the `loffset`.

Open-High-Low-Close (OHLC) resampling

In finance, a popular way to aggregate a time series is to compute four values for each bucket: the first (open), last (close), maximum (high), and minimal (low) values. By using the `ohlc` aggregate function you will obtain a DataFrame having columns containing these four aggregates, which are efficiently computed in a single sweep of the data:

```
In [222]: ts.resample('5min').ohlc()
Out[222]:
                     open  high  low  close
2000-01-01 00:00:00     0     4    0      4
2000-01-01 00:05:00     5     9    5      9
2000-01-01 00:10:00    10    11   10     11
```

Upsampling and Interpolation

When converting from a low frequency to a higher frequency, no aggregation is needed. Let's consider a DataFrame with some weekly data:

```
In [223]: frame = pd.DataFrame(np.random.randn(2, 4),
   .....:                      index=pd.date_range('1/1/2000', periods=2,
   .....:                                          freq='W-WED'),
   .....:                      columns=['Colorado', 'Texas', 'New York', 'Ohio'])

In [224]: frame
Out[224]:
            Colorado     Texas  New York      Ohio
2000-01-05 -0.896431  0.677263  0.036503  0.087102
2000-01-12 -0.046662  0.927238  0.482284 -0.867130
```

When you are using an aggregation function with this data, there is only one value per group, and missing values result in the gaps. We use the asfreq method to convert to the higher frequency without any aggregation:

```
In [225]: df_daily = frame.resample('D').asfreq()

In [226]: df_daily
Out[226]:
            Colorado     Texas  New York      Ohio
2000-01-05 -0.896431  0.677263  0.036503  0.087102
2000-01-06       NaN       NaN       NaN       NaN
2000-01-07       NaN       NaN       NaN       NaN
2000-01-08       NaN       NaN       NaN       NaN
2000-01-09       NaN       NaN       NaN       NaN
2000-01-10       NaN       NaN       NaN       NaN
2000-01-11       NaN       NaN       NaN       NaN
2000-01-12 -0.046662  0.927238  0.482284 -0.867130
```

Suppose you wanted to fill forward each weekly value on the non-Wednesdays. The same filling or interpolation methods available in the fillna and reindex methods are available for resampling:

```
In [227]: frame.resample('D').ffill()
Out[227]:
            Colorado     Texas  New York      Ohio
2000-01-05 -0.896431  0.677263  0.036503  0.087102
2000-01-06 -0.896431  0.677263  0.036503  0.087102
2000-01-07 -0.896431  0.677263  0.036503  0.087102
2000-01-08 -0.896431  0.677263  0.036503  0.087102
2000-01-09 -0.896431  0.677263  0.036503  0.087102
2000-01-10 -0.896431  0.677263  0.036503  0.087102
2000-01-11 -0.896431  0.677263  0.036503  0.087102
2000-01-12 -0.046662  0.927238  0.482284 -0.867130
```

You can similarly choose to only fill a certain number of periods forward to limit how far to continue using an observed value:

```
In [228]: frame.resample('D').ffill(limit=2)
Out[228]:
            Colorado    Texas  New York      Ohio
2000-01-05 -0.896431  0.677263  0.036503  0.087102
2000-01-06 -0.896431  0.677263  0.036503  0.087102
2000-01-07 -0.896431  0.677263  0.036503  0.087102
2000-01-08       NaN       NaN       NaN       NaN
2000-01-09       NaN       NaN       NaN       NaN
2000-01-10       NaN       NaN       NaN       NaN
2000-01-11       NaN       NaN       NaN       NaN
2000-01-12 -0.046662  0.927238  0.482284 -0.867130
```

Notably, the new date index need not overlap with the old one at all:

```
In [229]: frame.resample('W-THU').ffill()
Out[229]:
            Colorado    Texas  New York      Ohio
2000-01-06 -0.896431  0.677263  0.036503  0.087102
2000-01-13 -0.046662  0.927238  0.482284 -0.867130
```

Resampling with Periods

Resampling data indexed by periods is similar to timestamps:

```
In [230]: frame = pd.DataFrame(np.random.randn(24, 4),
   .....:                      index=pd.period_range('1-2000', '12-2001',
   .....:                                            freq='M'),
   .....:                      columns=['Colorado', 'Texas', 'New York', 'Ohio'])

In [231]: frame[:5]
Out[231]:
         Colorado     Texas  New York      Ohio
2000-01  0.493841 -0.155434  1.397286  1.507055
2000-02 -1.179442  0.443171  1.395676 -0.529658
2000-03  0.787358  0.248845  0.743239  1.267746
2000-04  1.302395 -0.272154 -0.051532 -0.467740
2000-05 -1.040816  0.426419  0.312945 -1.115689

In [232]: annual_frame = frame.resample('A-DEC').mean()

In [233]: annual_frame
Out[233]:
      Colorado     Texas  New York      Ohio
2000  0.556703  0.016631  0.111873 -0.027445
2001  0.046303  0.163344  0.251503 -0.157276
```

Upsampling is more nuanced, as you must make a decision about which end of the
timespan in the new frequency to place the values before resampling, just like the
asfreq method. The convention argument defaults to 'start' but can also be 'end':

```
# Q-DEC: Quarterly, year ending in December
In [234]: annual_frame.resample('Q-DEC').ffill()
Out[234]:
```

```
           Colorado    Texas  New York      Ohio
2000Q1     0.556703  0.016631  0.111873 -0.027445
2000Q2     0.556703  0.016631  0.111873 -0.027445
2000Q3     0.556703  0.016631  0.111873 -0.027445
2000Q4     0.556703  0.016631  0.111873 -0.027445
2001Q1     0.046303  0.163344  0.251503 -0.157276
2001Q2     0.046303  0.163344  0.251503 -0.157276
2001Q3     0.046303  0.163344  0.251503 -0.157276
2001Q4     0.046303  0.163344  0.251503 -0.157276

In [235]: annual_frame.resample('Q-DEC', convention='end').ffill()
Out[235]:
           Colorado    Texas  New York      Ohio
2000Q4     0.556703  0.016631  0.111873 -0.027445
2001Q1     0.556703  0.016631  0.111873 -0.027445
2001Q2     0.556703  0.016631  0.111873 -0.027445
2001Q3     0.556703  0.016631  0.111873 -0.027445
2001Q4     0.046303  0.163344  0.251503 -0.157276
```

Since periods refer to timespans, the rules about upsampling and downsampling are more rigid:

- In downsampling, the target frequency must be a *subperiod* of the source frequency.

- In upsampling, the target frequency must be a *superperiod* of the source frequency.

If these rules are not satisfied, an exception will be raised. This mainly affects the quarterly, annual, and weekly frequencies; for example, the timespans defined by Q-MAR only line up with A-MAR, A-JUN, A-SEP, and A-DEC:

```
In [236]: annual_frame.resample('Q-MAR').ffill()
Out[236]:
           Colorado    Texas  New York      Ohio
2000Q4     0.556703  0.016631  0.111873 -0.027445
2001Q1     0.556703  0.016631  0.111873 -0.027445
2001Q2     0.556703  0.016631  0.111873 -0.027445
2001Q3     0.556703  0.016631  0.111873 -0.027445
2001Q4     0.046303  0.163344  0.251503 -0.157276
2002Q1     0.046303  0.163344  0.251503 -0.157276
2002Q2     0.046303  0.163344  0.251503 -0.157276
2002Q3     0.046303  0.163344  0.251503 -0.157276
```

11.7 Moving Window Functions

An important class of array transformations used for time series operations are statistics and other functions evaluated over a sliding window or with exponentially decaying weights. This can be useful for smoothing noisy or gappy data. I call these *moving window functions*, even though it includes functions without a fixed-length window like exponentially weighted moving average. Like other statistical functions, these also automatically exclude missing data.

Before digging in, we can load up some time series data and resample it to business day frequency:

```
In [237]: close_px_all = pd.read_csv('examples/stock_px_2.csv',
   .....:                             parse_dates=True, index_col=0)

In [238]: close_px = close_px_all[['AAPL', 'MSFT', 'XOM']]

In [239]: close_px = close_px.resample('B').ffill()
```

I now introduce the rolling operator, which behaves similarly to resample and groupby. It can be called on a Series or DataFrame along with a window (expressed as a number of periods; see Figure 11-4 for the plot created):

```
In [240]: close_px.AAPL.plot()
Out[240]: <matplotlib.axes._subplots.AxesSubplot at 0x7ff6d0480e48>

In [241]: close_px.AAPL.rolling(250).mean().plot()
```

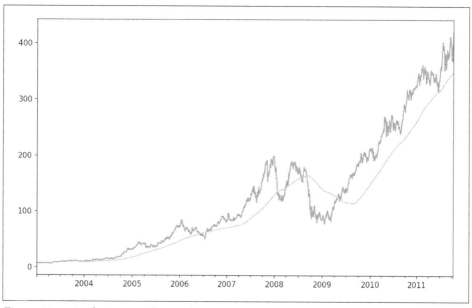

Figure 11-4. Apple Price with 250-day MA

The expression rolling(250) is similar in behavior to groupby, but instead of grouping it creates an object that enables grouping over a 250-day sliding window. So here we have the 250-day moving window average of Apple's stock price.

By default rolling functions require all of the values in the window to be non-NA. This behavior can be changed to account for missing data and, in particular, the fact that you will have fewer than window periods of data at the beginning of the time series (see Figure 11-5):

```
In [243]: appl_std250 = close_px.AAPL.rolling(250, min_periods=10).std()
```

```
In [244]: appl_std250[5:12]
Out[244]:
2003-01-09        NaN
2003-01-10        NaN
2003-01-13        NaN
2003-01-14        NaN
2003-01-15   0.077496
2003-01-16   0.074760
2003-01-17   0.112368
Freq: B, Name: AAPL, dtype: float64
```

```
In [245]: appl_std250.plot()
```

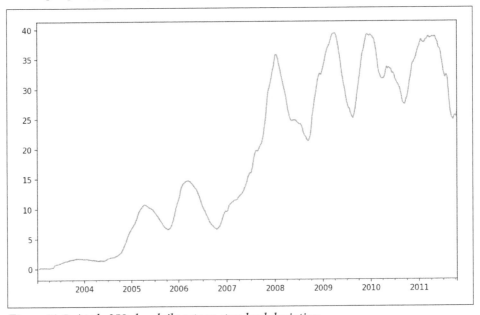

Figure 11-5. Apple 250-day daily return standard deviation

In order to compute an *expanding window mean*, use the expanding operator instead of rolling. The expanding mean starts the time window from the beginning of the time series and increases the size of the window until it encompasses the whole series. An expanding window mean on the apple_std250 time series looks like this:

```
In [246]: expanding_mean = appl_std250.expanding().mean()
```

Calling a moving window function on a DataFrame applies the transformation to each column (see Figure 11-6):

```
In [248]: close_px.rolling(60).mean().plot(logy=True)
```

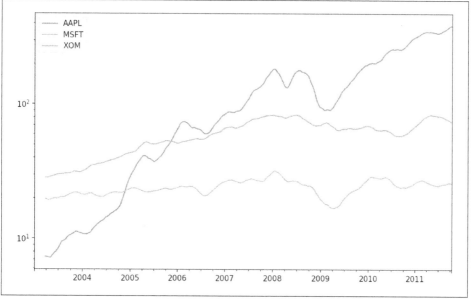

Figure 11-6. Stocks prices 60-day MA (log Y-axis)

The `rolling` function also accepts a string indicating a fixed-size time offset rather than a set number of periods. Using this notation can be useful for irregular time series. These are the same strings that you can pass to `resample`. For example, we could compute a 20-day rolling mean like so:

```
In [249]: close_px.rolling('20D').mean()
Out[249]:
                  AAPL       MSFT        XOM
2003-01-02    7.400000  21.110000  29.220000
2003-01-03    7.425000  21.125000  29.230000
2003-01-06    7.433333  21.256667  29.473333
2003-01-07    7.432500  21.425000  29.342500
2003-01-08    7.402000  21.402000  29.240000
2003-01-09    7.391667  21.490000  29.273333
2003-01-10    7.387143  21.558571  29.238571
2003-01-13    7.378750  21.633750  29.197500
2003-01-14    7.370000  21.717778  29.194444
2003-01-15    7.355000  21.757000  29.152000
...                ...        ...        ...
2011-10-03  398.002143  25.890714  72.413571
2011-10-04  396.802143  25.807857  72.427143
2011-10-05  395.751429  25.729286  72.422857
```

```
2011-10-06  394.099286  25.673571  72.375714
2011-10-07  392.479333  25.712000  72.454667
2011-10-10  389.351429  25.602143  72.527857
2011-10-11  388.505000  25.674286  72.835000
2011-10-12  388.531429  25.810000  73.400714
2011-10-13  388.826429  25.961429  73.905000
2011-10-14  391.038000  26.048667  74.185333
[2292 rows x 3 columns]
```

Exponentially Weighted Functions

An alternative to using a static window size with equally weighted observations is to specify a constant *decay factor* to give more weight to more recent observations. There are a couple of ways to specify the decay factor. A popular one is using a *span*, which makes the result comparable to a simple moving window function with window size equal to the span.

Since an exponentially weighted statistic places more weight on more recent observations, it "adapts" faster to changes compared with the equal-weighted version.

pandas has the `ewm` operator to go along with `rolling` and `expanding`. Here's an example comparing a 60-day moving average of Apple's stock price with an EW moving average with `span=60` (see Figure 11-7):

```
In [251]: aapl_px = close_px.AAPL['2006':'2007']

In [252]: ma60 = aapl_px.rolling(30, min_periods=20).mean()

In [253]: ewma60 = aapl_px.ewm(span=30).mean()

In [254]: ma60.plot(style='k--', label='Simple MA')
Out[254]: <matplotlib.axes._subplots.AxesSubplot at 0x7ff6b0a305c0>

In [255]: ewma60.plot(style='k-', label='EW MA')
Out[255]: <matplotlib.axes._subplots.AxesSubplot at 0x7ff6b0a305c0>

In [256]: plt.legend()
```

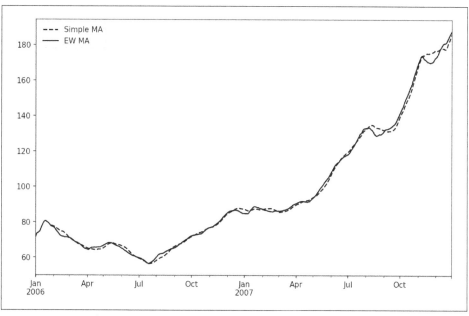

Figure 11-7. Simple moving average versus exponentially weighted

Binary Moving Window Functions

Some statistical operators, like correlation and covariance, need to operate on two time series. As an example, financial analysts are often interested in a stock's correlation to a benchmark index like the S&P 500. To have a look at this, we first compute the percent change for all of our time series of interest:

```
In [258]: spx_px = close_px_all['SPX']
```

```
In [259]: spx_rets = spx_px.pct_change()
```

```
In [260]: returns = close_px.pct_change()
```

The corr aggregation function after we call rolling can then compute the rolling correlation with spx_rets (see Figure 11-8 for the resulting plot):

```
In [261]: corr = returns.AAPL.rolling(125, min_periods=100).corr(spx_rets)
```

```
In [262]: corr.plot()
```

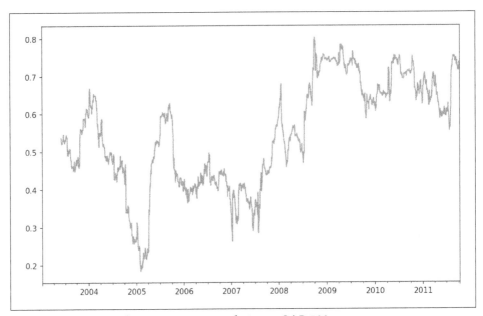

Figure 11-8. Six-month AAPL return correlation to S&P 500

Suppose you wanted to compute the correlation of the S&P 500 index with many stocks at once. Writing a loop and creating a new DataFrame would be easy but might get repetitive, so if you pass a Series and a DataFrame, a function like `rolling_corr` will compute the correlation of the Series (`spx_rets`, in this case) with each column in the DataFrame (see Figure 11-9 for the plot of the result):

```
In [264]: corr = returns.rolling(125, min_periods=100).corr(spx_rets)
```

```
In [265]: corr.plot()
```

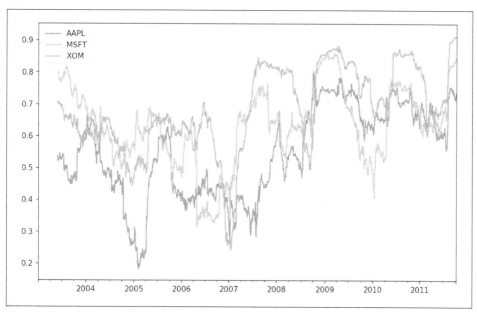

Figure 11-9. Six-month return correlations to S&P 500

User-Defined Moving Window Functions

The `apply` method on `rolling` and related methods provides a means to apply an array function of your own devising over a moving window. The only requirement is that the function produce a single value (a reduction) from each piece of the array. For example, while we can compute sample quantiles using `rolling(...).quantile(q)`, we might be interested in the percentile rank of a particular value over the sample. The `scipy.stats.percentileofscore` function does just this (see Figure 11-10 for the resulting plot):

```
In [267]: from scipy.stats import percentileofscore

In [268]: score_at_2percent = lambda x: percentileofscore(x, 0.02)

In [269]: result = returns.AAPL.rolling(250).apply(score_at_2percent)

In [270]: result.plot()
```

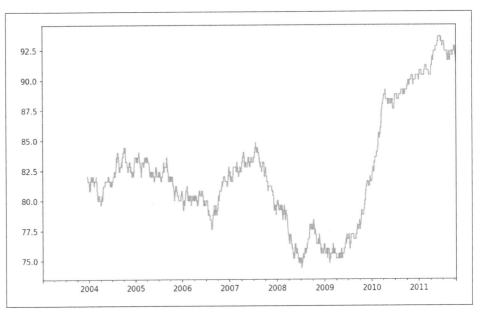

Figure 11-10. Percentile rank of 2% AAPL return over one-year window

If you don't have SciPy installed already, you can install it with conda or pip.

11.8 Conclusion

Time series data calls for different types of analysis and data transformation tools than the other types of data we have explored in previous chapters.

In the following chapters, we will move on to some advanced pandas methods and show how to start using modeling libraries like statsmodels and scikit-learn.

Advanced pandas

The preceding chapters have focused on introducing different types of data wrangling workflows and features of NumPy, pandas, and other libraries. Over time, pandas has developed a depth of features for power users. This chapter digs into a few more advanced feature areas to help you deepen your expertise as a pandas user.

12.1 Categorical Data

This section introduces the pandas `Categorical` type. I will show how you can achieve better performance and memory use in some pandas operations by using it. I also introduce some tools for using categorical data in statistics and machine learning applications.

Background and Motivation

Frequently, a column in a table may contain repeated instances of a smaller set of distinct values. We have already seen functions like `unique` and `value_counts`, which enable us to extract the distinct values from an array and compute their frequencies, respectively:

```
In [12]: import numpy as np; import pandas as pd

In [13]: values = pd.Series(['apple', 'orange', 'apple',
   ....:                      'apple'] * 2)

In [14]: values
Out[14]:
0     apple
1    orange
2     apple
3     apple
```

```
4    apple
5    orange
6    apple
7    apple
dtype: object

In [15]: pd.unique(values)
Out[15]: array(['apple', 'orange'], dtype=object)

In [16]: pd.value_counts(values)
Out[16]:
apple    6
orange   2
dtype: int64
```

Many data systems (for data warehousing, statistical computing, or other uses) have developed specialized approaches for representing data with repeated values for more efficient storage and computation. In data warehousing, a best practice is to use so-called *dimension tables* containing the distinct values and storing the primary observations as integer keys referencing the dimension table:

```
In [17]: values = pd.Series([0, 1, 0, 0] * 2)

In [18]: dim = pd.Series(['apple', 'orange'])

In [19]: values
Out[19]:
0    0
1    1
2    0
3    0
4    0
5    1
6    0
7    0
dtype: int64

In [20]: dim
Out[20]:
0    apple
1    orange
dtype: object
```

We can use the take method to restore the original Series of strings:

```
In [21]: dim.take(values)
Out[21]:
0    apple
1    orange
0    apple
0    apple
0    apple
1    orange
```

```
0       apple
0       apple
dtype: object
```

This representation as integers is called the *categorical* or *dictionary-encoded* representation. The array of distinct values can be called the *categories*, *dictionary*, or *levels* of the data. In this book we will use the terms *categorical* and *categories*. The integer values that reference the categories are called the *category codes* or simply *codes*.

The categorical representation can yield significant performance improvements when you are doing analytics. You can also perform transformations on the categories while leaving the codes unmodified. Some example transformations that can be made at relatively low cost are:

- Renaming categories
- Appending a new category without changing the order or position of the existing categories

Categorical Type in pandas

pandas has a special Categorical type for holding data that uses the integer-based categorical representation or *encoding*. Let's consider the example Series from before:

```
In [22]: fruits = ['apple', 'orange', 'apple', 'apple'] * 2

In [23]: N = len(fruits)

In [24]: df = pd.DataFrame({'fruit': fruits,
   ....:                    'basket_id': np.arange(N),
   ....:                    'count': np.random.randint(3, 15, size=N),
   ....:                    'weight': np.random.uniform(0, 4, size=N)},
   ....:                   columns=['basket_id', 'fruit', 'count', 'weight'])

In [25]: df
Out[25]:
   basket_id   fruit  count    weight
0          0   apple      5  3.858058
1          1  orange      8  2.612708
2          2   apple      4  2.995627
3          3   apple      7  2.614279
4          4   apple     12  2.990859
5          5  orange      8  3.845227
6          6   apple      5  0.033553
7          7   apple      4  0.425778
```

Here, df['fruit'] is an array of Python string objects. We can convert it to categorical by calling:

```
In [26]: fruit_cat = df['fruit'].astype('category')

In [27]: fruit_cat
Out[27]:
0     apple
1    orange
2     apple
3     apple
4     apple
5    orange
6     apple
7     apple
Name: fruit, dtype: category
Categories (2, object): [apple, orange]
```

The values for `fruit_cat` are not a NumPy array, but an instance of `pandas.Categorical`:

```
In [28]: c = fruit_cat.values

In [29]: type(c)
Out[29]: pandas.core.arrays.categorical.Categorical
```

The `Categorical` object has `categories` and `codes` attributes:

```
In [30]: c.categories
Out[30]: Index(['apple', 'orange'], dtype='object')

In [31]: c.codes
Out[31]: array([0, 1, 0, 0, 0, 1, 0, 0], dtype=int8)
```

You can convert a DataFrame column to categorical by assigning the converted result:

```
In [32]: df['fruit'] = df['fruit'].astype('category')

In [33]: df.fruit
Out[33]:
0     apple
1    orange
2     apple
3     apple
4     apple
5    orange
6     apple
7     apple
Name: fruit, dtype: category
Categories (2, object): [apple, orange]
```

You can also create `pandas.Categorical` directly from other types of Python sequences:

```
In [34]: my_categories = pd.Categorical(['foo', 'bar', 'baz', 'foo', 'bar'])

In [35]: my_categories
```

```
Out[35]:
[foo, bar, baz, foo, bar]
Categories (3, object): [bar, baz, foo]
```

If you have obtained categorical encoded data from another source, you can use the alternative `from_codes` constructor:

```
In [36]: categories = ['foo', 'bar', 'baz']

In [37]: codes = [0, 1, 2, 0, 0, 1]

In [38]: my_cats_2 = pd.Categorical.from_codes(codes, categories)

In [39]: my_cats_2
Out[39]:
[foo, bar, baz, foo, foo, bar]
Categories (3, object): [foo, bar, baz]
```

Unless explicitly specified, categorical conversions assume no specific ordering of the categories. So the `categories` array may be in a different order depending on the ordering of the input data. When using `from_codes` or any of the other constructors, you can indicate that the categories have a meaningful ordering:

```
In [40]: ordered_cat = pd.Categorical.from_codes(codes, categories,
   ....:                                         ordered=True)

In [41]: ordered_cat
Out[41]:
[foo, bar, baz, foo, foo, bar]
Categories (3, object): [foo < bar < baz]
```

The output [foo < bar < baz] indicates that 'foo' precedes 'bar' in the ordering, and so on. An unordered categorical instance can be made ordered with `as_ordered`:

```
In [42]: my_cats_2.as_ordered()
Out[42]:
[foo, bar, baz, foo, foo, bar]
Categories (3, object): [foo < bar < baz]
```

As a last note, categorical data need not be strings, even though I have only showed string examples. A categorical array can consist of any immutable value types.

Computations with Categoricals

Using `Categorical` in pandas compared with the non-encoded version (like an array of strings) generally behaves the same way. Some parts of pandas, like the `groupby` function, perform better when working with categoricals. There are also some functions that can utilize the `ordered` flag.

Let's consider some random numeric data, and use the `pandas.qcut` binning function. This return `pandas.Categorical`; we used `pandas.cut` earlier in the book but glossed over the details of how categoricals work:

```
In [43]: np.random.seed(12345)

In [44]: draws = np.random.randn(1000)

In [45]: draws[:5]
Out[45]: array([-0.2047,  0.4789, -0.5194, -0.5557,  1.9658])
```

Let's compute a quartile binning of this data and extract some statistics:

```
In [46]: bins = pd.qcut(draws, 4)

In [47]: bins
Out[47]:
[(-0.684, -0.0101], (-0.0101, 0.63], (-0.684, -0.0101], (-0.684, -0.0101], (0.63,
 3.928], ..., (-0.0101, 0.63], (-0.684, -0.0101], (-2.9499999999999997, -0.684],
(-0.0101, 0.63], (0.63, 3.928]]
Length: 1000
Categories (4, interval[float64]): [(-2.9499999999999997, -0.684] < (-0.684, -0.0
101] < (-0.0101, 0.63] <
                                    (0.63, 3.928]]
```

While useful, the exact sample quartiles may be less useful for producing a report than quartile names. We can achieve this with the `labels` argument to qcut:

```
In [48]: bins = pd.qcut(draws, 4, labels=['Q1', 'Q2', 'Q3', 'Q4'])

In [49]: bins
Out[49]:
[Q2, Q3, Q2, Q2, Q4, ..., Q3, Q2, Q1, Q3, Q4]
Length: 1000
Categories (4, object): [Q1 < Q2 < Q3 < Q4]

In [50]: bins.codes[:10]
Out[50]: array([1, 2, 1, 1, 3, 3, 2, 2, 3, 3], dtype=int8)
```

The labeled `bins` categorical does not contain information about the bin edges in the data, so we can use `groupby` to extract some summary statistics:

```
In [51]: bins = pd.Series(bins, name='quartile')

In [52]: results = (pd.Series(draws)
   ....:            .groupby(bins)
   ....:            .agg(['count', 'min', 'max'])
   ....:            .reset_index())

In [53]: results
Out[53]:
  quartile  count       min       max
0       Q1    250 -2.949343 -0.685484
```

```
1      Q2    250 -0.683066 -0.010115
2      Q3    250 -0.010032  0.628894
3      Q4    250  0.634238  3.927528
```

The 'quartile' column in the result retains the original categorical information, including ordering, from bins:

```
In [54]: results['quartile']
Out[54]:
0    Q1
1    Q2
2    Q3
3    Q4
Name: quartile, dtype: category
Categories (4, object): [Q1 < Q2 < Q3 < Q4]
```

Better performance with categoricals

If you do a lot of analytics on a particular dataset, converting to categorical can yield substantial overall performance gains. A categorical version of a DataFrame column will often use significantly less memory, too. Let's consider some Series with 10 million elements and a small number of distinct categories:

```
In [55]: N = 10000000
```

```
In [56]: draws = pd.Series(np.random.randn(N))
```

```
In [57]: labels = pd.Series(['foo', 'bar', 'baz', 'qux'] * (N // 4))
```

Now we convert labels to categorical:

```
In [58]: categories = labels.astype('category')
```

Now we note that labels uses significantly more memory than categories:

```
In [59]: labels.memory_usage()
Out[59]: 80000080
```

```
In [60]: categories.memory_usage()
Out[60]: 10000272
```

The conversion to category is not free, of course, but it is a one-time cost:

```
In [61]: %time _ = labels.astype('category')
CPU times: user 288 ms, sys: 60 ms, total: 348 ms
Wall time: 345 ms
```

GroupBy operations can be significantly faster with categoricals because the underlying algorithms use the integer-based codes array instead of an array of strings.

Categorical Methods

Series containing categorical data have several special methods similar to the `Ser` `ies.str` specialized string methods. This also provides convenient access to the categories and codes. Consider the Series:

```
In [62]: s = pd.Series(['a', 'b', 'c', 'd'] * 2)

In [63]: cat_s = s.astype('category')

In [64]: cat_s
Out[64]:
0    a
1    b
2    c
3    d
4    a
5    b
6    c
7    d
dtype: category
Categories (4, object): [a, b, c, d]
```

The special attribute `cat` provides access to categorical methods:

```
In [65]: cat_s.cat.codes
Out[65]:
0    0
1    1
2    2
3    3
4    0
5    1
6    2
7    3
dtype: int8

In [66]: cat_s.cat.categories
Out[66]: Index(['a', 'b', 'c', 'd'], dtype='object')
```

Suppose that we know the actual set of categories for this data extends beyond the four values observed in the data. We can use the `set_categories` method to change them:

```
In [67]: actual_categories = ['a', 'b', 'c', 'd', 'e']

In [68]: cat_s2 = cat_s.cat.set_categories(actual_categories)

In [69]: cat_s2
Out[69]:
0    a
1    b
```

```
2    c
3    d
4    a
5    b
6    c
7    d
dtype: category
Categories (5, object): [a, b, c, d, e]
```

While it appears that the data is unchanged, the new categories will be reflected in operations that use them. For example, value_counts respects the categories, if present:

```
In [70]: cat_s.value_counts()
Out[70]:
d    2
c    2
b    2
a    2
dtype: int64

In [71]: cat_s2.value_counts()
Out[71]:
d    2
c    2
b    2
a    2
e    0
dtype: int64
```

In large datasets, categoricals are often used as a convenient tool for memory savings and better performance. After you filter a large DataFrame or Series, many of the categories may not appear in the data. To help with this, we can use the remove_unused_categories method to trim unobserved categories:

```
In [72]: cat_s3 = cat_s[cat_s.isin(['a', 'b'])]

In [73]: cat_s3
Out[73]:
0    a
1    b
4    a
5    b
dtype: category
Categories (4, object): [a, b, c, d]

In [74]: cat_s3.cat.remove_unused_categories()
Out[74]:
0    a
1    b
4    a
5    b
```

```
dtype: category
Categories (2, object): [a, b]
```

See Table 12-1 for a listing of available categorical methods.

Table 12-1. Categorical methods for Series in pandas

Method	Description
add_categories	Append new (unused) categories at end of existing categories
as_ordered	Make categories ordered
as_unordered	Make categories unordered
remove_categories	Remove categories, setting any removed values to null
remove_unused_categories	Remove any category values which do not appear in the data
rename_categories	Replace categories with indicated set of new category names; cannot change the number of categories
reorder_categories	Behaves like rename_categories, but can also change the result to have ordered categories
set_categories	Replace the categories with the indicated set of new categories; can add or remove categories

Creating dummy variables for modeling

When you're using statistics or machine learning tools, you'll often transform categorical data into *dummy variables*, also known as *one-hot* encoding. This involves creating a DataFrame with a column for each distinct category; these columns contain 1s for occurrences of a given category and 0 otherwise.

Consider the previous example:

```
In [75]: cat_s = pd.Series(['a', 'b', 'c', 'd'] * 2, dtype='category')
```

As mentioned previously in Chapter 7, the `pandas.get_dummies` function converts this one-dimensional categorical data into a DataFrame containing the dummy variable:

```
In [76]: pd.get_dummies(cat_s)
Out[76]:
   a  b  c  d
0  1  0  0  0
1  0  1  0  0
2  0  0  1  0
3  0  0  0  1
4  1  0  0  0
5  0  1  0  0
6  0  0  1  0
7  0  0  0  1
```

12.2 Advanced GroupBy Use

While we've already discussed using the `groupby` method for Series and DataFrame in depth in Chapter 10, there are some additional techniques that you may find of use.

Group Transforms and "Unwrapped" GroupBys

In Chapter 10 we looked at the `apply` method in grouped operations for performing transformations. There is another built-in method called `transform`, which is similar to `apply` but imposes more constraints on the kind of function you can use:

- It can produce a scalar value to be broadcast to the shape of the group
- It can produce an object of the same shape as the input group
- It must not mutate its input

Let's consider a simple example for illustration:

```
In [77]: df = pd.DataFrame({'key': ['a', 'b', 'c'] * 4,
   ....:                     'value': np.arange(12.)})

In [78]: df
Out[78]:
    key  value
0     a    0.0
1     b    1.0
2     c    2.0
3     a    3.0
4     b    4.0
5     c    5.0
6     a    6.0
7     b    7.0
8     c    8.0
9     a    9.0
10    b   10.0
11    c   11.0
```

Here are the group means by key:

```
In [79]: g = df.groupby('key').value

In [80]: g.mean()
Out[80]:
key
a    4.5
b    5.5
c    6.5
Name: value, dtype: float64
```

Suppose instead we wanted to produce a Series of the same shape as df['value'] but with values replaced by the average grouped by 'key'. We can pass the function lambda x: x.mean() to transform:

```
In [81]: g.transform(lambda x: x.mean())
Out[81]:
0     4.5
1     5.5
2     6.5
3     4.5
4     5.5
5     6.5
6     4.5
7     5.5
8     6.5
9     4.5
10    5.5
11    6.5
Name: value, dtype: float64
```

For built-in aggregation functions, we can pass a string alias as with the GroupBy agg method:

```
In [82]: g.transform('mean')
Out[82]:
0     4.5
1     5.5
2     6.5
3     4.5
4     5.5
5     6.5
6     4.5
7     5.5
8     6.5
9     4.5
10    5.5
11    6.5
Name: value, dtype: float64
```

Like apply, transform works with functions that return Series, but the result must be the same size as the input. For example, we can multiply each group by 2 using a lambda function:

```
In [83]: g.transform(lambda x: x * 2)
Out[83]:
0      0.0
1      2.0
2      4.0
3      6.0
4      8.0
5     10.0
6     12.0
```

```
7      14.0
8      16.0
9      18.0
10     20.0
11     22.0
Name: value, dtype: float64
```

As a more complicated example, we can compute the ranks in descending order for each group:

```
In [84]: g.transform(lambda x: x.rank(ascending=False))
Out[84]:
0      4.0
1      4.0
2      4.0
3      3.0
4      3.0
5      3.0
6      2.0
7      2.0
8      2.0
9      1.0
10     1.0
11     1.0
Name: value, dtype: float64
```

Consider a group transformation function composed from simple aggregations:

```
def normalize(x):
    return (x - x.mean()) / x.std()
```

We can obtain equivalent results in this case either using transform or apply:

```
In [86]: g.transform(normalize)
Out[86]:
0      -1.161895
1      -1.161895
2      -1.161895
3      -0.387298
4      -0.387298
5      -0.387298
6       0.387298
7       0.387298
8       0.387298
9       1.161895
10      1.161895
11      1.161895
Name: value, dtype: float64

In [87]: g.apply(normalize)
Out[87]:
0      -1.161895
1      -1.161895
2      -1.161895
```

```
3     -0.387298
4     -0.387298
5     -0.387298
6      0.387298
7      0.387298
8      0.387298
9      1.161895
10     1.161895
11     1.161895
Name: value, dtype: float64
```

Built-in aggregate functions like 'mean' or 'sum' are often much faster than a general apply function. These also have a "fast past" when used with transform. This allows us to perform a so-called *unwrapped* group operation:

```
In [88]: g.transform('mean')
Out[88]:
0      4.5
1      5.5
2      6.5
3      4.5
4      5.5
5      6.5
6      4.5
7      5.5
8      6.5
9      4.5
10     5.5
11     6.5
Name: value, dtype: float64

In [89]: normalized = (df['value'] - g.transform('mean')) / g.transform('std')

In [90]: normalized
Out[90]:
0     -1.161895
1     -1.161895
2     -1.161895
3     -0.387298
4     -0.387298
5     -0.387298
6      0.387298
7      0.387298
8      0.387298
9      1.161895
10     1.161895
11     1.161895
Name: value, dtype: float64
```

While an unwrapped group operation may involve multiple group aggregations, the overall benefit of vectorized operations often outweighs this.

Grouped Time Resampling

For time series data, the `resample` method is semantically a group operation based on a time intervalization. Here's a small example table:

```
In [91]: N = 15

In [92]: times = pd.date_range('2017-05-20 00:00', freq='1min', periods=N)

In [93]: df = pd.DataFrame({'time': times,
   ....:                    'value': np.arange(N)})

In [94]: df
Out[94]:
                  time  value
0  2017-05-20 00:00:00      0
1  2017-05-20 00:01:00      1
2  2017-05-20 00:02:00      2
3  2017-05-20 00:03:00      3
4  2017-05-20 00:04:00      4
5  2017-05-20 00:05:00      5
6  2017-05-20 00:06:00      6
7  2017-05-20 00:07:00      7
8  2017-05-20 00:08:00      8
9  2017-05-20 00:09:00      9
10 2017-05-20 00:10:00     10
11 2017-05-20 00:11:00     11
12 2017-05-20 00:12:00     12
13 2017-05-20 00:13:00     13
14 2017-05-20 00:14:00     14
```

Here, we can index by `'time'` and then resample:

```
In [95]: df.set_index('time').resample('5min').count()
Out[95]:
                     value
time
2017-05-20 00:00:00      5
2017-05-20 00:05:00      5
2017-05-20 00:10:00      5
```

Suppose that a DataFrame contains multiple time series, marked by an additional group key column:

```
In [96]: df2 = pd.DataFrame({'time': times.repeat(3),
   ....:                     'key': np.tile(['a', 'b', 'c'], N),
   ....:                     'value': np.arange(N * 3.)})

In [97]: df2[:7]
Out[97]:
                  time key  value
0 2017-05-20 00:00:00   a    0.0
1 2017-05-20 00:00:00   b    1.0
```

```
2 2017-05-20 00:00:00   c   2.0
3 2017-05-20 00:01:00   a   3.0
4 2017-05-20 00:01:00   b   4.0
5 2017-05-20 00:01:00   c   5.0
6 2017-05-20 00:02:00   a   6.0
```

To do the same resampling for each value of `'key'`, we introduce the `pandas.Time Grouper` object:

```
In [98]: time_key = pd.TimeGrouper('5min')
```

We can then set the time index, group by `'key'` and `time_key`, and aggregate:

```
In [99]: resampled = (df2.set_index('time')
   ....:                  .groupby(['key', time_key])
   ....:                  .sum())

In [100]: resampled
Out[100]:
                           value
key time
a   2017-05-20 00:00:00     30.0
    2017-05-20 00:05:00    105.0
    2017-05-20 00:10:00    180.0
b   2017-05-20 00:00:00     35.0
    2017-05-20 00:05:00    110.0
    2017-05-20 00:10:00    185.0
c   2017-05-20 00:00:00     40.0
    2017-05-20 00:05:00    115.0
    2017-05-20 00:10:00    190.0

In [101]: resampled.reset_index()
Out[101]:
  key                time  value
0   a 2017-05-20 00:00:00   30.0
1   a 2017-05-20 00:05:00  105.0
2   a 2017-05-20 00:10:00  180.0
3   b 2017-05-20 00:00:00   35.0
4   b 2017-05-20 00:05:00  110.0
5   b 2017-05-20 00:10:00  185.0
6   c 2017-05-20 00:00:00   40.0
7   c 2017-05-20 00:05:00  115.0
8   c 2017-05-20 00:10:00  190.0
```

One constraint with using `TimeGrouper` is that the time must be the index of the Series or DataFrame.

12.3 Techniques for Method Chaining

When applying a sequence of transformations to a dataset, you may find yourself creating numerous temporary variables that are never used in your analysis. Consider this example, for instance:

```
df = load_data()
df2 = df[df['col2'] < 0]
df2['col1_demeaned'] = df2['col1'] - df2['col1'].mean()
result = df2.groupby('key').col1_demeaned.std()
```

While we're not using any real data here, this example highlights some new methods. First, the DataFrame.assign method is a *functional* alternative to column assignments of the form df[k] = v. Rather than modifying the object in-place, it returns a new DataFrame with the indicated modifications. So these statements are equivalent:

```
# Usual non-functional way
df2 = df.copy()
df2['k'] = v

# Functional assign way
df2 = df.assign(k=v)
```

Assigning in-place may execute faster than using assign, but assign enables easier method chaining:

```
result = (df2.assign(col1_demeaned=df2.col1 - df2.col2.mean())
          .groupby('key')
          .col1_demeaned.std())
```

I used the outer parentheses to make it more convenient to add line breaks.

One thing to keep in mind when doing method chaining is that you may need to refer to temporary objects. In the preceding example, we cannot refer to the result of load_data until it has been assigned to the temporary variable df. To help with this, assign and many other pandas functions accept function-like arguments, also known as *callables*.

To show callables in action, consider a fragment of the example from before:

```
df = load_data()
df2 = df[df['col2'] < 0]
```

This can be rewritten as:

```
df = (load_data()
      [lambda x: x['col2'] < 0])
```

Here, the result of load_data is not assigned to a variable, so the function passed into [] is then *bound* to the object at that stage of the method chain.

We can continue, then, and write the entire sequence as a single chained expression:

```
result = (load_data()
          [lambda x: x.col2 < 0]
          .assign(col1_demeaned=lambda x: x.col1 - x.col1.mean())
          .groupby('key')
          .col1_demeaned.std())
```

Whether you prefer to write code in this style is a matter of taste, and splitting up the expression into multiple steps may make your code more readable.

The pipe Method

You can accomplish a lot with built-in pandas functions and the approaches to method chaining with callables that we just looked at. However, sometimes you need to use your own functions or functions from third-party libraries. This is where the pipe method comes in.

Consider a sequence of function calls:

```
a = f(df, arg1=v1)
b = g(a, v2, arg3=v3)
c = h(b, arg4=v4)
```

When using functions that accept and return Series or DataFrame objects, you can rewrite this using calls to pipe:

```
result = (df.pipe(f, arg1=v1)
            .pipe(g, v2, arg3=v3)
            .pipe(h, arg4=v4))
```

The statement f(df) and df.pipe(f) are equivalent, but pipe makes chained invocation easier.

A potentially useful pattern for pipe is to generalize sequences of operations into reusable functions. As an example, let's consider substracting group means from a column:

```
g = df.groupby(['key1', 'key2'])
df['col1'] = df['col1'] - g.transform('mean')
```

Suppose that you wanted to be able to demean more than one column and easily change the group keys. Additionally, you might want to perform this transformation in a method chain. Here is an example implementation:

```
def group_demean(df, by, cols):
    result = df.copy()
    g = df.groupby(by)
    for c in cols:
        result[c] = df[c] - g[c].transform('mean')
    return result
```

Then it is possible to write:

```
result = (df[df.col1 < 0]
            .pipe(group_demean, ['key1', 'key2'], ['col1']))
```

12.4 Conclusion

pandas, like many open source software projects, is still changing and acquiring new and improved functionality. As elsewhere in this book, the focus here has been on the most stable functionality that is less likely to change over the next several years.

To deepen your expertise as a pandas user, I encourage you to explore the documentation (*http://pandas.pydata.org*) and read the release notes as the development team makes new open source releases. We also invite you to join in on pandas development: fixing bugs, building new features, and improving the documentation.

Introduction to Modeling Libraries
in Python

In this book, I have focused on providing a programming foundation for doing data analysis in Python. Since data analysts and scientists often report spending a disproportionate amount of time with data wrangling and preparation, the book's structure reflects the importance of mastering these techniques.

Which library you use for developing models will depend on the application. Many statistical problems can be solved by simpler techniques like ordinary least squares regression, while other problems may call for more advanced machine learning methods. Fortunately, Python has become one of the languages of choice for implementing analytical methods, so there are many tools you can explore after completing this book.

In this chapter, I will review some features of pandas that may be helpful when you're crossing back and forth between data wrangling with pandas and model fitting and scoring. I will then give short introductions to two popular modeling toolkits, statsmodels (*http://statsmodels.org*) and scikit-learn (*http://scikit-learn.org*). Since each of these projects is large enough to warrant its own dedicated book, I make no effort to be comprehensive and instead direct you to both projects' online documentation along with some other Python-based books on data science, statistics, and machine learning.

13.1 Interfacing Between pandas and Model Code

A common workflow for model development is to use pandas for data loading and cleaning before switching over to a modeling library to build the model itself. An important part of the model development process is called *feature engineering* in machine learning. This can describe any data transformation or analytics that extract information from a raw dataset that may be useful in a modeling context. The data aggregation and GroupBy tools we have explored in this book are used often in a feature engineering context.

While details of "good" feature engineering are out of scope for this book, I will show some methods to make switching between data manipulation with pandas and modeling as painless as possible.

The point of contact between pandas and other analysis libraries is usually NumPy arrays. To turn a DataFrame into a NumPy array, use the `.values` property:

```
In [12]: import pandas as pd

In [13]: import numpy as np

In [14]: data = pd.DataFrame({
   ....:         'x0': [1, 2, 3, 4, 5],
   ....:         'x1': [0.01, -0.01, 0.25, -4.1, 0.],
   ....:         'y': [-1.5, 0., 3.6, 1.3, -2.]})

In [15]: data
Out[15]:
   x0    x1    y
0   1  0.01 -1.5
1   2 -0.01  0.0
2   3  0.25  3.6
3   4 -4.10  1.3
4   5  0.00 -2.0

In [16]: data.columns
Out[16]: Index(['x0', 'x1', 'y'], dtype='object')

In [17]: data.values
Out[17]:
array([[ 1.  ,  0.01, -1.5 ],
       [ 2.  , -0.01,  0.  ],
       [ 3.  ,  0.25,  3.6 ],
       [ 4.  , -4.1 ,  1.3 ],
       [ 5.  ,  0.  , -2.  ]])
```

To convert back to a DataFrame, as you may recall from earlier chapters, you can pass a two-dimensional ndarray with optional column names:

```
In [18]: df2 = pd.DataFrame(data.values, columns=['one', 'two', 'three'])

In [19]: df2
Out[19]:
   one   two  three
0  1.0  0.01   -1.5
1  2.0 -0.01    0.0
2  3.0  0.25    3.6
```

```
3   4.0 -4.10   1.3
4   5.0  0.00  -2.0
```

 The `.values` attribute is intended to be used when your data is homogeneous—for example, all numeric types. If you have heterogeneous data, the result will be an ndarray of Python objects:

```
In [20]: df3 = data.copy()

In [21]: df3['strings'] = ['a', 'b', 'c', 'd', 'e']

In [22]: df3
Out[22]:
   x0    x1     y strings
0   1  0.01  -1.5       a
1   2 -0.01   0.0       b
2   3  0.25   3.6       c
3   4 -4.10   1.3       d
4   5  0.00  -2.0       e

In [23]: df3.values
Out[23]:
array([[1, 0.01, -1.5, 'a'],
       [2, -0.01, 0.0, 'b'],
       [3, 0.25, 3.6, 'c'],
       [4, -4.1, 1.3, 'd'],
       [5, 0.0, -2.0, 'e']], dtype=object)
```

For some models, you may only wish to use a subset of the columns. I recommend using `loc` indexing with `values`:

```
In [24]: model_cols = ['x0', 'x1']

In [25]: data.loc[:, model_cols].values
Out[25]:
array([[ 1.  ,  0.01],
       [ 2.  , -0.01],
       [ 3.  ,  0.25],
       [ 4.  , -4.1 ],
       [ 5.  ,  0.  ]])
```

Some libraries have native support for pandas and do some of this work for you automatically: converting to NumPy from DataFrame and attaching model parameter names to the columns of output tables or Series. In other cases, you will have to perform this "metadata management" manually.

In Chapter 12 we looked at pandas's `Categorical` type and the `pandas.get_dummies` function. Suppose we had a non-numeric column in our example dataset:

```
In [26]: data['category'] = pd.Categorical(['a', 'b', 'a', 'a', 'b'],
   ....:                                     categories=['a', 'b'])

In [27]: data
Out[27]:
   x0    x1    y category
0   1  0.01 -1.5        a
1   2 -0.01  0.0        b
2   3  0.25  3.6        a
3   4 -4.10  1.3        a
4   5  0.00 -2.0        b
```

If we wanted to replace the `'category'` column with dummy variables, we create dummy variables, drop the `'category'` column, and then join the result:

```
In [28]: dummies = pd.get_dummies(data.category, prefix='category')

In [29]: data_with_dummies = data.drop('category', axis=1).join(dummies)

In [30]: data_with_dummies
Out[30]:
   x0    x1    y  category_a  category_b
0   1  0.01 -1.5           1           0
1   2 -0.01  0.0           0           1
2   3  0.25  3.6           1           0
3   4 -4.10  1.3           1           0
4   5  0.00 -2.0           0           1
```

There are some nuances to fitting certain statistical models with dummy variables. It may be simpler and less error-prone to use Patsy (the subject of the next section) when you have more than simple numeric columns.

13.2 Creating Model Descriptions with Patsy

Patsy (*https://patsy.readthedocs.io/*) is a Python library for describing statistical models (especially linear models) with a small string-based "formula syntax," which is inspired by (but not exactly the same as) the formula syntax used by the R and S statistical programming languages.

Patsy is well supported for specifying linear models in statsmodels, so I will focus on some of the main features to help you get up and running. Patsy's *formulas* are a special string syntax that looks like:

```
y ~ x0 + x1
```

The syntax `a + b` does not mean to add `a` to `b`, but rather that these are *terms* in the *design matrix* created for the model. The `patsy.dmatrices` function takes a formula string along with a dataset (which can be a DataFrame or a dict of arrays) and produces design matrices for a linear model:

```
In [31]: data = pd.DataFrame({
   ....:     'x0': [1, 2, 3, 4, 5],
   ....:     'x1': [0.01, -0.01, 0.25, -4.1, 0.],
   ....:     'y': [-1.5, 0., 3.6, 1.3, -2.]})

In [32]: data
Out[32]:
   x0    x1    y
0   1  0.01 -1.5
1   2 -0.01  0.0
2   3  0.25  3.6
3   4 -4.10  1.3
4   5  0.00 -2.0

In [33]: import patsy

In [34]: y, X = patsy.dmatrices('y ~ x0 + x1', data)
```

Now we have:

```
In [35]: y
Out[35]:
DesignMatrix with shape (5, 1)
    y
 -1.5
  0.0
  3.6
  1.3
 -2.0
  Terms:
    'y' (column 0)

In [36]: X
Out[36]:
DesignMatrix with shape (5, 3)
  Intercept  x0     x1
          1   1   0.01
          1   2  -0.01
          1   3   0.25
          1   4  -4.10
          1   5   0.00
  Terms:
    'Intercept' (column 0)
    'x0' (column 1)
    'x1' (column 2)
```

These Patsy `DesignMatrix` instances are NumPy ndarrays with additional metadata:

```
In [37]: np.asarray(y)
Out[37]:
array([[-1.5],
       [ 0. ],
       [ 3.6],
```

```
        [ 1.3],
        [-2. ]])

In [38]: np.asarray(X)
Out[38]:
array([[ 1.  ,  1.  ,  0.01],
       [ 1.  ,  2.  , -0.01],
       [ 1.  ,  3.  ,  0.25],
       [ 1.  ,  4.  , -4.1 ],
       [ 1.  ,  5.  ,  0.  ]])
```

You might wonder where the `Intercept` term came from. This is a convention for linear models like ordinary least squares (OLS) regression. You can suppress the intercept by adding the term `+ 0` to the model:

```
In [39]: patsy.dmatrices('y ~ x0 + x1 + 0', data)[1]
Out[39]:
DesignMatrix with shape (5, 2)
  x0     x1
   1    0.01
   2   -0.01
   3    0.25
   4   -4.10
   5    0.00
  Terms:
    'x0' (column 0)
    'x1' (column 1)
```

The Patsy objects can be passed directly into algorithms like `numpy.linalg.lstsq`, which performs an ordinary least squares regression:

```
In [40]: coef, resid, _, _ = np.linalg.lstsq(X, y)
```

The model metadata is retained in the `design_info` attribute, so you can reattach the model column names to the fitted coefficients to obtain a Series, for example:

```
In [41]: coef
Out[41]:
array([[ 0.3129],
       [-0.0791],
       [-0.2655]])

In [42]: coef = pd.Series(coef.squeeze(), index=X.design_info.column_names)

In [43]: coef
Out[43]:
Intercept    0.312910
x0          -0.079106
x1          -0.265464
dtype: float64
```

Data Transformations in Patsy Formulas

You can mix Python code into your Patsy formulas; when evaluating the formula the library will try to find the functions you use in the enclosing scope:

```
In [44]: y, X = patsy.dmatrices('y ~ x0 + np.log(np.abs(x1) + 1)', data)

In [45]: X
Out[45]:
DesignMatrix with shape (5, 3)
  Intercept  x0  np.log(np.abs(x1) + 1)
          1   1                 0.00995
          1   2                 0.00995
          1   3                 0.22314
          1   4                 1.62924
          1   5                 0.00000
  Terms:
    'Intercept' (column 0)
    'x0' (column 1)
    'np.log(np.abs(x1) + 1)' (column 2)
```

Some commonly used variable transformations include standardizing (to mean 0 and variance 1) and centering (subtracting the mean). Patsy has built-in functions for this purpose:

```
In [46]: y, X = patsy.dmatrices('y ~ standardize(x0) + center(x1)', data)

In [47]: X
Out[47]:
DesignMatrix with shape (5, 3)
  Intercept  standardize(x0)  center(x1)
          1         -1.41421        0.78
          1         -0.70711        0.76
          1          0.00000        1.02
          1          0.70711       -3.33
          1          1.41421        0.77
  Terms:
    'Intercept' (column 0)
    'standardize(x0)' (column 1)
    'center(x1)' (column 2)
```

As part of a modeling process, you may fit a model on one dataset, then evaluate the model based on another. This might be a *hold-out* portion or new data that is observed later. When applying transformations like center and standardize, you should be careful when using the model to form predications based on new data. These are called *stateful* transformations, because you must use statistics like the mean or standard deviation of the original dataset when transforming a new dataset.

The `patsy.build_design_matrices` function can apply transformations to new *out-of-sample* data using the saved information from the original *in-sample* dataset:

```
In [48]: new_data = pd.DataFrame({
   ....:      'x0': [6, 7, 8, 9],
   ....:      'x1': [3.1, -0.5, 0, 2.3],
   ....:      'y': [1, 2, 3, 4]})

In [49]: new_X = patsy.build_design_matrices([X.design_info], new_data)

In [50]: new_X
Out[50]:
[DesignMatrix with shape (4, 3)
   Intercept  standardize(x0)  center(x1)
          1          2.12132        3.87
          1          2.82843        0.27
          1          3.53553        0.77
          1          4.24264        3.07
   Terms:
     'Intercept' (column 0)
     'standardize(x0)' (column 1)
     'center(x1)' (column 2)]
```

Because the plus symbol (+) in the context of Patsy formulas does not mean addition, when you want to add columns from a dataset by name, you must wrap them in the special *I* function:

```
In [51]: y, X = patsy.dmatrices('y ~ I(x0 + x1)', data)

In [52]: X
Out[52]:
DesignMatrix with shape (5, 2)
   Intercept  I(x0 + x1)
          1        1.01
          1        1.99
          1        3.25
          1       -0.10
          1        5.00
   Terms:
     'Intercept' (column 0)
     'I(x0 + x1)' (column 1)
```

Patsy has several other built-in transforms in the `patsy.builtins` module. See the online documentation for more.

Categorical data has a special class of transformations, which I explain next.

Categorical Data and Patsy

Non-numeric data can be transformed for a model design matrix in many different ways. A complete treatment of this topic is outside the scope of this book and would be best studied along with a course in statistics.

When you use non-numeric terms in a Patsy formula, they are converted to dummy variables by default. If there is an intercept, one of the levels will be left out to avoid collinearity:

```
In [53]: data = pd.DataFrame({
   ....:     'key1': ['a', 'a', 'b', 'b', 'a', 'b', 'a', 'b'],
   ....:     'key2': [0, 1, 0, 1, 0, 1, 0, 0],
   ....:     'v1': [1, 2, 3, 4, 5, 6, 7, 8],
   ....:     'v2': [-1, 0, 2.5, -0.5, 4.0, -1.2, 0.2, -1.7]
   ....: })

In [54]: y, X = patsy.dmatrices('v2 ~ key1', data)

In [55]: X
Out[55]:
DesignMatrix with shape (8, 2)
  Intercept   key1[T.b]
          1           0
          1           0
          1           1
          1           1
          1           0
          1           1
          1           0
          1           1
  Terms:
    'Intercept' (column 0)
    'key1' (column 1)
```

If you omit the intercept from the model, then columns for each category value will be included in the model design matrix:

```
In [56]: y, X = patsy.dmatrices('v2 ~ key1 + 0', data)

In [57]: X
Out[57]:
DesignMatrix with shape (8, 2)
  key1[a]   key1[b]
        1         0
        1         0
        0         1
        0         1
        1         0
        0         1
        1         0
        0         1
  Terms:
    'key1' (columns 0:2)
```

Numeric columns can be interpreted as categorical with the C function:

```
In [58]: y, X = patsy.dmatrices('v2 ~ C(key2)', data)
```

```
In [59]: X
Out[59]:
DesignMatrix with shape (8, 2)
  Intercept  C(key2)[T.1]
          1             0
          1             1
          1             0
          1             1
          1             0
          1             1
          1             0
          1             0
  Terms:
    'Intercept' (column 0)
    'C(key2)' (column 1)
```

When you're using multiple categorical terms in a model, things can be more complicated, as you can include interaction terms of the form key1:key2, which can be
used, for example, in analysis of variance (ANOVA) models:

```
In [60]: data['key2'] = data['key2'].map({0: 'zero', 1: 'one'})

In [61]: data
Out[61]:
  key1 key2 v1   v2
0    a zero  1 -1.0
1    a  one  2  0.0
2    b zero  3  2.5
3    b  one  4 -0.5
4    a zero  5  4.0
5    b  one  6 -1.2
6    a zero  7  0.2
7    b zero  8 -1.7

In [62]: y, X = patsy.dmatrices('v2 ~ key1 + key2', data)

In [63]: X
Out[63]:
DesignMatrix with shape (8, 3)
  Intercept  key1[T.b]  key2[T.zero]
          1          0             1
          1          0             0
          1          1             1
          1          1             0
          1          0             1
          1          1             0
          1          0             1
          1          1             1
  Terms:
    'Intercept' (column 0)
    'key1' (column 1)
    'key2' (column 2)
```

```
In [64]: y, X = patsy.dmatrices('v2 ~ key1 + key2 + key1:key2', data)

In [65]: X
Out[65]:
DesignMatrix with shape (8, 4)
  Intercept  key1[T.b]  key2[T.zero]  key1[T.b]:key2[T.zero]
          1          0             1                       0
          1          0             0                       0
          1          1             1                       1
          1          1             0                       0
          1          0             1                       0
          1          1             0                       0
          1          0             1                       0
          1          1             1                       1
  Terms:
    'Intercept' (column 0)
    'key1' (column 1)
    'key2' (column 2)
    'key1:key2' (column 3)
```

Patsy provides for other ways to transform categorical data, including transformations for terms with a particular ordering. See the online documentation for more.

13.3 Introduction to statsmodels

statsmodels (*http://www.statsmodels.org*) is a Python library for fitting many kinds of statistical models, performing statistical tests, and data exploration and visualization. Statsmodels contains more "classical" frequentist statistical methods, while Bayesian methods and machine learning models are found in other libraries.

Some kinds of models found in statsmodels include:

- Linear models, generalized linear models, and robust linear models
- Linear mixed effects models
- Analysis of variance (ANOVA) methods
- Time series processes and state space models
- Generalized method of moments

In the next few pages, we will use a few basic tools in statsmodels and explore how to use the modeling interfaces with Patsy formulas and pandas DataFrame objects.

Estimating Linear Models

There are several kinds of linear regression models in statsmodels, from the more basic (e.g., ordinary least squares) to more complex (e.g., iteratively reweighted least squares).

Linear models in statsmodels have two different main interfaces: array-based and formula-based. These are accessed through these API module imports:

```
import statsmodels.api as sm
import statsmodels.formula.api as smf
```

To show how to use these, we generate a linear model from some random data:

```
def dnorm(mean, variance, size=1):
    if isinstance(size, int):
        size = size,
    return mean + np.sqrt(variance) * np.random.randn(*size)

# For reproducibility
np.random.seed(12345)

N = 100
X = np.c_[dnorm(0, 0.4, size=N),
          dnorm(0, 0.6, size=N),
          dnorm(0, 0.2, size=N)]
eps = dnorm(0, 0.1, size=N)
beta = [0.1, 0.3, 0.5]

y = np.dot(X, beta) + eps
```

Here, I wrote down the "true" model with known parameters beta. In this case, dnorm is a helper function for generating normally distributed data with a particular mean and variance. So now we have:

```
In [68]: X[:5]
Out[68]:
array([[-0.1295, -1.2128,  0.5042],
       [ 0.3029, -0.4357, -0.2542],
       [-0.3285, -0.0253,  0.1384],
       [-0.3515, -0.7196, -0.2582],
       [ 1.2433, -0.3738, -0.5226]])

In [69]: y[:5]
Out[69]: array([ 0.4279, -0.6735, -0.0909, -0.4895, -0.1289])
```

A linear model is generally fitted with an intercept term as we saw before with Patsy. The sm.add_constant function can add an intercept column to an existing matrix:

```
In [70]: X_model = sm.add_constant(X)

In [71]: X_model[:5]
Out[71]:
array([[ 1.    , -0.1295, -1.2128,  0.5042],
       [ 1.    ,  0.3029, -0.4357, -0.2542],
       [ 1.    , -0.3285, -0.0253,  0.1384],
       [ 1.    , -0.3515, -0.7196, -0.2582],
       [ 1.    ,  1.2433, -0.3738, -0.5226]])
```

The sm.OLS class can fit an ordinary least squares linear regression:

```
In [72]: model = sm.OLS(y, X)
```

The model's fit method returns a regression results object containing estimated model parameters and other diagnostics:

```
In [73]: results = model.fit()
```

```
In [74]: results.params
Out[74]: array([0.1783, 0.223 , 0.501 ])
```

The summary method on results can print a model detailing diagnostic output of the model:

```
In [75]: print(results.summary())
                            OLS Regression Results
==============================================================================
Dep. Variable:                      y   R-squared:                       0.430
Model:                            OLS   Adj. R-squared:                  0.413
Method:                 Least Squares   F-statistic:                     24.42
Date:                Fri, 07 Sep 2018   Prob (F-statistic):           7.44e-12
Time:                        19:47:11   Log-Likelihood:                -34.305
No. Observations:                 100   AIC:                             74.61
Df Residuals:                      97   BIC:                             82.42
Df Model:                           3
Covariance Type:            nonrobust
==============================================================================
                 coef    std err          t      P>|t|      [0.025      0.975]
------------------------------------------------------------------------------
x1             0.1783      0.053      3.364      0.001       0.073       0.283
x2             0.2230      0.046      4.818      0.000       0.131       0.315
x3             0.5010      0.080      6.237      0.000       0.342       0.660
==============================================================================
Omnibus:                        4.662   Durbin-Watson:                   2.201
Prob(Omnibus):                  0.097   Jarque-Bera (JB):                4.098
Skew:                           0.481   Prob(JB):                        0.129
Kurtosis:                       3.243   Cond. No.                         1.74
==============================================================================

Warnings:
[1] Standard Errors assume that the covariance matrix of the errors is correctly
specified.
```

The parameter names here have been given the generic names x1, x2, and so on. Suppose instead that all of the model parameters are in a DataFrame:

```
In [76]: data = pd.DataFrame(X, columns=['col0', 'col1', 'col2'])
```

```
In [77]: data['y'] = y
```

```
In [78]: data[:5]
Out[78]:
        col0      col1      col2          y
```

```
0 -0.129468 -1.212753  0.504225  0.427863
1  0.302910 -0.435742 -0.254180 -0.673480
2 -0.328522 -0.025302  0.138351 -0.090878
3 -0.351475 -0.719605 -0.258215 -0.489494
4  1.243269 -0.373799 -0.522629 -0.128941
```

Now we can use the statsmodels formula API and Patsy formula strings:

```
In [79]: results = smf.ols('y ~ col0 + col1 + col2', data=data).fit()
```

```
In [80]: results.params
Out[80]:
Intercept    0.033559
col0         0.176149
col1         0.224826
col2         0.514808
dtype: float64
```

```
In [81]: results.tvalues
Out[81]:
Intercept    0.952188
col0         3.319754
col1         4.850730
col2         6.303971
dtype: float64
```

Observe how statsmodels has returned results as Series with the DataFrame column names attached. We also do not need to use add_constant when using formulas and pandas objects.

Given new out-of-sample data, you can compute predicted values given the estimated model parameters:

```
In [82]: results.predict(data[:5])
Out[82]:
0   -0.002327
1   -0.141904
2    0.041226
3   -0.323070
4   -0.100535
dtype: float64
```

There are many additional tools for analysis, diagnostics, and visualization of linear model results in statsmodels that you can explore. There are also other kinds of linear models beyond ordinary least squares.

Estimating Time Series Processes

Another class of models in statsmodels are for time series analysis. Among these are autoregressive processes, Kalman filtering and other state space models, and multivariate autoregressive models.

Let's simulate some time series data with an autoregressive structure and noise:

```
init_x = 4

import random
values = [init_x, init_x]
N = 1000

b0 = 0.8
b1 = -0.4
noise = dnorm(0, 0.1, N)
for i in range(N):
    new_x = values[-1] * b0 + values[-2] * b1 + noise[i]
    values.append(new_x)
```

This data has an AR(2) structure (two *lags*) with parameters 0.8 and –0.4. When you fit an AR model, you may not know the number of lagged terms to include, so you can fit the model with some larger number of lags:

```
In [84]: MAXLAGS = 5

In [85]: model = sm.tsa.AR(values)

In [86]: results = model.fit(MAXLAGS)
```

The estimated parameters in the results have the intercept first and the estimates for the first two lags next:

```
In [87]: results.params
Out[87]: array([-0.0062,  0.7845, -0.4085, -0.0136,  0.015 ,  0.0143])
```

Deeper details of these models and how to interpret their results is beyond what I can cover in this book, but there's plenty more to discover in the statsmodels documentation.

13.4 Introduction to scikit-learn

scikit-learn (*http://scikit-learn.org*) is one of the most widely used and trusted general-purpose Python machine learning toolkits. It contains a broad selection of standard supervised and unsupervised machine learning methods with tools for model selection and evaluation, data transformation, data loading, and model persistence. These models can be used for classification, clustering, prediction, and other common tasks.

There are excellent online and printed resources for learning about machine learning and how to apply libraries like scikit-learn and TensorFlow to solve real-world problems. In this section, I will give a brief flavor of the scikit-learn API style.

At the time of this writing, scikit-learn does not have deep pandas integration, though there are some add-on third-party packages that are still in development. pandas can be very useful for massaging datasets prior to model fitting, though.

As an example, I use a now-classic dataset from a Kaggle competition (*https://www.kaggle.com/c/titanic*) about passenger survival rates on the *Titanic*, which sank in 1912. We load the test and training dataset using pandas:

```
In [88]: train = pd.read_csv('datasets/titanic/train.csv')

In [89]: test = pd.read_csv('datasets/titanic/test.csv')

In [90]: train[:4]
Out[90]:
   PassengerId  Survived  Pclass  \
0            1         0       3
1            2         1       1
2            3         1       3
3            4         1       1
                                                 Name     Sex   Age  SibSp  \
0                             Braund, Mr. Owen Harris    male  22.0      1
1   Cumings, Mrs. John Bradley (Florence Briggs Thayer)  female  38.0      1
2                              Heikkinen, Miss. Laina  female  26.0      0
3        Futrelle, Mrs. Jacques Heath (Lily May Peel)  female  35.0      1
   Parch            Ticket     Fare Cabin Embarked
0      0         A/5 21171   7.2500   NaN        S
1      0          PC 17599  71.2833   C85        C
2      0  STON/O2. 3101282   7.9250   NaN        S
3      0            113803  53.1000  C123        S
```

Libraries like statsmodels and scikit-learn generally cannot be fed missing data, so we look at the columns to see if there are any that contain missing data:

```
In [91]: train.isnull().sum()
Out[91]:
PassengerId      0
Survived         0
Pclass           0
Name             0
Sex              0
Age            177
SibSp            0
Parch            0
Ticket           0
Fare             0
Cabin          687
Embarked         2
dtype: int64

In [92]: test.isnull().sum()
Out[92]:
PassengerId      0
```

```
Pclass          0
Name            0
Sex             0
Age            86
SibSp           0
Parch           0
Ticket          0
Fare            1
Cabin         327
Embarked        0
dtype: int64
```

In statistics and machine learning examples like this one, a typical task is to predict whether a passenger would survive based on features in the data. A model is fitted on a *training* dataset and then evaluated on an out-of-sample *testing* dataset.

I would like to use Age as a predictor, but it has missing data. There are a number of ways to do missing data imputation, but I will do a simple one and use the median of the training dataset to fill the nulls in both tables:

```
In [93]: impute_value = train['Age'].median()
```

```
In [94]: train['Age'] = train['Age'].fillna(impute_value)
```

```
In [95]: test['Age'] = test['Age'].fillna(impute_value)
```

Now we need to specify our models. I add a column IsFemale as an encoded version of the 'Sex' column:

```
In [96]: train['IsFemale'] = (train['Sex'] == 'female').astype(int)
```

```
In [97]: test['IsFemale'] = (test['Sex'] == 'female').astype(int)
```

Then we decide on some model variables and create NumPy arrays:

```
In [98]: predictors = ['Pclass', 'IsFemale', 'Age']
```

```
In [99]: X_train = train[predictors].values
```

```
In [100]: X_test = test[predictors].values
```

```
In [101]: y_train = train['Survived'].values
```

```
In [102]: X_train[:5]
Out[102]:
array([[ 3.,  0., 22.],
       [ 1.,  1., 38.],
       [ 3.,  1., 26.],
       [ 1.,  1., 35.],
       [ 3.,  0., 35.]])
```

```
In [103]: y_train[:5]
Out[103]: array([0, 1, 1, 1, 0])
```

I make no claims that this is a good model nor that these features are engineered properly. We use the `LogisticRegression` model from scikit-learn and create a model instance:

```
In [104]: from sklearn.linear_model import LogisticRegression
```

```
In [105]: model = LogisticRegression()
```

Similar to statsmodels, we can fit this model to the training data using the model's `fit` method:

```
In [106]: model.fit(X_train, y_train)
Out[106]:
LogisticRegression(C=1.0, class_weight=None, dual=False, fit_intercept=True,
          intercept_scaling=1, max_iter=100, multi_class='ovr', n_jobs=1,
          penalty='l2', random_state=None, solver='liblinear', tol=0.0001,
          verbose=0, warm_start=False)
```

Now, we can form predictions for the test dataset using `model.predict`:

```
In [107]: y_predict = model.predict(X_test)
```

```
In [108]: y_predict[:10]
Out[108]: array([0, 0, 0, 0, 1, 0, 1, 0, 1, 0])
```

If you had the true values for the test dataset, you could compute an accuracy percentage or some other error metric:

```
(y_true == y_predict).mean()
```

In practice, there are often many additional layers of complexity in model training. Many models have parameters that can be tuned, and there are techniques such as *cross-validation* that can be used for parameter tuning to avoid overfitting to the training data. This can often yield better predictive performance or robustness on new data.

Cross-validation works by splitting the training data to simulate out-of-sample prediction. Based on a model accuracy score like mean squared error, one can perform a grid search on model parameters. Some models, like logistic regression, have estimator classes with built-in cross-validation. For example, the `LogisticRegressionCV` class can be used with a parameter indicating how fine-grained of a grid search to do on the model regularization parameter C:

```
In [109]: from sklearn.linear_model import LogisticRegressionCV
```

```
In [110]: model_cv = LogisticRegressionCV(10)
```

```
In [111]: model_cv.fit(X_train, y_train)
Out[111]:
LogisticRegressionCV(Cs=10, class_weight=None, cv=None, dual=False,
          fit_intercept=True, intercept_scaling=1.0, max_iter=100,
```

```
multi_class='ovr', n_jobs=1, penalty='l2', random_state=None,
refit=True, scoring=None, solver='lbfgs', tol=0.0001, verbose=0)
```

To do cross-validation by hand, you can use the `cross_val_score` helper function, which handles the data splitting process. For example, to cross-validate our model with four non-overlapping splits of the training data, we can do:

```
In [112]: from sklearn.model_selection import cross_val_score

In [113]: model = LogisticRegression(C=10)

In [114]: scores = cross_val_score(model, X_train, y_train, cv=4)

In [115]: scores
Out[115]: array([0.7723, 0.8027, 0.7703, 0.7883])
```

The default scoring metric is model-dependent, but it is possible to choose an explicit scoring function. Cross-validated models take longer to train, but can often yield better model performance.

13.5 Continuing Your Education

While I have only skimmed the surface of some Python modeling libraries, there are more and more frameworks for various kinds of statistics and machine learning either implemented in Python or with a Python user interface.

This book is focused especially on data wrangling, but there are many others dedicated to modeling and data science tools. Some excellent ones are:

- *Introduction to Machine Learning with Python* by Andreas Mueller and Sarah Guido (O'Reilly)
- *Python Data Science Handbook* by Jake VanderPlas (O'Reilly)
- *Data Science from Scratch: First Principles with Python* by Joel Grus (O'Reilly)
- *Python Machine Learning* by Sebastian Raschka (Packt Publishing)
- *Hands-On Machine Learning with Scikit-Learn and TensorFlow* by Aurélien Géron (O'Reilly)

While books can be valuable resources for learning, they can sometimes grow out of date when the underlying open source software changes. It's a good idea to be familiar with the documentation for the various statistics or machine learning frameworks to stay up to date on the latest features and API.

Data Analysis Examples

Now that we've reached the end of this book's main chapters, we're going to take a look at a number of real-world datasets. For each dataset, we'll use the techniques presented in this book to extract meaning from the raw data. The demonstrated techniques can be applied to all manner of other datasets, including your own. This chapter contains a collection of miscellaneous example datasets that you can use for practice with the tools in this book.

The example datasets are found in the book's accompanying GitHub repository (*http://github.com/wesm/pydata-book*).

14.1 1.USA.gov Data from Bitly

In 2011, URL shortening service Bitly (*https://bitly.com/*) partnered with the US government website USA.gov (*https://www.usa.gov/*) to provide a feed of anonymous data gathered from users who shorten links ending with *.gov* or *.mil*. In 2011, a live feed as well as hourly snapshots were available as downloadable text files. This service is shut down at the time of this writing (2017), but we preserved one of the data files for the book's examples.

In the case of the hourly snapshots, each line in each file contains a common form of web data known as JSON, which stands for JavaScript Object Notation. For example, if we read just the first line of a file we may see something like this:

```
In [5]: path = 'datasets/bitly_usagov/example.txt'

In [6]: open(path).readline()
Out[6]: '{ "a": "Mozilla\\/5.0 (Windows NT 6.1; WOW64) AppleWebKit\\/535.11
(KHTML, like Gecko) Chrome\\/17.0.963.78 Safari\\/535.11", "c": "US", "nk": 1,
"tz": "America\\/New_York", "gr": "MA", "g": "A6qOVH", "h": "wfLQtf", "l":
"orofrog", "al": "en-US,en;q=0.8", "hh": "1.usa.gov", "r":
```

```
"http:\\/\\/www.facebook.com\\/l\\/7AQEFzjSi\\/1.usa.gov\\/wfLQtf", "u":
"http:\\/\\/www.ncbi.nlm.nih.gov\\/pubmed\\/22415991", "t": 1331923247, "hc":
1331822918, "cy": "Danvers", "ll": [ 42.576698, -70.954903 ] }\n'
```

Python has both built-in and third-party libraries for converting a JSON string into a Python dictionary object. Here we'll use the `json` module and its `loads` function invoked on each line in the sample file we downloaded:

```
import json
path = 'datasets/bitly_usagov/example.txt'
records = [json.loads(line) for line in open(path)]
```

The resulting object `records` is now a list of Python dicts:

```
In [18]: records[0]
Out[18]:
{'a': 'Mozilla/5.0 (Windows NT 6.1; WOW64) AppleWebKit/535.11 (KHTML, like Gecko)
Chrome/17.0.963.78 Safari/535.11',
 'al': 'en-US,en;q=0.8',
 'c': 'US',
 'cy': 'Danvers',
 'g': 'A6qOVH',
 'gr': 'MA',
 'h': 'wfLQtf',
 'hc': 1331822918,
 'hh': '1.usa.gov',
 'l': 'orofrog',
 'll': [42.576698, -70.954903],
 'nk': 1,
 'r': 'http://www.facebook.com/l/7AQEFzjSi/1.usa.gov/wfLQtf',
 't': 1331923247,
 'tz': 'America/New_York',
 'u': 'http://www.ncbi.nlm.nih.gov/pubmed/22415991'}
```

Counting Time Zones in Pure Python

Suppose we were interested in finding the most often-occurring time zones in the dataset (the `tz` field). There are many ways we could do this. First, let's extract a list of time zones again using a list comprehension:

```
In [14]: time_zones = [rec['tz'] for rec in records]
---------------------------------------------------------------------
KeyError                                  Traceback (most recent call last)
<ipython-input-14-db4fbd348da9> in <module>()
----> 1 time_zones = [rec['tz'] for rec in records]
<ipython-input-14-db4fbd348da9> in <listcomp>(.0)
----> 1 time_zones = [rec['tz'] for rec in records]
KeyError: 'tz'
```

Oops! Turns out that not all of the records have a time zone field. This is easy to handle, as we can add the check `if 'tz' in rec` at the end of the list comprehension:

```
In [15]: time_zones = [rec['tz'] for rec in records if 'tz' in rec]

In [16]: time_zones[:10]
Out[16]:
['America/New_York',
 'America/Denver',
 'America/New_York',
 'America/Sao_Paulo',
 'America/New_York',
 'America/New_York',
 'Europe/Warsaw',
 '',
 '',
 '']
```

Just looking at the first 10 time zones, we see that some of them are unknown (empty string). You can filter these out also, but I'll leave them in for now. Now, to produce counts by time zone I'll show two approaches: the harder way (using just the Python standard library) and the easier way (using pandas). One way to do the counting is to use a dict to store counts while we iterate through the time zones:

```python
def get_counts(sequence):
    counts = {}
    for x in sequence:
        if x in counts:
            counts[x] += 1
        else:
            counts[x] = 1
    return counts
```

Using more advanced tools in the Python standard library, you can write the same thing more briefly:

```python
from collections import defaultdict

def get_counts2(sequence):
    counts = defaultdict(int) # values will initialize to 0
    for x in sequence:
        counts[x] += 1
    return counts
```

I put this logic in a function just to make it more reusable. To use it on the time zones, just pass the time_zones list:

```
In [19]: counts = get_counts(time_zones)

In [20]: counts['America/New_York']
Out[20]: 1251

In [21]: len(time_zones)
Out[21]: 3440
```

If we wanted the top 10 time zones and their counts, we can do a bit of dictionary acrobatics:

```
def top_counts(count_dict, n=10):
    value_key_pairs = [(count, tz) for tz, count in count_dict.items()]
    value_key_pairs.sort()
    return value_key_pairs[-n:]
```

We have then:

```
In [23]: top_counts(counts)
Out[23]:
[(33, 'America/Sao_Paulo'),
 (35, 'Europe/Madrid'),
 (36, 'Pacific/Honolulu'),
 (37, 'Asia/Tokyo'),
 (74, 'Europe/London'),
 (191, 'America/Denver'),
 (382, 'America/Los_Angeles'),
 (400, 'America/Chicago'),
 (521, ''),
 (1251, 'America/New_York')]
```

If you search the Python standard library, you may find the `collections.Counter` class, which makes this task a lot easier:

```
In [24]: from collections import Counter

In [25]: counts = Counter(time_zones)

In [26]: counts.most_common(10)
Out[26]:
[('America/New_York', 1251),
 ('', 521),
 ('America/Chicago', 400),
 ('America/Los_Angeles', 382),
 ('America/Denver', 191),
 ('Europe/London', 74),
 ('Asia/Tokyo', 37),
 ('Pacific/Honolulu', 36),
 ('Europe/Madrid', 35),
 ('America/Sao_Paulo', 33)]
```

Counting Time Zones with pandas

Creating a DataFrame from the original set of records is as easy as passing the list of records to `pandas.DataFrame`:

```
In [27]: import pandas as pd

In [28]: frame = pd.DataFrame(records)

In [29]: frame.info()
```

```
<class 'pandas.core.frame.DataFrame'>
RangeIndex: 3560 entries, 0 to 3559
Data columns (total 18 columns):
_heartbeat_    120 non-null float64
a              3440 non-null object
al             3094 non-null object
c              2919 non-null object
cy             2919 non-null object
g              3440 non-null object
gr             2919 non-null object
h              3440 non-null object
hc             3440 non-null float64
hh             3440 non-null object
kw             93 non-null object
l              3440 non-null object
ll             2919 non-null object
nk             3440 non-null float64
r              3440 non-null object
t              3440 non-null float64
tz             3440 non-null object
u              3440 non-null object
dtypes: float64(4), object(14)
memory usage: 500.7+ KB

In [30]: frame['tz'][:10]
Out[30]:
0       America/New_York
1         America/Denver
2       America/New_York
3      America/Sao_Paulo
4       America/New_York
5       America/New_York
6          Europe/Warsaw
7
8
9
Name: tz, dtype: object
```

The output shown for the `frame` is the *summary view*, shown for large DataFrame objects. We can then use the `value_counts` method for Series:

```
In [31]: tz_counts = frame['tz'].value_counts()

In [32]: tz_counts[:10]
Out[32]:
America/New_York       1251
                        521
America/Chicago         400
America/Los_Angeles     382
America/Denver          191
Europe/London            74
Asia/Tokyo               37
Pacific/Honolulu         36
```

```
Europe/Madrid              35
America/Sao_Paulo          33
Name: tz, dtype: int64
```

We can visualize this data using matplotlib. You can do a bit of munging to fill in a substitute value for unknown and missing time zone data in the records. We replace the missing values with the `fillna` method and use boolean array indexing for the empty strings:

```
In [33]: clean_tz = frame['tz'].fillna('Missing')

In [34]: clean_tz[clean_tz == ''] = 'Unknown'

In [35]: tz_counts = clean_tz.value_counts()

In [36]: tz_counts[:10]
Out[36]:
America/New_York       1251
Unknown                 521
America/Chicago         400
America/Los_Angeles     382
America/Denver          191
Missing                 120
Europe/London            74
Asia/Tokyo               37
Pacific/Honolulu         36
Europe/Madrid            35
Name: tz, dtype: int64
```

At this point, we can use the seaborn package (*http://seaborn.pydata.org/*) to make a horizontal bar plot (see Figure 14-1 for the resulting visualization):

```
In [38]: import seaborn as sns

In [39]: subset = tz_counts[:10]

In [40]: sns.barplot(y=subset.index, x=subset.values)
```

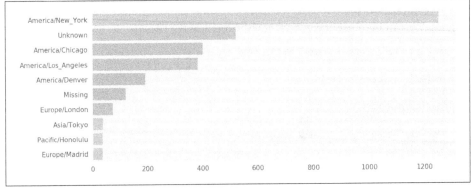

Figure 14-1. Top time zones in the 1.usa.gov sample data

The a field contains information about the browser, device, or application used to perform the URL shortening:

```
In [41]: frame['a'][1]
Out[41]: 'GoogleMaps/RochesterNY'

In [42]: frame['a'][50]
Out[42]: 'Mozilla/5.0 (Windows NT 5.1; rv:10.0.2) Gecko/20100101 Firefox/10.0.2'

In [43]: frame['a'][51][:50]  # long line
Out[43]: 'Mozilla/5.0 (Linux; U; Android 2.2.2; en-us; LG-P9'
```

Parsing all of the interesting information in these "agent" strings may seem like a daunting task. One possible strategy is to split off the first token in the string (corresponding roughly to the browser capability) and make another summary of the user behavior:

```
In [44]: results = pd.Series([x.split()[0] for x in frame.a.dropna()])

In [45]: results[:5]
Out[45]:
0                Mozilla/5.0
1    GoogleMaps/RochesterNY
2                Mozilla/4.0
3                Mozilla/5.0
4                Mozilla/5.0
dtype: object

In [46]: results.value_counts()[:8]
Out[46]:
Mozilla/5.0                 2594
Mozilla/4.0                  601
GoogleMaps/RochesterNY       121
Opera/9.80                    34
TEST_INTERNET_AGENT           24
GoogleProducer                21
Mozilla/6.0                    5
BlackBerry8520/5.0.0.681       4
dtype: int64
```

Now, suppose you wanted to decompose the top time zones into Windows and non-Windows users. As a simplification, let's say that a user is on Windows if the string 'Windows' is in the agent string. Since some of the agents are missing, we'll exclude these from the data:

```
In [47]: cframe = frame[frame.a.notnull()]
```

We want to then compute a value for whether each row is Windows or not:

```
In [49]: cframe['os'] = np.where(cframe['a'].str.contains('Windows'),
   ....:                         'Windows', 'Not Windows')

In [50]: cframe['os'][:5]
```

```
Out[50]:
0        Windows
1    Not Windows
2        Windows
3    Not Windows
4        Windows
Name: os, dtype: object
```

Then, you can group the data by its time zone column and this new list of operating systems:

```
In [51]: by_tz_os = cframe.groupby(['tz', 'os'])
```

The group counts, analogous to the value_counts function, can be computed with size. This result is then reshaped into a table with unstack:

```
In [52]: agg_counts = by_tz_os.size().unstack().fillna(0)

In [53]: agg_counts[:10]
Out[53]:
os                              Not Windows  Windows
tz
                                    245.0    276.0
Africa/Cairo                          0.0      3.0
Africa/Casablanca                     0.0      1.0
Africa/Ceuta                          0.0      2.0
Africa/Johannesburg                   0.0      1.0
Africa/Lusaka                         0.0      1.0
America/Anchorage                     4.0      1.0
America/Argentina/Buenos_Aires        1.0      0.0
America/Argentina/Cordoba             0.0      1.0
America/Argentina/Mendoza             0.0      1.0
```

Finally, let's select the top overall time zones. To do so, I construct an indirect index array from the row counts in agg_counts:

```
# Use to sort in ascending order
In [54]: indexer = agg_counts.sum(1).argsort()

In [55]: indexer[:10]
Out[55]:
tz
                                    24
Africa/Cairo                        20
Africa/Casablanca                   21
Africa/Ceuta                        92
Africa/Johannesburg                 87
Africa/Lusaka                       53
America/Anchorage                   54
America/Argentina/Buenos_Aires      57
America/Argentina/Cordoba           26
America/Argentina/Mendoza           55
dtype: int64
```

I use take to select the rows in that order, then slice off the last 10 rows (largest values):

```
In [56]: count_subset = agg_counts.take(indexer[-10:])

In [57]: count_subset
Out[57]:
os                        Not Windows  Windows
tz
America/Sao_Paulo                13.0     20.0
Europe/Madrid                    16.0     19.0
Pacific/Honolulu                  0.0     36.0
Asia/Tokyo                         2.0     35.0
Europe/London                    43.0     31.0
America/Denver                  132.0     59.0
America/Los_Angeles            130.0    252.0
America/Chicago                115.0    285.0
                                245.0    276.0
America/New_York               339.0    912.0
```

pandas has a convenience method called nlargest that does the same thing:

```
In [58]: agg_counts.sum(1).nlargest(10)
Out[58]:
tz
America/New_York         1251.0
                          521.0
America/Chicago           400.0
America/Los_Angeles       382.0
America/Denver            191.0
Europe/London              74.0
Asia/Tokyo                 37.0
Pacific/Honolulu           36.0
Europe/Madrid              35.0
America/Sao_Paulo          33.0
dtype: float64
```

Then, as shown in the preceding code block, this can be plotted in a bar plot; I'll make it a stacked bar plot by passing an additional argument to seaborn's barplot function (see Figure 14-2):

```
# Rearrange the data for plotting
In [60]: count_subset = count_subset.stack()

In [61]: count_subset.name = 'total'

In [62]: count_subset = count_subset.reset_index()

In [63]: count_subset[:10]
Out[63]:
                 tz           os  total
0  America/Sao_Paulo  Not Windows   13.0
1  America/Sao_Paulo      Windows   20.0
```

```
2       Europe/Madrid   Not Windows   16.0
3       Europe/Madrid       Windows   19.0
4    Pacific/Honolulu   Not Windows    0.0
5    Pacific/Honolulu       Windows   36.0
6          Asia/Tokyo   Not Windows    2.0
7          Asia/Tokyo       Windows   35.0
8       Europe/London   Not Windows   43.0
9       Europe/London       Windows   31.0

In [64]: sns.barplot(x='total', y='tz', hue='os',  data=count_subset)
```

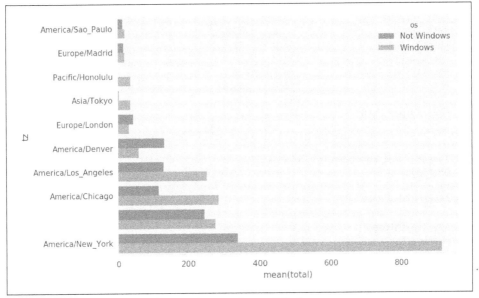

Figure 14-2. Top time zones by Windows and non-Windows users

The plot doesn't make it easy to see the relative percentage of Windows users in the smaller groups, so let's normalize the group percentages to sum to 1:

```
def norm_total(group):
    group['normed_total'] = group.total / group.total.sum()
    return group

results = count_subset.groupby('tz').apply(norm_total)
```

Then plot this in Figure 14-3:

```
In [67]: sns.barplot(x='normed_total', y='tz', hue='os',  data=results)
```

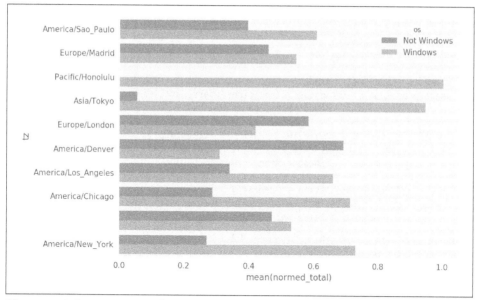

Figure 14-3. Percentage Windows and non-Windows users in top-occurring time zones

We could have computed the normalized sum more efficiently by using the `trans form` method with `groupby`:

```
In [68]: g = count_subset.groupby('tz')

In [69]: results2 = count_subset.total / g.total.transform('sum')
```

14.2 MovieLens 1M Dataset

GroupLens Research (*http://www.grouplens.org/node/73*) provides a number of collections of movie ratings data collected from users of MovieLens in the late 1990s and early 2000s. The data provide movie ratings, movie metadata (genres and year), and demographic data about the users (age, zip code, gender identification, and occupation). Such data is often of interest in the development of recommendation systems based on machine learning algorithms. While we do not explore machine learning techniques in detail in this book, I will show you how to slice and dice datasets like these into the exact form you need.

The MovieLens 1M dataset contains 1 million ratings collected from 6,000 users on 4,000 movies. It's spread across three tables: ratings, user information, and movie information. After extracting the data from the ZIP file, we can load each table into a pandas DataFrame object using `pandas.read_table`:

```
import pandas as pd

# Make display smaller
pd.options.display.max_rows = 10

unames = ['user_id', 'gender', 'age', 'occupation', 'zip']
users = pd.read_table('datasets/movielens/users.dat', sep='::',
                      header=None, names=unames)

rnames = ['user_id', 'movie_id', 'rating', 'timestamp']
ratings = pd.read_table('datasets/movielens/ratings.dat', sep='::',
                        header=None, names=rnames)

mnames = ['movie_id', 'title', 'genres']
movies = pd.read_table('datasets/movielens/movies.dat', sep='::',
                       header=None, names=mnames)
```

You can verify that everything succeeded by looking at the first few rows of each
DataFrame with Python's slice syntax:

```
In [71]: users[:5]
Out[71]:
   user_id gender  age  occupation    zip
0        1      F    1          10  48067
1        2      M   56          16  70072
2        3      M   25          15  55117
3        4      M   45           7  02460
4        5      M   25          20  55455

In [72]: ratings[:5]
Out[72]:
   user_id  movie_id  rating   timestamp
0        1      1193       5   978300760
1        1       661       3   978302109
2        1       914       3   978301968
3        1      3408       4   978300275
4        1      2355       5   978824291

In [73]: movies[:5]
Out[73]:
   movie_id                               title                        genres
0         1                    Toy Story (1995)   Animation|Children's|Comedy
1         2                      Jumanji (1995)  Adventure|Children's|Fantasy
2         3             Grumpier Old Men (1995)                Comedy|Romance
3         4            Waiting to Exhale (1995)                  Comedy|Drama
4         5  Father of the Bride Part II (1995)                        Comedy

In [74]: ratings
Out[74]:
        user_id  movie_id  rating   timestamp
0             1      1193       5   978300760
1             1       661       3   978302109
2             1       914       3   978301968
```

```
3                1        3408      4  978300275
4                1        2355      5  978824291
...              ...      ...       ...      ...
1000204       6040        1091      1  956716541
1000205       6040        1094      5  956704887
1000206       6040         562      5  956704746
1000207       6040        1096      4  956715648
1000208       6040        1097      4  956715569
[1000209 rows x 4 columns]
```

Note that ages and occupations are coded as integers indicating groups described in the dataset's *README* file. Analyzing the data spread across three tables is not a simple task; for example, suppose you wanted to compute mean ratings for a particular movie by sex and age. As you will see, this is much easier to do with all of the data merged together into a single table. Using pandas's merge function, we first merge ratings with users and then merge that result with the movies data. pandas infers which columns to use as the merge (or *join*) keys based on overlapping names:

```
In [75]: data = pd.merge(pd.merge(ratings, users), movies)

In [76]: data
Out[76]:
          user_id  movie_id  rating   timestamp gender  age  occupation   zip \
0               1      1193       5   978300760      F    1          10  48067
1               2      1193       5   978298413      M   56          16  70072
2              12      1193       4   978220179      M   25          12  32793
3              15      1193       4   978199279      M   25           7  22903
4              17      1193       5   978158471      M   50           1  95350
...           ...       ...     ...         ...    ...  ...         ...    ...
1000204      5949      2198       5   958846401      M   18          17  47901
1000205      5675      2703       3   976029116      M   35          14  30030
1000206      5780      2845       1   958153068      M   18          17  92886
1000207      5851      3607       5   957756608      F   18          20  55410
1000208      5938      2909       4   957273353      M   25           1  35401

                                          title                genres
0                One Flew Over the Cuckoo's Nest (1975)          Drama
1                One Flew Over the Cuckoo's Nest (1975)          Drama
2                One Flew Over the Cuckoo's Nest (1975)          Drama
3                One Flew Over the Cuckoo's Nest (1975)          Drama
4                One Flew Over the Cuckoo's Nest (1975)          Drama
...                                            ...                ...
1000204                        Modulations (1998)           Documentary
1000205                     Broken Vessels (1998)                 Drama
1000206                        White Boys (1999)                  Drama
1000207                 One Little Indian (1973)   Comedy|Drama|Western
1000208   Five Wives, Three Secretaries and Me (1998)         Documentary
[1000209 rows x 10 columns]

In [77]: data.iloc[0]
Out[77]:
user_id                              1
```

```
movie_id                                           1193
rating                                                5
timestamp                                     978300760
gender                                                F
age                                                   1
occupation                                           10
zip                                               48067
title           One Flew Over the Cuckoo's Nest (1975)
genres                                            Drama
Name: 0, dtype: object
```

To get mean movie ratings for each film grouped by gender, we can use the pivot_table method:

```
In [78]: mean_ratings = data.pivot_table('rating', index='title',
   ....:                                  columns='gender', aggfunc='mean')

In [79]: mean_ratings[:5]
Out[79]:
gender                             F         M
title
$1,000,000 Duck (1971)       3.375000  2.761905
'Night Mother (1986)         3.388889  3.352941
'Til There Was You (1997)    2.675676  2.733333
'burbs, The (1989)           2.793478  2.962085
...And Justice for All (1979) 3.828571  3.689024
```

This produced another DataFrame containing mean ratings with movie titles as row labels (the "index") and gender as column labels. I first filter down to movies that received at least 250 ratings (a completely arbitrary number); to do this, I then group the data by title and use size() to get a Series of group sizes for each title:

```
In [80]: ratings_by_title = data.groupby('title').size()

In [81]: ratings_by_title[:10]
Out[81]:
title
$1,000,000 Duck (1971)                  37
'Night Mother (1986)                    70
'Til There Was You (1997)               52
'burbs, The (1989)                     303
...And Justice for All (1979)          199
1-900 (1994)                             2
10 Things I Hate About You (1999)      700
101 Dalmatians (1961)                  565
101 Dalmatians (1996)                  364
12 Angry Men (1957)                    616
dtype: int64

In [82]: active_titles = ratings_by_title.index[ratings_by_title >= 250]

In [83]: active_titles
```

```
Out[83]:
Index([''burbs, The (1989)', '10 Things I Hate About You (1999)',
       '101 Dalmatians (1961)', '101 Dalmatians (1996)', '12 Angry Men (1957)',
       '13th Warrior, The (1999)', '2 Days in the Valley (1996)',
       '20,000 Leagues Under the Sea (1954)', '2001: A Space Odyssey (1968)',
       '2010 (1984)',
       ...
       'X-Men (2000)', 'Year of Living Dangerously (1982)',
       'Yellow Submarine (1968)', 'You've Got Mail (1998)',
       'Young Frankenstein (1974)', 'Young Guns (1988)',
       'Young Guns II (1990)', 'Young Sherlock Holmes (1985)',
       'Zero Effect (1998)', 'eXistenZ (1999)'],
      dtype='object', name='title', length=1216)
```

The index of titles receiving at least 250 ratings can then be used to select rows from mean_ratings:

```
# Select rows on the index
In [84]: mean_ratings = mean_ratings.loc[active_titles]

In [85]: mean_ratings
Out[85]:
gender                                          F         M
title
'burbs, The (1989)                       2.793478  2.962085
10 Things I Hate About You (1999)        3.646552  3.311966
101 Dalmatians (1961)                    3.791444  3.500000
101 Dalmatians (1996)                    3.240000  2.911215
12 Angry Men (1957)                      4.184397  4.328421
...                                           ...       ...
Young Guns (1988)                        3.371795  3.425620
Young Guns II (1990)                     2.934783  2.904025
Young Sherlock Holmes (1985)             3.514706  3.363344
Zero Effect (1998)                       3.864407  3.723140
eXistenZ (1999)                          3.098592  3.289086
[1216 rows x 2 columns]
```

To see the top films among female viewers, we can sort by the F column in descending order:

```
In [87]: top_female_ratings = mean_ratings.sort_values(by='F', ascending=False)

In [88]: top_female_ratings[:10]
Out[88]:
gender                                                        F         M
title
Close Shave, A (1995)                                  4.644444  4.473795
Wrong Trousers, The (1993)                             4.588235  4.478261
Sunset Blvd. (a.k.a. Sunset Boulevard) (1950)          4.572650  4.464589
Wallace & Gromit: The Best of Aardman Animation (1996) 4.563107  4.385075
Schindler's List (1993)                                4.562602  4.491415
Shawshank Redemption, The (1994)                       4.539075  4.560625
Grand Day Out, A (1992)                                4.537879  4.293255
```

```
To Kill a Mockingbird (1962)                        4.536667  4.372611
Creature Comforts (1990)                            4.513889  4.272277
Usual Suspects, The (1995)                          4.513317  4.518248
```

Measuring Rating Disagreement

Suppose you wanted to find the movies that are most divisive between male and female viewers. One way is to add a column to mean_ratings containing the difference in means, then sort by that:

```
In [89]: mean_ratings['diff'] = mean_ratings['M'] - mean_ratings['F']
```

Sorting by 'diff' yields the movies with the greatest rating difference so that we can see which ones were preferred by women:

```
In [90]: sorted_by_diff = mean_ratings.sort_values(by='diff')

In [91]: sorted_by_diff[:10]
Out[91]:
gender                                     F         M      diff
title
Dirty Dancing (1987)                3.790378  2.959596 -0.830782
Jumpin' Jack Flash (1986)           3.254717  2.578358 -0.676359
Grease (1978)                       3.975265  3.367041 -0.608224
Little Women (1994)                 3.870588  3.321739 -0.548849
Steel Magnolias (1989)              3.901734  3.365957 -0.535777
Anastasia (1997)                    3.800000  3.281609 -0.518391
Rocky Horror Picture Show, The (1975)  3.673016  3.160131 -0.512885
Color Purple, The (1985)            4.158192  3.659341 -0.498851
Age of Innocence, The (1993)        3.827068  3.339506 -0.487561
Free Willy (1993)                   2.921348  2.438776 -0.482573
```

Reversing the order of the rows and again slicing off the top 10 rows, we get the movies preferred by men that women didn't rate as highly:

```
# Reverse order of rows, take first 10 rows
In [92]: sorted_by_diff[::-1][:10]
Out[92]:
gender                                          F         M      diff
title
Good, The Bad and The Ugly, The (1966)   3.494949  4.221300  0.726351
Kentucky Fried Movie, The (1977)         2.878788  3.555147  0.676359
Dumb & Dumber (1994)                     2.697987  3.336595  0.638608
Longest Day, The (1962)                  3.411765  4.031447  0.619682
Cable Guy, The (1996)                    2.250000  2.863787  0.613787
Evil Dead II (Dead By Dawn) (1987)       3.297297  3.909283  0.611985
Hidden, The (1987)                       3.137931  3.745098  0.607167
Rocky III (1982)                         2.361702  2.943503  0.581801
Caddyshack (1980)                        3.396135  3.969737  0.573602
For a Few Dollars More (1965)            3.409091  3.953795  0.544704
```

Suppose instead you wanted the movies that elicited the most disagreement among viewers, independent of gender identification. Disagreement can be measured by the variance or standard deviation of the ratings:

```
# Standard deviation of rating grouped by title
In [93]: rating_std_by_title = data.groupby('title')['rating'].std()

# Filter down to active_titles
In [94]: rating_std_by_title = rating_std_by_title.loc[active_titles]

# Order Series by value in descending order
In [95]: rating_std_by_title.sort_values(ascending=False)[:10]
Out[95]:
title
Dumb & Dumber (1994)                      1.321333
Blair Witch Project, The (1999)           1.316368
Natural Born Killers (1994)               1.307198
Tank Girl (1995)                          1.277695
Rocky Horror Picture Show, The (1975)     1.260177
Eyes Wide Shut (1999)                     1.259624
Evita (1996)                              1.253631
Billy Madison (1995)                      1.249970
Fear and Loathing in Las Vegas (1998)     1.246408
Bicentennial Man (1999)                   1.245533
Name: rating, dtype: float64
```

You may have noticed that movie genres are given as a pipe-separated (|) string. If you wanted to do some analysis by genre, more work would be required to transform the genre information into a more usable form.

14.3 US Baby Names 1880–2010

The United States Social Security Administration (SSA) has made available data on the frequency of baby names from 1880 through the present. Hadley Wickham, an author of several popular R packages, has often made use of this dataset in illustrating data manipulation in R.

We need to do some data wrangling to load this dataset, but once we do that we will have a DataFrame that looks like this:

```
In [4]: names.head(10)
Out[4]:
        name sex  births  year
0       Mary   F    7065  1880
1       Anna   F    2604  1880
2       Emma   F    2003  1880
3  Elizabeth   F    1939  1880
4     Minnie   F    1746  1880
5   Margaret   F    1578  1880
6        Ida   F    1472  1880
```

```
7      Alice   F    1414    1880
8      Bertha  F    1320    1880
9       Sarah  F    1288    1880
```

There are many things you might want to do with the dataset:

- Visualize the proportion of babies given a particular name (your own, or another name) over time
- Determine the relative rank of a name
- Determine the most popular names in each year or the names whose popularity has advanced or declined the most
- Analyze trends in names: vowels, consonants, length, overall diversity, changes in spelling, first and last letters
- Analyze external sources of trends: biblical names, celebrities, demographic changes

With the tools in this book, many of these kinds of analyses are within reach, so I will walk you through some of them.

As of this writing, the US Social Security Administration makes available data files, one per year, containing the total number of births for each sex/name combination. The raw archive of these files can be obtained from *http://www.ssa.gov/oact/baby names/limits.html*.

In the event that this page has been moved by the time you're reading this, it can most likely be located again by an internet search. After downloading the "National data" file *names.zip* and unzipping it, you will have a directory containing a series of files like *yob1880.txt*. I use the Unix head command to look at the first 10 lines of one of the files (on Windows, you can use the more command or open it in a text editor):

```
In [96]: !head -n 10 datasets/babynames/yob1880.txt
Mary,F,7065
Anna,F,2604
Emma,F,2003
Elizabeth,F,1939
Minnie,F,1746
Margaret,F,1578
Ida,F,1472
Alice,F,1414
Bertha,F,1320
Sarah,F,1288
```

As this is already in a nicely comma-separated form, it can be loaded into a Data-Frame with pandas.read_csv:

```
In [97]: import pandas as pd

In [98]: names1880 = pd.read_csv('datasets/babynames/yob1880.txt',
   ....:                          names=['name', 'sex', 'births'])

In [99]: names1880
Out[99]:
             name sex  births
0            Mary   F    7065
1            Anna   F    2604
2            Emma   F    2003
3       Elizabeth   F    1939
4          Minnie   F    1746
...           ...  ..     ...
1995       Woodie   M       5
1996       Worthy   M       5
1997       Wright   M       5
1998         York   M       5
1999    Zachariah   M       5
[2000 rows x 3 columns]
```

These files only contain names with at least five occurrences in each year, so for simplicity's sake we can use the sum of the births column by sex as the total number of births in that year:

```
In [100]: names1880.groupby('sex').births.sum()
Out[100]:
sex
F     90993
M    110493
Name: births, dtype: int64
```

Since the dataset is split into files by year, one of the first things to do is to assemble all of the data into a single DataFrame and further to add a year field. You can do this using pandas.concat:

```
years = range(1880, 2011)

pieces = []
columns = ['name', 'sex', 'births']

for year in years:
    path = 'datasets/babynames/yob%d.txt' % year
    frame = pd.read_csv(path, names=columns)

    frame['year'] = year
    pieces.append(frame)

# Concatenate everything into a single DataFrame
names = pd.concat(pieces, ignore_index=True)
```

There are a couple things to note here. First, remember that concat glues the Data-Frame objects together row-wise by default. Secondly, you have to pass ignore_index=True because we're not interested in preserving the original row numbers returned from read_csv. So we now have a very large DataFrame containing all of the names data:

```
In [102]: names
Out[102]:
              name sex  births  year
0             Mary   F    7065  1880
1             Anna   F    2604  1880
2             Emma   F    2003  1880
3        Elizabeth   F    1939  1880
4           Minnie   F    1746  1880
...            ...  ..     ...   ...
1690779    Zymaire   M       5  2010
1690780     Zyonne   M       5  2010
1690781   Zyquarius   M      5  2010
1690782      Zyran   M       5  2010
1690783      Zzyzx   M       5  2010
[1690784 rows x 4 columns]
```

With this data in hand, we can already start aggregating the data at the year and sex level using groupby or pivot_table (see Figure 14-4):

```
In [103]: total_births = names.pivot_table('births', index='year',
   .....:                                   columns='sex', aggfunc=sum)

In [104]: total_births.tail()
Out[104]:
sex          F        M
year
2006   1896468  2050234
2007   1916888  2069242
2008   1883645  2032310
2009   1827643  1973359
2010   1759010  1898382

In [105]: total_births.plot(title='Total births by sex and year')
```

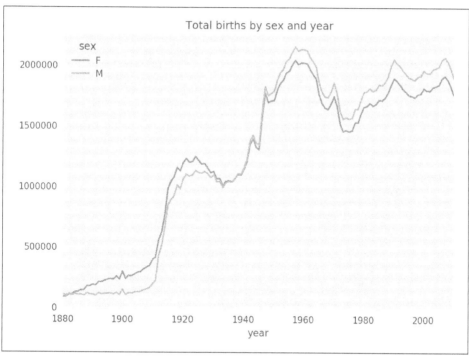

Figure 14-4. Total births by sex and year

Next, let's insert a column prop with the fraction of babies given each name relative to the total number of births. A prop value of 0.02 would indicate that 2 out of every 100 babies were given a particular name. Thus, we group the data by year and sex, then add the new column to each group:

```
def add_prop(group):
    group['prop'] = group.births / group.births.sum()
    return group
names = names.groupby(['year', 'sex']).apply(add_prop)
```

The resulting complete dataset now has the following columns:

```
In [107]: names
Out[107]:
              name sex  births  year      prop
0             Mary   F    7065  1880  0.077643
1             Anna   F    2604  1880  0.028618
2             Emma   F    2003  1880  0.022013
3        Elizabeth   F    1939  1880  0.021309
4           Minnie   F    1746  1880  0.019188
...            ...  ..     ...   ...       ...
1690779     Zymaire  M       5  2010  0.000003
1690780      Zyonne  M       5  2010  0.000003
1690781    Zyquarius  M      5  2010  0.000003
```

```
1690782      Zyran   M    5  2010  0.000003
1690783      Zzyzx   M    5  2010  0.000003
[1690784 rows x 5 columns]
```

When performing a group operation like this, it's often valuable to do a sanity check, like verifying that the prop column sums to 1 within all the groups:

```
In [108]: names.groupby(['year', 'sex']).prop.sum()
Out[108]:
year  sex
1880  F      1.0
      M      1.0
1881  F      1.0
      M      1.0
1882  F      1.0
            ...
2008  M      1.0
2009  F      1.0
      M      1.0
2010  F      1.0
      M      1.0
Name: prop, Length: 262, dtype: float64
```

Now that this is done, I'm going to extract a subset of the data to facilitate further analysis: the top 1,000 names for each sex/year combination. This is yet another group operation:

```
def get_top1000(group):
    return group.sort_values(by='births', ascending=False)[:1000]
grouped = names.groupby(['year', 'sex'])
top1000 = grouped.apply(get_top1000)
# Drop the group index, not needed
top1000.reset_index(inplace=True, drop=True)
```

If you prefer a do-it-yourself approach, try this instead:

```
pieces = []
for year, group in names.groupby(['year', 'sex']):
    pieces.append(group.sort_values(by='births', ascending=False)[:1000])
top1000 = pd.concat(pieces, ignore_index=True)
```

The resulting dataset is now quite a bit smaller:

```
In [110]: top1000
Out[110]:
             name sex  births  year      prop
0            Mary   F    7065  1880  0.077643
1            Anna   F    2604  1880  0.028618
2            Emma   F    2003  1880  0.022013
3       Elizabeth   F    1939  1880  0.021309
4          Minnie   F    1746  1880  0.019188
...           ...  ..     ...   ...       ...
261872     Camilo   M     194  2010  0.000102
261873     Destin   M     194  2010  0.000102
```

```
261874    Jaquan   M    194  2010  0.000102
261875    Jaydan   M    194  2010  0.000102
261876    Maxton   M    193  2010  0.000102
[261877 rows x 5 columns]
```

We'll use this Top 1,000 dataset in the following investigations into the data.

Analyzing Naming Trends

With the full dataset and Top 1,000 dataset in hand, we can start analyzing various naming trends of interest. Splitting the Top 1,000 names into the boy and girl portions is easy to do first:

```
In [111]: boys = top1000[top1000.sex == 'M']
```

```
In [112]: girls = top1000[top1000.sex == 'F']
```

Simple time series, like the number of Johns or Marys for each year, can be plotted but require a bit of munging to be more useful. Let's form a pivot table of the total number of births by year and name:

```
In [113]: total_births = top1000.pivot_table('births', index='year',
   ....:                                      columns='name',
   ....:                                      aggfunc=sum)
```

Now, this can be plotted for a handful of names with DataFrame's plot method (Figure 14-5 shows the result):

```
In [114]: total_births.info()
<class 'pandas.core.frame.DataFrame'>
Int64Index: 131 entries, 1880 to 2010
Columns: 6868 entries, Aaden to Zuri
dtypes: float64(6868)
memory usage: 6.9 MB
```

```
In [115]: subset = total_births[['John', 'Harry', 'Mary', 'Marilyn']]
```

```
In [116]: subset.plot(subplots=True, figsize=(12, 10), grid=False,
   ....:              title="Number of births per year")
```

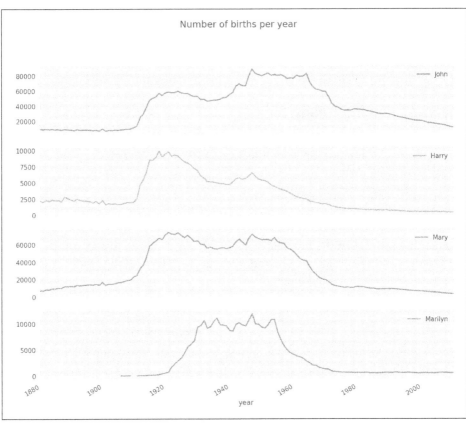

Figure 14-5. A few boy and girl names over time

On looking at this, you might conclude that these names have grown out of favor with the American population. But the story is actually more complicated than that, as will be explored in the next section.

Measuring the increase in naming diversity

One explanation for the decrease in plots is that fewer parents are choosing common names for their children. This hypothesis can be explored and confirmed in the data. One measure is the proportion of births represented by the top 1,000 most popular names, which I aggregate and plot by year and sex (Figure 14-6 shows the resulting plot):

```
In [118]: table = top1000.pivot_table('prop', index='year',
     .....:                            columns='sex', aggfunc=sum)
```

```
In [119]: table.plot(title='Sum of table1000.prop by year and sex',
     .....:           yticks=np.linspace(0, 1.2, 13), xticks=range(1880, 2020, 10)
)
```

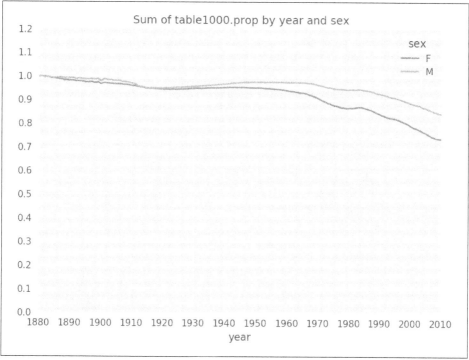

Figure 14-6. Proportion of births represented in top 1000 names by sex

You can see that, indeed, there appears to be increasing name diversity (decreasing total proportion in the top 1,000). Another interesting metric is the number of distinct names, taken in order of popularity from highest to lowest, in the top 50% of births. This number is a bit more tricky to compute. Let's consider just the boy names from 2010:

```
In [120]: df = boys[boys.year == 2010]
```

```
In [121]: df
Out[121]:
           name sex  births  year      prop
260877    Jacob   M   21875  2010  0.011523
260878    Ethan   M   17866  2010  0.009411
260879  Michael   M   17133  2010  0.009025
260880   Jayden   M   17030  2010  0.008971
260881  William   M   16870  2010  0.008887
```

```
    ...        ...    ..    ...     ...       ...
261872  Camilo   M   194  2010  0.000102
261873  Destin   M   194  2010  0.000102
261874  Jaquan   M   194  2010  0.000102
261875  Jaydan   M   194  2010  0.000102
261876  Maxton   M   193  2010  0.000102
[1000 rows x 5 columns]
```

After sorting prop in descending order, we want to know how many of the most popular names it takes to reach 50%. You could write a for loop to do this, but a vectorized NumPy way is a bit more clever. Taking the cumulative sum, cumsum, of prop and then calling the method searchsorted returns the position in the cumulative sum at which 0.5 would need to be inserted to keep it in sorted order:

```
In [122]: prop_cumsum = df.sort_values(by='prop', ascending=False).prop.cumsum()
```

```
In [123]: prop_cumsum[:10]
Out[123]:
260877    0.011523
260878    0.020934
260879    0.029959
260880    0.038930
260881    0.047817
260882    0.056579
260883    0.065155
260884    0.073414
260885    0.081528
260886    0.089621
Name: prop, dtype: float64
```

```
In [124]: prop_cumsum.values.searchsorted(0.5)
Out[124]: 116
```

Since arrays are zero-indexed, adding 1 to this result gives you a result of 117. By contrast, in 1900 this number was much smaller:

```
In [125]: df = boys[boys.year == 1900]
```

```
In [126]: in1900 = df.sort_values(by='prop', ascending=False).prop.cumsum()
```

```
In [127]: in1900.values.searchsorted(0.5) + 1
Out[127]: 25
```

You can now apply this operation to each year/sex combination, groupby those fields, and apply a function returning the count for each group:

```
def get_quantile_count(group, q=0.5):
    group = group.sort_values(by='prop', ascending=False)
    return group.prop.cumsum().values.searchsorted(q) + 1

diversity = top1000.groupby(['year', 'sex']).apply(get_quantile_count)
diversity = diversity.unstack('sex')
```

This resulting DataFrame `diversity` now has two time series, one for each sex, indexed by year. This can be inspected in IPython and plotted as before (see Figure 14-7):

```
In [130]: diversity.head()
Out[130]:
sex     F   M
year
1880   38  14
1881   38  14
1882   38  15
1883   39  15
1884   39  16

In [131]: diversity.plot(title="Number of popular names in top 50%")
```

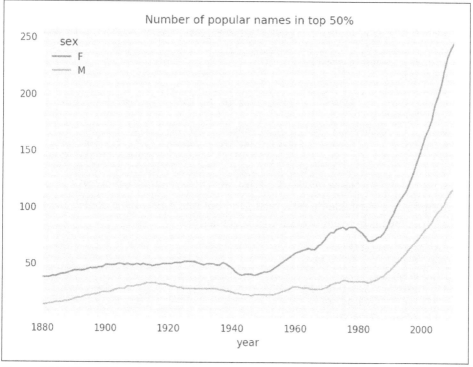

Figure 14-7. Plot of diversity metric by year

As you can see, girl names have always been more diverse than boy names, and they have only become more so over time. Further analysis of what exactly is driving the diversity, like the increase of alternative spellings, is left to the reader.

The "last letter" revolution

In 2007, baby name researcher Laura Wattenberg pointed out on her website (*http://www.babynamewizard.com*) that the distribution of boy names by final letter has changed significantly over the last 100 years. To see this, we first aggregate all of the births in the full dataset by year, sex, and final letter:

```
# extract last letter from name column
get_last_letter = lambda x: x[-1]
last_letters = names.name.map(get_last_letter)
last_letters.name = 'last_letter'

table = names.pivot_table('births', index=last_letters,
                          columns=['sex', 'year'], aggfunc=sum)
```

Then we select out three representative years spanning the history and print the first few rows:

```
In [133]: subtable = table.reindex(columns=[1910, 1960, 2010], level='year')
```

```
In [134]: subtable.head()
Out[134]:
sex                F                            M
year            1910      1960      2010      1910       1960       2010
last_letter
a           108376.0  691247.0  670605.0     977.0     5204.0    28438.0
b                NaN     694.0     450.0     411.0     3912.0    38859.0
c                5.0      49.0     946.0     482.0    15476.0    23125.0
d             6750.0    3729.0    2607.0   22111.0   262112.0    44398.0
e           133569.0  435013.0  313833.0   28655.0   178823.0   129012.0
```

Next, normalize the table by total births to compute a new table containing proportion of total births for each sex ending in each letter:

```
In [135]: subtable.sum()
Out[135]:
sex  year
F    1910     396416.0
     1960    2022062.0
     2010    1759010.0
M    1910     194198.0
     1960    2132588.0
     2010    1898382.0
dtype: float64
```

```
In [136]: letter_prop = subtable / subtable.sum()
```

```
In [137]: letter_prop
Out[137]:
sex                F                            M
year            1910      1960      2010      1910       1960       2010
last_letter
a           0.273390  0.341853  0.381240  0.005031  0.002440   0.014980
```

```
b           NaN  0.000343  0.000256  0.002116  0.001834  0.020470
c      0.000013  0.000024  0.000538  0.002482  0.007257  0.012181
d      0.017028  0.001844  0.001482  0.113858  0.122908  0.023387
e      0.336941  0.215133  0.178415  0.147556  0.083853  0.067959
...         ...       ...       ...       ...       ...       ...
v           NaN  0.000060  0.000117  0.000113  0.000037  0.001434
w      0.000020  0.000031  0.001182  0.006329  0.007711  0.016148
x      0.000015  0.000037  0.000727  0.003965  0.001851  0.008614
y      0.110972  0.152569  0.116828  0.077349  0.160987  0.058168
z      0.002439  0.000659  0.000704  0.000170  0.000184  0.001831
[26 rows x 6 columns]
```

With the letter proportions now in hand, we can make bar plots for each sex broken down by year (see Figure 14-8):

```python
import matplotlib.pyplot as plt

fig, axes = plt.subplots(2, 1, figsize=(10, 8))
letter_prop['M'].plot(kind='bar', rot=0, ax=axes[0], title='Male')
letter_prop['F'].plot(kind='bar', rot=0, ax=axes[1], title='Female',
                      legend=False)
```

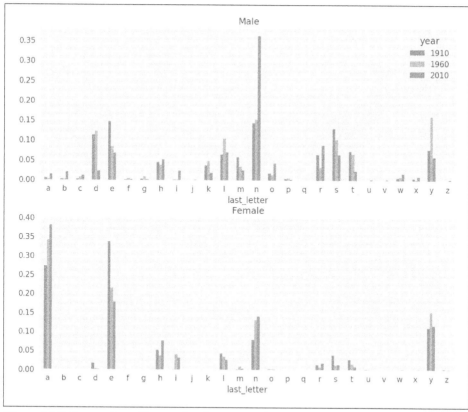

Figure 14-8. Proportion of boy and girl names ending in each letter

As you can see, boy names ending in *n* have experienced significant growth since the 1960s. Going back to the full table created before, I again normalize by year and sex and select a subset of letters for the boy names, finally transposing to make each column a time series:

```
In [140]: letter_prop = table / table.sum()
```

```
In [141]: dny_ts = letter_prop.loc[['d', 'n', 'y'], 'M'].T
```

```
In [142]: dny_ts.head()
Out[142]:
last_letter         d         n         y
year
1880         0.083055  0.153213  0.075760
1881         0.083247  0.153214  0.077451
1882         0.085340  0.149560  0.077537
1883         0.084066  0.151646  0.079144
1884         0.086120  0.149915  0.080405
```

With this DataFrame of time series in hand, I can make a plot of the trends over time again with its `plot` method (see Figure 14-9):

```
In [145]: dny_ts.plot()
```

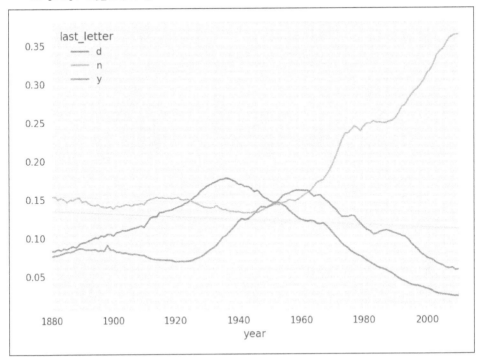

Figure 14-9. Proportion of boys born with names ending in d/n/y over time

Boy names that became girl names (and vice versa)

Another fun trend is looking at boy names that were more popular with one sex earlier in the sample but have "changed sexes" in the present. One example is the name Lesley or Leslie. Going back to the `top1000` DataFrame, I compute a list of names occurring in the dataset starting with "lesl":

```
In [146]: all_names = pd.Series(top1000.name.unique())

In [147]: lesley_like = all_names[all_names.str.lower().str.contains('lesl')]

In [148]: lesley_like
Out[148]:
632       Leslie
2294      Lesley
4262      Leslee
4728       Lesli
6103       Lesly
dtype: object
```

From there, we can filter down to just those names and sum births grouped by name to see the relative frequencies:

```
In [149]: filtered = top1000[top1000.name.isin(lesley_like)]

In [150]: filtered.groupby('name').births.sum()
Out[150]:
name
Leslee        1082
Lesley       35022
Lesli          929
Leslie      370429
Lesly        10067
Name: births, dtype: int64
```

Next, let's aggregate by sex and year and normalize within year:

```
In [151]: table = filtered.pivot_table('births', index='year',
   .....:                               columns='sex', aggfunc='sum')

In [152]: table = table.div(table.sum(1), axis=0)

In [153]: table.tail()
Out[153]:
sex      F   M
year
2006   1.0 NaN
2007   1.0 NaN
2008   1.0 NaN
2009   1.0 NaN
2010   1.0 NaN
```

Lastly, it's now possible to make a plot of the breakdown by sex over time (Figure 14-10):

```
In [155]: table.plot(style={'M': 'k-', 'F': 'k--'})
```

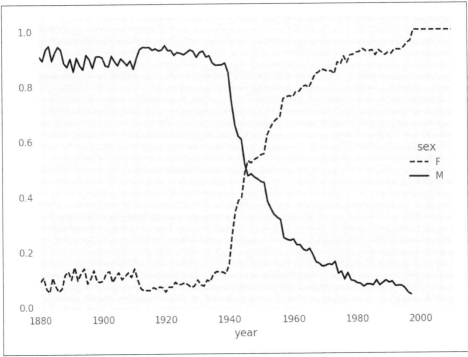

Figure 14-10. Proportion of male/female Lesley-like names over time

14.4 USDA Food Database

The US Department of Agriculture makes available a database of food nutrient information. Programmer Ashley Williams made available a version of this database in JSON format. The records look like this:

```
{
  "id": 21441,
  "description": "KENTUCKY FRIED CHICKEN, Fried Chicken, EXTRA CRISPY,
Wing, meat and skin with breading",
  "tags": ["KFC"],
  "manufacturer": "Kentucky Fried Chicken",
  "group": "Fast Foods",
  "portions": [
    {
      "amount": 1,
      "unit": "wing, with skin",
      "grams": 68.0
```

```
    },

    ...
  ],
  "nutrients": [
    {
      "value": 20.8,
      "units": "g",
      "description": "Protein",
      "group": "Composition"
    },

    ...
  ]
}
```

Each food has a number of identifying attributes along with two lists of nutrients and portion sizes. Data in this form is not particularly amenable to analysis, so we need to do some work to wrangle the data into a better form.

After downloading and extracting the data from the link, you can load it into Python with any JSON library of your choosing. I'll use the built-in Python `json` module:

```
In [156]: import json

In [157]: db = json.load(open('datasets/usda_food/database.json'))

In [158]: len(db)
Out[158]: 6636
```

Each entry in `db` is a dict containing all the data for a single food. The `'nutrients'` field is a list of dicts, one for each nutrient:

```
In [159]: db[0].keys()
Out[159]: dict_keys(['id', 'description', 'tags', 'manufacturer', 'group', 'porti
ons', 'nutrients'])

In [160]: db[0]['nutrients'][0]
Out[160]:
{'description': 'Protein',
 'group': 'Composition',
 'units': 'g',
 'value': 25.18}

In [161]: nutrients = pd.DataFrame(db[0]['nutrients'])

In [162]: nutrients[:7]
Out[162]:
                     description        group units    value
0                        Protein  Composition     g    25.18
1              Total lipid (fat)  Composition     g    29.20
2   Carbohydrate, by difference  Composition     g     3.06
3                            Ash        Other     g     3.28
```

```
4                 Energy      Energy  kcal    376.00
5                 Water   Composition     g     39.28
6                 Energy      Energy    kJ   1573.00
```

When converting a list of dicts to a DataFrame, we can specify a list of fields to extract. We'll take the food names, group, ID, and manufacturer:

```
In [163]: info_keys = ['description', 'group', 'id', 'manufacturer']

In [164]: info = pd.DataFrame(db, columns=info_keys)

In [165]: info[:5]
Out[165]:
                           description                    group    id  \
0                       Cheese, caraway  Dairy and Egg Products  1008
1                       Cheese, cheddar  Dairy and Egg Products  1009
2                          Cheese, edam  Dairy and Egg Products  1018
3                          Cheese, feta  Dairy and Egg Products  1019
4  Cheese, mozzarella, part skim milk  Dairy and Egg Products  1028
  manufacturer
0
1
2
3
4

In [166]: info.info()
<class 'pandas.core.frame.DataFrame'>
RangeIndex: 6636 entries, 0 to 6635
Data columns (total 4 columns):
description     6636 non-null object
group          6636 non-null object
id             6636 non-null int64
manufacturer   5195 non-null object
dtypes: int64(1), object(3)
memory usage: 207.5+ KB
```

You can see the distribution of food groups with value_counts:

```
In [167]: pd.value_counts(info.group)[:10]
Out[167]:
Vegetables and Vegetable Products    812
Beef Products                        618
Baked Products                       496
Breakfast Cereals                    403
Fast Foods                           365
Legumes and Legume Products          365
Lamb, Veal, and Game Products        345
Sweets                               341
Pork Products                        328
Fruits and Fruit Juices              328
Name: group, dtype: int64
```

Now, to do some analysis on all of the nutrient data, it's easiest to assemble the nutrients for each food into a single large table. To do so, we need to take several steps. First, I'll convert each list of food nutrients to a DataFrame, add a column for the food id, and append the DataFrame to a list. Then, these can be concatenated together with concat:

```
nutrients = []

for rec in db:
    fnuts = pd.DataFrame(rec['nutrients'])
    fnuts['id'] = rec['id']
    nutrients.append(fnuts)

nutrients = pd.concat(nutrients, ignore_index=True)
```

If all goes well, nutrients should look like this:

```
In [169]: nutrients
Out[169]:
                               description        group units    value     id
0                                  Protein  Composition     g   25.180   1008
1                         Total lipid (fat)  Composition     g   29.200   1008
2            Carbohydrate, by difference  Composition     g    3.060   1008
3                                      Ash        Other     g    3.280   1008
4                                   Energy       Energy  kcal  376.000   1008
...                                    ...          ...   ...      ...    ...
389350                     Vitamin B-12, added     Vitamins   mcg    0.000  43546
389351                           Cholesterol        Other    mg    0.000  43546
389352         Fatty acids, total saturated        Other     g    0.072  43546
389353   Fatty acids, total monounsaturated        Other     g    0.028  43546
389354   Fatty acids, total polyunsaturated        Other     g    0.041  43546
[389355 rows x 5 columns]
```

I noticed that there are duplicates in this DataFrame, so it makes things easier to drop them:

```
In [170]: nutrients.duplicated().sum()  # number of duplicates
Out[170]: 14179
```

```
In [171]: nutrients = nutrients.drop_duplicates()
```

Since 'group' and 'description' are in both DataFrame objects, we can rename for clarity:

```
In [172]: col_mapping = {'description' : 'food',
   .....:                 'group'       : 'fgroup'}
```

```
In [173]: info = info.rename(columns=col_mapping, copy=False)
```

```
In [174]: info.info()
<class 'pandas.core.frame.DataFrame'>
RangeIndex: 6636 entries, 0 to 6635
Data columns (total 4 columns):
```

```
food           6636 non-null object
fgroup         6636 non-null object
id             6636 non-null int64
manufacturer   5195 non-null object
dtypes: int64(1), object(3)
memory usage: 207.5+ KB

In [175]: col_mapping = {'description' : 'nutrient',
   .....:                'group' : 'nutgroup'}

In [176]: nutrients = nutrients.rename(columns=col_mapping, copy=False)

In [177]: nutrients
Out[177]:
                                 nutrient      nutgroup units    value     id
0                                 Protein   Composition     g   25.180   1008
1                       Total lipid (fat)   Composition     g   29.200   1008
2             Carbohydrate, by difference   Composition     g    3.060   1008
3                                     Ash         Other     g    3.280   1008
4                                  Energy        Energy  kcal  376.000   1008
...                                   ...           ...   ...      ...    ...
389350                  Vitamin B-12, added      Vitamins   mcg    0.000  43546
389351                          Cholesterol        Other    mg    0.000  43546
389352            Fatty acids, total saturated        Other     g    0.072  43546
389353      Fatty acids, total monounsaturated        Other     g    0.028  43546
389354      Fatty acids, total polyunsaturated        Other     g    0.041  43546
[375176 rows x 5 columns]
```

With all of this done, we're ready to merge `info` with `nutrients`:

```
In [178]: ndata = pd.merge(nutrients, info, on='id', how='outer')

In [179]: ndata.info()
<class 'pandas.core.frame.DataFrame'>
Int64Index: 375176 entries, 0 to 375175
Data columns (total 8 columns):
nutrient       375176 non-null object
nutgroup       375176 non-null object
units          375176 non-null object
value          375176 non-null float64
id             375176 non-null int64
food           375176 non-null object
fgroup         375176 non-null object
manufacturer   293054 non-null object
dtypes: float64(1), int64(1), object(6)
memory usage: 25.8+ MB

In [180]: ndata.iloc[30000]
Out[180]:
nutrient                        Glycine
nutgroup                    Amino Acids
units                                 g
value                              0.04
```

```
id                                                      6158
food            Soup, tomato bisque, canned, condensed
fgroup                    Soups, Sauces, and Gravies
manufacturer
Name: 30000, dtype: object
```

We could now make a plot of median values by food group and nutrient type (see Figure 14-11):

```
In [182]: result = ndata.groupby(['nutrient', 'fgroup'])['value'].quantile(0.5)
```

```
In [183]: result['Zinc, Zn'].sort_values().plot(kind='barh')
```

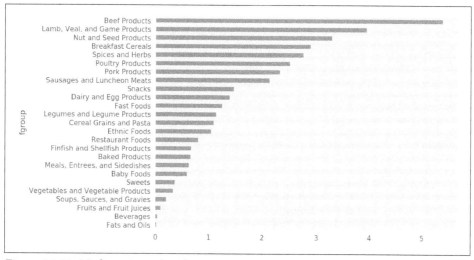

Figure 14-11. Median zinc values by nutrient group

With a little cleverness, you can find which food is most dense in each nutrient:

```
by_nutrient = ndata.groupby(['nutgroup', 'nutrient'])

get_maximum = lambda x: x.loc[x.value.idxmax()]
get_minimum = lambda x: x.loc[x.value.idxmin()]

max_foods = by_nutrient.apply(get_maximum)[['value', 'food']]

# make the food a little smaller
max_foods.food = max_foods.food.str[:50]
```

The resulting DataFrame is a bit too large to display in the book; here is only the `'Amino Acids'` nutrient group:

```
In [185]: max_foods.loc['Amino Acids']['food']
Out[185]:
nutrient
Alanine                         Gelatins, dry powder, unsweetened
Arginine                         Seeds, sesame flour, low-fat
```

```
Aspartic acid                                    Soy protein isolate
Cystine                 Seeds, cottonseed flour, low fat (glandless)
Glutamic acid                                    Soy protein isolate
                                 ...
Serine                  Soy protein isolate, PROTEIN TECHNOLOGIES INTERNAT
Threonine               Soy protein isolate, PROTEIN TECHNOLOGIES INTERNAT
Tryptophan                  Sea lion, Steller, meat with fat (Alaska Native)
Tyrosine                Soy protein isolate, PROTEIN TECHNOLOGIES INTERNAT
Valine                  Soy protein isolate, PROTEIN TECHNOLOGIES INTERNAT
Name: food, Length: 19, dtype: object
```

14.5 2012 Federal Election Commission Database

The US Federal Election Commission publishes data on contributions to political campaigns. This includes contributor names, occupation and employer, address, and contribution amount. An interesting dataset is from the 2012 US presidential election. A version of the dataset I downloaded in June 2012 is a 150 megabyte CSV file *P00000001-ALL.csv* (see the book's data repository), which can be loaded with pandas.read_csv:

```
In [186]: fec = pd.read_csv('datasets/fec/P00000001-ALL.csv')
```

```
In [187]: fec.info()
<class 'pandas.core.frame.DataFrame'>
RangeIndex: 1001731 entries, 0 to 1001730
Data columns (total 16 columns):
cmte_id             1001731 non-null object
cand_id             1001731 non-null object
cand_nm             1001731 non-null object
contbr_nm           1001731 non-null object
contbr_city         1001712 non-null object
contbr_st           1001727 non-null object
contbr_zip          1001620 non-null object
contbr_employer     988002 non-null object
contbr_occupation   993301 non-null object
contb_receipt_amt   1001731 non-null float64
contb_receipt_dt    1001731 non-null object
receipt_desc        14166 non-null object
memo_cd             92482 non-null object
memo_text           97770 non-null object
form_tp             1001731 non-null object
file_num            1001731 non-null int64
dtypes: float64(1), int64(1), object(14)
memory usage: 122.3+ MB
```

A sample record in the DataFrame looks like this:

```
In [188]: fec.iloc[123456]
Out[188]:
cmte_id             C00431445
cand_id             P80003338
```

```
cand_nm            Obama, Barack
contbr_nm          ELLMAN, IRA
contbr_city              TEMPE
                         ...
receipt_desc               NaN
memo_cd                    NaN
memo_text                  NaN
form_tp                  SA17A
file_num                772372
Name: 123456, Length: 16, dtype: object
```

You may think of some ways to start slicing and dicing this data to extract informative statistics about donors and patterns in the campaign contributions. I'll show you a number of different analyses that apply techniques in this book.

You can see that there are no political party affiliations in the data, so this would be useful to add. You can get a list of all the unique political candidates using unique:

```
In [189]: unique_cands = fec.cand_nm.unique()

In [190]: unique_cands
Out[190]:
array(['Bachmann, Michelle', 'Romney, Mitt', 'Obama, Barack',
       "Roemer, Charles E. 'Buddy' III", 'Pawlenty, Timothy',
       'Johnson, Gary Earl', 'Paul, Ron', 'Santorum, Rick',
       'Cain, Herman', 'Gingrich, Newt', 'McCotter, Thaddeus G',
       'Huntsman, Jon', 'Perry, Rick'], dtype=object)

In [191]: unique_cands[2]
Out[191]: 'Obama, Barack'
```

One way to indicate party affiliation is using a dict:[1]

```
parties = {'Bachmann, Michelle': 'Republican',
           'Cain, Herman': 'Republican',
           'Gingrich, Newt': 'Republican',
           'Huntsman, Jon': 'Republican',
           'Johnson, Gary Earl': 'Republican',
           'McCotter, Thaddeus G': 'Republican',
           'Obama, Barack': 'Democrat',
           'Paul, Ron': 'Republican',
           'Pawlenty, Timothy': 'Republican',
           'Perry, Rick': 'Republican',
           "Roemer, Charles E. 'Buddy' III": 'Republican',
           'Romney, Mitt': 'Republican',
           'Santorum, Rick': 'Republican'}
```

---

1 This makes the simplifying assumption that Gary Johnson is a Republican even though he later became the Libertarian party candidate.

Now, using this mapping and the `map` method on Series objects, you can compute an array of political parties from the candidate names:

```
In [193]: fec.cand_nm[123456:123461]
Out[193]:
123456     Obama, Barack
123457     Obama, Barack
123458     Obama, Barack
123459     Obama, Barack
123460     Obama, Barack
Name: cand_nm, dtype: object

In [194]: fec.cand_nm[123456:123461].map(parties)
Out[194]:
123456     Democrat
123457     Democrat
123458     Democrat
123459     Democrat
123460     Democrat
Name: cand_nm, dtype: object

# Add it as a column
In [195]: fec['party'] = fec.cand_nm.map(parties)

In [196]: fec['party'].value_counts()
Out[196]:
Democrat       593746
Republican     407985
Name: party, dtype: int64
```

A couple of data preparation points. First, this data includes both contributions and refunds (negative contribution amount):

```
In [197]: (fec.contb_receipt_amt > 0).value_counts()
Out[197]:
True      991475
False      10256
Name: contb_receipt_amt, dtype: int64
```

To simplify the analysis, I'll restrict the dataset to positive contributions:

```
In [198]: fec = fec[fec.contb_receipt_amt > 0]
```

Since Barack Obama and Mitt Romney were the main two candidates, I'll also prepare a subset that just has contributions to their campaigns:

```
In [199]: fec_mrbo = fec[fec.cand_nm.isin(['Obama, Barack', 'Romney, Mitt'])]
```

Donation Statistics by Occupation and Employer

Donations by occupation is another oft-studied statistic. For example, lawyers (attorneys) tend to donate more money to Democrats, while business executives tend to donate more to Republicans. You have no reason to believe me; you can see for your-self in the data. First, the total number of donations by occupation is easy:

```
In [200]: fec.contbr_occupation.value_counts()[:10]
Out[200]:
RETIRED                                 233990
INFORMATION REQUESTED                    35107
ATTORNEY                                 34286
HOMEMAKER                                29931
PHYSICIAN                                23432
INFORMATION REQUESTED PER BEST EFFORTS   21138
ENGINEER                                 14334
TEACHER                                  13990
CONSULTANT                               13273
PROFESSOR                                12555
Name: contbr_occupation, dtype: int64
```

You will notice by looking at the occupations that many refer to the same basic job type, or there are several variants of the same thing. The following code snippet illus-trates a technique for cleaning up a few of them by mapping from one occupation to another; note the "trick" of using dict.get to allow occupations with no mapping to "pass through":

```
occ_mapping = {
   'INFORMATION REQUESTED PER BEST EFFORTS' : 'NOT PROVIDED',
   'INFORMATION REQUESTED' : 'NOT PROVIDED',
   'INFORMATION REQUESTED (BEST EFFORTS)' : 'NOT PROVIDED',
   'C.E.O.': 'CEO'
}

# If no mapping provided, return x
f = lambda x: occ_mapping.get(x, x)
fec.contbr_occupation = fec.contbr_occupation.map(f)
```

I'll also do the same thing for employers:

```
emp_mapping = {
   'INFORMATION REQUESTED PER BEST EFFORTS' : 'NOT PROVIDED',
   'INFORMATION REQUESTED' : 'NOT PROVIDED',
   'SELF' : 'SELF-EMPLOYED',
   'SELF EMPLOYED' : 'SELF-EMPLOYED',
}

# If no mapping provided, return x
f = lambda x: emp_mapping.get(x, x)
fec.contbr_employer = fec.contbr_employer.map(f)
```

Now, you can use pivot_table to aggregate the data by party and occupation, then filter down to the subset that donated at least $2 million overall:

```
In [203]: by_occupation = fec.pivot_table('contb_receipt_amt',
   .....:                                  index='contbr_occupation',
   .....:                                  columns='party', aggfunc='sum')
```

```
In [204]: over_2mm = by_occupation[by_occupation.sum(1) > 2000000]

In [205]: over_2mm
Out[205]:
party                   Democrat     Republican
contbr_occupation
ATTORNEY            11141982.97    7.477194e+06
CEO                  2074974.79    4.211041e+06
CONSULTANT           2459912.71    2.544725e+06
ENGINEER              951525.55    1.818374e+06
EXECUTIVE            1355161.05    4.138850e+06
...                        ...             ...
PRESIDENT            1878509.95    4.720924e+06
PROFESSOR            2165071.08    2.967027e+05
REAL ESTATE           528902.09    1.625902e+06
RETIRED            25305116.38     2.356124e+07
SELF-EMPLOYED         672393.40    1.640253e+06
[17 rows x 2 columns]
```

It can be easier to look at this data graphically as a bar plot ('barh' means horizontal bar plot; see Figure 14-12):

```
In [207]: over_2mm.plot(kind='barh')
```

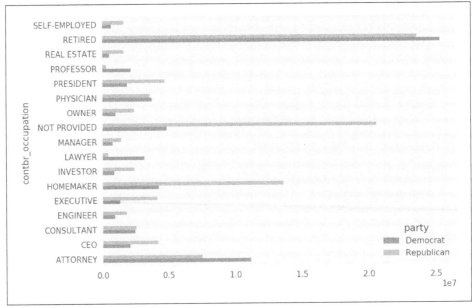

Figure 14-12. Total donations by party for top occupations

You might be interested in the top donor occupations or top companies that donated to Obama and Romney. To do this, you can group by candidate name and use a variant of the top method from earlier in the chapter:

```
def get_top_amounts(group, key, n=5):
    totals = group.groupby(key)['contb_receipt_amt'].sum()
    return totals.nlargest(n)
```

Then aggregate by occupation and employer:

```
In [209]: grouped = fec_mrbo.groupby('cand_nm')

In [210]: grouped.apply(get_top_amounts, 'contbr_occupation', n=7)
Out[210]:
cand_nm         contbr_occupation
Obama, Barack   RETIRED                  25305116.38
                ATTORNEY                 11141982.97
                INFORMATION REQUESTED     4866973.96
                HOMEMAKER                 4248875.80
                PHYSICIAN                 3735124.94
                                              ...
Romney, Mitt    HOMEMAKER                 8147446.22
                ATTORNEY                  5364718.82
                PRESIDENT                 2491244.89
                EXECUTIVE                 2300947.03
                C.E.O.                    1968386.11
Name: contb_receipt_amt, Length: 14, dtype: float64

In [211]: grouped.apply(get_top_amounts, 'contbr_employer', n=10)
Out[211]:
cand_nm         contbr_employer
Obama, Barack   RETIRED                  22694358.85
                SELF-EMPLOYED            17080985.96
                NOT EMPLOYED              8586308.70
                INFORMATION REQUESTED     5053480.37
                HOMEMAKER                 2605408.54
                                              ...
Romney, Mitt    CREDIT SUISSE             281150.00
                MORGAN STANLEY            267266.00
                GOLDMAN SACH & CO.        238250.00
                BARCLAYS CAPITAL          162750.00
                H.I.G. CAPITAL            139500.00
Name: contb_receipt_amt, Length: 20, dtype: float64
```

Bucketing Donation Amounts

A useful way to analyze this data is to use the cut function to discretize the contributor amounts into buckets by contribution size:

```
In [212]: bins = np.array([0, 1, 10, 100, 1000, 10000,
   .....:                   100000, 1000000, 10000000])
```

```
In [213]: labels = pd.cut(fec_mrbo.contb_receipt_amt, bins)

In [214]: labels
Out[214]:
411          (10, 100]
412          (100, 1000]
413          (100, 1000]
414          (10, 100]
415          (10, 100]
               ...
701381       (10, 100]
701382       (100, 1000]
701383       (1, 10]
701384       (10, 100]
701385       (100, 1000]
Name: contb_receipt_amt, Length: 694282, dtype: category
Categories (8, interval[int64]): [(0, 1] < (1, 10] < (10, 100] < (100, 1000] < (1
000, 10000] <
                                  (10000, 100000] < (100000, 1000000] < (1000000,
10000000]]
```

We can then group the data for Obama and Romney by name and bin label to get a histogram by donation size:

```
In [215]: grouped = fec_mrbo.groupby(['cand_nm', labels])

In [216]: grouped.size().unstack(0)
Out[216]:
cand_nm                  Obama, Barack   Romney, Mitt
contb_receipt_amt
(0, 1]                          493.0           77.0
(1, 10]                       40070.0         3681.0
(10, 100]                    372280.0        31853.0
(100, 1000]                  153991.0        43357.0
(1000, 10000]                 22284.0        26186.0
(10000, 100000]                   2.0            1.0
(100000, 1000000]                 3.0            NaN
(1000000, 10000000]               4.0            NaN
```

This data shows that Obama received a significantly larger number of small donations than Romney. You can also sum the contribution amounts and normalize within buckets to visualize percentage of total donations of each size by candidate (Figure 14-13 shows the resulting plot):

```
In [218]: bucket_sums = grouped.contb_receipt_amt.sum().unstack(0)

In [219]: normed_sums = bucket_sums.div(bucket_sums.sum(axis=1), axis=0)

In [220]: normed_sums
Out[220]:
cand_nm                  Obama, Barack   Romney, Mitt
contb_receipt_amt
(0, 1]                       0.805182       0.194818
```

```
(1, 10]                    0.918767      0.081233
(10, 100]                  0.910769      0.089231
(100, 1000]                0.710176      0.289824
(1000, 10000]              0.447326      0.552674
(10000, 100000]            0.823120      0.176880
(100000, 1000000]          1.000000           NaN
(1000000, 10000000]        1.000000           NaN

In [221]: normed_sums[:-2].plot(kind='barh')
```

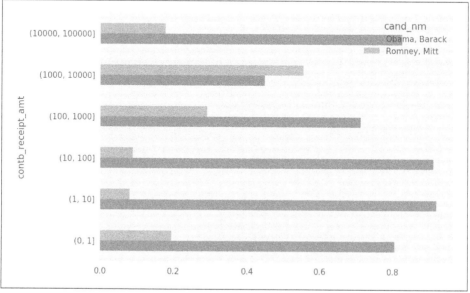

Figure 14-13. Percentage of total donations received by candidates for each donation size

I excluded the two largest bins as these are not donations by individuals.

This analysis can be refined and improved in many ways. For example, you could aggregate donations by donor name and zip code to adjust for donors who gave many small amounts versus one or more large donations. I encourage you to download and explore the dataset yourself.

Donation Statistics by State

Aggregating the data by candidate and state is a routine affair:

```
In [222]: grouped = fec_mrbo.groupby(['cand_nm', 'contbr_st'])

In [223]: totals = grouped.contb_receipt_amt.sum().unstack(0).fillna(0)

In [224]: totals = totals[totals.sum(1) > 100000]

In [225]: totals[:10]
```

```
Out[225]:
cand_nm     Obama, Barack  Romney, Mitt
contbr_st
AK            281840.15      86204.24
AL            543123.48     527303.51
AR            359247.28     105556.00
AZ           1506476.98    1888436.23
CA          23824984.24   11237636.60
CO           2132429.49    1506714.12
CT           2068291.26    3499475.45
DC           4373538.80    1025137.50
DE            336669.14      82712.00
FL           7318178.58    8338458.81
```

If you divide each row by the total contribution amount, you get the relative percentage of total donations by state for each candidate:

```
In [226]: percent = totals.div(totals.sum(1), axis=0)
```

```
In [227]: percent[:10]
Out[227]:
cand_nm     Obama, Barack  Romney, Mitt
contbr_st
AK             0.765778      0.234222
AL             0.507390      0.492610
AR             0.772902      0.227098
AZ             0.443745      0.556255
CA             0.679498      0.320502
CO             0.585970      0.414030
CT             0.371476      0.628524
DC             0.810113      0.189887
DE             0.802776      0.197224
FL             0.467417      0.532583
```

14.6 Conclusion

We've reached the end of the book's main chapters. I have included some additional content you may find useful in the appendixes.

In the five years since the first edition of this book was published, Python has become a popular and widespread language for data analysis. The programming skills you have developed here will stay relevant for a long time into the future. I hope the programming tools and libraries we've explored serve you well in your work.

Advanced NumPy

In this appendix, I will go deeper into the NumPy library for array computing. This will include more internal detail about the ndarray type and more advanced array manipulations and algorithms.

This appendix contains miscellaneous topics and does not necessarily need to be read linearly.

A.1 ndarray Object Internals

The NumPy ndarray provides a means to interpret a block of homogeneous data (either contiguous or strided) as a multidimensional array object. The data type, or *dtype*, determines how the data is interpreted as being floating point, integer, boolean, or any of the other types we've been looking at.

Part of what makes ndarray flexible is that every array object is a *strided* view on a block of data. You might wonder, for example, how the array view arr[::2, ::-1] does not copy any data. The reason is that the ndarray is more than just a chunk of memory and a dtype; it also has "striding" information that enables the array to move through memory with varying step sizes. More precisely, the ndarray internally consists of the following:

- A *pointer to data*—that is, a block of data in RAM or in a memory-mapped file
- The *data type* or dtype, describing fixed-size value cells in the array
- A tuple indicating the array's *shape*
- A tuple of *strides*, integers indicating the number of bytes to "step" in order to advance one element along a dimension

See Figure A-1 for a simple mockup of the ndarray innards.

For example, a 10 × 5 array would have shape (10, 5):

```
In [12]: np.ones((10, 5)).shape
Out[12]: (10, 5)
```

A typical (C order) 3 × 4 × 5 array of float64 (8-byte) values has strides (160, 40, 8) (knowing about the strides can be useful because, in general, the larger the strides on a particular axis, the more costly it is to perform computation along that axis):

```
In [13]: np.ones((3, 4, 5), dtype=np.float64).strides
Out[13]: (160, 40, 8)
```

While it is rare that a typical NumPy user would be interested in the array strides, they are the critical ingredient in constructing "zero-copy" array views. Strides can even be negative, which enables an array to move "backward" through memory (this would be the case, for example, in a slice like obj[::-1] or obj[:, ::-1]).

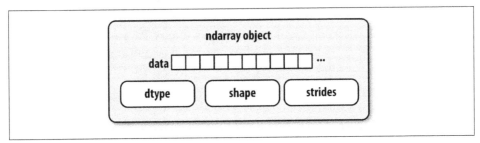

Figure A-1. The NumPy ndarray object

NumPy dtype Hierarchy

You may occasionally have code that needs to check whether an array contains integers, floating-point numbers, strings, or Python objects. Because there are multiple types of floating-point numbers (float16 through float128), checking that the dtype is among a list of types would be very verbose. Fortunately, the dtypes have superclasses such as np.integer and np.floating, which can be used in conjunction with the np.issubdtype function:

```
In [14]: ints = np.ones(10, dtype=np.uint16)

In [15]: floats = np.ones(10, dtype=np.float32)

In [16]: np.issubdtype(ints.dtype, np.integer)
Out[16]: True

In [17]: np.issubdtype(floats.dtype, np.floating)
Out[17]: True
```

You can see all of the parent classes of a specific dtype by calling the type's mro method:

```
In [18]: np.float64.mro()
Out[18]:
[numpy.float64,
 numpy.floating,
 numpy.inexact,
 numpy.number,
 numpy.generic,
 float,
 object]
```

Therefore, we also have:

```
In [19]: np.issubdtype(ints.dtype, np.number)
Out[19]: True
```

Most NumPy users will never have to know about this, but it occasionally comes in handy. See Figure A-2 for a graph of the dtype hierarchy and parent–subclass relationships.[1]

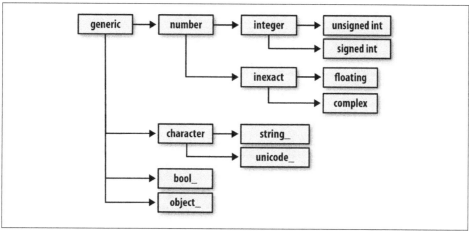

Figure A-2. The NumPy dtype class hierarchy

A.2 Advanced Array Manipulation

There are many ways to work with arrays beyond fancy indexing, slicing, and boolean subsetting. While much of the heavy lifting for data analysis applications is handled by higher-level functions in pandas, you may at some point need to write a data algorithm that is not found in one of the existing libraries.

---

1 Some of the dtypes have trailing underscores in their names. These are there to avoid variable name conflicts between the NumPy-specific types and the Python built-in ones.

Reshaping Arrays

In many cases, you can convert an array from one shape to another without copying any data. To do this, pass a tuple indicating the new shape to the `reshape` array instance method. For example, suppose we had a one-dimensional array of values that we wished to rearrange into a matrix (the is illustrated in Figure A-3):

```
In [20]: arr = np.arange(8)

In [21]: arr
Out[21]: array([0, 1, 2, 3, 4, 5, 6, 7])

In [22]: arr.reshape((4, 2))
Out[22]:
array([[0, 1],
       [2, 3],
       [4, 5],
       [6, 7]])
```

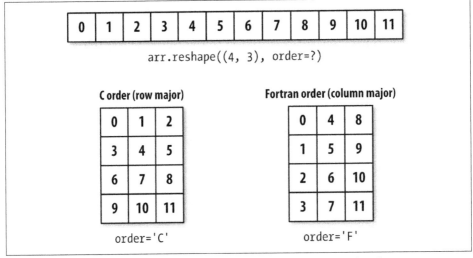

Figure A-3. Reshaping in C (row major) or Fortran (column major) order

A multidimensional array can also be reshaped:

```
In [23]: arr.reshape((4, 2)).reshape((2, 4))
Out[23]:
array([[0, 1, 2, 3],
       [4, 5, 6, 7]])
```

One of the passed shape dimensions can be –1, in which case the value used for that dimension will be inferred from the data:

```
In [24]: arr = np.arange(15)
```

```
In [25]: arr.reshape((5, -1))
Out[25]:
array([[ 0,  1,  2],
       [ 3,  4,  5],
       [ 6,  7,  8],
       [ 9, 10, 11],
       [12, 13, 14]])
```

Since an array's shape attribute is a tuple, it can be passed to reshape, too:

```
In [26]: other_arr = np.ones((3, 5))
```

```
In [27]: other_arr.shape
Out[27]: (3, 5)
```

```
In [28]: arr.reshape(other_arr.shape)
Out[28]:
array([[ 0,  1,  2,  3,  4],
       [ 5,  6,  7,  8,  9],
       [10, 11, 12, 13, 14]])
```

The opposite operation of reshape from one-dimensional to a higher dimension is typically known as *flattening* or *raveling*:

```
In [29]: arr = np.arange(15).reshape((5, 3))
```

```
In [30]: arr
Out[30]:
array([[ 0,  1,  2],
       [ 3,  4,  5],
       [ 6,  7,  8],
       [ 9, 10, 11],
       [12, 13, 14]])
```

```
In [31]: arr.ravel()
Out[31]: array([ 0,  1,  2,  3,  4,  5,  6,  7,  8,  9, 10, 11, 12, 13, 14])
```

ravel does not produce a copy of the underlying values if the values in the result were contiguous in the original array. The flatten method behaves like ravel except it always returns a copy of the data:

```
In [32]: arr.flatten()
Out[32]: array([ 0,  1,  2,  3,  4,  5,  6,  7,  8,  9, 10, 11, 12, 13, 14])
```

The data can be reshaped or raveled in different orders. This is a slightly nuanced topic for new NumPy users and is therefore the next subtopic.

C Versus Fortran Order

NumPy gives you control and flexibility over the layout of your data in memory. By default, NumPy arrays are created in *row major* order. Spatially this means that if you have a two-dimensional array of data, the items in each row of the array are stored in adjacent memory locations. The alternative to row major ordering is *column major* order, which means that values within each column of data are stored in adjacent memory locations.

For historical reasons, row and column major order are also know as C and Fortran order, respectively. In the FORTRAN 77 language, matrices are all column major.

Functions like `reshape` and `ravel` accept an `order` argument indicating the order to use the data in the array. This is usually set to `'C'` or `'F'` in most cases (there are also less commonly used options `'A'` and `'K'`; see the NumPy documentation, and refer back to Figure A-3 for an illustration of these options):

```
In [33]: arr = np.arange(12).reshape((3, 4))

In [34]: arr
Out[34]:
array([[ 0,  1,  2,  3],
       [ 4,  5,  6,  7],
       [ 8,  9, 10, 11]])

In [35]: arr.ravel()
Out[35]: array([ 0,  1,  2,  3,  4,  5,  6,  7,  8,  9, 10, 11])

In [36]: arr.ravel('F')
Out[36]: array([ 0,  4,  8,  1,  5,  9,  2,  6, 10,  3,  7, 11])
```

Reshaping arrays with more than two dimensions can be a bit mind-bending (see Figure A-3). The key difference between C and Fortran order is the way in which the dimensions are walked:

C/row major order
> Traverse higher dimensions *first* (e.g., axis 1 before advancing on axis 0).

Fortran/column major order
> Traverse higher dimensions *last* (e.g., axis 0 before advancing on axis 1).

Concatenating and Splitting Arrays

`numpy.concatenate` takes a sequence (tuple, list, etc.) of arrays and joins them together in order along the input axis:

```
In [37]: arr1 = np.array([[1, 2, 3], [4, 5, 6]])

In [38]: arr2 = np.array([[7, 8, 9], [10, 11, 12]])
```

```
In [39]: np.concatenate([arr1, arr2], axis=0)
Out[39]:
array([[ 1,  2,  3],
       [ 4,  5,  6],
       [ 7,  8,  9],
       [10, 11, 12]])

In [40]: np.concatenate([arr1, arr2], axis=1)
Out[40]:
array([[ 1,  2,  3,  7,  8,  9],
       [ 4,  5,  6, 10, 11, 12]])
```

There are some convenience functions, like vstack and hstack, for common kinds of concatenation. The preceding operations could have been expressed as:

```
In [41]: np.vstack((arr1, arr2))
Out[41]:
array([[ 1,  2,  3],
       [ 4,  5,  6],
       [ 7,  8,  9],
       [10, 11, 12]])

In [42]: np.hstack((arr1, arr2))
Out[42]:
array([[ 1,  2,  3,  7,  8,  9],
       [ 4,  5,  6, 10, 11, 12]])
```

split, on the other hand, slices apart an array into multiple arrays along an axis:

```
In [43]: arr = np.random.randn(5, 2)

In [44]: arr
Out[44]:
array([[-0.2047,  0.4789],
       [-0.5194, -0.5557],
       [ 1.9658,  1.3934],
       [ 0.0929,  0.2817],
       [ 0.769 ,  1.2464]])

In [45]: first, second, third = np.split(arr, [1, 3])

In [46]: first
Out[46]: array([[-0.2047,  0.4789]])

In [47]: second
Out[47]:
array([[-0.5194, -0.5557],
       [ 1.9658,  1.3934]])

In [48]: third
Out[48]:
array([[0.0929, 0.2817],
       [0.769 , 1.2464]])
```

The value [1, 3] passed to np.split indicate the indices at which to split the array into pieces.

See Table A-1 for a list of all relevant concatenation and splitting functions, some of which are provided only as a convenience of the very general-purpose concatenate.

Table A-1. Array concatenation functions

Function	Description
concatenate	Most general function, concatenates collection of arrays along one axis
vstack, row_stack	Stack arrays row-wise (along axis 0)
hstack	Stack arrays column-wise (along axis 1)
column_stack	Like hstack, but converts 1D arrays to 2D column vectors first
dstack	Stack arrays "depth"-wise (along axis 2)
split	Split array at passed locations along a particular axis
hsplit/vsplit	Convenience functions for splitting on axis 0 and 1, respectively

Stacking helpers: r_ and c_

There are two special objects in the NumPy namespace, r_ and c_, that make stacking arrays more concise:

```
In [49]: arr = np.arange(6)

In [50]: arr1 = arr.reshape((3, 2))

In [51]: arr2 = np.random.randn(3, 2)

In [52]: np.r_[arr1, arr2]
Out[52]:
array([[ 0.    ,  1.    ],
       [ 2.    ,  3.    ],
       [ 4.    ,  5.    ],
       [ 1.0072, -1.2962],
       [ 0.275 ,  0.2289],
       [ 1.3529,  0.8864]])

In [53]: np.c_[np.r_[arr1, arr2], arr]
Out[53]:
array([[ 0.    ,  1.    ,  0.    ],
       [ 2.    ,  3.    ,  1.    ],
       [ 4.    ,  5.    ,  2.    ],
       [ 1.0072, -1.2962,  3.    ],
       [ 0.275 ,  0.2289,  4.    ],
       [ 1.3529,  0.8864,  5.    ]])
```

These additionally can translate slices to arrays:

```
In [54]: np.c_[1:6, -10:-5]
Out[54]:
```

```
array([[  1, -10],
       [  2,  -9],
       [  3,  -8],
       [  4,  -7],
       [  5,  -6]])
```

See the docstring for more on what you can do with c_ and r_.

Repeating Elements: tile and repeat

Two useful tools for repeating or replicating arrays to produce larger arrays are the
repeat and tile functions. repeat replicates each element in an array some number
of times, producing a larger array:

```
In [55]: arr = np.arange(3)

In [56]: arr
Out[56]: array([0, 1, 2])

In [57]: arr.repeat(3)
Out[57]: array([0, 0, 0, 1, 1, 1, 2, 2, 2])
```

> The need to replicate or repeat arrays can be less common with
> NumPy than it is with other array programming frameworks like
> MATLAB. One reason for this is that *broadcasting* often fills this
> need better, which is the subject of the next section.

By default, if you pass an integer, each element will be repeated that number of times.
If you pass an array of integers, each element can be repeated a different number of
times:

```
In [58]: arr.repeat([2, 3, 4])
Out[58]: array([0, 0, 1, 1, 1, 2, 2, 2, 2])
```

Multidimensional arrays can have their elements repeated along a particular axis.

```
In [59]: arr = np.random.randn(2, 2)

In [60]: arr
Out[60]:
array([[-2.0016, -0.3718],
       [ 1.669 , -0.4386]])

In [61]: arr.repeat(2, axis=0)
Out[61]:
array([[-2.0016, -0.3718],
       [-2.0016, -0.3718],
       [ 1.669 , -0.4386],
       [ 1.669 , -0.4386]])
```

Note that if no axis is passed, the array will be flattened first, which is likely not what you want. Similarly, you can pass an array of integers when repeating a multidimensional array to repeat a given slice a different number of times:

```
In [62]: arr.repeat([2, 3], axis=0)
Out[62]:
array([[-2.0016, -0.3718],
       [-2.0016, -0.3718],
       [ 1.669 , -0.4386],
       [ 1.669 , -0.4386],
       [ 1.669 , -0.4386]])

In [63]: arr.repeat([2, 3], axis=1)
Out[63]:
array([[-2.0016, -2.0016, -0.3718, -0.3718, -0.3718],
       [ 1.669 ,  1.669 , -0.4386, -0.4386, -0.4386]])
```

tile, on the other hand, is a shortcut for stacking copies of an array along an axis. Visually you can think of it as being akin to "laying down tiles":

```
In [64]: arr
Out[64]:
array([[-2.0016, -0.3718],
       [ 1.669 , -0.4386]])

In [65]: np.tile(arr, 2)
Out[65]:
array([[-2.0016, -0.3718, -2.0016, -0.3718],
       [ 1.669 , -0.4386,  1.669 , -0.4386]])
```

The second argument is the number of tiles; with a scalar, the tiling is made row by row, rather than column by column. The second argument to tile can be a tuple indicating the layout of the "tiling":

```
In [66]: arr
Out[66]:
array([[-2.0016, -0.3718],
       [ 1.669 , -0.4386]])

In [67]: np.tile(arr, (2, 1))
Out[67]:
array([[-2.0016, -0.3718],
       [ 1.669 , -0.4386],
       [-2.0016, -0.3718],
       [ 1.669 , -0.4386]])

In [68]: np.tile(arr, (3, 2))
Out[68]:
array([[-2.0016, -0.3718, -2.0016, -0.3718],
       [ 1.669 , -0.4386,  1.669 , -0.4386],
       [-2.0016, -0.3718, -2.0016, -0.3718],
       [ 1.669 , -0.4386,  1.669 , -0.4386],
```

```
         [-2.0016, -0.3718, -2.0016, -0.3718],
         [ 1.669 , -0.4386,  1.669 , -0.4386]])
```

Fancy Indexing Equivalents: take and put

As you may recall from Chapter 4, one way to get and set subsets of arrays is by *fancy* indexing using integer arrays:

```
In [69]: arr = np.arange(10) * 100

In [70]: inds = [7, 1, 2, 6]

In [71]: arr[inds]
Out[71]: array([700, 100, 200, 600])
```

There are alternative ndarray methods that are useful in the special case of only making a selection on a single axis:

```
In [72]: arr.take(inds)
Out[72]: array([700, 100, 200, 600])

In [73]: arr.put(inds, 42)

In [74]: arr
Out[74]: array([  0,  42,  42, 300, 400, 500,  42,  42, 800, 900])

In [75]: arr.put(inds, [40, 41, 42, 43])

In [76]: arr
Out[76]: array([  0,  41,  42, 300, 400, 500,  43,  40, 800, 900])
```

To use take along other axes, you can pass the axis keyword:

```
In [77]: inds = [2, 0, 2, 1]

In [78]: arr = np.random.randn(2, 4)

In [79]: arr
Out[79]:
array([[-0.5397,  0.477 ,  3.2489, -1.0212],
       [-0.5771,  0.1241,  0.3026,  0.5238]])

In [80]: arr.take(inds, axis=1)
Out[80]:
array([[ 3.2489, -0.5397,  3.2489,  0.477 ],
       [ 0.3026, -0.5771,  0.3026,  0.1241]])
```

put does not accept an axis argument but rather indexes into the flattened (one-dimensional, C order) version of the array. Thus, when you need to set elements using an index array on other axes, it is often easiest to use fancy indexing.

A.3 Broadcasting

Broadcasting describes how arithmetic works between arrays of different shapes. It can be a powerful feature, but one that can cause confusion, even for experienced users. The simplest example of broadcasting occurs when combining a scalar value with an array:

```
In [81]: arr = np.arange(5)

In [82]: arr
Out[82]: array([0, 1, 2, 3, 4])

In [83]: arr * 4
Out[83]: array([ 0,  4,  8, 12, 16])
```

Here we say that the scalar value 4 has been *broadcast* to all of the other elements in the multiplication operation.

For example, we can demean each column of an array by subtracting the column means. In this case, it is very simple:

```
In [84]: arr = np.random.randn(4, 3)

In [85]: arr.mean(0)
Out[85]: array([-0.3928, -0.3824, -0.8768])

In [86]: demeaned = arr - arr.mean(0)

In [87]: demeaned
Out[87]:
array([[ 0.3937,  1.7263,  0.1633],
       [-0.4384, -1.9878, -0.9839],
       [-0.468 ,  0.9426, -0.3891],
       [ 0.5126, -0.6811,  1.2097]])

In [88]: demeaned.mean(0)
Out[88]: array([-0.,  0., -0.])
```

See Figure A-4 for an illustration of this operation. Demeaning the rows as a broadcast operation requires a bit more care. Fortunately, broadcasting potentially lower dimensional values across any dimension of an array (like subtracting the row means from each column of a two-dimensional array) is possible as long as you follow the rules.

This brings us to:

The Broadcasting Rule

Two arrays are compatible for broadcasting if for each *trailing dimension* (i.e., starting from the end) the axis lengths match or if either of the lengths is 1. Broadcasting is then performed over the missing or length 1 dimensions.

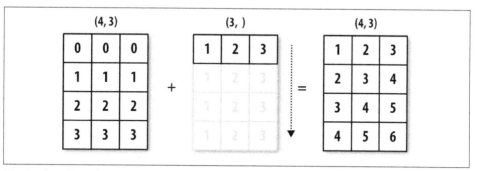

Figure A-4. Broadcasting over axis 0 with a 1D array

Even as an experienced NumPy user, I often find myself having to pause and draw a diagram as I think about the broadcasting rule. Consider the last example and suppose we wished instead to subtract the mean value from each row. Since arr.mean(0) has length 3, it is compatible for broadcasting across axis 0 because the trailing dimension in arr is 3 and therefore matches. According to the rules, to subtract over axis 1 (i.e., subtract the row mean from each row), the smaller array must have shape (4, 1):

```
In [89]: arr
Out[89]:
array([[ 0.0009,  1.3438, -0.7135],
       [-0.8312, -2.3702, -1.8608],
       [-0.8608,  0.5601, -1.2659],
       [ 0.1198, -1.0635,  0.3329]])

In [90]: row_means = arr.mean(1)

In [91]: row_means.shape
Out[91]: (4,)

In [92]: row_means.reshape((4, 1))
Out[92]:
array([[ 0.2104],
       [-1.6874],
       [-0.5222],
       [-0.2036]])
```

```
In [93]: demeaned = arr - row_means.reshape((4, 1))

In [94]: demeaned.mean(1)
Out[94]: array([ 0., -0.,  0.,  0.])
```

See Figure A-5 for an illustration of this operation.

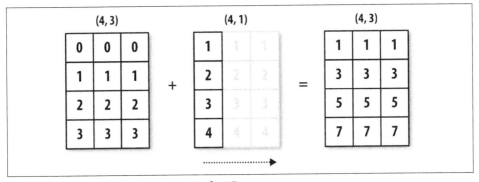

Figure A-5. Broadcasting over axis 1 of a 2D array

See Figure A-6 for another illustration, this time adding a two-dimensional array to a three-dimensional one across axis 0.

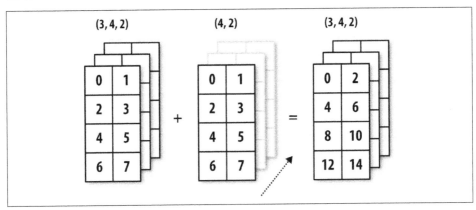

Figure A-6. Broadcasting over axis 0 of a 3D array

Broadcasting Over Other Axes

Broadcasting with higher dimensional arrays can seem even more mind-bending, but it is really a matter of following the rules. If you don't, you'll get an error like this:

```
In [95]: arr - arr.mean(1)
-----------------------------------------------------------------------
ValueError                                Traceback (most recent call last)
<ipython-input-95-7b87b85a20b2> in <module>()
----> 1 arr - arr.mean(1)
ValueError: operands could not be broadcast together with shapes (4,3) (4,)
```

It's quite common to want to perform an arithmetic operation with a lower dimensional array across axes other than axis 0. According to the broadcasting rule, the "broadcast dimensions" must be 1 in the smaller array. In the example of row demeaning shown here, this meant reshaping the row means to be shape (4, 1) instead of (4,):

```
In [96]: arr - arr.mean(1).reshape((4, 1))
Out[96]:
array([[-0.2095,  1.1334, -0.9239],
       [ 0.8562, -0.6828, -0.1734],
       [-0.3386,  1.0823, -0.7438],
       [ 0.3234, -0.8599,  0.5365]])
```

In the three-dimensional case, broadcasting over any of the three dimensions is only a matter of reshaping the data to be shape-compatible. Figure A-7 nicely visualizes the shapes required to broadcast over each axis of a three-dimensional array.

A common problem, therefore, is needing to add a new axis with length 1 specifically for broadcasting purposes. Using reshape is one option, but inserting an axis requires constructing a tuple indicating the new shape. This can often be a tedious exercise. Thus, NumPy arrays offer a special syntax for inserting new axes by indexing. We use the special np.newaxis attribute along with "full" slices to insert the new axis:

```
In [97]: arr = np.zeros((4, 4))

In [98]: arr_3d = arr[:, np.newaxis, :]

In [99]: arr_3d.shape
Out[99]: (4, 1, 4)

In [100]: arr_1d = np.random.normal(size=3)

In [101]: arr_1d[:, np.newaxis]
Out[101]:
array([[-2.3594],
       [-0.1995],
       [-1.542 ]])

In [102]: arr_1d[np.newaxis, :]
Out[102]: array([[-2.3594, -0.1995, -1.542 ]])
```

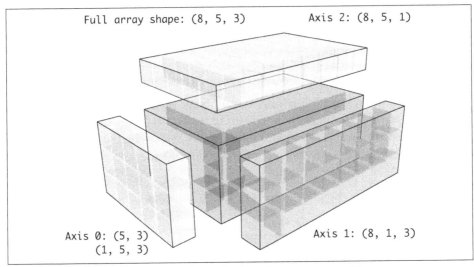

Figure A-7. Compatible 2D array shapes for broadcasting over a 3D array

Thus, if we had a three-dimensional array and wanted to demean axis 2, say, we would need to write:

```
In [103]: arr = np.random.randn(3, 4, 5)

In [104]: depth_means = arr.mean(2)

In [105]: depth_means
Out[105]:
array([[-0.4735,  0.3971, -0.0228,  0.2001],
       [-0.3521, -0.281 , -0.071 , -0.1586],
       [ 0.6245,  0.6047,  0.4396, -0.2846]])

In [106]: depth_means.shape
Out[106]: (3, 4)

In [107]: demeaned = arr - depth_means[:, :, np.newaxis]

In [108]: demeaned.mean(2)
Out[108]:
array([[ 0.,  0., -0., -0.],
       [ 0.,  0., -0.,  0.],
       [ 0.,  0., -0., -0.]])
```

You might be wondering if there's a way to generalize demeaning over an axis without sacrificing performance. There is, but it requires some indexing gymnastics:

```
def demean_axis(arr, axis=0):
    means = arr.mean(axis)

    # This generalizes things like [:, :, np.newaxis] to N dimensions
    indexer = [slice(None)] * arr.ndim
    indexer[axis] = np.newaxis
    return arr - means[indexer]
```

Setting Array Values by Broadcasting

The same broadcasting rule governing arithmetic operations also applies to setting values via array indexing. In a simple case, we can do things like:

```
In [109]: arr = np.zeros((4, 3))

In [110]: arr[:] = 5

In [111]: arr
Out[111]:
array([[5., 5., 5.],
       [5., 5., 5.],
       [5., 5., 5.],
       [5., 5., 5.]])
```

However, if we had a one-dimensional array of values we wanted to set into the columns of the array, we can do that as long as the shape is compatible:

```
In [112]: col = np.array([1.28, -0.42, 0.44, 1.6])

In [113]: arr[:] = col[:, np.newaxis]

In [114]: arr
Out[114]:
array([[ 1.28,  1.28,  1.28],
       [-0.42, -0.42, -0.42],
       [ 0.44,  0.44,  0.44],
       [ 1.6 ,  1.6 ,  1.6 ]])

In [115]: arr[:2] = [[-1.37], [0.509]]

In [116]: arr
Out[116]:
array([[-1.37 , -1.37 , -1.37 ],
       [ 0.509,  0.509,  0.509],
       [ 0.44 ,  0.44 ,  0.44 ],
       [ 1.6  ,  1.6  ,  1.6  ]])
```

A.4 Advanced ufunc Usage

While many NumPy users will only make use of the fast element-wise operations provided by the universal functions, there are a number of additional features that occasionally can help you write more concise code without loops.

ufunc Instance Methods

Each of NumPy's binary ufuncs has special methods for performing certain kinds of special vectorized operations. These are summarized in Table A-2, but I'll give a few concrete examples to illustrate how they work.

reduce takes a single array and aggregates its values, optionally along an axis, by performing a sequence of binary operations. For example, an alternative way to sum elements in an array is to use np.add.reduce:

```
In [117]: arr = np.arange(10)

In [118]: np.add.reduce(arr)
Out[118]: 45

In [119]: arr.sum()
Out[119]: 45
```

The starting value (0 for add) depends on the ufunc. If an axis is passed, the reduction is performed along that axis. This allows you to answer certain kinds of questions in a concise way. As a less trivial example, we can use np.logical_and to check whether the values in each row of an array are sorted:

```
In [120]: np.random.seed(12346)  # for reproducibility

In [121]: arr = np.random.randn(5, 5)

In [122]: arr[::2].sort(1) # sort a few rows

In [123]: arr[:, :-1] < arr[:, 1:]
Out[123]:
array([[ True,  True,  True,  True],
       [False,  True, False, False],
       [ True,  True,  True,  True],
       [ True, False,  True,  True],
       [ True,  True,  True,  True]])

In [124]: np.logical_and.reduce(arr[:, :-1] < arr[:, 1:], axis=1)
Out[124]: array([ True, False,  True, False,  True])
```

Note that logical_and.reduce is equivalent to the all method.

accumulate is related to reduce like cumsum is related to sum. It produces an array of the same size with the intermediate "accumulated" values:

```
In [125]: arr = np.arange(15).reshape((3, 5))

In [126]: np.add.accumulate(arr, axis=1)
Out[126]:
array([[ 0,  1,  3,  6, 10],
       [ 5, 11, 18, 26, 35],
       [10, 21, 33, 46, 60]])
```

outer performs a pairwise cross-product between two arrays:

```
In [127]: arr = np.arange(3).repeat([1, 2, 2])

In [128]: arr
Out[128]: array([0, 1, 1, 2, 2])

In [129]: np.multiply.outer(arr, np.arange(5))
Out[129]:
array([[0, 0, 0, 0, 0],
       [0, 1, 2, 3, 4],
       [0, 1, 2, 3, 4],
       [0, 2, 4, 6, 8],
       [0, 2, 4, 6, 8]])
```

The output of outer will have a dimension that is the concatenation of the dimensions of the inputs:

```
In [130]: x, y = np.random.randn(3, 4), np.random.randn(5)

In [131]: result = np.subtract.outer(x, y)

In [132]: result.shape
Out[132]: (3, 4, 5)
```

The last method, reduceat, performs a "local reduce," in essence an array groupby operation in which slices of the array are aggregated together. It accepts a sequence of "bin edges" that indicate how to split and aggregate the values:

```
In [133]: arr = np.arange(10)

In [134]: np.add.reduceat(arr, [0, 5, 8])
Out[134]: array([10, 18, 17])
```

The results are the reductions (here, sums) performed over arr[0:5], arr[5:8], and arr[8:]. As with the other methods, you can pass an axis argument:

```
In [135]: arr = np.multiply.outer(np.arange(4), np.arange(5))

In [136]: arr
Out[136]:
array([[ 0,  0,  0,  0,  0],
       [ 0,  1,  2,  3,  4],
       [ 0,  2,  4,  6,  8],
       [ 0,  3,  6,  9, 12]])
```

```
In [137]: np.add.reduceat(arr, [0, 2, 4], axis=1)
Out[137]:
array([[ 0,  0,  0],
       [ 1,  5,  4],
       [ 2, 10,  8],
       [ 3, 15, 12]])
```

See Table A-2 for a partial listing of ufunc methods.

Table A-2. ufunc methods

Method	Description
reduce(x)	Aggregate values by successive applications of the operation
accumulate(x)	Aggregate values, preserving all partial aggregates
reduceat(x, bins)	"Local" reduce or "group by"; reduce contiguous slices of data to produce aggregated array
outer(x, y)	Apply operation to all pairs of elements in x and y; the resulting array has shape x.shape + y.shape

Writing New ufuncs in Python

There are a number of facilities for creating your own NumPy ufuncs. The most general is to use the NumPy C API, but that is beyond the scope of this book. In this section, we will look at pure Python ufuncs.

numpy.frompyfunc accepts a Python function along with a specification for the number of inputs and outputs. For example, a simple function that adds element-wise would be specified as:

```
In [138]: def add_elements(x, y):
     ....:     return x + y

In [139]: add_them = np.frompyfunc(add_elements, 2, 1)

In [140]: add_them(np.arange(8), np.arange(8))
Out[140]: array([0, 2, 4, 6, 8, 10, 12, 14], dtype=object)
```

Functions created using frompyfunc always return arrays of Python objects, which can be inconvenient. Fortunately, there is an alternative (but slightly less featureful) function, numpy.vectorize, that allows you to specify the output type:

```
In [141]: add_them = np.vectorize(add_elements, otypes=[np.float64])

In [142]: add_them(np.arange(8), np.arange(8))
Out[142]: array([ 0.,  2.,  4.,  6.,  8., 10., 12., 14.])
```

These functions provide a way to create ufunc-like functions, but they are very slow because they require a Python function call to compute each element, which is a lot slower than NumPy's C-based ufunc loops:

```
In [143]: arr = np.random.randn(10000)

In [144]: %timeit add_them(arr, arr)
1.73 ms +- 10.5 us per loop (mean +- std. dev. of 7 runs, 1000 loops each)

In [145]: %timeit np.add(arr, arr)
3.09 us +- 86.9 ns per loop (mean +- std. dev. of 7 runs, 100000 loops each)
```

Later in this chapter we'll show how to create fast ufuncs in Python using the Numba project (*http://numba.pydata.org/*).

A.5 Structured and Record Arrays

You may have noticed up until now that ndarray is a *homogeneous* data container; that is, it represents a block of memory in which each element takes up the same number of bytes, determined by the dtype. On the surface, this would appear to not allow you to represent heterogeneous or tabular-like data. A *structured* array is an ndarray in which each element can be thought of as representing a *struct* in C (hence the "structured" name) or a row in a SQL table with multiple named fields:

```
In [146]: dtype = [('x', np.float64), ('y', np.int32)]

In [147]: sarr = np.array([(1.5, 6), (np.pi, -2)], dtype=dtype)

In [148]: sarr
Out[148]: array([(1.5    , 6), (3.1416, -2)], dtype=[('x', '<f8'), ('y', '<i4')])
```

There are several ways to specify a structured dtype (see the online NumPy documentation). One typical way is as a list of tuples with (field_name, field_data_type). Now, the elements of the array are tuple-like objects whose elements can be accessed like a dictionary:

```
In [149]: sarr[0]
Out[149]: (1.5, 6)

In [150]: sarr[0]['y']
Out[150]: 6
```

The field names are stored in the dtype.names attribute. When you access a field on the structured array, a strided view on the data is returned, thus copying nothing:

```
In [151]: sarr['x']
Out[151]: array([1.5    , 3.1416])
```

Nested dtypes and Multidimensional Fields

When specifying a structured dtype, you can additionally pass a shape (as an int or tuple):

```
In [152]: dtype = [('x', np.int64, 3), ('y', np.int32)]

In [153]: arr = np.zeros(4, dtype=dtype)

In [154]: arr
Out[154]:
array([([0, 0, 0], 0), ([0, 0, 0], 0), ([0, 0, 0], 0), ([0, 0, 0], 0)],
      dtype=[('x', '<i8', (3,)), ('y', '<i4')])
```

In this case, the x field now refers to an array of length 3 for each record:

```
In [155]: arr[0]['x']
Out[155]: array([0, 0, 0])
```

Conveniently, accessing `arr['x']` then returns a two-dimensional array instead of a one-dimensional array as in prior examples:

```
In [156]: arr['x']
Out[156]:
array([[0, 0, 0],
       [0, 0, 0],
       [0, 0, 0],
       [0, 0, 0]])
```

This enables you to express more complicated, nested structures as a single block of memory in an array. You can also nest dtypes to make more complex structures. Here is an example:

```
In [157]: dtype = [('x', [('a', 'f8'), ('b', 'f4')]), ('y', np.int32)]

In [158]: data = np.array([((1, 2), 5), ((3, 4), 6)], dtype=dtype)

In [159]: data['x']
Out[159]: array([(1., 2.), (3., 4.)], dtype=[('a', '<f8'), ('b', '<f4')])

In [160]: data['y']
Out[160]: array([5, 6], dtype=int32)

In [161]: data['x']['a']
Out[161]: array([1., 3.])
```

pandas DataFrame does not support this feature directly, though it is similar to hierarchical indexing.

Why Use Structured Arrays?

Compared with, say, a pandas DataFrame, NumPy structured arrays are a comparatively low-level tool. They provide a means to interpreting a block of memory as a tabular structure with arbitrarily complex nested columns. Since each element in the array is represented in memory as a fixed number of bytes, structured arrays provide a very fast and efficient way of writing data to and from disk (including memory maps), transporting it over the network, and other such uses.

As another common use for structured arrays, writing data files as fixed-length record byte streams is a common way to serialize data in C and C++ code, which is commonly found in legacy systems in industry. As long as the format of the file is known (the size of each record and the order, byte size, and data type of each element), the data can be read into memory with `np.fromfile`. Specialized uses like this are beyond the scope of this book, but it's worth knowing that such things are possible.

A.6 More About Sorting

Like Python's built-in list, the ndarray `sort` instance method is an *in-place* sort, meaning that the array contents are rearranged without producing a new array:

```
In [162]: arr = np.random.randn(6)

In [163]: arr.sort()

In [164]: arr
Out[164]: array([-1.082 ,  0.3759,  0.8014,  1.1397,  1.2888,  1.8413])
```

When sorting arrays in-place, remember that if the array is a view on a different ndarray, the original array will be modified:

```
In [165]: arr = np.random.randn(3, 5)

In [166]: arr
Out[166]:
array([[-0.3318, -1.4711,  0.8705, -0.0847, -1.1329],
       [-1.0111, -0.3436,  2.1714,  0.1234, -0.0189],
       [ 0.1773,  0.7424,  0.8548,  1.038 , -0.329 ]])

In [167]: arr[:, 0].sort()  # Sort first column values in-place

In [168]: arr
Out[168]:
array([[-1.0111, -1.4711,  0.8705, -0.0847, -1.1329],
       [-0.3318, -0.3436,  2.1714,  0.1234, -0.0189],
       [ 0.1773,  0.7424,  0.8548,  1.038 , -0.329 ]])
```

On the other hand, `numpy.sort` creates a new, sorted copy of an array. Otherwise, it accepts the same arguments (such as `kind`) as `ndarray.sort`:

```
In [169]: arr = np.random.randn(5)

In [170]: arr
Out[170]: array([-1.1181, -0.2415, -2.0051,  0.7379, -1.0614])

In [171]: np.sort(arr)
Out[171]: array([-2.0051, -1.1181, -1.0614, -0.2415,  0.7379])
```

```
In [172]: arr
Out[172]: array([-1.1181, -0.2415, -2.0051,  0.7379, -1.0614])
```

All of these sort methods take an axis argument for sorting the sections of data along the passed axis independently:

```
In [173]: arr = np.random.randn(3, 5)

In [174]: arr
Out[174]:
array([[ 0.5955, -0.2682,  1.3389, -0.1872,  0.9111],
       [-0.3215,  1.0054, -0.5168,  1.1925, -0.1989],
       [ 0.3969, -1.7638,  0.6071, -0.2222, -0.2171]])

In [175]: arr.sort(axis=1)

In [176]: arr
Out[176]:
array([[-0.2682, -0.1872,  0.5955,  0.9111,  1.3389],
       [-0.5168, -0.3215, -0.1989,  1.0054,  1.1925],
       [-1.7638, -0.2222, -0.2171,  0.3969,  0.6071]])
```

You may notice that none of the sort methods have an option to sort in descending order. This is a problem in practice because array slicing produces views, thus not producing a copy or requiring any computational work. Many Python users are familiar with the "trick" that for a list values, values[::-1] returns a list in reverse order. The same is true for ndarrays:

```
In [177]: arr[:, ::-1]
Out[177]:
array([[ 1.3389,  0.9111,  0.5955, -0.1872, -0.2682],
       [ 1.1925,  1.0054, -0.1989, -0.3215, -0.5168],
       [ 0.6071,  0.3969, -0.2171, -0.2222, -1.7638]])
```

Indirect Sorts: argsort and lexsort

In data analysis you may need to reorder datasets by one or more keys. For example, a table of data about some students might need to be sorted by last name, then by first name. This is an example of an *indirect* sort, and if you've read the pandas-related chapters you have already seen many higher-level examples. Given a key or keys (an array of values or multiple arrays of values), you wish to obtain an array of integer *indices* (I refer to them colloquially as *indexers*) that tells you how to reorder the data to be in sorted order. Two methods for this are argsort and numpy.lexsort. As an example:

```
In [178]: values = np.array([5, 0, 1, 3, 2])

In [179]: indexer = values.argsort()

In [180]: indexer
Out[180]: array([1, 2, 4, 3, 0])
```

```
In [181]: values[indexer]
Out[181]: array([0, 1, 2, 3, 5])
```

As a more complicated example, this code reorders a two-dimensional array by its
first row:

```
In [182]: arr = np.random.randn(3, 5)
```

```
In [183]: arr[0] = values
```

```
In [184]: arr
Out[184]:
array([[ 5.    ,  0.    ,  1.    ,  3.    ,  2.    ],
       [-0.3636, -0.1378,  2.1777, -0.4728,  0.8356],
       [-0.2089,  0.2316,  0.728 , -1.3918,  1.9956]])
```

```
In [185]: arr[:, arr[0].argsort()]
Out[185]:
array([[ 0.    ,  1.    ,  2.    ,  3.    ,  5.    ],
       [-0.1378,  2.1777,  0.8356, -0.4728, -0.3636],
       [ 0.2316,  0.728 ,  1.9956, -1.3918, -0.2089]])
```

lexsort is similar to argsort, but it performs an indirect *lexicographical* sort on multiple key arrays. Suppose we wanted to sort some data identified by first and last
names:

```
In [186]: first_name = np.array(['Bob', 'Jane', 'Steve', 'Bill', 'Barbara'])
```

```
In [187]: last_name = np.array(['Jones', 'Arnold', 'Arnold', 'Jones', 'Walters'])
```

```
In [188]: sorter = np.lexsort((first_name, last_name))
```

```
In [189]: sorter
Out[189]: array([1, 2, 3, 0, 4])
```

```
In [190]: list(zip(last_name[sorter], first_name[sorter]))
Out[190]:
[('Arnold', 'Jane'),
 ('Arnold', 'Steve'),
 ('Jones', 'Bill'),
 ('Jones', 'Bob'),
 ('Walters', 'Barbara')]
```

lexsort can be a bit confusing the first time you use it because the order in which the
keys are used to order the data starts with the *last* array passed. Here, last_name was
used before first_name.

pandas methods like Series's and DataFrame's `sort_values` method are implemented with variants of these functions (which also must take into account missing values).

Alternative Sort Algorithms

A *stable* sorting algorithm preserves the relative position of equal elements. This can be especially important in indirect sorts where the relative ordering is meaningful:

```
In [191]: values = np.array(['2:first', '2:second', '1:first', '1:second',
   .....:                     '1:third'])

In [192]: key = np.array([2, 2, 1, 1, 1])

In [193]: indexer = key.argsort(kind='mergesort')

In [194]: indexer
Out[194]: array([2, 3, 4, 0, 1])

In [195]: values.take(indexer)
Out[195]:
array(['1:first', '1:second', '1:third', '2:first', '2:second'],
      dtype='<U8')
```

The only stable sort available is *mergesort*, which has guaranteed O(n log n) performance (for complexity buffs), but its performance is on average worse than the default quicksort method. See Table A-3 for a summary of available methods and their relative performance (and performance guarantees). This is not something that most users will ever have to think about, but it's useful to know that it's there.

Table A-3. Array sorting methods

Kind	Speed	Stable	Work space	Worst case
'quicksort'	1	No	0	O(n^2)
'mergesort'	2	Yes	n / 2	O(n log n)
'heapsort'	3	No	0	O(n log n)

Partially Sorting Arrays

One of the goals of sorting can be to determine the largest or smallest elements in an array. NumPy has optimized methods, `numpy.partition` and `np.argpartition`, for partitioning an array around the k-th smallest element:

```
In [196]: np.random.seed(12345)

In [197]: arr = np.random.randn(20)
```

```
In [198]: arr
Out[198]:
array([-0.2047,  0.4789, -0.5194, -0.5557,  1.9658,  1.3934,  0.0929,
        0.2817,  0.769 ,  1.2464,  1.0072, -1.2962,  0.275 ,  0.2289,
        1.3529,  0.8864, -2.0016, -0.3718,  1.669 , -0.4386])

In [199]: np.partition(arr, 3)
Out[199]:
array([-2.0016, -1.2962, -0.5557, -0.5194, -0.3718, -0.4386, -0.2047,
        0.2817,  0.769 ,  0.4789,  1.0072,  0.0929,  0.275 ,  0.2289,
        1.3529,  0.8864,  1.3934,  1.9658,  1.669 ,  1.2464])
```

After you call partition(arr, 3), the first three elements in the result are the smallest three values in no particular order. numpy.argpartition, similar to numpy.argsort, returns the indices that rearrange the data into the equivalent order:

```
In [200]: indices = np.argpartition(arr, 3)

In [201]: indices
Out[201]:
array([16, 11,  3,  2, 17, 19,  0,  7,  8,  1, 10,  6, 12, 13, 14, 15,  5,
        4, 18,  9])

In [202]: arr.take(indices)
Out[202]:
array([-2.0016, -1.2962, -0.5557, -0.5194, -0.3718, -0.4386, -0.2047,
        0.2817,  0.769 ,  0.4789,  1.0072,  0.0929,  0.275 ,  0.2289,
        1.3529,  0.8864,  1.3934,  1.9658,  1.669 ,  1.2464])
```

numpy.searchsorted: Finding Elements in a Sorted Array

searchsorted is an array method that performs a binary search on a sorted array, returning the location in the array where the value would need to be inserted to maintain sortedness:

```
In [203]: arr = np.array([0, 1, 7, 12, 15])

In [204]: arr.searchsorted(9)
Out[204]: 3
```

You can also pass an array of values to get an array of indices back:

```
In [205]: arr.searchsorted([0, 8, 11, 16])
Out[205]: array([0, 3, 3, 5])
```

You might have noticed that searchsorted returned 0 for the 0 element. This is because the default behavior is to return the index at the left side of a group of equal values:

```
In [206]: arr = np.array([0, 0, 0, 1, 1, 1, 1])

In [207]: arr.searchsorted([0, 1])
```

```
Out[207]: array([0, 3])

In [208]: arr.searchsorted([0, 1], side='right')
Out[208]: array([3, 7])
```

As another application of searchsorted, suppose we had an array of values between 0 and 10,000, and a separate array of "bucket edges" that we wanted to use to bin the data:

```
In [209]: data = np.floor(np.random.uniform(0, 10000, size=50))

In [210]: bins = np.array([0, 100, 1000, 5000, 10000])

In [211]: data
Out[211]:
array([9940., 6768., 7908., 1709.,  268., 8003., 9037.,  246., 4917.,
       5262., 5963.,  519., 8950., 7282., 8183., 5002., 8101.,  959.,
       2189., 2587., 4681., 4593., 7095., 1780., 5314., 1677., 7688.,
       9281., 6094., 1501., 4896., 3773., 8486., 9110., 3838., 3154.,
       5683., 1878., 1258., 6875., 7996., 5735., 9732., 6340., 8884.,
       4954., 3516., 7142., 5039., 2256.])
```

To then get a labeling of which interval each data point belongs to (where 1 would mean the bucket [0, 100)), we can simply use searchsorted:

```
In [212]: labels = bins.searchsorted(data)

In [213]: labels
Out[213]:
array([4, 4, 4, 3, 2, 4, 4, 2, 3, 4, 4, 2, 4, 4, 4, 4, 4, 2, 3, 3, 3, 3,
       4, 3, 4, 3, 4, 4, 4, 3, 3, 3, 4, 4, 3, 3, 4, 3, 3, 4, 4, 4, 4, 4,
       4, 3, 3, 4, 4, 3])
```

This, combined with pandas's groupby, can be used to bin data:

```
In [214]: pd.Series(data).groupby(labels).mean()
Out[214]:
2     498.000000
3    3064.277778
4    7389.035714
dtype: float64
```

A.7 Writing Fast NumPy Functions with Numba

Numba (*http://numba.pydata.org/*) is an open source project that creates fast functions for NumPy-like data using CPUs, GPUs, or other hardware. It uses the LLVM Project (*http://llvm.org/*) to translate Python code into compiled machine code.

To introduce Numba, let's consider a pure Python function that computes the expression (x - y).mean() using a for loop:

```
import numpy as np

def mean_distance(x, y):
    nx = len(x)
    result = 0.0
    count = 0
    for i in range(nx):
        result += x[i] - y[i]
        count += 1
    return result / count
```

This function is very slow:

```
In [209]: x = np.random.randn(10000000)

In [210]: y = np.random.randn(10000000)

In [211]: %timeit mean_distance(x, y)
1 loop, best of 3: 2 s per loop

In [212]: %timeit (x - y).mean()
100 loops, best of 3: 14.7 ms per loop
```

The NumPy version is over 100 times faster. We can turn this function into a compiled Numba function using the numba.jit function:

```
In [213]: import numba as nb

In [214]: numba_mean_distance = nb.jit(mean_distance)
```

We could also have written this as a decorator:

```
@nb.jit
def mean_distance(x, y):
    nx = len(x)
    result = 0.0
    count = 0
    for i in range(nx):
        result += x[i] - y[i]
        count += 1
    return result / count
```

The resulting function is actually faster than the vectorized NumPy version:

```
In [215]: %timeit numba_mean_distance(x, y)
100 loops, best of 3: 10.3 ms per loop
```

Numba cannot compile arbitrary Python code, but it supports a significant subset of pure Python that is most useful for writing numerical algorithms.

Numba is a deep library, supporting different kinds of hardware, modes of compilation, and user extensions. It is also able to compile a substantial subset of the NumPy Python API without explicit for loops. Numba is able to recognize constructs that can be compiled to machine code, while substituting calls to the CPython API for functions that it does not know how to compile. Numba's `jit` function has an option, `nopython=True`, which restricts allowed code to Python code that can be compiled to LLVM without any Python C API calls. `jit(nopython=True)` has a shorter alias `numba.njit`.

In the previous example, we could have written:

```
from numba import float64, njit

@njit(float64(float64[:], float64[:]))
def mean_distance(x, y):
    return (x - y).mean()
```

I encourage you to learn more by reading the online documentation for Numba (*http://numba.pydata.org/*). The next section shows an example of creating custom NumPy ufunc objects.

Creating Custom numpy.ufunc Objects with Numba

The `numba.vectorize` function creates compiled NumPy ufuncs, which behave like built-in ufuncs. Let's consider a Python implementation of `numpy.add`:

```
from numba import vectorize

@vectorize
def nb_add(x, y):
    return x + y
```

Now we have:

```
In [13]: x = np.arange(10)

In [14]: nb_add(x, x)
Out[14]: array([  0.,   2.,   4.,   6.,   8.,  10.,  12.,  14.,  16.,  18.])

In [15]: nb_add.accumulate(x, 0)
Out[15]: array([  0.,   1.,   3.,   6.,  10.,  15.,  21.,  28.,  36.,  45.])
```

A.8 Advanced Array Input and Output

In Chapter 4, we became acquainted with `np.save` and `np.load` for storing arrays in binary format on disk. There are a number of additional options to consider for more sophisticated use. In particular, memory maps have the additional benefit of enabling you to work with datasets that do not fit into RAM.

Memory-Mapped Files

A *memory-mapped* file is a method for interacting with binary data on disk as though it is stored in an in-memory array. NumPy implements a `memmap` object that is ndarray-like, enabling small segments of a large file to be read and written without reading the whole array into memory. Additionally, a memmap has the same methods as an in-memory array and thus can be substituted into many algorithms where an ndarray would be expected.

To create a new memory map, use the function np.memmap and pass a file path, dtype, shape, and file mode:

```
In [216]: mmap = np.memmap('mymmap', dtype='float64', mode='w+',
   .....:                   shape=(10000, 10000))

In [217]: mmap
Out[217]:
memmap([[0., 0., 0., ..., 0., 0., 0.],
        [0., 0., 0., ..., 0., 0., 0.],
        [0., 0., 0., ..., 0., 0., 0.],
        ...,
        [0., 0., 0., ..., 0., 0., 0.],
        [0., 0., 0., ..., 0., 0., 0.],
        [0., 0., 0., ..., 0., 0., 0.]])
```

Slicing a memmap returns views on the data on disk:

```
In [218]: section = mmap[:5]
```

If you assign data to these, it will be buffered in memory (like a Python file object), but you can write it to disk by calling flush:

```
In [219]: section[:] = np.random.randn(5, 10000)

In [220]: mmap.flush()

In [221]: mmap
Out[221]:
memmap([[ 0.7584, -0.6605,  0.8626, ...,  0.6046, -0.6212,  2.0542],
        [-1.2113, -1.0375,  0.7093, ..., -1.4117, -0.1719, -0.8957],
        [-0.1419, -0.3375,  0.4329, ...,  1.2914, -0.752 , -0.44  ],
        ...,
        [ 0.    ,  0.    ,  0.    , ...,  0.    ,  0.    ,  0.    ],
        [ 0.    ,  0.    ,  0.    , ...,  0.    ,  0.    ,  0.    ],
        [ 0.    ,  0.    ,  0.    , ...,  0.    ,  0.    ,  0.    ]])

In [222]: del mmap
```

Whenever a memory map falls out of scope and is garbage-collected, any changes will be flushed to disk also. When *opening an existing memory map*, you still have to specify the dtype and shape, as the file is only a block of binary data with no metadata on disk:

```
In [223]: mmap = np.memmap('mymmap', dtype='float64', shape=(10000, 10000))

In [224]: mmap
```

```
Out[224]:
memmap([[ 0.7584, -0.6605,  0.8626, ...,  0.6046, -0.6212,  2.0542],
        [-1.2113, -1.0375,  0.7093, ..., -1.4117, -0.1719, -0.8957],
        [-0.1419, -0.3375,  0.4329, ...,  1.2914, -0.752 , -0.44  ],
        ...,
        [ 0.    ,  0.    ,  0.    , ...,  0.    ,  0.    ,  0.    ],
        [ 0.    ,  0.    ,  0.    , ...,  0.    ,  0.    ,  0.    ],
        [ 0.    ,  0.    ,  0.    , ...,  0.    ,  0.    ,  0.    ]])
```

Memory maps also work with structured or nested dtypes as described in a previous section.

HDF5 and Other Array Storage Options

PyTables and h5py are two Python projects providing NumPy-friendly interfaces for storing array data in the efficient and compressible HDF5 format (HDF stands for *hierarchical data format*). You can safely store hundreds of gigabytes or even terabytes of data in HDF5 format. To learn more about using HDF5 with Python, I recommend reading the pandas online documentation (*http://pandas.pydata.org*).

A.9 Performance Tips

Getting good performance out of code utilizing NumPy is often straightforward, as array operations typically replace otherwise comparatively extremely slow pure Python loops. The following list briefly summarizes some things to keep in mind:

- Convert Python loops and conditional logic to array operations and boolean array operations
- Use broadcasting whenever possible
- Use arrays views (slicing) to avoid copying data
- Utilize ufuncs and ufunc methods

If you can't get the performance you require after exhausting the capabilities provided by NumPy alone, consider writing code in C, Fortran, or Cython. I use Cython (*http://cython.org*) frequently in my own work as an easy way to get C-like performance with minimal development.

The Importance of Contiguous Memory

While the full extent of this topic is a bit outside the scope of this book, in some applications the memory layout of an array can significantly affect the speed of computations. This is based partly on performance differences having to do with the cache hierarchy of the CPU; operations accessing contiguous blocks of memory (e.g., summing the rows of a C order array) will generally be the fastest because the memory subsystem will buffer the appropriate blocks of memory into the ultrafast L1 or

L2 CPU cache. Also, certain code paths inside NumPy's C codebase have been optimized for the contiguous case in which generic strided memory access can be avoided.

To say that an array's memory layout is *contiguous* means that the elements are stored in memory in the order that they appear in the array with respect to Fortran (column major) or C (row major) ordering. By default, NumPy arrays are created as *C-contiguous* or just simply contiguous. A column major array, such as the transpose of a C-contiguous array, is thus said to be Fortran-contiguous. These properties can be explicitly checked via the `flags` attribute on the ndarray:

```
In [227]: arr_c = np.ones((1000, 1000), order='C')

In [228]: arr_f = np.ones((1000, 1000), order='F')

In [229]: arr_c.flags
Out[229]:
  C_CONTIGUOUS : True
  F_CONTIGUOUS : False
  OWNDATA : True
  WRITEABLE : True
  ALIGNED : True
  WRITEBACKIFCOPY : False
  UPDATEIFCOPY : False

In [230]: arr_f.flags
Out[230]:
  C_CONTIGUOUS : False
  F_CONTIGUOUS : True
  OWNDATA : True
  WRITEABLE : True
  ALIGNED : True
  WRITEBACKIFCOPY : False
  UPDATEIFCOPY : False

In [231]: arr_f.flags.f_contiguous
Out[231]: True
```

In this example, summing the rows of these arrays should, in theory, be faster for `arr_c` than `arr_f` since the rows are contiguous in memory. Here I check for sure using `%timeit` in IPython:

```
In [232]: %timeit arr_c.sum(1)
344 us +- 8.93 us per loop (mean +- std. dev. of 7 runs, 1000 loops each)

In [233]: %timeit arr_f.sum(1)
433 us +- 8.56 us per loop (mean +- std. dev. of 7 runs, 1000 loops each)
```

When you're looking to squeeze more performance out of NumPy, this is often a place to invest some effort. If you have an array that does not have the desired memory order, you can use copy and pass either `'C'` or `'F'`:

```
In [234]: arr_f.copy('C').flags
Out[234]:
  C_CONTIGUOUS : True
  F_CONTIGUOUS : False
  OWNDATA : True
  WRITEABLE : True
  ALIGNED : True
  WRITEBACKIFCOPY : False
  UPDATEIFCOPY : False
```

When constructing a view on an array, keep in mind that the result is not guaranteed to be contiguous:

```
In [235]: arr_c[:50].flags.contiguous
Out[235]: True

In [236]: arr_c[:, :50].flags
Out[236]:
  C_CONTIGUOUS : False
  F_CONTIGUOUS : False
  OWNDATA : False
  WRITEABLE : True
  ALIGNED : True
  WRITEBACKIFCOPY : False
  UPDATEIFCOPY : False
```

More on the IPython System

In Chapter 2 we looked at the basics of using the IPython shell and Jupyter notebook. In this chapter, we explore some deeper functionality in the IPython system that can either be used from the console or within Jupyter.

B.1 Using the Command History

IPython maintains a small on-disk database containing the text of each command that you execute. This serves various purposes:

- Searching, completing, and executing previously executed commands with minimal typing
- Persisting the command history between sessions
- Logging the input/output history to a file

These features are more useful in the shell than in the notebook, since the notebook by design keeps a log of the input and output in each code cell.

Searching and Reusing the Command History

The IPython shell lets you search and execute previous code or other commands. This is useful, as you may often find yourself repeating the same commands, such as a %run command or some other code snippet. Suppose you had run:

```
In[7]: %run first/second/third/data_script.py
```

and then explored the results of the script (assuming it ran successfully) only to find that you made an incorrect calculation. After figuring out the problem and modifying *data_script.py*, you can start typing a few letters of the %run command and then press either the Ctrl-P key combination or the up arrow key. This will search the command history for the first prior command matching the letters you typed. Pressing either Ctrl-P or the up arrow key multiple times will continue to search through the history. If you pass over the command you wish to execute, fear not. You can move *forward* through the command history by pressing either Ctrl-N or the down arrow key. After doing this a few times, you may start pressing these keys without thinking!

Using Ctrl-R gives you the same partial incremental searching capability provided by the readline used in Unix-style shells, such as the bash shell. On Windows, readline functionality is emulated by IPython. To use this, press Ctrl-R and then type a few characters contained in the input line you want to search for:

```
In [1]: a_command = foo(x, y, z)

(reverse-i-search)`com': a_command = foo(x, y, z)
```

Pressing Ctrl-R will cycle through the history for each line matching the characters you've typed.

Input and Output Variables

Forgetting to assign the result of a function call to a variable can be very annoying. An IPython session stores references to *both* the input commands and output Python objects in special variables. The previous two outputs are stored in the _ (one underscore) and __ (two underscores) variables, respectively:

```
In [24]: 2 ** 27
Out[24]: 134217728

In [25]: _
Out[25]: 134217728
```

Input variables are stored in variables named like _iX, where X is the input line number. For each input variable there is a corresponding output variable _X. So after input line 27, say, there will be two new variables _27 (for the output) and _i27 for the input:

```
In [26]: foo = 'bar'

In [27]: foo
Out[27]: 'bar'

In [28]: _i27
Out[28]: u'foo'

In [29]: _27
Out[29]: 'bar'
```

Since the input variables are strings they can be executed again with the Python `eval` keyword:

```
In [30]: eval(_i27)
Out[30]: 'bar'
```

Here `_i27` refers to the code input in `In [27]`.

Several magic functions allow you to work with the input and output history. `%hist` is capable of printing all or part of the input history, with or without line numbers. `%reset` is for clearing the interactive namespace and optionally the input and output caches. The `%xdel` magic function is intended for removing all references to a *particular* object from the IPython machinery. See the documentation for both of these magics for more details.

 When working with very large datasets, keep in mind that IPython's input and output history causes any object referenced there to not be garbage-collected (freeing up the memory), even if you delete the variables from the interactive namespace using the `del` keyword. In such cases, careful usage of `%xdel` and `%reset` can help you avoid running into memory problems.

B.2 Interacting with the Operating System

Another feature of IPython is that it allows you to seamlessly access the filesystem and operating system shell. This means, among other things, that you can perform most standard command-line actions as you would in the Windows or Unix (Linux, macOS) shell without having to exit IPython. This includes shell commands, changing directories, and storing the results of a command in a Python object (list or string). There are also simple command aliasing and directory bookmarking features.

See Table B-1 for a summary of magic functions and syntax for calling shell commands. I'll briefly visit these features in the next few sections.

Table B-1. IPython system-related commands

Command	Description
`!cmd`	Execute cmd in the system shell
`output = !cmd args`	Run cmd and store the stdout in `output`
`%alias alias_name cmd`	Define an alias for a system (shell) command
`%bookmark`	Utilize IPython's directory bookmarking system
`%cd directory`	Change system working directory to passed directory
`%pwd`	Return the current system working directory
`%pushd directory`	Place current directory on stack and change to target directory
`%popd`	Change to directory popped off the top of the stack

Command	Description
`%dirs`	Return a list containing the current directory stack
`%dhist`	Print the history of visited directories
`%env`	Return the system environment variables as a dict
`%matplotlib`	Configure matplotlib integration options

Shell Commands and Aliases

Starting a line in IPython with an exclamation point !, or bang, tells IPython to execute everything after the bang in the system shell. This means that you can delete files (using rm or del, depending on your OS), change directories, or execute any other process.

You can store the console output of a shell command in a variable by assigning the expression escaped with ! to a variable. For example, on my Linux-based machine connected to the internet via ethernet, I can get my IP address as a Python variable:

```
In [1]: ip_info = !ifconfig wlan0 | grep "inet "

In [2]: ip_info[0].strip()
Out[2]: 'inet addr:10.0.0.11  Bcast:10.0.0.255  Mask:255.255.255.0'
```

The returned Python object ip_info is actually a custom list type containing various versions of the console output.

IPython can also substitute in Python values defined in the current environment when using !. To do this, preface the variable name by the dollar sign $:

```
In [3]: foo = 'test*'

In [4]: !ls $foo
test4.py  test.py  test.xml
```

The %alias magic function can define custom shortcuts for shell commands. As a simple example:

```
In [1]: %alias ll ls -l

In [2]: ll /usr
total 332
drwxr-xr-x   2 root root  69632 2012-01-29 20:36 bin/
drwxr-xr-x   2 root root   4096 2010-08-23 12:05 games/
drwxr-xr-x 123 root root  20480 2011-12-26 18:08 include/
drwxr-xr-x 265 root root 126976 2012-01-29 20:36 lib/
drwxr-xr-x  44 root root  69632 2011-12-26 18:08 lib32/
lrwxrwxrwx   1 root root      3 2010-08-23 16:02 lib64 -> lib/
drwxr-xr-x  15 root root   4096 2011-10-13 19:03 local/
drwxr-xr-x   2 root root  12288 2012-01-12 09:32 sbin/
drwxr-xr-x 387 root root  12288 2011-11-04 22:53 share/
drwxrwsr-x  24 root src    4096 2011-07-17 18:38 src/
```

You can execute multiple commands just as on the command line by separating them with semicolons:

```
In [558]: %alias test_alias (cd examples; ls; cd ..)

In [559]: test_alias
macrodata.csv  spx.csv  tips.csv
```

You'll notice that IPython "forgets" any aliases you define interactively as soon as the session is closed. To create permanent aliases, you will need to use the configuration system.

Directory Bookmark System

IPython has a simple directory bookmarking system to enable you to save aliases for common directories so that you can jump around very easily. For example, suppose you wanted to create a bookmark that points to the supplementary materials for this book:

```
In [6]: %bookmark py4da /home/wesm/code/pydata-book
```

Once you've done this, when we use the %cd magic, we can use any bookmarks we've defined:

```
In [7]: cd py4da
(bookmark:py4da) -> /home/wesm/code/pydata-book
/home/wesm/code/pydata-book
```

If a bookmark name conflicts with a directory name in your current working directory, you can use the -b flag to override and use the bookmark location. Using the -l option with %bookmark lists all of your bookmarks:

```
In [8]: %bookmark -l
Current bookmarks:
py4da -> /home/wesm/code/pydata-book-source
```

Bookmarks, unlike aliases, are automatically persisted between IPython sessions.

B.3 Software Development Tools

In addition to being a comfortable environment for interactive computing and data exploration, IPython can also be a useful companion for general Python software development. In data analysis applications, it's important first to have *correct* code. Fortunately, IPython has closely integrated and enhanced the built-in Python pdb debugger. Secondly you want your code to be *fast*. For this IPython has easy-to-use code timing and profiling tools. I will give an overview of these tools in detail here.

Interactive Debugger

IPython's debugger enhances pdb with tab completion, syntax highlighting, and context for each line in exception tracebacks. One of the best times to debug code is right after an error has occurred. The %debug command, when entered immediately after an exception, invokes the "post-mortem" debugger and drops you into the stack frame where the exception was raised:

```
In [2]: run examples/ipython_bug.py
---------------------------------------------------------------------
AssertionError                           Traceback (most recent call last)
/home/wesm/code/pydata-book/examples/ipython_bug.py in <module>()
     13     throws_an_exception()
     14
---> 15 calling_things()

/home/wesm/code/pydata-book/examples/ipython_bug.py in calling_things()
     11 def calling_things():
     12     works_fine()
---> 13     throws_an_exception()
     14
     15 calling_things()

/home/wesm/code/pydata-book/examples/ipython_bug.py in throws_an_exception()
      7     a = 5
      8     b = 6
----> 9     assert(a + b == 10)
     10
     11 def calling_things():

AssertionError:

In [3]: %debug
> /home/wesm/code/pydata-book/examples/ipython_bug.py(9)throws_an_exception()
      8     b = 6
----> 9     assert(a + b == 10)
     10

ipdb>
```

Once inside the debugger, you can execute arbitrary Python code and explore all of the objects and data (which have been "kept alive" by the interpreter) inside each stack frame. By default you start in the lowest level, where the error occurred. By pressing u (up) and d (down), you can switch between the levels of the stack trace:

```
ipdb> u
> /home/wesm/code/pydata-book/examples/ipython_bug.py(13)calling_things()
     12     works_fine()
---> 13     throws_an_exception()
     14
```

Executing the %pdb command makes it so that IPython automatically invokes the debugger after any exception, a mode that many users will find especially useful.

It's also easy to use the debugger to help develop code, especially when you wish to set breakpoints or step through the execution of a function or script to examine the state at each stage. There are several ways to accomplish this. The first is by using %run with the -d flag, which invokes the debugger before executing any code in the passed script. You must immediately press s (step) to enter the script:

```
In [5]: run -d examples/ipython_bug.py
Breakpoint 1 at /home/wesm/code/pydata-book/examples/ipython_bug.py:1
NOTE: Enter 'c' at the ipdb>  prompt to start your script.
> <string>(1)<module>()

ipdb> s
--Call--
> /home/wesm/code/pydata-book/examples/ipython_bug.py(1)<module>()
1---> 1 def works_fine():
      2     a = 5
      3     b = 6
```

After this point, it's up to you how you want to work your way through the file. For example, in the preceding exception, we could set a breakpoint right before calling the works_fine method and run the script until we reach the breakpoint by pressing c (continue):

```
ipdb> b 12
ipdb> c
> /home/wesm/code/pydata-book/examples/ipython_bug.py(12)calling_things()
     11 def calling_things():
2--> 12     works_fine()
     13     throws_an_exception()
```

At this point, you can step into works_fine() or execute works_fine() by pressing n (next) to advance to the next line:

```
ipdb> n
> /home/wesm/code/pydata-book/examples/ipython_bug.py(13)calling_things()
2    12     works_fine()
---> 13     throws_an_exception()
     14
```

Then, we could step into throws_an_exception and advance to the line where the error occurs and look at the variables in the scope. Note that debugger commands take precedence over variable names; in such cases, preface the variables with ! to examine their contents:

```
ipdb> s
--Call--
> /home/wesm/code/pydata-book/examples/ipython_bug.py(6)throws_an_exception()
      5
```

```
----> 6 def throws_an_exception():
      7     a = 5

ipdb> n
> /home/wesm/code/pydata-book/examples/ipython_bug.py(7)throws_an_exception()
      6 def throws_an_exception():
----> 7     a = 5
      8     b = 6

ipdb> n
> /home/wesm/code/pydata-book/examples/ipython_bug.py(8)throws_an_exception()
      7     a = 5
----> 8     b = 6
      9     assert(a + b == 10)

ipdb> n
> /home/wesm/code/pydata-book/examples/ipython_bug.py(9)throws_an_exception()
      8     b = 6
----> 9     assert(a + b == 10)
     10

ipdb> !a
5
ipdb> !b
6
```

Developing proficiency with the interactive debugger is largely a matter of practice and experience. See Table B-2 for a full catalog of the debugger commands. If you are accustomed to using an IDE, you might find the terminal-driven debugger to be a bit unforgiving at first, but that will improve in time. Some of the Python IDEs have excellent GUI debuggers, so most users can find something that works for them.

Table B-2. (I)Python debugger commands

Command	Action
h(elp)	Display command list
help *command*	Show documentation for *command*
c(ontinue)	Resume program execution
q(uit)	Exit debugger without executing any more code
b(reak) *number*	Set breakpoint at *number* in current file
b *path/to/file.py:number*	Set breakpoint at line *number* in specified file
s(tep)	Step *into* function call
n(ext)	Execute current line and advance to next line at current level
u(p)/d(own)	Move up/down in function call stack
a(rgs)	Show arguments for current function
debug *statement*	Invoke statement *statement* in new (recursive) debugger
l(ist) *statement*	Show current position and context at current level of stack
w(here)	Print full stack trace with context at current position

Other ways to make use of the debugger

There are a couple of other useful ways to invoke the debugger. The first is by using a special `set_trace` function (named after `pdb.set_trace`), which is basically a "poor man's breakpoint." Here are two small recipes you might want to put somewhere for your general use (potentially adding them to your IPython profile as I do):

```
from IPython.core.debugger import Pdb

def set_trace():
    Pdb(color_scheme='Linux').set_trace(sys._getframe().f_back)

def debug(f, *args, **kwargs):
    pdb = Pdb(color_scheme='Linux')
    return pdb.runcall(f, *args, **kwargs)
```

The first function, `set_trace`, is very simple. You can use a `set_trace` in any part of your code that you want to temporarily stop in order to more closely examine it (e.g., right before an exception occurs):

```
In [7]: run examples/ipython_bug.py
> /home/wesm/code/pydata-book/examples/ipython_bug.py(16)calling_things()
     15         set_trace()
---> 16         throws_an_exception()
     17
```

Pressing c (continue) will cause the code to resume normally with no harm done.

The `debug` function we just looked at enables you to invoke the interactive debugger easily on an arbitrary function call. Suppose we had written a function like the following and we wished to step through its logic:

```
def f(x, y, z=1):
    tmp = x + y
    return tmp / z
```

Ordinarily using f would look like f(1, 2, z=3). To instead step into f, pass f as the first argument to debug followed by the positional and keyword arguments to be passed to f:

```
In [6]: debug(f, 1, 2, z=3)
> <ipython-input>(2)f()
      1 def f(x, y, z):
----> 2     tmp = x + y
      3     return tmp / z

ipdb>
```

I find that these two simple recipes save me a lot of time on a day-to-day basis.

Lastly, the debugger can be used in conjunction with %run. By running a script with %run -d, you will be dropped directly into the debugger, ready to set any breakpoints and start the script:

```
In [1]: %run -d examples/ipython_bug.py
Breakpoint 1 at /home/wesm/code/pydata-book/examples/ipython_bug.py:1
NOTE: Enter 'c' at the ipdb>  prompt to start your script.
> <string>(1)<module>()

ipdb>
```

Adding -b with a line number starts the debugger with a breakpoint set already:

```
In [2]: %run -d -b2 examples/ipython_bug.py
Breakpoint 1 at /home/wesm/code/pydata-book/examples/ipython_bug.py:2
NOTE: Enter 'c' at the ipdb>  prompt to start your script.
> <string>(1)<module>()

ipdb> c
> /home/wesm/code/pydata-book/examples/ipython_bug.py(2)works_fine()
      1 def works_fine():
1---> 2     a = 5
      3     b = 6

ipdb>
```

Timing Code: %time and %timeit

For larger-scale or longer-running data analysis applications, you may wish to measure the execution time of various components or of individual statements or function calls. You may want a report of which functions are taking up the most time in a complex process. Fortunately, IPython enables you to get this information very easily while you are developing and testing your code.

Timing code by hand using the built-in time module and its functions time.clock and time.time is often tedious and repetitive, as you must write the same uninteresting boilerplate code:

```
import time
start = time.time()
for i in range(iterations):
    # some code to run here
elapsed_per = (time.time() - start) / iterations
```

Since this is such a common operation, IPython has two magic functions, %time and %timeit, to automate this process for you.

%time runs a statement once, reporting the total execution time. Suppose we had a large list of strings and we wanted to compare different methods of selecting all strings starting with a particular prefix. Here is a simple list of 600,000 strings and two identical methods of selecting only the ones that start with 'foo':

```
# a very large list of strings
strings = ['foo', 'foobar', 'baz', 'qux',
           'python', 'Guido Van Rossum'] * 100000

method1 = [x for x in strings if x.startswith('foo')]

method2 = [x for x in strings if x[:3] == 'foo']
```

It looks like they should be about the same performance-wise, right? We can check for sure using %time:

```
In [561]: %time method1 = [x for x in strings if x.startswith('foo')]
CPU times: user 0.19 s, sys: 0.00 s, total: 0.19 s
Wall time: 0.19 s

In [562]: %time method2 = [x for x in strings if x[:3] == 'foo']
CPU times: user 0.09 s, sys: 0.00 s, total: 0.09 s
Wall time: 0.09 s
```

The Wall time (short for "wall-clock time") is the main number of interest. So, it looks like the first method takes more than twice as long, but it's not a very precise measurement. If you try %time-ing those statements multiple times yourself, you'll find that the results are somewhat variable. To get a more precise measurement, use the %timeit magic function. Given an arbitrary statement, it has a heuristic to run a statement multiple times to produce a more accurate average runtime:

```
In [563]: %timeit [x for x in strings if x.startswith('foo')]
10 loops, best of 3: 159 ms per loop

In [564]: %timeit [x for x in strings if x[:3] == 'foo']
10 loops, best of 3: 59.3 ms per loop
```

This seemingly innocuous example illustrates that it is worth understanding the performance characteristics of the Python standard library, NumPy, pandas, and other libraries used in this book. In larger-scale data analysis applications, those milliseconds will start to add up!

%timeit is especially useful for analyzing statements and functions with very short execution times, even at the level of microseconds (millionths of a second) or nanoseconds (billionths of a second). These may seem like insignificant amounts of time, but of course a 20 microsecond function invoked 1 million times takes 15 seconds longer than a 5 microsecond function. In the preceding example, we could very directly compare the two string operations to understand their performance characteristics:

```
In [565]: x = 'foobar'
```

```
In [566]: y = 'foo'

In [567]: %timeit x.startswith(y)
1000000 loops, best of 3: 267 ns per loop

In [568]: %timeit x[:3] == y
10000000 loops, best of 3: 147 ns per loop
```

Basic Profiling: %prun and %run -p

Profiling code is closely related to timing code, except it is concerned with determining *where* time is spent. The main Python profiling tool is the cProfile module, which is not specific to IPython at all. cProfile executes a program or any arbitrary block of code while keeping track of how much time is spent in each function.

A common way to use cProfile is on the command line, running an entire program and outputting the aggregated time per function. Suppose we had a simple script that does some linear algebra in a loop (computing the maximum absolute eigenvalues of a series of 100×100 matrices):

```
import numpy as np
from numpy.linalg import eigvals

def run_experiment(niter=100):
    K = 100
    results = []
    for _ in range(niter):
        mat = np.random.randn(K, K)
        max_eigenvalue = np.abs(eigvals(mat)).max()
        results.append(max_eigenvalue)
    return results
some_results = run_experiment()
print('Largest one we saw: {0}'.format(np.max(some_results)))
```

You can run this script through cProfile using the following in the command line:

```
python -m cProfile cprof_example.py
```

If you try that, you'll find that the output is sorted by function name. This makes it a bit hard to get an idea of where the most time is spent, so it's very common to specify a *sort order* using the -s flag:

```
$ python -m cProfile -s cumulative cprof_example.py
Largest one we saw: 11.923204422
        15116 function calls (14927 primitive calls) in 0.720 seconds

Ordered by: cumulative time

ncalls  tottime  percall  cumtime  percall filename:lineno(function)
     1    0.001    0.001    0.721    0.721 cprof_example.py:1(<module>)
   100    0.003    0.000    0.586    0.006 linalg.py:702(eigvals)
```

```
200    0.572    0.003    0.572    0.003 {numpy.linalg.lapack_lite.dgeev}
  1    0.002    0.002    0.075    0.075 __init__.py:106(<module>)
100    0.059    0.001    0.059    0.001 {method 'randn')
  1    0.000    0.000    0.044    0.044 add_newdocs.py:9(<module>)
  2    0.001    0.001    0.037    0.019 __init__.py:1(<module>)
  2    0.003    0.002    0.030    0.015 __init__.py:2(<module>)
  1    0.000    0.000    0.030    0.030 type_check.py:3(<module>)
  1    0.001    0.001    0.021    0.021 __init__.py:15(<module>)
  1    0.013    0.013    0.013    0.013 numeric.py:1(<module>)
  1    0.000    0.000    0.009    0.009 __init__.py:6(<module>)
  1    0.001    0.001    0.008    0.008 __init__.py:45(<module>)
262    0.005    0.000    0.007    0.000 function_base.py:3178(add_newdoc)
100    0.003    0.000    0.005    0.000 linalg.py:162(_assertFinite)
...
```

Only the first 15 rows of the output are shown. It's easiest to read by scanning down the cumtime column to see how much total time was spent *inside* each function. Note that if a function calls some other function, *the clock does not stop running*. cProfile records the start and end time of each function call and uses that to produce the timing.

In addition to the command-line usage, cProfile can also be used programmatically to profile arbitrary blocks of code without having to run a new process. IPython has a convenient interface to this capability using the %prun command and the -p option to %run. %prun takes the same "command-line options" as cProfile but will profile an arbitrary Python statement instead of a whole *.py* file:

```
In [4]: %prun -l 7 -s cumulative run_experiment()
        4203 function calls in 0.643 seconds

Ordered by: cumulative time
List reduced from 32 to 7 due to restriction <7>

ncalls  tottime  percall  cumtime  percall filename:lineno(function)
     1    0.000    0.000    0.643    0.643 <string>:1(<module>)
     1    0.001    0.001    0.643    0.643 cprof_example.py:4(run_experiment)
   100    0.003    0.000    0.583    0.006 linalg.py:702(eigvals)
   200    0.569    0.003    0.569    0.003 {numpy.linalg.lapack_lite.dgeev}
   100    0.058    0.001    0.058    0.001 {method 'randn'}
   100    0.003    0.000    0.005    0.000 linalg.py:162(_assertFinite)
   200    0.002    0.000    0.002    0.000 {method 'all' of 'numpy.ndarray'}
```

Similarly, calling %run -p -s cumulative cprof_example.py has the same effect as the command-line approach, except you never have to leave IPython.

In the Jupyter notebook, you can use the %%prun magic (two % signs) to profile an entire code block. This pops up a separate window with the profile output. This can be useful in getting possibly quick answers to questions like, "Why did that code block take so long to run?"

There are other tools available that help make profiles easier to understand when you are using IPython or Jupyter. One of these is SnakeViz (*https://github.com/jiffyclub/ snakeviz/*), which produces an interactive visualization of the profile results using d3.js.

Profiling a Function Line by Line

In some cases the information you obtain from %prun (or another cProfile-based profile method) may not tell the whole story about a function's execution time, or it may be so complex that the results, aggregated by function name, are hard to interpret. For this case, there is a small library called line_profiler (obtainable via PyPI or one of the package management tools). It contains an IPython extension enabling a new magic function %lprun that computes a line-by-line-profiling of one or more functions. You can enable this extension by modifying your IPython configuration (see the IPython documentation or the section on configuration later in this chapter) to include the following line:

```
# A list of dotted module names of IPython extensions to load.
c.TerminalIPythonApp.extensions = ['line_profiler']
```

You can also run the command:

```
%load_ext line_profiler
```

line_profiler can be used programmatically (see the full documentation), but it is perhaps most powerful when used interactively in IPython. Suppose you had a module prof_mod with the following code doing some NumPy array operations:

```
from numpy.random import randn

def add_and_sum(x, y):
    added = x + y
    summed = added.sum(axis=1)
    return summed

def call_function():
    x = randn(1000, 1000)
    y = randn(1000, 1000)
    return add_and_sum(x, y)
```

If we wanted to understand the performance of the add_and_sum function, %prun gives us the following:

```
In [569]: %run prof_mod

In [570]: x = randn(3000, 3000)

In [571]: y = randn(3000, 3000)

In [572]: %prun add_and_sum(x, y)
```

```
      4 function calls in 0.049 seconds
   Ordered by: internal time
   ncalls  tottime  percall  cumtime  percall filename:lineno(function)
        1    0.036    0.036    0.046    0.046 prof_mod.py:3(add_and_sum)
        1    0.009    0.009    0.009    0.009 {method 'sum' of 'numpy.ndarray'}
        1    0.003    0.003    0.049    0.049 <string>:1(<module>)
```

This is not especially enlightening. With the line_profiler IPython extension activated, a new command %lprun is available. The only difference in usage is that we must instruct %lprun which function or functions we wish to profile. The general syntax is:

```
%lprun -f func1 -f func2 statement_to_profile
```

In this case, we want to profile add_and_sum, so we run:

```
In [573]: %lprun -f add_and_sum add_and_sum(x, y)
Timer unit: 1e-06 s
File: prof_mod.py
Function: add_and_sum at line 3
Total time: 0.045936 s
Line #      Hits         Time   Per Hit   % Time  Line Contents
==============================================================
     3                                             def add_and_sum(x, y):
     4         1        36510   36510.0     79.5      added = x + y
     5         1         9425    9425.0     20.5      summed = added.sum(axis=1)
     6         1            1       1.0      0.0      return summed
```

This can be much easier to interpret. In this case we profiled the same function we used in the statement. Looking at the preceding module code, we could call call_function and profile that as well as add_and_sum, thus getting a full picture of the performance of the code:

```
In [574]: %lprun -f add_and_sum -f call_function call_function()
Timer unit: 1e-06 s
File: prof_mod.py
Function: add_and_sum at line 3
Total time: 0.005526 s
Line #      Hits         Time   Per Hit   % Time  Line Contents
==============================================================
     3                                             def add_and_sum(x, y):
     4         1         4375    4375.0     79.2      added = x + y
     5         1         1149    1149.0     20.8      summed = added.sum(axis=1)
     6         1            2       2.0      0.0      return summed
File: prof_mod.py
Function: call_function at line 8
Total time: 0.121016 s
Line #      Hits         Time   Per Hit   % Time  Line Contents
==============================================================
     8                                             def call_function():
     9         1        57169   57169.0     47.2      x = randn(1000, 1000)
```

```
10        1      58304  58304.0    48.2    y = randn(1000, 1000)
11        1       5543   5543.0     4.6    return add_and_sum(x, y)
```

As a general rule of thumb, I tend to prefer %prun (cProfile) for "macro" profiling and %lprun (line_profiler) for "micro" profiling. It's worthwhile to have a good understanding of both tools.

 The reason that you must explicitly specify the names of the functions you want to profile with %lprun is that the overhead of "tracing" the execution time of each line is substantial. Tracing functions that are not of interest has the potential to significantly alter the profile results.

B.4 Tips for Productive Code Development Using IPython

Writing code in a way that makes it easy to develop, debug, and ultimately *use* interactively may be a paradigm shift for many users. There are procedural details like code reloading that may require some adjustment as well as coding style concerns.

Therefore, implementing most of the strategies described in this section is more of an art than a science and will require some experimentation on your part to determine a way to write your Python code that is effective for you. Ultimately you want to structure your code in a way that makes it easy to use iteratively and to be able to explore the results of running a program or function as effortlessly as possible. I have found software designed with IPython in mind to be easier to work with than code intended only to be run as as standalone command-line application. This becomes especially important when something goes wrong and you have to diagnose an error in code that you or someone else might have written months or years beforehand.

Reloading Module Dependencies

In Python, when you type import some_lib, the code in some_lib is executed and all the variables, functions, and imports defined within are stored in the newly created some_lib module namespace. The next time you type import some_lib, you will get a reference to the existing module namespace. The potential difficulty in interactive IPython code development comes when you, say, %run a script that depends on some other module where you may have made changes. Suppose I had the following code in *test_script.py*:

```
import some_lib

x = 5
y = [1, 2, 3, 4]
result = some_lib.get_answer(x, y)
```

If you were to execute %run `test_script.py` then modify *some_lib.py*, the next time you execute %run `test_script.py` you will still get the *old version* of *some_lib.py* because of Python's "load-once" module system. This behavior differs from some other data analysis environments, like MATLAB, which automatically propagate code changes.[1] To cope with this, you have a couple of options. The first way is to use the `reload` function in the `importlib` module in the standard library:

```
import some_lib
import importlib

importlib.reload(some_lib)
```

This guarantees that you will get a fresh copy of *some_lib.py* every time you run *test_script.py*. Obviously, if the dependencies go deeper, it might be a bit tricky to be inserting usages of `reload` all over the place. For this problem, IPython has a special `dreload` function (*not* a magic function) for "deep" (recursive) reloading of modules. If I were to run *some_lib.py* then type `dreload(some_lib)`, it will attempt to reload `some_lib` as well as all of its dependencies. This will not work in all cases, unfortunately, but when it does it beats having to restart IPython.

Code Design Tips

There's no simple recipe for this, but here are some high-level principles I have found effective in my own work.

Keep relevant objects and data alive

It's not unusual to see a program written for the command line with a structure somewhat like the following trivial example:

```
from my_functions import g

def f(x, y):
    return g(x + y)

def main():
    x = 6
    y = 7.5
    result = x + y

if __name__ == '__main__':
    main()
```

---

[1] Since a module or package may be imported in many different places in a particular program, Python caches a module's code the first time it is imported rather than executing the code in the module every time. Otherwise, modularity and good code organization could potentially cause inefficiency in an application.

Do you see what might go wrong if we were to run this program in IPython? After it's done, none of the results or objects defined in the `main` function will be accessible in the IPython shell. A better way is to have whatever code is in `main` execute directly in the module's global namespace (or in the `if __name__ == '__main__':` block, if you want the module to also be importable). That way, when you `%run` the code, you'll be able to look at all of the variables defined in `main`. This is equivalent to defining top-level variables in cells in the Jupyter notebook.

Flat is better than nested

Deeply nested code makes me think about the many layers of an onion. When testing or debugging a function, how many layers of the onion must you peel back in order to reach the code of interest? The idea that "flat is better than nested" is a part of the Zen of Python, and it applies generally to developing code for interactive use as well. Making functions and classes as decoupled and modular as possible makes them easier to test (if you are writing unit tests), debug, and use interactively.

Overcome a fear of longer files

If you come from a Java (or another such language) background, you may have been told to keep files short. In many languages, this is sound advice; long length is usually a bad "code smell," indicating refactoring or reorganization may be necessary. However, while developing code using IPython, working with 10 small but interconnected files (under, say, 100 lines each) is likely to cause you more headaches in general than two or three longer files. Fewer files means fewer modules to reload and less jumping between files while editing, too. I have found maintaining larger modules, each with high *internal* cohesion, to be much more useful and Pythonic. After iterating toward a solution, it sometimes will make sense to refactor larger files into smaller ones.

Obviously, I don't support taking this argument to the extreme, which would to be to put all of your code in a single monstrous file. Finding a sensible and intuitive module and package structure for a large codebase often takes a bit of work, but it is especially important to get right in teams. Each module should be internally cohesive, and it should be as obvious as possible where to find functions and classes responsible for each area of functionality.

B.5 Advanced IPython Features

Making full use of the IPython system may lead you to write your code in a slightly different way, or to dig into the configuration.

Making Your Own Classes IPython-Friendly

IPython makes every effort to display a console-friendly string representation of any object that you inspect. For many objects, like dicts, lists, and tuples, the built-in pprint module is used to do the nice formatting. In user-defined classes, however, you have to generate the desired string output yourself. Suppose we had the following simple class:

```
class Message:
    def __init__(self, msg):
        self.msg = msg
```

If you wrote this, you would be disappointed to discover that the default output for your class isn't very nice:

```
In [576]: x = Message('I have a secret')

In [577]: x
Out[577]: <__main__.Message instance at 0x60ebbd8>
```

IPython takes the string returned by the __repr__ magic method (by doing output = repr(obj)) and prints that to the console. Thus, we can add a simple __repr__ method to the preceding class to get a more helpful output:

```
class Message:
    def __init__(self, msg):
        self.msg = msg

    def __repr__(self):
        return 'Message: %s' % self.msg

In [579]: x = Message('I have a secret')

In [580]: x
Out[580]: Message: I have a secret
```

Profiles and Configuration

Most aspects of the appearance (colors, prompt, spacing between lines, etc.) and behavior of the IPython and Jupyter environments are configurable through an extensive configuration system. Here are some things you can do via configuration:

- Change the color scheme
- Change how the input and output prompts look, or remove the blank line after Out and before the next In prompt
- Execute an arbitrary list of Python statements (e.g., imports that you use all the time or anything else you want to happen each time you launch IPython)
- Enable always-on IPython extensions, like the %lprun magic in line_profiler

- Enabling Jupyter extensions
- Define your own magics or system aliases

Configurations for the IPython shell are specified in special *ipython_config.py* files, which are usually found in the *.ipython/* directory in your user home directory. Configuration is performed based on a particular *profile*. When you start IPython normally, you load up, by default, the *default profile*, stored in the *profile_default* directory. Thus, on my Linux OS the full path to my default IPython configuration file is:

```
/home/wesm/.ipython/profile_default/ipython_config.py
```

To initialize this file on your system, run in the terminal:

```
ipython profile create
```

I'll spare you the gory details of what's in this file. Fortunately it has comments describing what each configuration option is for, so I will leave it to the reader to tinker and customize. One additional useful feature is that it's possible to have *multiple profiles*. Suppose you wanted to have an alternative IPython configuration tailored for a particular application or project. Creating a new profile is as simple as typing something like the following:

```
ipython profile create secret_project
```

Once you've done this, edit the config files in the newly created *profile_secret_project* directory and then launch IPython like so:

```
$ ipython --profile=secret_project
Python 3.5.1 | packaged by conda-forge | (default, May 20 2016, 05:22:56)
Type "copyright", "credits" or "license" for more information.

IPython 5.1.0 -- An enhanced Interactive Python.
?         -> Introduction and overview of IPython's features.
%quickref -> Quick reference.
help      -> Python's own help system.
object?   -> Details about 'object', use 'object??' for extra details.

IPython profile: secret_project
```

As always, the online IPython documentation is an excellent resource for more on profiles and configuration.

Configuration for Jupyter works a little differently because you can use its notebooks with languages other than Python. To create an analogous Jupyter config file, run:

```
jupyter notebook --generate-config
```

This writes a default config file to the *.jupyter/jupyter_notebook_config.py* directory in your home directory. After editing this to suit your needs, you may rename it to a different file, like:

```
$ mv ~/.jupyter/jupyter_notebook_config.py ~/.jupyter/my_custom_config.py
```

When launching Jupyter, you can then add the `--config` argument:

```
jupyter notebook --config=~/.jupyter/my_custom_config.py
```

B.6 Conclusion

As you work through the code examples in this book and grow your skills as a Python programmer, I encourage you to keep learning about the IPython and Jupyter ecosystems. Since these projects have been designed to assist user productivity, you may discover tools that enable you to do your work more easily than using the Python language and its computational libraries by themselves.

You can also find a wealth of interesting Jupyter notebooks on the nbviewer website (*https://nbviewer.jupyter.org/*).

Index

D

writing fast functions with Numba, 482-484

O

object data type, 93
object introspection, 23-24
object model, 31
objectify function, 183-185
objects (see Python objects)
OHLC (Open-High-Low-Close) resampling, 357
ohlc aggregate function, 357
Oliphant, Travis, 88
OLS (ordinary least squares) regression, 318, 394
OLS class, 401
Olson database, 341
ones function, 91-92
ones_like function, 92
open built-in function, 80, 84
openpyxl package, 188
operating system, IPython interacting with, 491-493
or keyword, 43, 103
OS X, setting up Python on, 9
outer join type, 233
outer method, 473
outliers, detecting and filtering, 209
output variables, 490

P

%p datetime format, 327
packages, installing or updating, 10
pad method, 223
%page magic function, 29
pairplot function, 287
pairs plot, 287
pandas library, 4
    (see also data wrangling)
    about, 4, 125
    arithmetic and data alignment, 148-154
    as time zone naive, 341
    binary data formats, 185-189
    categorical data and, 369-378
    data structures for, 126-138
    drop method, 140
    filtering in, 142-147
    function application and mapping, 154
    group operations and, 379-384
    indexes in, 142-147, 159

integer indexing, 147
interacting with databases, 191
interacting with Web APIs, 189
interfacing with model code, 389
JSON data, 180-181
method chaining, 384-386
nested data types and, 476
plotting with, 273-291
ranking data in, 156-159
reading and writing data in text format, 169-177
reductions in, 160-167
reindex method, 138-140
selecting data in, 142-147
sorting considerations, 156-159, 480, 482
summary statistics in, 160-167
vectorized string methods in, 220-223
Web scraping, 181-185
working with delimited formats, 178-180
pandas-datareader package, 163
parentheses (), 32, 51
parse method, 188, 326
partial argument application, 74
partial function, 75
partition method, 480
pass statement, 48
%paste magic function, 26, 29
patches, defined, 271
Patsy library
    about, 392
    categorical data and, 396-399
    creating model descriptions with, 392-394
    data transformations in Patsy formulas, 395
pct_change method, 163, 317
%pdb magic function, 29, 80, 495
percent sign (%), 28, 501
percentileofscore function, 367
Pérez, Fernando, 6
period (.), 21
Period class, 345
PeriodIndex class, 346, 351
periods of dates and times
    about, 345
    converting frequencies, 346
    converting timestamps to/from, 350
    creating PeriodIndex from arrays, 351
    fixed periods, 323
    quarterly period frequencies, 348
    resampling with, 359

About the Author

Wes McKinney is a New York-based software developer and entrepreneur. After finishing his undergraduate degree in mathematics at MIT in 2007, he went on to do quantitative finance work at AQR Capital Management in Greenwich, CT. Frustrated by cumbersome data analysis tools, he learned Python and started building what would later become the pandas project. He's now an active member of the Python data community and is an advocate for the use of Python in data analysis, finance, and statistical computing applications.

Wes was later the cofounder and CEO of DataPad, whose technology assets and team were acquired by Cloudera in 2014. He has since become involved in big data technology, joining the Project Management Committees for the Apache Arrow and Apache Parquet projects in the Apache Software Foundation. In 2016, he joined Two Sigma Investments in New York City, where he continues working to make data analysis faster and easier through open source software.

Colophon

The animal on the cover of *Python for Data Analysis* is a golden-tailed, or pen-tailed, tree shrew (*Ptilocercus lowii*). The golden-tailed tree shrew is the only one of its species in the genus *Ptilocercus* and family *Ptilocercidae*; all the other tree shrews are of the family *Tupaiidae*. Tree shrews are identified by their long tails and soft red-brown fur. As nicknamed, the golden-tailed tree shrew has a tail that resembles the feather on a quill pen. Tree shrews are omnivores, feeding primarily on insects, fruit, seeds, and small vertebrates.

Found predominantly in Indonesia, Malaysia, and Thailand, these wild mammals are known for their chronic consumption of alcohol. Malaysian tree shrews were found to spend several hours consuming the naturally fermented nectar of the bertam palm, equalling about 10 to 12 glasses of wine with 3.8% alcohol content. Despite this, no golden-tailed tree shrew has ever been intoxicated, thanks largely to their impressive ability to break down ethanol, which includes metabolizing the alcohol in a way not used by humans. Also more impressive than any of their mammal counterparts, including humans? Brain-to-body mass ratio.

Despite these mammals' name, the golden-tailed shrew is not a true shrew, instead more closely related to primates. Because of their close relation, tree shrews have become an alternative to primates in medical experimentation for myopia, psychosocial stress, and hepatitis.

The cover image is from *Cassell's Natural History*. The cover fonts are URW Typewriter and Guardian Sans. The text font is Adobe Minion Pro; the heading font is Adobe Myriad Condensed; and the code font is Dalton Maag's Ubuntu Mono.

Learn from experts.
Find the answers you need.

Sign up for a **10-day free trial** to get **unlimited access** to all of the content on Safari, including Learning Paths, interactive tutorials, and curated playlists that draw from thousands of ebooks and training videos on a wide range of topics, including data, design, DevOps, management, business—and much more.

Start your free trial at:

oreilly.com/safari

(No credit card required)

©2016 O'Reilly Media Inc. O'Reilly is a registered trademark of O'Reilly Media Inc. D25c1